MORE WIVES THAN ONE

KATHRYN M. DAYNES

More Wives
Than One

TRANSFORMATION OF THE MORMON

MARRIAGE SYSTEM, 1840–1910

UNIVERSITY OF ILLINOIS PRESS

URBANA AND CHICAGO

First Illinois paperback, 2008
© 2001 by the Board of Trustees
of the University of Illinois
All rights reserved
Manufactured in the United States of America
1 2 3 4 5 C P 5 4 3 2 1

∞ This book is printed on acid-free paper.

The Library of Congress cataloged the cloth edition
as follows:
Daynes, Kathryn M.
More wives than one: transformation of the Mormon
marriage system, 1840–1910 / Kathryn M. Daynes.
p.   cm.
Includes bibliographical references and index.
ISBN 0-252-02681-0 (cloth : alk. paper)
1. Polygamy—United States—History. 2. Marriage
Religious aspects—Mormon Church—History of
doctrines. 3. Church of Jesus Christ of Latter-day Saints—
History. I. Title.
BX8641.D39   2001
306.84'23'088283—dc21   2001000826

PAPERBACK ISBN 978-0-252-07560-5

For Bill,

who has made thirty-four years of monogamy

so ideal that it has made much more difficult

the task of understanding why my great-grandmother

and great-great grandmother entered plural marriage

Contents

Acknowledgments   ix

Introduction   1

PART 1: GENESIS TO REVELATION: INTRODUCTION OF
PLURAL MARRIAGE TO THE MANIFESTO

1.   *Kirtland and Nauvoo: Beginnings of Plural Marriage*   17
2.   *Plural Marriage under Mormon Control*   36

PART 2: I LEVITICUS: LEGAL AND ECCLESIASTICAL
FRAMEWORK FOR MARRIAGE

3.   *Nineteenth-Century Marriage Law in Utah*   55
4.   *The Nature of Mormon Marriages*   67

PART 3: NUMBERS: AN ANALYSIS OF THE MARRIAGE
PATTERNS OF MANTI WOMEN

5.   *The Marriage Market*   91
6.   *Women Who Became Plural Wives*   116
7.   *Economics and Plural Marriage*   128

PART 4: II LEVITICUS: LEGAL AND ECCLESIASTICAL
FRAMEWORK FOR DIVORCE

8. Civil and Ecclesiastical Divorce   *141*

9. Incidence of Divorce and Remarriage   *160*

PART 5: ACTS AND JUDGES: THE MORMON MARRIAGE
SYSTEM AND ITS DEMISE

10. The Decline of Plural Marriage   *173*

11. The Nineteenth-Century Mormon Marriage System   *188*

Appendix: Description of Demographic Data   *215*

Notes   *223*

Selected Bibliography   *283*

Index   *297*

Illustrations follow page *52*

Acknowledgments

Along the way to completion of this study, I have incurred many debts. Jeri Woodward first awakened my interest in Mormon history, and she, Clair Woodward, and Martha Taysom have all helped by listening to and commenting on various ideas. Sheila Cooper provided advice and encouragement that made the project easier.

The archivists, librarians, and staffs of Special Collections at the Harold B. Lee Library of Brigham Young University, the LDS Church Archives, the Manti City Library, and the Family History Library were all helpful and accommodating. The Sanpete County Clerk's Office gave me access to its Basement Archives. John Lunceford of the Terre Haute Family History Center also provided important assistance by generously sharing his extensive knowledge about tracing families and the types of sources available for LDS families. Without that knowledge, the Manti data set would have been much less complete.

For help on legal matters, I turned to Christopher A. Newton, who read portions of preliminary drafts and offered advice, and to George Ryskamp. Thomas G. Alexander read an early draft and shared his extensive knowledge of both Mormon and Utah history. Clayne Pope gave me the names of Manti heads of households from his computerized list of the 1850, 1860, and 1870 Utah censuses, which aided me considerably in the early phases of my research.

This book began as a dissertation, and a Graduate School Research Grant from Indiana University facilitated this project, allowing me to obtain microfilms and other sources of data needed to reconstruct the families of Manti. My debt is especially large to those who served on my dissertation committee and read the early drafts. David Thelen and Ellen Dwyer offered helpful suggestions. M. Jeanne Peterson not only made my prose clearer but also, by making me think more deeply about various issues, made the final draft a tighter, more complete work. But my debt to her is much greater than this. The knowledge and skills I learned from her through classes as well as from her comments on term and seminar papers have informed the way I study history. Beyond that, her professional help and personal encouragement opened the way for me to complete my graduate studies. George Alter's aid, from sharing his knowledge of family history to helping me with the demographic methods used in this study, was vital.

Jan Shipps offered invaluable advice from the conception of this project to its conclusion. She helped refine ideas at their inception as well as encouraged and advised me as the manuscript was considerably revised and reorganized for publication. Her support as a teacher, adviser, and friend has been indispensable.

Mark Grandstaff and Richard Bushman read and commented on portions of the manuscript, and Mary Richards helped tighten my argument. Dean May and Walter Nugent carefully read the manuscript and made helpful suggestions. I also benefited from Joe Olsen's help preparing the graphs and from the research assistance given by Megan McRae, Warren Daynes, and Marie Burt, the last of whom also helped initially edit the manuscript and index the book. Liz Dulany of the University of Illinois Press has been particularly helpful in moving this work from manuscript to published book, and Jane Mohraz improved it by her careful editing and perceptive suggestions. I alone, however, am responsible for the book's content and interpretation.

My children, Austen, Marie, and Warren, were patient and encouraging through the long gestation of this project. It, however, never would have been begun, much less completed, without the untiring assistance and support of Bill Daynes. To him my debt of gratitude is especially great.

MORE WIVES THAN ONE

Introduction

Hugging the Wasatch Plateau, whose mountain streams sustain life in that semiarid land, the small town of Manti reached its peak population at the beginning of the twentieth century. It then began a slow decline as it yielded up its sons and daughters to the economic opportunities of urban, industrial America. A few remained to carry on the names and the religion of the nineteenth-century pioneers who had found the Sanpete Valley to be "both wilderness of Sinai and Promised Land." In 1998, 80 percent of Sanpete residents still adhered to the same church as their Mormon forebears.[1]

A few, however, argued that the latter-day Mormons were not carrying on the religion of their pioneer forefathers. Moving from Salt Lake to the isolated town of Manti in 1990, James Harmston began to teach that the Church of Jesus Christ of Latter-day Saints was in apostasy, having abandoned, among other practices, plural marriage. Four years later, about fifty families, including the Harmstons, were excommunicated and formed the True and Living Church of Jesus Christ of Saints of the Last Days (TLC). Manti burgeoned, doubling in three years by one estimate, as converts moved to the Zion of the newly formed fundamentalist church. Believing that Harmston had been ordained by Enoch, Noah, Abraham, and Moses, the group of about three hundred members acknowledged him as their prophet.[2]

In the year of its organization, 1994, half of the church's male members became practicing polygamists. The media flocked to Manti wanting to learn about the group's sleeping arrangements. In 1998, the church finally posted on its Web site an article about plural marriage, written by John Pratt in response to a query by a secondary schoolteacher in England. Using arguments reminiscent of nineteenth-century Mormon sermons—not surprising, because TLC members assiduously study them—Pratt claimed polygamy was a religious imperative. He explained that while a few men had wives living in separate dwellings, most plural families resided together in a single household. Circumstances and desires determined arrangements in the house. Each wife had her own bedroom, which might be shared with a child or two. Some men had their own bedrooms, while others slept in the different rooms of their wives, "with no children present, of course." Denying that husbands ever slept with more than one wife at a time, the article maintained that the conjugal relations of the husband and wife were strictly private. No intimate details were to be shared even with other wives. As far as jealousy among the wives was concerned, Pratt claimed, the main issue for women was receiving "assurance that her husband still maintains his affectionate feelings for her."[3]

All was not well within the church, however. In 1995, after a power struggle won by Harmston, 40 percent of the church's membership left. Two years later, a former apostle of the church, one of his wives, and another woman were excommunicated. They did not go quietly. Claiming that church leaders had failed to fulfill their promise that the three would meet face-to-face with Jesus Christ, they sued the church in 1998 for a return of over $250,000 they claimed they had given the church. That same month, Manti residents obtained a taped sermon by Harmston in which he divulged intimate matters, although without details. One of his wives, still in her teens, was not a good lover, he said, but "she's the most cuddling little thing you ever saw in all your life."[4] Believing that the end of the earth is near, however, may have alleviated any anxieties the group had about these matters.

How is it that men such as Harmston can openly live with his eight wives, have his picture with them published in the *New York Times*, and fear no prosecution in a state in which the prohibition against polygamy is embedded in its constitution? Harmston's answer is simple: "In today's society . . . we find that the liberal government is far more permissive of non-traditional families."[5]

His point is an important one. A marriage system—"the sets of rules used in societies to govern the establishment, continuance, and dissolution of marriage"[6]—is determined not solely by the law but also by the way that law is enforced. Moreover, as the TLC example shows, religious belief also has an important impact on the nature of marriages.

That laws and religion make a difference in choices about marriage and divorce seems obvious; yet in most historical studies of the family, the roles of law and religion are often overlooked, while the impact of social and economic factors are explored in depth.[7] Gerald F. Moran and Maris A. Vinovskis lament this imbalance, stating that "historians of the family have paid very little attention to the role of religion in the lives of individuals or their families." Yet, according to them, "one of the most promising areas for achieving an integrated view of the family in history is that of religion, since the life of the family and the life of the spirit have intersected at numerous points."[8] Similarly, Tamara K. Hareven, in assessing the progress and state of family history, writes that scholars need "to pursue topics which have not received sufficient attention," among which are "a more systematic study of the family in relation to religion, the state, and the legal system."[9]

Such systematic studies need to go beyond straightforward accounts of laws and religious doctrines to the examination of the interaction of laws and religion, on the one hand, with individuals and families, on the other. Moreover, individual-level data on behavior need to replace generalizations about families. For nineteenth-century America, Mormon Utah is particularly suitable for such study. The Mormons not only possess the richness of family and church records necessary for such a study but also are a significant group in American history.[10] As a religious movement, Mormonism is by far the largest of the indigenous religious movements that arose in the United States, having "outlasted or outdistanced every other sect and communitarian movement brought into being in America."[11] In addition, Mormons were important in the settlement of the American West, creating a unique American subculture in Utah and surrounding states that has persisted to the present. In their distinctiveness, Mormons tested the ability of a group to withstand the pressures of the dominant society in America as well as the limits of dissent.[12] The homogeneity of the population and the distinctiveness of Utah law and Mormon doctrine on marriage and divorce provide a test case against which other populations may be compared. Moreover, changes in marriage law imposed by the federal government and change in marriage policy by the Mormon church provide prime opportunities to assess the interaction of law and religion with the family.

In the light of currently accepted family models of progress from the patriarchal family of early colonial times to the companionate family of today, plural marriage seems an anachronism. But that model of evolution between those family types has recently been questioned as scholars move beyond the fiction and prescriptive literature upon which the models are based. The models are no longer seen as so monolithic or the movement from one type to the other so linear as they had previously been described. Class and ethnicity especially have had a profound impact on configurations of families.[13]

Religion, too, has had a crucial influence. Marriage not only occupies a central place in Mormon theology but also plays an important role in Mormon religious practice. To be sure, other religions are familistic in their doctrines; that is, in Carle C. Zimmerman's words, "they are concerned with the sanctity of family relations *more than any other mundane subject.*"[14] For Mormons, however, family relationships and marriage are not only mundane, or of this world, but also crucial for one's place in the hereafter.

In Mormon theology, unconditional or general salvation, consisting of being resurrected, comes to all through God's grace. The degree of glory the resurrected being will receive, however, depends on one's righteousness and obedience to the gospel in mortal life. The highest—and most desirable—degree of glory is exaltation. Because exaltation is the continuation of the family unit throughout eternity, an individual must be married to become exalted.[15] As Jan Shipps succinctly explained it, while the "unit of salvation" in Mormonism is the individual, the "unit of exaltation" is the family.[16]

Many nineteenth-century Americans believed that families would be reunited in heaven, and one scholar contended that "among non-evangelical groups, the out-and-out supporters of a domestic heaven were dominant." Elizabeth Stuart Phelps's novel *Beyond the Gates* pictured the narrator's heavenly home as a small, quiet, but charming house where her deceased father waited for her. For Mormons, the family in heaven is more than a part of a new type of consolation literature. It is even more than a central doctrine. It is in fact embedded in the most sacred of Mormon religious rituals, including marriage for eternity.[17]

Because marriage is requisite for exaltation, the marriage must be valid in eternity, not merely for mortal life. According to Mormon doctrine, a marriage "till death us do part" has no efficacy in the hereafter. To be valid, the marriage must be performed by someone with the authority to bind in heaven as well as on earth. Mormons call such authority the sealing power. Marriages valid for eternity performed by someone with the sealing power are called sealings and are the only marriages that qualify a person for exaltation. Such sealings, Mormons believe, are performed only on earth.[18] Although living persons may act as proxies for the dead in sealing ceremonies, many Latter-day Saints in the nineteenth century believed they should be married for eternity, or sealed, during their lifetimes if they hoped to be exalted.

Eternal marriage, or celestial marriage as it was often called, was thus more than a part of the belief system.[19] It affected in practice whether one married, whom one married, and the ceremony by which one was married. It also provided one rationale for plural marriage. A man who was sealed to his wife for eternity might remarry after his first wife's death. He would then have two wives: one in heaven and one on earth. If he was also sealed to his second wife, he could expect to have two wives in heaven. Although a woman also might remarry, she was sealed to only one husband. Plural marriage, also called patriarchal marriage or the principle, was explicitly modeled after the biblical patriarchs Abraham and Jacob.[20] It was thus a patriarchal familial structure, with a man presiding over his wives and children.

Plural marriages created a set of relationships in the family that differed from those in companionate marriage, which was increasingly the ideal in nineteenth-century America.[21] The mutual dependence of a man and woman in a companionate marriage might exist for a polygamist and one of his wives, but in general the belief in the patriarchal nature of the marriage, with the concomitant view that the man held superior power and authority, precluded companionate marriages.[22]

With the relationship between husbands and plural wives weakened, women intensified the strength of the bonds they forged with their children. The significance of this stronger bond was not emotional alone, for Mormon doctrine teaches not only that marriages in the temple (or Endowment House) seal the husband-wife relationship for eternity but also that children born of such unions are likewise sealed to their parents for eternity.

To summarize, the Mormon marriage system rested on a distinctively Mormon doctrine of family perpetuation through the eternities that not only sacralizes family relationships but also makes eternal marriage requisite for exaltation to godhood. Persons, *male as well as female,* not married for eternity by being sealed on earth have no possibility of being exalted. It is important to note, however, that the ritual sacralization of the marriage union does not guarantee exaltation in the hereafter since exaltation of the family unit occurs only if both partners are righteous, or "worthy."[23]

Divorce was the mechanism to dissolve a marriage to an unrighteous spouse because it barred an eternal marriage with a worthy one; hence, a divorce cannot be treated as evidence that the marriage failed in the traditional sense. Even as it served a religious purpose, however, divorce allowed individuals to remove themselves from relationships characterized by conflict and alienation so that they could seek marriages in which they could develop the Christian qualities of harmony, unity, and love. Divorce was not a sign that the system had failed but was a mechanism that adjusted the problems encountered within the marriage system.

Because Mormon polygamy was an unusual family form in nineteenth-century America, it has received extensive scholarly attention. Richard Van Wagoner's *Mormon Polygamy* provides an overview of polygamy. A more theoretical account is Lawrence Foster's *Religion and Sexuality*, a comparative study of marriage and the family among the Shakers, Oneida Perfectionists, and Mormons. It offers a sociological explanation of the introduction of their alternative marriage systems and an insightful assessment of their success in terms of their own objectives. Through biographies of Joseph Smith's wives, Todd Compton's *In Sacred Loneliness* treats in depth some of the first women to become plural wives and the introduction of plural marriage in Nauvoo.[24]

The quality of relationships in plural families is effectively portrayed in Kimball Young's *Isn't One Wife Enough?* and Jessie Embry's *Mormon Polygamous Families.* Because the two sets of interviews upon which their works are based were conducted in the 1930s and between 1976 and 1984, these present a picture of Mormon polygamy during the last phase of its existence, thus ignoring change over time. In studying the religious activity of Mormon families and the reaction of families to the federal prosecution of polygamists in the 1880s, these books touch on the impact of law and religion on the family, but that topic remains inchoate.[25]

Eugene Campbell and Bruce Campbell, in their important article "Divorce among Mormon Polygamists," account for the social origins of divorce among Mormon polygamists by declaring that "the context of Mormon polygamy was a state of anomie or normlessness caused by their millennialist belief system and the instability of their lives in colonizing the Great Basin." Although their article is an important source for the number of divorces granted, it does not present enough data on individuals to establish a valid estimate of the extent of divorce among the Saints.[26] To provide more accurate figures, Phillip R. Kunz, in "One Wife or Several? A Comparative Study of Late Nineteenth-Century Marriage in Utah," uses family group records, which are reconstitutions of ancestors' families that church members submitted to the Family History Library in Salt Lake City. He does not, however, place Mormon divorce in the larger religious or legal context. Richard Aaron's "Mormon Divorce and the Statute of 1852: Questions for Divorce in the 1980s" deals with divorce law in Utah but does not have the individual-level data to explicate the relationship between the law and individual families.[27]

The most complete individual data for the Mormon population is that collected by the Mormon Historical Demography Project. This project involved computerizing the genealogies of all individuals in the family group records that included at least one event (birth or death) in Utah or along the Mormon Pioneer Trail. The data set includes approximately 1.2 million individuals in 185,000 families. Scholars using this data base have concentrated on studying fertility, to which the information derived from the family group records best lends itself. They have explored such topics as fertility on the frontier and in polygynous societies. In stressing the similarities between the Mormon population and other populations to which their findings may apply, these scholars tend to downplay the peculiarities of Mormon Utah. While some investigators have assessed the impact of religion on fertility patterns—indicating that religion may have affected levels of fertility but not trends in fertility decline—they have not systematically investigated the effect of religion and law on nuptiality and divorce.[28]

Two works treat the tortuous route church leaders took in accommodating to American marriage norms at the turn of the century. D. Michael Quinn's "LDS Church Authority and New Plural Marriages, 1890–1904" and B. Carmon Hardy's *Solemn Covenant* both document in detail marriages taking place just before and long after the Woodruff Manifesto was announced in 1890. Hardy's book covers plural marriage from its commencement to its end, but his analysis of individual marriages is confined to the late period.[29]

The work of Stanley Ivins in "Notes on Mormon Polygamy" stands out not only because it was among the first to examine plural marriage quantitatively but also because it deals with change over time. Nevertheless, Ivins makes little attempt to assess the accuracy or the representativeness of the sources he uses.[30] In "Polygyny and Fertility in Nineteenth-Century America," James E. Smith and Phillip R. Kunz also estimate the incidence of polygamy but acknowledge that their estimates, as well as those by previous scholars, are crude. More recently, Lowell "Ben" Bennion, in "The Incidence of Mormon Polygamy in 1880: 'Dixie' versus Davis Stake," uses the 1880 manuscript census to calculate the incidence of plural marriage among Mormons. He concludes that the number of plural families varied from one location to another but that most previous calculations have been made on the basis of incomplete data and hence underestimated its prevalence. In "How Common the Principle? Women as Plural Wives in 1860," Marie Cornwall, Camela Courtright, and Laga Van Beek present data on three wards in Salt Lake City in 1860 that show a high incidence of plural marriage.[31]

Larry M. Logue, in his research on the town of St. George, Utah, reconstitutes the families of St. George from its founding in 1861 to 1880 and connects the experiences of their family lives to Mormon doctrine. Logue's *Sermon in the Desert: Belief and Behavior in Early St. George, Utah* demonstrates the value of studying one community intensively to delineate the relationship between religion and family life. By using individual-level data, he goes beyond anecdotes, generalizations, and prescribed conduct to describe the behavior of individuals and families. Moreover, he is able to relate that behavior to their religious beliefs as well as to economic conditions.[32]

Nevertheless, the narrow time frame of his study, from 1861 to 1880, limits examination of change over time and excludes two periods when change was most likely to occur: the period of initial settlement in Utah and the prosecutions of polygamists in the 1880s. Moreover, creation of and changes in laws during those periods provide opportunities for studying the interaction of families with the state and legal system as well as with religion.

This study uses individual-level data to elucidate the nature of the Mormon marriage system. It seeks to verify and to extend our knowledge about such questions as whether marriage rates changed over time, whether the number of women entering plural marriage decreased considerably over time (as Ivins contends), whether plural marriage was pervasive in the 1880s (as Logue argues), and whether the social context of divorce laws and church practice was normlessness (as the Campbells assert). It also explores the types of women who entered plural marriage, the incidence of divorce among polygamists, and the effects of inheritance laws on families.

Researching these topics has required analyzing a variety of records. First, federal and territorial laws on marriage and divorce have been essential, as have court cases at the local and territorial levels. Second, this study uses church pronouncements about marriage and divorce as well as records indicating how the church dealt with problems concerning marriage and divorce. Third, to produce high quality data on a large number of individuals has required different types of records, including censuses, family group records, church membership records, cemetery records, and marriage licenses. Focusing on families in a single community has made such a study feasible by limiting the number of records that had to be searched; it also provides boundaries within which I could ascertain the completeness of the data. An elaborate data set from a single community may not represent the entire LDS population in every respect, but such data represent a real and complete community and can thus reveal more than a nonrandom, biased data set based on accidental availability of information. In contrast, diaries and other personal accounts as well as oral interviews provide important insights into attitudes and the qualitative relationships within families, but elites, the well-educated, and those still living when the oral interviews started are over-represented. Experiences of the illiterate, the foreign-born, and the ordinary members have remained obscure because so few left accounts. A complete data set for a community helps rectify the lack of traditional sources for such people.

Since plural marriage was practiced for just a short time, only a community settled early would allow the study of change in marriage and divorce patterns over time, but the community had to have remained small enough to make a complete study of its families feasible. Manti, Utah, fit both criteria. This community, among the first western settlements Mormons established outside the Salt Lake Valley, was settled in 1849, soon enough to be included in the 1850 census (taken in 1851 in Utah). It did not, however, grow so large as to make it an unmanageable subject of study; its population in 1900 was 2,425.[33] Notwithstanding its size, Manti's significance is indicated by its being chosen as the site for the first Mormon temple in central Utah. More important for this study, during the nineteenth century it was typical—to the extent any town can be typical—of Mormon villages in the incidence of plural marriage.[34] In addition, although Salt Lake City was the main locus of settlement in 1850, from 1860 to 1900 about three-quarters of the Saints resided in Mormon villages or in rural areas.[35] Manti, then, was characteristic of the locations in which most nineteenth-century Utah Saints lived. However much Manti may be known today for its modern-day polygamists, the town was not chosen for that reason. Collection of data for this project began before the Harmstons and others were excommunicated from the LDS Church and reinstituted polygyny. Their presence makes the choice fortuitous, although their "God-ordered silence" makes it difficult to compare past practices with those of today.[36]

The reconstituted families of Manti form an important source for this study, and the wide variety of sources used has produced a data set of high quality.[37] The census data and family group records were particularly valuable for the early years. The first step in the research plan was compiling a list of everyone who lived in Manti from 1849 to 1910. Those who came in 1849 were enumerated by Adelia Sidwell, who arrived that first year.[38] To examine the impact of the Manifesto, the study extends to 1910. Names from the manuscript censuses for 1850, 1860, 1870, 1880, 1900, and 1910 form the basic core of the list. Names from membership records of the LDS Church, the 1890 tax assessment rolls, and the Manti cemetery record help fill in the lacunas caused by the loss of the 1890 manuscript census in a fire. A variety of other sources provided additional names of those who once resided in Manti.

Family group records augment the information about families on the basic list. Other sources—including marriage license records, court records, immigration indexes, and diaries—permitted reconstitution of families who had no family group records and corrected or provided additional information for those having such records.[39]

Unfortunately, not all the relevant information needed for this study is currently available to scholars. Church court records, temple sealing (marriage) records, and cancellations of temple sealings (church divorces) are now restricted. Nevertheless, enough information is available, though not necessarily easily accessible, to explore in depth patterns of nuptiality and divorce among Mormons.

From the Manti data base, I created a subset of polygamous men and all their first and plural wives. In this study, the term *plural wife* refers to a woman who was a second or higher-order wife and thus is distinguished from a first wife, who was in a monogamous marriage before her husband married subsequent wives. First and plural wives are collectively referred to as polygamous wives. Monogamous wives, as indicated by dates of death and divorce, were not included in the polygamy subset unless they had been first or plural wives at some point during their lifetimes. I found 155 men who entered plural marriage before or during their residence in Manti. Among these polygamists were four men who were in plural marriages before moving to Manti but were monogamous during their residence there. Also included in the subset were two men in nominal plural marriages and two others whose plural wives appeared to have been sealed for eternity only.

Mormons recognized several types of marriages with various rights and obligations. Most couples in the subset were married, or sealed, for time and eternity. Such marriages, now as well as in the nineteenth century, involve full conjugal rights and obligations on earth, and Mormons believe the marriage will continue in force after both husband and wife have died. Some women in the nineteenth century, however, were sealed to husbands for eternity only. Such sealings entailed few or no marital rights or obligations on earth. In addition, some women were sealed to their husbands for eternity only but used their husbands' surnames. These marriages appear to have conferred no right to sexual access but may have carried some responsibility for husbands to provide some financial assistance and protection to the women. In this study, such marriages are called nominal plural marriages.[40]

The 155 polygamists and their 444 wives who were in plural marriage constitute the Manti subset regardless of whether those wives ever lived in Manti. Wives' names were compiled from husbands' family group records and the *International Genealogical Index* (now named the *Ordinance Index*), though a few wives' names were found in other sources. The goal was to include all first and plural wives, not just those whose records were easily accessible, as has usually been done in studies of plural marriage. Of the 444 wives, 21 appear to have been in eternity-only or nominal plural marriages. Others may also have belonged in those categories, but such women were not so classified if they lived in their husbands' households and used their surnames, even if age and affinity suggested that their marriages were for eternity only.

The subset yields men and women whose backgrounds and experiences in plural marriage were diverse. Although included because of the husbands' residence in Manti, the wives in the subset lived in a variety of Mormon settlements over their lifetimes, including Nauvoo and Salt Lake City and communities in southern Utah, Arizona, Colorado, and Mexico. The men and women, including two Native American plural wives, in the subset came from North America and northern Europe, those areas from which Mormonism drew most of its converts in the nineteenth century: England, Wales, Scotland, Ireland, Denmark, Sweden, Norway, Germany, Switzerland, upper Canada, as well as all parts of the United States.[41] The subset includes those who were illiterate as well as those who left extensive diaries, those who held high positions in the LDS Church hierarchy as well as those who apostatized, those who possessed considerable wealth and those who possessed too little to be on tax rolls. The experiences of these Saints who lived in Manti or were married to a man residing in Manti are equally diverse. The subset includes those who lived over half a century in plural marriage and those whose plural marriage lasted only three months, as well as those in marriages where there were multiple wives and those who were sealed for eternity only. The data set is thus far more representative of participants in plural marriage than its origins in Manti might at first suggest.

I traced the histories of these men and women over their lifetimes to compile as complete a marital history for each as was possible. Finding the necessary information for this project involved linking individuals across a variety of records. This is, at best, a difficult and time-consuming process, because of the inconsistent spellings of names and the changes of women's surnames with each marriage. Sporadic use of patronymics by both Scandinavian men and women in the subset exacerbated this problem. Moreover, tracing the women was considerably more difficult than tracing the men. For example, the woman whose maiden name was Ane Catherine Elizabeth Bischoff was also listed under the names Ane Larsen (Crossing the Ocean Index), Christina Madsen (1880 census), Katrine Madsen (Sanpete County marriage records), Hannah Marker (1900 census), and Anna C. Marker (cemetery records).[42] Despite such complications, I was able to find information for 98 percent (436) of the wives.

The data in the Manti data set, derived by linking multiple records, are more complete and more accurate than information collected from one or two sources. Scholars assessing data from family groups records have shown that these records are of high quality.[43] Reconstituting additional families through census, cemetery, and church records overcomes the problem of the nonrepresentativeness of the family group records. In addition, the immigration data gathered on individuals and families make the data set unusual because such information is rarely available. With this wealth of data, it is possible to study the impact of law and religion on patterns of marriage and divorce in this nineteenth-century Mormon population.

Over the years I have studied the residents of Manti, I have come to know many of them well. Much about these people is revealed not only in what they said but also in how they said it. I therefore have been faithful to their spelling and punctuation without the constant use of *sic* and have added only that punctuation that seemed necessary to make the meaning clear. Spellings of individuals' names are often not consistent across several records, although such evidence as age or presence of other family members shows that the various spellings refer to the same person. I have used what I believe is the proper spelling in the text, but in the notes I have given the spelling written on the record cited.

Part 1 provides an outline of Mormon history in the nineteenth century, sketching the genesis of plural marriage—protopolygamy in Nauvoo—as well as its development and the amount of autonomy the Saints had to create their distinctive marriage patterns in Utah. It concludes with the Woodruff Manifesto, which began the LDS Church's abandonment of polygamy. Part 2, called Leviticus after the biblical book containing priestly law, describes Mormon doctrine and Utah laws on marriage and considers how these were applied in people's lives. Material in this section shows how studying individuals illuminates a range of marriage types—the limits of Mormon marriage practice—that is not discernible by using only statutes and religious prescriptive literature. Part 3 considers the impact the law and Mormon doctrine had on aggregate marriage behavior (marriage rates and the mean age of women at marriage) over time as well as their indirect effect through plural marriage on all women. It also discusses the types of women who became plural wives, who disproportionately were drawn from groups likely to be economically disadvantaged. This section emphasizes women because heretofore little quantitative work has been done comparing plural wives and other women. Part 4, II Leviticus, does for divorce what part 2 does for marriage: it discusses the impact the law in Utah and Mormon church doctrine had on divorce and relates this to individuals' lives and subsequent marital patterns. It also reassesses the extent of divorce among polygamists. Part 5, the final section, discusses the decline of plural marriage in the face of federal legislation and changing church practice and delineates the rules of the Mormon marriage system.

The nineteenth-century Mormon marriage system was actually a system; that is, it had its own rules governing the establishment and dissolution of marriage, although these changed over time. At first these rules were lenient, for the policy of the church encouraged marriage, but authority for both the establishment and cancellation of sealings was centralized and came from the president of the church. Both the church and the laws established by the Utah Territory worked together initially in encouraging marriage.

Under increasing pressure from the federal government, the marriage system changed: marriage and divorce came firmly under the jurisdiction of the state, and the church was left with jurisdiction over only that part of the sealing ceremony having to do with eternity. From the 1870s, the law also increasingly tightened the rules regulating divorce. During the next decade, the federal government stepped up enforcement of its anti-polygamy legislation. Believing the choice was between maintaining plural marriage or continuing the sacred temple ceremonies for the living and the dead,[44] church leaders chose the latter and issued the Manifesto, which withdrew official sanction for future plural marriages. Although plural marriage lingered for some time after 1890, the laws and official church policy governing the distinctive nineteenth-century Mormon marriage system were replaced by those consonant with laws elsewhere in the United States.

While the Mormon marriage system was in place, however, the church's influence on families was decisive. The impact of plural marriage reached beyond those who entered it. When many women became plural wives, as they did in the late 1850s, the entire marriage market was affected, and the average age of all brides decreased. In addition, the church's lenient divorce policy and plural marriage provided opportunities for women who wished to remarry. Moreover, as the richer men took economically disadvantaged women—the widowed, the divorced, and the fatherless—as plural wives, the wealth per capita within families became more evenly distributed. Plural marriage thus promoted the goals of the church: it supplied all women who wanted to marry an opportunity to do so; it fostered a more equal distribution of wealth; and it provided aid to financially disadvantaged women by transferring economic resources from wealthier men.

As long as the Saints controlled the making and interpretation of those civil laws that governed the family, the laws of Utah also encouraged marriage and made divorce accessible. That changed, however, with the federal legislation aimed at abolishing plural marriage and with the court rulings that upheld that legislation. Plural families suffered the most, but all families were affected because the Edmunds-Tucker Act also put marriage firmly under the control of the state. Federal law thus firmly established its supremacy over both church and family and thereby changed the nature of both in Utah.

Families' interaction with the church and the law also shaped the marriage system. As women became increasingly reluctant to enter plural marriage after the 1860s, the marriage age of Utah brides gradually rose. Moreover, this reluctance created a younger generation that was, in general, monogamous by the time the Manifesto was issued. This made it easier for younger, if not older, Saints to accept the return to a monogamic system. Moreover, unhappy couples, accepting at face value the idea that they should not beget children when their feelings were alienated from each other, insisted on divorces when they could not live in peace and happiness. They therefore prompted the church president to grant permission for more divorces than he preferred.

Nor were families passive in the face of the law. Some plural families used a Utah law to circumvent dower rights mandated by Congress and thus were able to preserve a share of polygamists' property for plural wives and their children. They also used a variety of means to circumvent the antipolygamy laws. Some used secrecy, others moved one family out of state or out of the country, while others moved entire plural families to Mexico.

Both the old and the new marriage systems were shaped by the interaction of the church, the law, and the family. Church doctrine and the law served to expand or restrict the range of choices within the marriage system and to give validity to the rules that governed it. What was permissible in these marriage systems, however, may be found not necessarily in doctrinal statements or legislative acts but rather in the way the church and the legal system enforced the rules. The realities of the system, in short, are found only at the place where church, law, and the lives of individuals intersected.

PART I

Genesis to Revelation: Introduction of Plural Marriage to the Manifesto

In the celestial glory there are three heavens or
   degrees;
And in order to obtain the highest, a man must enter
   into this order of the priesthood [meaning the new
   and everlasting covenant of marriage];
And if he does not, he cannot obtain it.

—Doctrine and Covenants 131:1–3

Inasmuch as laws have been enacted by Congress for-
bidding plural marriages, which laws have been pronounced constitutional by the court of last resort, I
hereby declare my intention to submit to those laws,
and to use my influence with the members of the
Church over which I preside to have them do likewise.

—Wilford Woodruff, Doctrine and Covenants,
   Official Declaration 1

1 *Kirtland and Nauvoo:*
Beginnings of Plural Marriage

Jane Eyre, almost penniless, fled from Thornfield Hall and its brooding, Byronic master, Mr. Rochester, when she learned that the marriage he offered her was a bigamous one. Mr. Rochester's first wife was not only insane but also violent, and he averred to Jane that he had never loved the woman who was legally his wife.[1] Although under English law it was extremely difficult for him to obtain a divorce, Jane believed it would be wrong in the eyes of God either to marry him or to live with him.[2] The fictional heroine therefore fled into the night from the man she loved.

About the time Charlotte Brontë was creating *Jane Eyre* in her father's Yorkshire parsonage, a real Yorkshire lass was beginning a journey opposite from that of the fictional Jane. Mercy Pitchforth was born in 1831 in Brighouse, a village less than fifteen miles from Haworth, where the Brontës lived.[3] When Mormon missionaries came to the area in the early 1840s, Mercy, along with other members of her family, believed their message and joined the new church. Responding to the call to gather with the main body of the Saints, Mercy, her mother, and her siblings sailed for America, leaving behind their unbelieving father. When they began their journey to Nauvoo, Illinois, the Pitchforths were probably unaware that the doctrine of plural marriage was then being introduced into the church.

Having cast their lot with the Saints, the Pitchforths suffered along with others when the Mormon prophet Joseph Smith was murdered and his followers were driven from their homes in the Latter-day Saint kingdom on the Mississippi.[4] Their mother died soon after they started west in 1846, and Mercy and her two sisters lived with their brother and his wife.[5] After arriving in the Salt Lake Valley as a faithful Latter-day Saint, seventeen-year-old Mercy, believing it right in the eyes of God, willingly became the plural wife of Samuel Harvey Marble.[6] Unlike Jane's journey, Mercy's had led her toward, not away from, becoming the second wife of a man whose first wife was still living.

Like Mr. Rochester's first marriage, Mercy's marriage was not a satisfactory one. She was more fortunate than Mr. Rochester, however, because in Utah she could obtain a divorce. At about age twenty-two, she married a second time, this time as a monogamous wife. Eight years after she remarried, however, her second husband married a plural wife, who then moved next door to Mercy.[7]

The two marriage systems—the way marriages are formed, continued, and dissolved—in which the fictional Jane Eyre and the real Mercy Pitchforth lived were very different from each other, both in the types of marriages allowed and the accessibility of divorce. The laws in Britain and the practices of the Church of England supported a system that mandated monogamy and severely restricted divorce; the laws in Utah permitted both polygamy and divorce.[8] Moreover, the doctrine of the Church of Jesus Christ of Latter-day Saints declared that plural marriage was the highest form of marriage.[9] Living in two such different marriage systems, the two women who both came from the Yorkshire moors made opposite choices about marriage.

To be sure, the marriage systems in the various states in America were generally more flexible in recognizing unions as marriages and allowing divorces than in England, but monogamy was equally well entrenched in the United States. The reasons why Mormons, imbued as they were with beliefs in monogamy and strict sexual purity, espoused and practiced plural marriage is inexplicable without an understanding of, first, Latter-day Saint belief in divine revelation both to individuals and to Joseph Smith as a prophet; second, belief in the restoration of all things; and third, Mormonism's millenarian outlook, including the necessity of the gathering of the Saints.

On April 6, 1830, in Fayette, New York, six men whose average age was twenty-four—Joseph Smith, Oliver Cowdery, Hyrum Smith, David Whitmer, Samuel H. Smith, and Peter Whitmer Jr.—organized the Church of Jesus Christ of Latter-day Saints.[10] The church was founded only a few days after the appearance of a new book of scripture, the Book of Mormon. Mormonism, nicknamed after this foundational text, was a religion of the book. But from its very inception it was more than this. The account Joseph Smith wrote about the beginnings of the church makes it clear that his visions and revelatory experiences were as important as the new book of scripture was in establishing the religious authority of the church. This account of his religious history supported the divine origin of the book by relating how an angel gave him the golden plates from which he translated the new scripture. During the process of translation, he found mention of the baptism for the remission of sins. He and his scribe, Oliver Cowdery, retired to pray, inquiring about the concept. A heavenly messenger appeared, who conferred upon the two men the priesthood, the authority to perform baptisms and to act in the name of God. This and later visitations conferred upon Joseph Smith the keys to perform the ordinances necessary for salvation.[11] These miraculous events, detailed in the account he later wrote, established within the church Joseph's preeminent (although not unchallenged) authority to be the conduit through which new revelation came from God and his commission to use the priesthood power restored from heaven.

Like other restorationists of his time, Joseph Smith believed that the primitive church was to be restored, there having been an apostasy. But unlike other frontier restorationists, such as Alexander Campbell and Barton Stone, the Mormon prophet believed that the primitive church was not the New Testament church alone but the "restitution of all things" (Acts 3:21) from all dispensations back to Adam.[12] For Joseph Smith, the restoration of the ancient church was literal. Heavenly messengers appeared to him and conferred upon him God's power through the priesthood, power that Joseph could give to others by laying his hands on their heads and conferring upon them the priesthood. In contrast, for other restorationists, as for most Protestants, the priesthood was a endowment from God to believers.[13] Mormons' belief in the immediacy of God's word and power set them apart from not only other restorationists but also other Bible-believing Americans. Although other Latter-day Saints received personal revelation and were involved in the restoration of priesthood power, only revelations through Joseph Smith (occasionally accompanied by others) were given scriptural status by the church.

As the prophet and leader of the new church, Joseph Smith soon moved its headquarters to Kirtland, Ohio, where a community of recent converts lived, including Isaac Morley, founding father of Manti. According to Danel Bachman, who did path-breaking research on the beginnings of plural marriage, it was probably there in 1831, when the Mormon prophet was studying and emending the Old Testament, that he questioned why the ancient prophets Abraham, Isaac, Jacob, and Moses had two or more wives at the same time. The answer, recorded over a decade later, was "because they did none other things than that which they were commanded."[14] This doctrine—that plural marriage was not only acceptable but also mandatory if commanded by God—was little known by members of the church at that early date. W. W. Phelps later recalled that in 1831 Smith had stated, "It is my will, that in time, ye should take unto you wives of the Lamanites and Nephites [Native Americans]." Wondering how married men could wed Indian wives, Phelps asked Smith for clarification about three years later. According to Phelps, he replied, "In the same manner that Abraham took Hagar and Keturah; and Jacob took Rachel, Bilhah and Zilpha; by revelation—the saints of the Lord are always directed by revelations."[15] Belief in revelation was the key to change.

Rumors about polygamy among the Mormons were prevalent enough that on August 17, 1835, the General Assembly of the church approved the "Chapter of Rules for Marriage among the Saints," which was included in the 1835 edition of the Doctrine and Covenants, a book accepted as scripture by the Saints. The chapter read in part, "Inasmuch as this church of Christ has been reproached with the crime of fornication, and polygamy, we declare that we believe, that one man should have one wife; and one woman, but one husband, except in the case of death, when either is at liberty to marry again." This had been adopted while Joseph Smith was absent, although he did nothing to alter this part of the statement before it was published.[16] Whatever revelations he had on marriage remained private, and the status quo, monogamy, became the official policy of the church.

Some evidence suggests the article on marriage was adopted shortly after Joseph Smith's first plural marriage was discovered. The evidence is sketchy, but several later accounts consider the relationship with Fanny Alger as a polygamous marriage, and a second-hand account by Mosiah Hancock tells the story of his father, Levi, performing the ceremony. The relationship was brief, terminated by Emma, Joseph Smith's wife, when she learned about it. Fanny left Ohio in 1836 with her family and on November 17, 1836, married Solomon Custer in Indiana.[17]

That the revelation about plural marriage is connected with Joseph Smith's study of the Bible, particularly the Old Testament, manifests Mormonism's early emphasis on the "restoration of all things," from the Old Testament as well as the New Testament. The church's stay in Kirtland began what Jan Shipps calls "a latter-day recapitulation of the ancient Patriarchal Age."[18] Beyond the reintroduction of plural marriage, Joseph Smith's father was called as the first Patriarch with the responsibility of pronouncing patriarchal blessings on individual Saints.[19] This recapitulation also identified the Saints as part of the House of Israel. Increasingly Mormons stressed that they were literally of the blood of Israel, not merely adopted into the seed of Abraham by their faithfulness. As the elect—the House of Israel—they were to be gathered out of the world to Kirtland or to Zion, the New Jerusalem designated as Independence, Missouri.[20] It was not in Zion, however, but in Kirtland that the first temple was built. Reminiscent of the temple in Jerusalem, it was the most sacred of locations, a place where God communed with man.[21] Even animal sacrifice, a part of ancient temple worship, may have been contemplated in the restoration of all things. Wandle Mace wrote that he heard Joseph Smith instruct some of the Twelve Apostles to "cleanse and purify a certain room" in the Kirtland Temple and to "kill a lamb and offer a sacrifice unto the Lord which should prepare them to ordain Willard Richard a member of the Quorum of the Twelve Apostles."[22] It appears that the instructions were not carried out because a year later in 1840 Joseph Smith preached—in the future tense—that such sacrifices "will when the temple of the Lord shall be built and the Sons Levi be purified be fully restored and attended to."[23] All these innovations—appointing a patriarch who gave patriarchal blessings, restoring Israel and gathering to a new Zion, building a temple and reestablishing its accompanying ceremonies, and reintroducing plural marriage—were part of the "restitution of all things," with an emphasis on Old Testament practices.

Coupled with the restoration of practices of the ancient church was an apocalyptic worldview, encompassing the expectation of Christ's second coming in the near future and the establishment of his kingdom on earth. As part of that worldview, Saints believed that the earth was steeped in sin and thus ripe for destruction. To be spared, Mormons believed that they must forsake the world and gather together where they could be saved along with other Saints. These views led to a dualistic outlook: a person was either among the saved Saints or among the unbelievers in the evil world, among the elect who "harden not their hearts" or among the wicked who "will not hear my voice but harden their hearts."[24] Such dualism predisposed the Saints to expect opposition, and in this they were not disappointed, although opposition came from within the church as well as from without.[25]

In both Kirtland and Missouri, persecution reached a peak between 1837 and 1839, though the main causes were not plural marriage.[26] Opposition to Joseph Smith centered on the failure of the Mormon bank, the Kirtland Safety Anti-banking Company, but its roots went deeper. A number of church members, including some of its top leaders, were concerned about the growing conflation of religious power with political and economic control. Failure of the bank, however, united opposition to the Smith. Unable to quell the dissenters and believing his life was in danger, he fled to Missouri in January 1838.

Although the Kirtland dissenters had made insinuations about the Alger affair, in Missouri Smith was directly confronted with questions about rumors that he had committed adultery with Fanny Alger. In 1837, two apostles, Thomas Marsh and David Patten, were concerned enough that they approached Oliver Cowdery, an early leader in the church hierarchy, to ask if the rumors were true. Cowdery implied they were. That autumn, however, Smith met Cowdery in the presence of Marsh and George W. Harris. Cowdery again "seemed to insinuate that Joseph Smith jr was guilty of adultery." Cowdery did say, however, that Smith had never *acknowledged* being guilty of adultery. Marsh and Harris were so satisfied with Smith's innocence that they signed statements about the meeting, which were printed in a church publication.[27]

Oliver Cowdery, however, viewed the meeting differently. He wrote his brothers in Kirtland vehemently denying that he had confessed to lying about Joseph Smith. "When [Joseph Smith] was here," he wrote, "we had some conversation in which in every instance, I did not fail to affirm that what I had said was strictly true. A dirty, nasty, filthy affair of his and Fanny Alger's was talked over in which I strictly declared that I had never deviated from the truth in the matter."[28] Harris's comment that Oliver Cowdery insinuated Joseph Smith was guilty supports Cowdery's account of the meeting. What others at the meeting remembered and emphasized, however, was Cowdery's confession that Joseph Smith had not in fact acknowledged being guilty of adultery. Rejecting the idea that plural marriage was adultery, Joseph Smith would never have made such an acknowledgment.

Nevertheless, Cowdery was a man intensely concerned about his honor and took umbrage at being accused of telling lies. Upon being told that Joseph Smith was so accusing him, Cowdery immediately wrote a letter to his erstwhile friend demanding he refute his previous statements that Cowdery had willfully lied.[29] This difficulty created a rift between the two men, but three months later, just before the trial that resulted in his excommunication, Cowdery wrote that he wished charges against him "might have been deferred until after my interview with President Smith," implying that such an interview might have produced a rapprochement. By the time of Cowdery's trial, however, his alienation from the church had been completed by the Far West High Council's bringing charges against him for selling lots in Jackson County, Missouri, from which the Saints had been driven five years earlier. Cowdery wrote, "I told them that if I had property, while I lived and was sane, I would not be dictated influenced or controlled, by any man or set of men. . . ." Although during the trial, the High Council rejected the charge of his selling Jackson County land, Cowdery was already disaffected by what he considered an attempt by the church to control his temporal affairs.[30]

While plural marriage was only partly responsible for Oliver Cowdery's leaving the church, it was even less significant for other leaders. The reasons for the apostasy and splits in the leadership were rooted in the dissenters' objection to "a concentration of authority at the top and authority's increasing control of every aspect of life." Those who left the church during this period "wanted a more open society, closer to the values and traditions of evangelical Protestantism," than appeared to be the case as the church became more involved in economic and political activities.[31] David Whitmer, one of the six men who organized the church in 1830, claimed that he had doubted Joseph Smith had any connection with the spiritual wife doctrine until years later when he read the first issue of the *True Latter Day Saints' Herald*.[32] In the last three chapters of his history, John Whitmer, David's brother, wrote scathingly of "adultery, wickedness, and abominations," but those chapters were written sometime in the mid-1840s. In March 1838, when John Whitmer was excommunicated from the church, his history made no mention of plural marriage.[33]

Thomas Marsh, president of the Quorum of the Twelve Apostles, had zealously pursued various charges against Cowdery and the Whitmers in church courts. But he, too, soon left the church, although not over plural marriage. He had been satisfied by Oliver Cowdery's response that Joseph Smith had not admitted being guilty of adultery. Marsh did confess that when he thought of returning to the church in 1857, the doctrine of plurality was a "great bugbear" to him; in spite of that doctrine, he struggled to get to Florence, Nebraska, so that he could be rebaptized into the church. Like others who left the church in 1837 and 1838, he was concerned with Joseph Smith's increasing power. Joseph Smith had presided at a trial at which Marsh's wife was found guilty of dishonesty. Marsh became embittered and said, "Joseph Had no business in the High Council, etc." Only when Marsh accepted "the propriety of God's vesting the authority in one man" did he decide to rejoin the church.[34]

The dissent of these and other leaders shook the church. The cumulative effect of the apostasies of 1837 and 1838 divested the church of much of its leadership. Among Joseph Smith's two counselors in the First Presidency, the Quorum of the Twelve Apostles, and the Stake Presidency at the town of Far West, over half left the church or became disaffected.

Of the three witnesses who testified God had told them the Book of Mormon was translated by his gift and power and the eight witnesses who attested they had handled the gold plates from which that book of scripture was translated, not one outside of Joseph Smith's family remained in the church.[35]

In the wake of this crisis in leadership, the church suffered a greater crisis that threatened its very existence. Many Saints abandoned Kirtland following the dissension there and moved to Missouri, settling not only in the Mormon enclave in Caldwell County but in surrounding counties as well. Escalating hostilities, owing to increasing political and economic rivalry, expanded into war between the Mormons and the Missourians. On October 31, 1838, more than twenty-five hundred Missouri militiamen were in formation to attack Far West, which had only six to eight hundred Mormon defenders. The Saints surrendered, but the terms dictated to them were onerous: they were to give up their arms; their leaders were to be tried and punished, while the remainder were to leave the state; and they were to sign their property over to the state of Missouri to pay for the militia called out against them.[36]

In accordance with these terms, Joseph Smith and the other leaders, including Isaac Morley, were taken to prison. Because no evidence of wrongdoing could be found against Morley and some others, they were released and were able to help their families move east to Illinois early the next spring. While the main body of the Saints settled at a bend in the Mississippi River that they named Nauvoo, Morley and his extended family, along with a few other Mormons, moved to Morley's Settlement and once again carved out farms.[37]

The apostasy of so many leaders and the subsequent expulsion of the Mormons from Missouri were not caused by the introduction of polygamy, but the acceptance of plural marriage within the Mormon community was facilitated by these events. First, those leaders who opposed the concentration of power in Joseph Smith's hands and who favored more open decision making were no longer in the church. Second, the high costs of disloyalty were emblazoned on the minds of those members who remained in the church. Partly because former Latter-day Saints had turned against the church, Joseph Smith and other leaders had almost been summarily executed, and many Saints had lost their farms and then suffered from cold and deprivation as they fled from Missouri.[38]

Loyalty was thus a vital issue to members of the church. Soon after Smith's escape from Missouri, he admonished the Twelve Apostles: "See to it that you do not betray heaven, that you do not betray Jesus Christ, that you do not betray your Brethren, & that you do not betray the revelations of God, . . . but whatever you do do not betray your Friend."[39] Many Mormons believed that the Saints' surrender of Far West and their leaders' imprisonment were the results of betrayal by Colonel George M. Hinkle, commander of the Mormon militia, and that the Mormons who had testified against the church before Judge Austin A. King were at least partially responsible for the calamity that had befallen the Saints in Missouri.[40] Loyalty to the church and its leaders was thus a concern.

The sociologist Robert Wuthnow contends uncertainty fosters rituals that promote moral obligations in social relationships, including familial ones.[41] In Nauvoo, Joseph Smith introduced religious rituals essential to obtaining eternal life. A side effect of these was to make the moral obligations to the church and to other Mormons more solemn and more binding. Among those rituals was the "endowment," in which participants receive the gift of knowledge Mormons believe necessary for returning to God. Also during this ceremony participants vow to be faithful Latter-day Saints.[42] Although Mormons have maintained that these rituals are too sacred to be openly discussed, Apostle Heber C. Kimball stated, "Do [Latter-day Saints] hold their covenants sacred, those they made when they received their endowments, when they covenanted not to speak evil of one another, nor of the Lord's anointed [the head of the church], nor of those that lead them?"[43] On another occasion when speaking about these rituals, he remarked, "It is not for us to reproach the Lord's anointed, nor to speak evil of him; all have covenanted not to do it."[44] These rituals strengthened loyalty through solemn promises made not "to speak evil" of one another, especially not of the church's leaders.

Among these rituals were those binding, or sealing, families together. According to Mormon belief, family units must be sealed together by the authority of the priesthood (restored through Joseph Smith) to have validity after death. One ordinance seals parents and children to each other. Because most early Mormons were children of unbaptized members, however, many were "adopted to" prominent men in the church. Isaac Morley, for example, was adopted as a son to Brigham Young, although fifteen years his senior. These family ties carried with them all the moral obligations that inhere in family relationships, strengthening the bonds of loyalty among the leading families.[45]

The other sealing ordinance seals husbands and wives together for eternity, not just "till death us do part." Because this ordinance permitted a man to be sealed to more than one woman at a time, it was the religious ritual that created plural marriages. When the sealing took place between members of families, it also cemented ties of loyalty among church leaders by making them a part of one another's extended families.⁴⁶ For example, Joseph Smith became the son-in-law of Apostle Heber C. Kimball by marrying his daughter, and he became the brother-in-law of Apostle Brigham Young by marrying Young's sister. Marriage among other Mormons expanded these relationships, such as when Isaac Morley's daughter Theressa became a plural wife of Heber C. Kimball. Morley thus became the father-in-law of the father-in-law of Joseph Smith.⁴⁷

In addition to creating such affinal relationships among Mormons, the sealing of a woman to Joseph Smith brought her blessings of exaltation and conferred those blessings on her family. Helen Mar Kimball became Joseph Smith's plural wife because he had taught, "If you will take this step, it will ensure your eternal salvation & exaltation and that of your father's household & all your kindred." Similar promises were made to the families of Sarah Ann Whitney and Lucy Walker when they became Joseph Smith's plural wives.⁴⁸ Believing that one's eternal exaltation depended on Joseph Smith ensured loyalty to him, especially when his power extended not only to his plural wives but also to their families.⁴⁹ Mormons' concern with their salvation was strong and immediate because of their millenarian belief that the end of the world and the second coming of Christ would happen, not imminently but in the not-too-far-distant future.

Sealing also fostered loyalty in more complex ways because the act of accepting plural marriage was itself a dramatic sign of loyalty to the community's leaders. Entering plural marriage in Nauvoo caused considerable anguish, because it was secret and because it countered the monogamous tradition in the Western world and within the church in its earliest days. Brigham Young recalled that "it was the first time in my life that I had desired the grave, and I could hardly get over it for a long time. And when I saw a funeral, I felt to envy the corpse its situation, and to regret that I was not in the coffin." His fellow apostle John Taylor remembered that when he first heard of the new doctrine, "it made my flesh crawl." Heber C. Kimball's daughter wrote that it "had a similar effect to a sudden shock of a small earthquake" when it was proposed that she become a plural wife of Joseph Smith.⁵⁰

Despite these feelings, these three, as well as others, entered plural marriage because in the end they were loyal to Joseph Smith and believed in his role as a prophet and revelator of God's word. The language of loyalty pervaded the discussions of plural marriage. When teaching Mary Rollins Lightner about plural marriage, Joseph Smith asked her if she "was going to be a *traitor.*" While introducing the new doctrine of marriage to Emily Partridge, he said, "Emily if you will not *betray* me, I will tell you something for your benefit."[51] Both women had experienced the results of betrayal in Missouri. Neither chose to betray their prophet in Nauvoo, and they both entered plural marriage. Isaac Morley had already shown his loyalty by giving considerable property to the church and offering his life in exchange for the safety of the Mormon community in Independence, Missouri. On January 14, 1844, he again demonstrated that loyalty by taking as his plural wife a widow who lived in his settlement.[52]

Some reported having spiritual experiences that confirmed plural marriage was a righteous principle. This not only helped them decide to enter plural marriage but also strengthened their belief in and loyalty to their prophet. The case of Lucy Walker is illustrative. "In the year of 1842," she wrote, "President Joseph Smith sought an interview with me and said: 'I have a message for you. I have been commanded of God to take another wife, and you are the woman.' My astonishment knew no bounds. This announcement was indeed a thunderbolt to me. He asked me if I believed him to be a prophet of God. 'Most assuredly I do,' I replied. He fully explained to me the principle of plural or celestial marriage. Said this principle was again to be restored for the benefit of the human family. That it would prove an everlasting blessing to my father's house, and form a chain that could never be broken, worlds without end."[53]

The marriage Joseph Smith proposed was not preceded by a romantic relationship or physical love-making. Instead, it was proposed in a religious context. It not only promised blessings to her and her family but also was a commandment of God coming through the person Walker acknowledged as the prophet of God, that is, the person through whom revelations from God came. Essential, then, to understanding why Latter-day Saints did not immediately and vociferously reject such proposals so repugnant to their ingrained traditions is their central belief that God revealed his will to humans and that Joseph Smith as his prophet was the conduit through whom such revelations were received.

Mormons also believed, however, that they could receive revelation in answer to their own prayers. Despite her initial aversion to the idea of becoming the wife of a married man, Walker's belief in Joseph Smith's role as prophet was strong enough that she spent many hours in earnest prayer to determine her answer. Her answer—"my soul was filled with a calm, sweet peace that 'I never knew' . . . and I received a powerful and irresistible testimony of the truth of plural marriage"—fulfilled the prophet's prediction that she would "have a manifestation of the will of God concerning you. . . . It shall be that joy and peace that you never knew." Not only did Lucy Walker consent to enter plural marriage, but also the experience strengthened her belief in Joseph Smith as a prophet of God.[54]

Such spiritual experiences intensified individual Saints' allegiance to Joseph Smith. In addition, entering plural marriage entailed sacrifice. With their monogamous tradition, many Mormons, like Lucy Walker, accepted the ancient but newly restored marriage practice only after agonizing over the decision, and entering polygamy was difficult because the marriages were secret and their existence vigorously denied in public.[55] Sacrifice is one mechanism that increases commitment. According to the "Lectures on Faith," "a religion that does not require the sacrifice of all things never has power sufficient to produce the faith necessary unto life and salvation." For many, entering plural marriage in Nauvoo was a great sacrifice; hence their faith in and commitment to the church and its prophet was commensurately increased.[56]

The tenacity with which Joseph Smith attempted to reinstitutionalize plural marriage among the Saints evinces his religious motivations. Many have been quick to attribute the cause to Smith's libidinous desires, but Lawrence Foster has cogently argued that is too simplistic. It would have been easier to have followed the example of John C. Bennett, the church leader who was excommunicated because he seduced compliant women by telling them that God had sanctioned their love and its consummation. Instead, Smith introduced not only women to the restored order of marriage but also many leaders of the church, commanding them also to take plural wives. Even those who left the church acknowledged the seriousness with which Joseph Smith undertook instituting plural marriage.[57]

The reasons for taking plural wives do not entirely fit the four motivations for marriage one historian of the family proposed: economic or political reasons, romantic love, companionship, or sexual attraction.[58] To be sure, the marriages were political in the sense that they created lateral links within the Mormon community, binding families to church leaders, a practice that has been labeled dynasticism.[59] These marriages ritualized bonds of loyalty, bonds that were freighted with eternal as well as temporal significance. But no evidence points to marriages entered into solely because of romantic love, companionship, or sexual attraction, although these may have developed as a result of the marriage. Lucy Walker specifically states that her marriage was "not a love matter. . . . But simply the giving up of myself as a sacrifice to establish that grand and glorious principle that God had revealed to the world."[60] Nor did the men entering plural marriage desire companionship. Joseph Smith and Heber C. Kimball, for example, showed in both word and deed that their companionship with their first wives was more important than with subsequent wives. Sexual attraction, if it had a role, appears to have come *after* the individuals had accepted the possibility of plural marriage rather than before they had done so. Heber C. Kimball contemplated taking the two "elderly Sisters Pitkin" as his first plural wives because he thought his marriage to them would cause his first wife less grief. Joseph Smith, however, counseled him to marry a widow ten years his junior whose husband had deserted her.[61]

While plural marriage linked families in an eternal bond that was necessary "for their exaltation in the eternal worlds," Joseph Smith's counseling Kimball to marry a fecund woman is consonant with a second reason for plural marriage: "to multiply and replenish the earth, according to my commandment."[62] Plural marriage thus had two major purposes, only *one* of which involved sexuality. Some historians have assumed that because some plural marriages involved sexuality, probably most, if not all, did so, a conclusion that goes beyond documentary evidence.[63] That is particularly the case in the Nauvoo period. Although contemporary evidence is amply sufficient to establish that plural marriage was practiced in Nauvoo, most of the evidence about the quality of those marriages comes from documents produced later—sometimes much later. Memory is not a storehouse of facts but rather a process that, for example, conflates details or shapes a view of the distant past based on intervening events or understandings.[64] Moreover, much of the evidence about plural marriage in Nauvoo is ambiguous or second hand.

This problematic nature of the evidence has made the history of plural marriage in Nauvoo contested terrain. Perhaps nothing is less understood than Joseph Smith's sealings to women already married, because the evidence supports conflicting interpretations. For example, in 1915 Josephine F. Fisher, daughter of Sylvia Sessions, signed the following statement: "Just prior to my mothers death in 1882 she called me to her bedside and told me that her days on earth were about numbered and before she passed away from mortality she desired to tell me something which she had kept as an entire secret from me and from all others but which she now desired to communicate to me. She then told me that I was the daughter of the Prophet Joseph Smith, she having been sealed to the Prophet at the time her husband Mr. Lyon was out of fellowship with the Church."[65] This statement, not surprisingly, has generally been interpreted to mean simply that Joseph Smith was involved in a polyandrous relationship with Sylvia Sessions and fathered a child by her.[66] If Sessions knew that Fisher was Joseph Smith's biological child, however, she could have been having sexual relations only with Smith, not with Windsor

Lyon. That is, her marriages were polyandrous in name only because she could be certain of her child's paternity only if she restricted her sexual relationship to one husband at a time. The timing of the births of Sylvia Sessions's children lends some credence to her having denied Lyon cohabitation rights if Joseph Smith was the father of Fisher. Married to Lyon in March 1838, she gave birth to their first child sixteen months later, in July 1839. Their second child was born twenty-three months later, in June 1841, and another thirty months later their third child was born and died the same day, in December 1842, one month after Lyon had been excommunicated from the church. The next child, the purported daughter of Joseph Smith, was born in February 1844, fourteen months after Sessions's third child, a common interval between children when the previous child died as an infant. The child after Fisher, however, was not born until forty-two months later, in September 1847, over three years after Smith's death and nineteen months after Lyon was rebaptized a member of the church. Sessions's sixth and last child was born only eleven months after the fifth, a surprisingly short interval.[67] Only Fisher was conceived during the entire time Lyon was excommunicated from the church, and the spacing between Fisher and the next child is a year longer than any of the other birth intervals—all of which is consonant with Sessions's having denied Lyon sexual relations while he was out of the church and thus with her having only one de facto husband at a time.

Rex Cooper, however, has questioned the interpretation that Smith was Fisher's biological father. He posits that because Fisher's mother was sealed to Smith, Fisher was his daughter only in a spiritual sense.[68] Given the extant evidence, both interpretations are plausible. Fisher believed she was the biological daughter, and most historians have based their interpretation on that belief. It is, however, second-hand evidence based on what Fisher thought she heard from her mother. More problematic is whether there is a discrepancy between what Fisher understood and what her mother meant. That is, did Fisher interpret her mother's remarks to mean that she was the biological daughter of Joseph Smith and thus state that with more certitude than was warranted, when in fact her mother meant only that in the hereafter Fisher would belong to Joseph Smith's family through Sessions's sealing to him? Because Sessions was on her deathbed, when one's thoughts naturally turn to the hereafter, the latter is a reasonable explanation. Moreover, the intervals between Sessions's children could easily be the vagaries of conception while she cohabited solely with Lyon. In short, even seemingly straightforward statements about Nauvoo plural marriages are often problematic and can reasonably support more than one interpretation.

While the inner workings of these marriages are shrouded in the problems of memory and ambiguity of the documents, it is clear that these marriages lack most of the elements generally associated with marriage. No plural wife in Nauvoo took her husband's name and was known by it. Polygamous couples did not openly cohabit, nor was there acknowledgment of the marriage beyond a small circle of people, and the polygamous couples certainly never acquired a reputation in the community as husband and wife. Nevertheless, polygamous husbands apparently fulfilled the role of provider when possible. Benjamin Johnson later wrote that he perceived that Delcena Johnson Sherman and Louisa Beeman, two plural wives of Joseph Smith, "were both in his care, and that he provided for their comfort."[69] Moreover, in most cases some evidence of a marriage ceremony exists. Also, evidence from several of Joseph Smith's plural wives and the acknowledged births to plural wives of other men clearly attest to the sexual nature of at least some of these marriages. Because these Nauvoo marriages were secret, however, they incorporated only some aspects of marriage. It is therefore preferable to designate this period as protopolygamy (*proto* meaning giving rise to or being ancestral to), to distinguish it from the later Utah period when polygamy was openly practiced.

These Mormon plural marriages stood outside the long Anglo-American tradition of monogamy. Moreover, these sealings that extended family units were in direct opposition to those ideas increasingly accepted by the new urban middle class, which emphasized the intense, intimate social relations in the conjugal family. The economic and social circumstances of the Mormon community precluded the movement toward privatization of the family then taking place in cities of upstate New York, the area from which the earliest Mormons had come. By the 1830s in Rochester, for example, the household economy, where workers lived in the employers' households, was quickly passing out of existence as the scale of business enterprises greatly increased. Nuclear families, with the addition of only personal servants, became the norm.[70]

Social and economic conditions among the Mormons for the first several decades of the church's existence proved quite different. Nauvoo grew from a few families in 1839 to one of the largest cities in Illinois by the time the Mormons abandoned it in 1846, swelled not only by Mormons fleeing from Missouri but also by increasing numbers of converts from Britain.[71] Adequate housing remained a problem in Nauvoo, as it had been in Kirtland and Missouri and as it would become in Utah.[72] Members already established in an area took in new arrivals, so that households often contained not only the nuclear family but also kin and nonkin. As in other Mormon centers, this resulted in a variety of household arrangements that intensified the closeness to and dependence on those outside the nuclear family.

Parley P. Pratt's experience may not have been typical, but it illustrates some of the housing conditions Mormons experienced as they moved from place to place. When Pratt went on proselyting missions in the 1830s, he often lodged with acquaintances, while at home his wife boarded with friends. He spent one winter in Missouri in a log cabin occupied by ten families. He and his family, along with some other Mormons, lived in the open air when they first arrived in Nauvoo. In Kirtland, his mother joined his family; in Nauvoo, his wife's sister did so.[73] Although the presence of nonnuclear family members in households did not make plural marriage easy to introduce among the Mormons, their experience with various household arrangements was more conducive to accepting other wives into the family than if the community had experienced the economic and ideological changes—nucleation and privatization—that were transforming urban middle-class homes elsewhere.[74]

While twenty-nine men besides Joseph Smith took plural wives before the prophet's death on June 27, 1844, the practice was not acknowledged before any body of the church until it was announced on August 12, 1843, in a meeting of the Nauvoo High Council, a governing body of the church in the city. To be sure, John C. Bennett, a mercurial man who quickly rose in the Mormon leadership after his baptism in 1840, had written an exposé of the practice in 1842, bringing much criticism of the church and causing some Mormons to leave. The church, however, was able to weather the storm, battered but still afloat. Mormon leaders excommunicated Bennett and vociferously denied the church engaged in the practice, denials whose plausibility was increased by his exaggerated accounts. Dissension in the church leadership, promoted by announcing the doctrine to the Nauvoo High Council in August 1843, however, set in motion events that led to the prophet's death.[75]

Heretofore, Joseph Smith, who regarded "every thing acording to the circumstances of the case, and every person according to their intrinsic worth," had carefully selected and prepared the Saints to whom he introduced the restored practice of plural marriage. Hyrum Smith, Joseph's brother and also assistant president of the church, was more attuned to principles than to people.[76] Hyrum, a recent convert to the principle of plural marriage, told Joseph to write the revelation on celestial marriage, which Hyrum would then take to the prophet's recalcitrant wife and convince her of the truth of the principle.[77] Although Emma remained unconvinced, despite its stern warning that all who had the principle revealed to them must obey it, the revelation provided the framework and the justification for plural marriage that remained essentially unchanged. Now recorded in Doctrine and Covenants 132, the revelation states that marriages not sealed by God's word through the priesthood will not be in force after death. Those whose marriages are so sealed, however, will rise in the first resurrection and be exalted: "they shall be gods, because they have no end." At any one time only one man on earth, at that time Joseph Smith, would hold the priesthood keys necessary to seal such marriages. Turning then to plural marriage, the revelation declares Abraham, Isaac, and Jacob were justified in taking plural wives "because they did none other things than that which they were commanded." Plural marriage was not adultery because a man could not commit adultery with wives who belonged to him. Finally, the revelation indicates the purpose of plural marriage in mortality was to "multiply and replenish the earth."[78] These elements—the biblical justification, the necessity of eternal marriage to receive exaltation, and procreation as an important purpose of plural marriage—remained central Mormon defenses of plural marriage, while the prophet alone holding the sealing keys continued to be crucial to its practice.

This was the revelation Hyrum Smith read to the Nauvoo High Council, and not surprisingly some members of the Nauvoo High Council reacted negatively to it. Austin A. Cowles resigned from his position a month later and joined with others, including William Law of the First Presidency of the church, who opposed plural marriage as well as the prophet's increasing political and economic power in Nauvoo. The opposition coalesced around Law in the next few months. In April 1844, he, his wife, and his brother were excommunicated, and ten days later they and other dissenters formed their own church. The next month, Law filed a suit in the county circuit court accusing Joseph Smith of living in adultery with Maria Lawrence, one of his plural wives. Then, on June 7, the dissidents denounced plural marriage and called Joseph Smith a fallen prophet in the first and only issue of the *Nauvoo Expositor*.

This crisis was more serious than Bennett's exposé because it affected cohesion within the church and relations with those outside the faith. Declaring the newspaper libelous, the Nauvoo City Council decided after long debate that the press itself was a nuisance and should be destroyed. The destruction of the press, however, escalated tensions with surrounding communities and brought the governor of the state into the

fray. Governor Thomas Ford insisted that Joseph Smith go to the county
seat at Carthage to stand trial. Knowing his life was in danger, Smith gave
himself up to the authorities. Although he was released after his preliminary hearing for perjury, he was immediately charged with treason and
placed in the Carthage jail. There, on June 27, 1844, men from a neighboring town's disbanded militia stormed the jail and killed Joseph Smith
and his brother Hyrum.[79]

Dissension split the church and, combined with internal and external concern over Joseph Smith's growing political and economic power,
resulted in the death of the prophet.[80] After his death, the church frag-
mented into several groups, but its demise, confidently expected by its
enemies, did not occur. The largest group of Mormons accepted the leadership of Brigham Young and the Twelve Apostles, nine of whom had
received the fulness of the priesthood ordinances and seven of whom had
already taken plural wives. The temple ordinances, along with sealings
to plural wives, had been unable to ensure the loyalty to Joseph Smith
that would preserve his life, but a majority of the apostles remained loyal so that these legacies from the founding prophet would continue after
his death.[81]

When it had become clear at the beginning of 1844 that William Law
and his associates had turned against the church and would create problems for it, the number of new plural marriages had decreased. In the first
half of 1844, before Joseph and Hyrum died, only ten new plural marriages
were contracted, and Joseph himself took no more wives during that
period. Clearly the dissent and attendant threat to the prophet's life reduced the expansion of plural marriage. His death, however, reinvigorated
it. In the last half of 1844, thirty-nine new plural marriages were contracted, and the number of such marriages burgeoned when the temple was
opened for ordinances in the late winter of 1845.[82]

Before the completion of the temple, however, the uneasy peace between the Mormons and their neighbors broke down in September 1845,
and the church's enemies began burning Mormon homes in the outlying settlements, intensifying the sense of crisis created by the murder of
Joseph and Hyrum Smith. Morley's Settlement was the first to be at-
tacked, and in September 1845 Isaac Morley, his families, and his neighbors fled to Nauvoo with the few possessions they could carry, while
mobsters burned their homes and farm buildings.[83]

Because of the escalating tensions, the Saints had two tasks during
the winter of 1845–46: to finish the temple and to prepare for their exodus from Nauvoo. By December, the temple was opened for the perfor-
mance of the sacred rituals. Sealings for adoption and plural marriages

are religious ceremonies performed for spiritual reasons, but they also organized people into family groups for the trek west. Because the Saints were abandoning Nauvoo and the new temple, the number of plural marriages increased dramatically during those three months the temple was used for ordinances. Mercy Pitchforth's mother from the Yorkshire moors was sealed as the fourth wife of John Taylor, future president of the church. Isaac Morley was also sealed to five additional wives after the temple's completion: Nancy Bache, Eleanor Mills, and Betsey Bradford, who were all widows; Hannah Libbey, whose former husband had never joined the church; and Harriet Cox, whose husband had deserted her. In addition, on January 27, 1846, Morley's daughter Cordelia became the third wife of Frederick W. Cox, a former resident of Morley's Settlement. By the time the Saints left Illinois in 1846, 153 men had entered plural marriage with 587 wives.[84]

Before his death, Joseph Smith had asked Cordelia Morley to become his plural wife, but she had declined. When she knelt at the altar to be married to Cox, Apostle Heber C. Kimball reminded her of the prophet's request. She consented to be sealed to Joseph Smith for eternity and was married to Cox for "time," or for mortal life only.[85]

A few days later, on February 4, Isaac Morley and his family, along with other Saints, began crossing the Mississippi River and trudging west across Iowa. They endured bitter cold in February and faced almost impassable mud when spring came. What was worse, many were poorly provisioned. The 130-day trek across Iowa was so full of delays and difficulties that the Saints decided to stay a year on the banks of the Missouri River before attempting the longer move to the Salt Lake Valley.[86]

The Nauvoo period is crucial to an understanding of Mormon plural marriage. There the distinctive doctrines buttressing it were fully developed and explicated. There the millenarian worldview, the sense of crisis produced by tensions inside and outside the church, and the beliefs in Joseph Smith's role as God's messenger and in personal revelation all conjoined to create an atmosphere in which plural marriage could be introduced and accepted. Being introduced in secret, it could not be lived openly, no matter how open the secret. Only when the Saints were sufficiently isolated could the protopolygamy of Nauvoo become the open and acknowledged plural marriage characteristic of nineteenth-century Utah. There many more Mormons entered plural marriage, including Mercy Pitchforth, who, unlike the fictional Jane Eyre, believed that God not only sanctioned plural marriages but also sanctified those unions in which a man had more wives than one.

2 *Plural Marriage under Mormon Control*

Even before Isaac Morley led his pioneer band into the Y-shaped Sanpete Valley to settle Manti in 1849 and Orson Pratt publicly announced the Latter-day Saints' belief in and practice of plural marriage on August 29, 1852, polygamy was already well established among the Latter-day Saints. Even after the federal government imprisoned many polygamists in the 1880s and the church officially renounced new plural marriages in 1890, some church leaders continued to sanction some plural marriages. The religious doctrines undergirding the principle of plural marriage were developed and taught before the Saints left their homes in Nauvoo; they continued to be believed long after Utah became a state in 1896. But the political autonomy to establish a legal system in which the practice of plural marriage could flourish was short: it lasted from the time Utah was first settled in 1847 until, at the latest, 1882, when the federal government disfranchised all polygamists.

The Saints did not know how measured their political autonomy would be, of course, as they ferried across the Mississippi River and trudged through the mud of Iowa. Nor did they realize how hard life could be as they journeyed to the frontier and settled in along the Missouri as the cold weather arrived. Life in Winter Quarters was punctuated by cold, hunger, disease, and death. Moving a community of nearly nine thousand people who had sacrificed much of their property in Illinois produced administrative headaches for the leaders and caused suffering for the individuals.

Suffering as they did, the Mormons sought some form of assistance from the federal government. The Mormons' emissary arrived in Washington in the spring of 1846, just as the James K. Polk administration was planning its strategy and preparing for war against Mexico. The compromise over Oregon had not yet been reached with Britain, and the emissary hinted that if the United States did not conciliate the westward-emigrating Mormons, they might make overtures to the British. Early in June, the president authorized the enlistment of five hundred Mormons in a battalion to march to California under Colonel Stephen W. Kearny. The clothing allowance and pay for the men amounted to over $50,000, a fair amount of which went into the community's coffers. It purchased provisions for the Saints and paid for land acquired in Utah.[1]

What helped the state and the church, however, was often a hardship on the families of the men who joined this military unit. Esther Smith, for example, whose family members were among the first settlers of Manti, was left with three children aged fourteen, twelve, and two when her husband, Albert, and her older son, Azariah, enlisted. Luther T. Tuttle, another settler of Manti, marched away three days after his marriage, leaving his wife with her mother. The church had agreed to care for the families of the men in the battalion, but some were dissatisfied with the housing provided and others complained that the church received too much of the soldiers' pay.[2] No woman whose husband enlisted during that time of scarcity found it an easy eighteen months.

While the absence of men in the battalion directly affected only some, disease and death touched almost every family. Between June 1846 and May 1847, one person in twelve died. The deathrate was lower in subsequent years in the Missouri River settlements but nonetheless took a high toll on the remaining family members. Over half of those who died were children, but many families lost husbands, wives, mothers, and fathers. Lucy Morley, Isaac's first wife, who had supported him through proselyting missions, persecution, imprisonment, and plural marriage, died in January 1848, just before the Morley family began its trek to the Salt Lake Valley. Sophia Sweat, who became the plural wife of the Manti settler John Carter, grieved over her mother's death in Iowa in 1846; her father then died in 1850 as he attempted to cross the plains to Utah.[3] The large number of deaths not only grieved families but also disrupted them.

The Saints felt more autonomous in thinly populated Iowa than in Illinois, and after their exodus from Nauvoo they no longer hid their plural marriages. Some were enthusiastic about being able to acknowledge these relationships openly, but others felt the sting of prejudice.[4] Curious people came by to see the "spiritual child" born to Brigham Young's plural wife Emily Partridge. One woman was surprised to see that the child was as smart as he was because she shared the commonly held belief that children born to plural marriages were not as bright as other children. Partridge wrote, "There was a good deal of that spirit at that time and sometimes it was very oppressive."[5]

But Iowa did not provide sufficient political autonomy for the Saints, and with openness also came the first prosecutions for polygamy. In the fall of 1851, Frederick W. Cox, Isaac Morley's son-in-law, was summoned to the Mills County court and told that he could not lawfully keep his two younger wives. Cox firmly refused to desert his plural wives, defending himself by saying that the religious freedom his grandfather had fought for in the Revolutionary War gave him the right to practice his religion. The court agreed to let his case rest if he would move his plural wives out of the county by January 15. He found a small house in Pottawatamie County into which he moved his younger wives. Much to their horror, they soon learned the attitude that non-Mormons maintained toward them: the gold-diggers returning from California thought of plural wives as prostitutes, and the young women had to be vigilant to protect themselves from unwanted attention.[6] By the time plural marriage was first publicly announced as a doctrine of the church in 1852 in Salt Lake City, it was already lived openly by the Saints and had had its first confrontation with the courts.

The announcement, made by Apostle Orson Pratt, put the doctrine within its religious framework, drawing on the main points in the revelation Joseph Smith dictated on July 12, 1843. Pratt declared that because the spirits who will inhabit the bodies of humankind are already created and awaiting their opportunity to come to earth, it is incumbent on those now in mortality to prepare bodies for those spirits. Marriage, especially marriage that lasted eternally, was ordained by God as the means through which those spirits could come to earth. The great blessing given to the Patriarch Abraham was numerous progeny, and the means for that was his having three wives. The blessing of Abraham, a large posterity, was given to other righteous men. To create "a numerous and faithful posterity," the Saints would use the same means as Abraham—plural marriage. Because plural marriage was "necessary for our exaltation to the fulness of the Lord's glory in the eternal world," the U.S. government, with the First Amendment right to freedom of religion, could not pass laws to restrict its practice. Although less important to his reasoning, Pratt also adduced secular arguments to buttress his case. Polygamy was believed in by four-fifths of the world's population, but monogamy, being unnatural, fostered prostitution.[7] By insisting that plural marriage was integral to Mormon doctrine, by positing the unconstitutionality of governmental interference, and by suggesting the reformation of society by its practice, Pratt's announcement delineated arguments that remained the main contours of the Mormons' defense of their peculiar marriage system.[8]

Although the religious argument remained at the core of the Mormon defense, some felt it necessary to justify it within the context of nineteenth-century ideas. Using the widely held belief that men's sexual drives are greater than women's, George Q. Cannon argued that polygamy allowed the "demands of nature" to be met with "decency and propriety," an implicit indictment of the prostitution flourishing in monogamic societies.[9] Belinda Pratt put forth a variation on this argument. Drawing on the belief then current that a woman's thoughts and environment affect the nature of the child she carried in her womb or nursed, Pratt, like other Americans, believed a woman's passions should not be aroused during pregnancy or lactation. Proscribing sexual intercourse during those times promoted the "sound health and morals in the constitutions of their offspring." Men, having no such "draw back on their strength," could have their needs met by practicing plural marriage while protecting their unborn and infant children from unwanted influences.[10] The advice against intercourse during pregnancy given by family moralists elsewhere hardened into stricture among the Mormons.[11] Heber C. Kimball, for example, exhorted the Saints not to "weary the tree while it is maturing fruit" or "excite adultery" by taking "that course at the most improper and unwise times, and thereby seriously injure their offspring."[12] Mormons perceived their system as more moral than that of other Americans, and hence their beliefs and regulations about sexuality became exacting.

Not surprising, other Americans dismissed these defenses. For them, the solution for men's greater sexual drive was self-control, not plural marriage. Sexual indulgence once each lunar month was most healthy for all concerned, advised William Alcott. The prevailing view was that "the social order rest[ed] on man's ability to control sexual desire."[13] In the changing economy of nineteenth-century America, individual families' economic well-being depended on self-control to limit size of families. A man might be denied credit because of his "large and expensive family." Infrequent coitus, combined with rudimentary means of birth control, was sufficient to decrease the number of children for white women in the United States from 7.04 in 1800 to 5.42 in 1850 and 3.56 in 1900.[14] The American middle class, advocating sexual self-control to limit its fertility, was hardly likely to be amenable to Mormon arguments that the male sex drive was best kept in bounds by adding more wives and providing more tabernacles for waiting spirits.

Nor were the patriarchal underpinnings of polygamy likely to find a receptive audience among the middle class of the 1850s. In western New York of the 1820s and 1830s, the birthplace of Mormonism, religious magazines assumed that the family was patriarchal, that authority and obedience were the preferred relations between husband/father and his wife and children, and that the boundaries between the household and the larger society were porous. The Saints carried those ideas with them as they moved west and became increasingly isolated from mainstream American society. In the 1830s, however, American views about the family began to change, and by the 1850s the home had become the "empire of the mother," who was enthroned in an isolated refuge from the larger society. Women's domain included rearing the children, controlling the frequency of sexual relations, and guarding the morals of the home. While the ideology was undoubtedly in advance of the practice, it provided a mind-set among the growing middle class that was antithetical to marriage that was either patriarchal or plural. In particular, women, who were crucial in defining a family's middle-class status, were unwilling to countenance such a different male sexual standard or accept women not upholding middle-class morality.[15] In such a climate, Orson Pratt could not possibly devise arguments supporting plural marriage that would persuade most Americans.

Initially, however, the Mormons' isolation in the Salt Lake Valley, where the first pioneers settled in July 1847, provided sufficient autonomy for them to establish their own social and economic system, which included plural marriage. They did not attain as complete self-government as they sought, however. As part of the Compromise of 1850 to paper over the growing chasm between free and slave states, Congress denied Utah statehood and instead made it a territory.

Before Utah was made a territory, the Saints simply governed themselves through the already established organization of the church, including its court system. Disputes between members were to be settled between themselves, if possible, but if that failed, local officials, called teachers, tried to mediate the difficulty. If that did not produce reconciliation, the case would go to a bishop's court, in which the bishop—leader of the local congregation, the ward—and his two counselors sat as judges. This decision could be appealed to the stake high council (a stake is composed of several wards), consisting of the stake presidency and twelve high councillors. If a satisfactory judgment was still not reached, the case could be appealed to the highest court of the church, the First

Presidency sitting with the Quorum of the Twelve Apostles. This court system had a number of advantages for the early Saints. Its procedures were simple: a case could be initiated by writing a complaint and the defendant being notified. At the hearing, both plaintiff and defendant presented their cases and brought their witnesses. No lawyers were present, and the costs of trying the case were minimal. The emphasis was on providing justice, not on following prescribed procedures. Church leaders insisted that the church court system have exclusive jurisdiction over all civil cases in which all parties were Latter-day Saints. Until the first decade of the twentieth century, church courts heard and decided a wide variety of cases: land disputes, collection of debt, estate settlements, conflicts in polygamous families, and divorces, to name a few.[16]

After Congress created the Utah Territory, with its district courts and federally appointed judges, the church emphasized the exclusive jurisdiction of the church courts, but the territorial legislature also greatly expanded the powers of the county probate courts. In the United States, the jurisdiction of probate courts was limited to settling decedents' estates and providing guardianship for minors and the mentally ill, but in 1852 the Utah legislature gave these courts original jurisdiction in civil and criminal cases, making their jurisdiction concurrent with that of the district courts. Because the territorial legislature usually selected the probate judges from among local ecclesiastical leaders, the Mormons were able to continue exercising considerable control over the civil court system. This control was not maintained to foster Mormons' interests over non-Mormons'. Studies show that the justice in these courts was impartial. The Saints wanted to have the courts under their control so that they could protect distinctive Mormon institutions, such as plural marriage.[17] In 1874, however, Congress passed the Poland Act, which stripped the probate courts of their jurisdiction over civil and criminal cases, although those courts retained concurrent jurisdiction over divorces arising from statutory causes.[18]

Not only did Congress curtail the power of the Mormons, but also Latter-day Saints were limited by the resources available in their new location. Early difficulties in growing sufficient crops to support the burgeoning LDS population prevented the immediate migration of all the Saints from the Missouri River settlements.[19] By 1852, when those settlements were finally abandoned, communities had been pioneered outside of Salt Lake City, and Manti was already almost three years old.[20]

Some of the early Manti settlers were volunteers, some were selected because they possessed skills needed for pioneering a new area, some had lived at Morley's Settlement in Illinois, and some were related to Isaac

Morley. Four of his plural wives had adult children who came to Manti: the Tuttles, Merriams, Buchanans, and Carters all made contributions to the settlement.[21] In addition, two of Morley's sons-in-law, Frederick W. Cox and Joseph S. Allen, came with their plural families. Several men who had been in the Mormon Battalion also moved to Manti, including Captain Nelson Higgins, who was in charge of military affairs. To ensure good relations with the Indians, Dimick B. Huntington, an Indian interpreter, came, as did Barney Ward, who had married an Indian woman.[22]

Both Utes and Mormons began with high expectations for establishing a good relationship with each other. The Mormons had settled in Sanpete Valley at the invitation of Chief Wahkara (anglicized Walker), and he and over a hundred members of his tribe were baptized by the Mormons in 1850.[23] But because of differences in culture and misunderstandings, conflict was endemic. For many years, the Utes had sold children captured from other tribes to Spanish traders. As the Indian agent in Utah, Brigham Young had Spanish traders in Sanpete County arrested in 1851.[24] Because the Spanish discontinued buying slave children in Utah, Arapeen, Chief Wahkara's brother, argued that the Mormons should buy the children. When one Mormon tried to convince him of his wrongdoing, Arapeen became angry. He grabbed one of the captive children, dashed his brains out on the hard earth, threw the corpse at the stunned Mormons, and chastised them by saying, "You have no heart or you would have bought [the child] and saved [his] life."[25]

In 1852, the Utah legislature passed an act authorizing select men in their respective counties to obtain Indian prisoners and apprentice them to responsible families.[26] Even before this, however, some Manti residents, usually those who already had polygamous families, had purchased such children and taken them into their homes. These children were generally listed as servants on subsequent censuses, but some appear to have been treated more like nephews and nieces. Madison D. Hambleton, for example, left a legacy to Harriet, the Indian girl he had taken into his home, though it was less than that left to his own children. Christian Nielsen willed his Native American "heir" one yearling colt, while he left his daughter and one son ten dollars each, although he left his other son considerably more. Manuscript censuses show that many of the children remained in the community, and at least one of the girls became a plural wife.[27]

The slave trade remained a point of contention between the Utes and the Mormons and was one of the underlying causes of the Walker War in 1853–54.[28] Because the Indians killed several Manti men, the residents of Manti became concerned for their safety. They had initially built their one-room cabins on the one-acre city plots each family had been assigned. In 1852, responding to the threat from the Indians, men from the community erected a small stone fort, with cabins as close together as possible inside. In 1854, they built a larger stone fort, but housing conditions were still crowded.[29] The crowding was exacerbated in the fall of 1853, when Brigham Young sent the first large company of immigrating Danes to Sanpete County to strengthen the settlements there. Many Manti residents invited Danish families to live in their already small quarters. Flora Washburn, a plural wife, and her three young children, who lived in one large room, divided their home with two newly married Danish couples. Although neither the Danes nor the Americans could speak the others' language, they shared the room and one fireplace for some time.[30]

Two sixteen-foot rooms were all Frederick W. Cox had for his family of three wives and thirteen children when he moved into the fort. In October, he added another wife, Lydia, to his family and fortunately was able to acquire another room.[31] His daughter Emerette described the living conditions in the fort: "Aunt Emeline's room was lighted by one small window, one door and an open fireplace, and had room for two beds with the foot boards coming close together. There was scarcely room for her family to gather around the fire opposite the beds. The next room being the corner one had a door facing the east, . . . Aunt Jemima had two beds in here and Aunt Lydia one. They had no fireplace but used a stepstone for cooking and heating. They did all their work, lived and ate in this same room. Mama had a small bedroom a little more than half way up the side of the fort. In it there was a corner fireplace with room for mother's half chair where she sat to knit and we gathered around her and the fire."[32]

By the end of 1855, Emeline, Cox's first wife, had six children in her small room. Jemima and Lydia, not only sister wives but sisters by birth, shared one room. In 1856, Jemima was the mother of four children, Lydia mother of one. Cordelia, Emerette's mother, lived with her four children in her small room. As others began moving out of the fort in 1857 and 1858, the Cox family probably acquired more space; but they remained in the fort nine years, until Cox was able to build a large stone house for his family.[33] In short, the Indian threat imposed considerable hardships on the young colony, causing families to live, work, and beget children in overcrowded spaces.

Chief Wahkara also precipitated a plural marriage in Manti. No sooner had he signed the treaty ending the Walker War than the war chief asked Brigham Young for a white plural wife. Chief Wahkara had already been ordained an elder in the Mormon priesthood,[34] and the church president granted his request, provided he could find a willing woman. He apparently already had in mind Mary Artemisia Lowry, the comely twenty-year-old daughter of Manti's bishop. While the men were out working in the fields and Lowry was home alone tending her paralytic grandmother, the chief came to make his proposals. One of Lowry's contemporaries—with no little prejudice against Native Americans—described his offer of marriage:

> He poured into her ears the tale of a splendidly elegant and imposing wickiup he would build for her, told her how rich he was, what numberless droves of horses he owned, and how he would furnish her future home in such barbaric splendor as should astonish all beholders—nicest buffalo robes, costly furs, seal, ermine, sable (skunks) and bearskins, sheep pelts and cowhides from the Tesican ranges—long horns, hair and hoofs on all. He was willing to promise never to take her to the mountains as he did his other squaws, but she could always live in his wigwam and he would learn the white man's ways and live with her.[35]

These riches appealed to her no more than their owner did. She despairingly considered the choices before her. She dared not trust her future happiness to a man who had beaten his own mother.[36] Neither did she dare refuse, knowing that the frustrated war chief might well make the entire town suffer for his unrequited love.

She cut the Gordian knot by asserting that she was married to George Peacock, her sister's husband. Chief Wahkara was deterred, but to indicate what Judge Peacock might expect, the chief plunged his hunting knife into the pine table. When her father came from the fields, Lowry told him the whole story. Realizing the peril she and Peacock faced, he determined that her word would be made good. He summoned Peacock and told him the news. He then found Isaac Morley—the only one in Manti who had the authority to seal plural marriages—and the couple quickly swore their marriage vows. To avoid the war chief's wrath, they hurried into hiding in Salt Lake City. Chief Wahkara died five months later; George and Mary Peacock's twenty-four-year marriage produced ten children.[37]

The motive for this marriage was not lust or even romantic love. Rather, it was a product of the narrow choices Lowry faced as she and the other Mormon settlers pioneered the Sanpete Valley. Moreover, her complete rejection of marriage to a Native American, even one as powerful as Chief Wahkara, reflects the prejudice and separateness that prevailed in relationships between the Utes and the Mormons.

In the early years, the Indians clearly had a greater impact on the Manti settlers' daily lives than did laws emanating from the nation's capitol. The colony was established at Chief Wahkara's request, the settlers lived in an overcrowded fort because they feared an Indian attack, some women were left without husbands and some children without fathers when men were killed during Indian raids, and Chief Wahkara's proposals even precipitated a plural marriage.

Arapeen, who succeeded Wahkara as chief, sold the Sanpete Valley to the church in 1856, but the Indians still continued to influence events there. Long-standing difficulties between Indians and Mormons, as Native Americans resisted displacement by the expanding white population, flared into the war in 1865, after an Indian was insulted by John Lowry in Manti. The town's men served in the militia, and the community welcomed into its midst settlers who had had to abandon settlements in the Sevier Valley.[38] In speaking of the conflicts with the Indians, one early settler wrote that "a number of people living in Salt Lake and Utah counties . . . express a wonder why Manti, being such an old settlement, is not farther advanced in improvement, etc. To such I would say that had they participated in those labors and troubles, and been robbed and plundered of property accumulated by years of toil, they would readily understand some of the causes for this lack of improvement."[39] The Mormons transformed the Utes' way of life, but in turn the Native Americans, as they fought settlers and raided their cattle, had a significant impact on Manti residents.

Nature also took its toll. Because of heavy snows in 1849–50, the Saints lost all but 100 of the 240 head of cattle they had brought with them to Sanpete, and only provisions sent by the church the next spring kept the colony from starvation. Their first harvest was frost bitten and extremely scant, but the colony was saved by an arrangement to exchange shingles for provisions from the parent colony. Economic cooperation among the Mormons made colonization possible; the semiarid, plague-prone nature of the Great Basin made settlement difficult. No sooner had the Manti settlers survived the unproductive first years of pioneering and the Walker War than came the grasshopper invasions in the summers of 1855 and 1856 and a severe winter in between.[40] The parent colony could offer no help because all Utah suffered. One church leader wrote, "Dollars and cents do not count now, in these times, for they are the tightest that I have ever seen in the Territory of Utah."[41] In Manti, the Saints survived by eating the one plant the grasshoppers did not eat: pigweed, or wild spinach, which grew at the foot of Temple Hill. Every day the children took knives and cut the weeds close to the ground so they would grow again. One day they would go to the north, the next to the east, and so forth, and by the fourth day the weeds had grown enough that they could again cut them to the north.[42]

In these times of deprivation, the Mormon reformation began, continuing from the fall of 1856 to the spring of 1857. Like the prophets in the Old Testament and the Puritan divines in early New England, Mormon leaders blamed the calamities on the unfaithfulness of the people and called them to repent.[43] The resulting reformation was a series of revivals enjoining the Saints to confess and repent of their sins as well as to fulfill more completely the covenants they had made at baptism. One sin of omission forcefully brought to the attention of church members was their failure to enter plural marriages more readily. In the heady atmosphere of millenarian fervor, a considerable number did obey the injunction to marry additional wives.[44] One Danish resident of Sanpete County was among them, but as he wrote, "Now we had lots of preaching and council, but some of it vent little to far to be from the highest authority, some of this was about plural marriage, I was obeydient but not wise, I married a girl, but she did it more of fright than of love, for that reason it could not last long only about 9 months then she was divorced in 1858."[45] He was not alone in finding that it was easier to enter plural marriage than it was to live in it.

Orson Hyde, the apostle with responsibility for Sanpete County, later said the reformation "was not all pure water; but [I] compared it to the snow melting and thus increasing the water but at the same time we had more filth, etc."[46] While defending its virtues, Hyde hinted at some of the reformation's excesses. In subsequent years, leaders still enjoined members to enter plural marriage, though rarely so intensely, but the numbers who heeded that message were never so great.

While the Mormons were preaching the virtues of plural marriage in the Utah Territory, the Republicans in the rest of the nation were condemning it. In its 1856 platform, the newly founded party proclaimed Congress had "the right and the imperative duty . . . to prohibit in the Territories those twin relics of barbarism—Polygamy, and Slavery."[47] When the Republicans became the majority party, they tried to do just that. In a reprise of Reconstruction, the federal government began limiting the autonomy of the Utah Territory. Radical Republicans spearheaded reconstruction of Utah as well as the South.[48]

Like the South, Utah had its "carpetbaggers." Just as some Union soldiers saw undeveloped coal and iron ore resources near Chattanooga and went back after the Civil War to take advantage of them, so too did soldiers in Utah exploit the mining opportunities found nearby. In 1863, Colonel Conner, commander of the California Volunteers stationed in Utah, encouraged his soldiers' efforts to discover and develop mines, in hopes of attracting other males to the state to overwhelm Mormons at the ballot box.[49] Such a ploy was doomed to failure. The Utah legislature extended the franchise to women in 1870, overwhelming the vote of primarily male mining communities.

The same year Abraham Lincoln issued the preliminary proclamation emancipating slaves, Congress passed the Morrill Anti-Bigamy Act. Sponsored by a Republican congressman from Vermont, this 1862 law provided penalties for persons found guilty of bigamy, invalidated territorial laws incorporating the Church of Jesus Christ of Latter-day Saints, and made it unlawful for religious organizations in U.S. territories to hold real property over fifty thousand dollars.[50] With Mormon juries, however, the law was difficult to enforce.

Having more immediate impact on Utah was the passage that same year of another Republican bill providing for a transcontinental railroad. Building it provided work for men in Utah, and the completed line, combined with the change from sailing ships to steamships in 1868, made immigration to the territory much easier.[51] For example, in 1853, the Fosgren Company sailed from Liverpool on January 16 and did not arrive in Salt Lake City until September 30; in 1869, the year the transcontinental railroad was completed, Richard Hayes and his family sailed from England on June 2 and arrived in Ogden, Utah, on June 25.[52] In 1870, Salt Lake City was connected by rail to Ogden so that immigrants could go from England to the Mormons' capital in just over three weeks.[53] At the same time, the railroad threatened to erode the distinctiveness of Mormon life, but the Saints tried to counter this by organizing cooperatives so that they could maintain control of their own society.

To justify Reconstruction in the South, Congress in 1866 accepted Richard Henry Dana's argument that the federal government should hold the former Confederate states in the "grasp of war" for a limited time.[54] Similarly, George F. Edmunds in 1873 argued that the federal government exercised "sovereign dominion . . . over territory it has acquired" and thus had the power to legislate for Utah.[55]

Congress accepted Edmund's argument, and as Reconstruction was ending in the South, it began in Utah. In 1874, the Poland bill transferred jurisdiction of criminal, civil, and chancery cases from probate courts, whose judges were often Mormon bishops, to federal courts. It also gave federal judges considerable power over the selection of jurors.[56] One purpose was to curtail Mormon power; another was to open the way for the successful prosecution of polygamists.

The Saints believed the Morrill Anti-Bigamy Law violated their First Amendment rights to exercise freely their religion; and George Reynolds, secretary to Brigham Young, was prosecuted to test the law. In 1879, the

U.S. Supreme Court issued the landmark decision *Reynolds v. United States*. Alleging that polygamy was antirepublican because it led to patriarchy, Chief Justice Morrison R. Waite, writing for the majority, stated, "Laws are made for the government of actions, and while they cannot interfere with mere religious belief and opinions, they may with practices."[57] This distinction between belief and practice prepared the way for further prosecutions of polygamists.

In 1882, the Edmunds Act made it easier to procure convictions. It not only designated polygamy as a crime but also made cohabiting with more than one woman a misdemeanor, punishable by a fine of three hundred dollars and/or imprisonment for up to six months.[58] To facilitate convictions, the law made *belief* in polygamy grounds for challenging a juror.[59]

Moreover, Congress attempted to shift political power in Utah. In 1867, it had enfranchised freedmen in an attempt to empower African Americans and to build a Republican majority in the South; in 1882, it disfranchised polygamists to produce non-Mormon voting majorities in Utah. The Edmunds Act also barred women cohabiting with polygamists from voting and established the Utah Commission to enforce this law.[60]

Latter-day Saints were outraged at the way the law was enforced. John Taylor, president of the church, declared that James T. Little, deputy registrar, could not let his own father, formerly a polygamist but a monogamist by 1882, register to vote. By the rules then in place, however, Little could register Kate Flint, "a notorious courtesan." At about the same time, a non-Mormon, after reading part of the test oath, declared he could not sign it because he had a wife but also kept a mistress. The registrar advised him to read on. When the prospective voter came to the words *"in the marriage relation,"* he affirmed that he could honestly take the oath and so was registered to vote.[61]

This inconsistency, so hypocritical in Mormon eyes, was consistent with nineteenth-century law. Lawrence M. Friedman has called nineteenth-century law regarding moral issues, particularly sexual behavior, the "Victorian compromise."[62] Lawmakers did not try to stamp out adultery or fornication; they simply tried to keep it out of sight. Some sexual acts were crimes only if they were flaunted. In 1872, for example, California legislators made adultery a crime when a person lived "in a state of open and notorious cohabitation and adultery," and the next year the state supreme court reversed a conviction, stating that although the evidence pointed to the defendant's having committed adultery, "there is not the slightest proof of a living with her in a state of notorious adultery or cohabitation." In 1848, the Alabama Supreme Court ruled that "an occasional act of criminal intimacy" did not fall under the wording of the Alabama statute, but adultery was punishable when it became "open and notorious" and an "outrage upon decency and morality."[63] The problem for the Latter-day Saints was not that polygamous men had sexual relations with more than one woman but that they insisted on openly acknowledging plural wives as spouses. While the Saints condemned non-Mormons for having mistresses but not acknowledging them, Americans punished Mormons for so flagrantly violating the Victorian compromise. When the Edmunds Act failed to produce the desired results, Congress disfranchised all women in Utah in 1887 and in 1890 threatened to disfranchise all Mormon men, as had already been done in Idaho.[64]

Although the disfranchisement of polygamists began when the Utah Commission was appointed in 1882, intense prosecution of polygamists, known as "The Raid," did not commence until 1885. Polygamists, including the church's president, went into hiding, or "underground." Some were called on foreign missions to get them out of the way of federal marshals, and some fled to Mexico to find freedom of religion. Trying to avoid prosecution, others moved one wife to Canada or to a state or territory surrounding Utah. Plural wives also went underground so they could not be found to testify against their husbands (sometimes naming their children Exile as a memorial to their plight). By 1895, 780 had been imprisoned for unlawful cohabitation, 146 for adultery, 13 for polygamy, and 1 for incest.[65]

Despite the disruptions to the Mormon community when many of its leaders went underground, the church did not capitulate. Then in 1887 Congress passed the Edmunds-Tucker Act, which not only strengthened provisions against polygamists but also sought to destroy the economic and political power of the church.[66] It dissolved the corporation of the Church of Jesus Christ of Latter-day Saints and directed the U.S. attorney general to escheat its property holdings over $50,000.[67] It also dissolved and escheated the property of the Perpetual Emigrating Fund Company, the church organization that provided financial assistance to converts emigrating from Europe. The escheated property was to be used for the common schools, presumably to ensure that Mormon children were given a secular education so that they would not follow in the footsteps of their elders.[68] Moreover, to dilute the Mormon vote, all women in the Utah Territory were disfranchised.[69]

By 1890, over a million dollars worth of church property was in the hands of the government receiver, and in *The Late Corporation of the Church of Jesus Christ of Latter-day Saints v. United States,* the U.S. Supreme Court upheld the constitutionality of the Edmunds-Tucker

Act.[70] In addition, the Liberal Party, the non-Mormon party in Utah, gained control of two of Utah's largest cities. The U.S. Supreme Court had upheld Idaho's test oath that required voters to swear they did not believe in plural marriage or belong to a church that advocated it. Congress was considering the Cullom-Strubble bill, which would have applied a similar test oath in Utah. Beleaguered, the Saints sought an agreement with the federal government. Finally on September 25, 1890, Wilford Woodruff, president of the church, issued what became known as the Manifesto, announcing that the church would submit to the laws of the land. It was accepted by vote at the church's semiannual conference on October 6.[71] To be readmitted to the Union, former Confederate states had to ratify the Fourteenth Amendment, which they all accomplished by 1870; for Utah to be admitted as a state, the LDS Church had to abandon plural marriage, which it officially began to do in 1890.

The Manifesto was ambiguous, but, in the words of Jan Shipps, "Whatever else it did, the Manifesto announced that the old order would have to pass away."[72] Henceforth, the church's economic and political power was fundamentally altered, and future plural marriages in the United States were no longer officially sanctioned by the church.[73] In 1896, Utah became a state, but the state constitution had to contain the clause that "polygamous or plural marriages are forever prohibited."[74] Mormons finally obtained the statehood they had so long sought, but under circumstances that circumscribed the autonomy they desired.

While Congress and the courts were reconstructing Utah, economic developments were transforming the lives of its citizens. Manti, long a part of the regional economy, was now integrated into the national economy.[75] Advertisements for national products in the local newspapers and the extension of the railroad to Manti in 1890 were some of the visible signs. So were the products sold in Sanpete. In the 1890s, "buggies, organs, pianos, 'States' carpets, upholstered furniture with festooned 'tidies' and draperies hung over the upholstery" became marks of wealth and refinement, while "homemade carpets with straw padding underneath next to the board floor" were relegated to barn lofts.[76]

Never during their history were the Mormons free from the *influence* of outsiders. While in the Midwest, they were subjected to the political situations in those states and the hostility of the surrounding communities. In the Great Basin, the federal government curtailed the Saints' autonomy. From the establishment of the Utah Territory in 1850, federally appointed officials held some political power, and for most of the period after 1857 contingents of the U.S. army were stationed there.[77] By the 1880s, the federal government was intervening directly—and repressively—into the territorial governing process. Even the Indians, though technically not outsiders after so many had been baptized into the church, affected the Saints' lives. Despite the many assaults on their freedom of action, however, the Saints enjoyed sufficient autonomy during the first thirty-five years in the Great Basin to establish plural marriage as a family form and to create the legal system necessary to promote it.

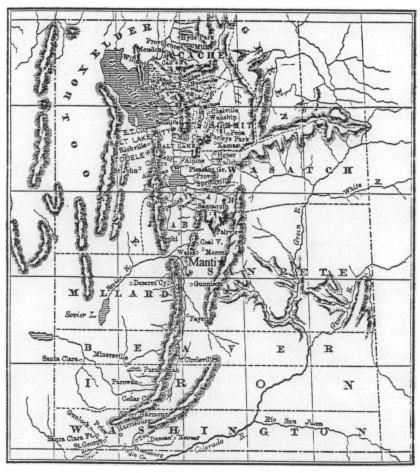

Map of principal settlements in Utah, 1862. (Adapted from Hubert Howe
Bancroft, *History of Utah, 1540–1887* [San Francisco: History Company,
1890])

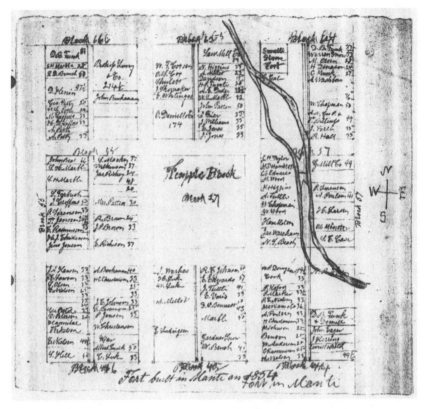

Manti Fort, 1854. Built because of hostile Native Americans, the fort superimposed crowded housing onto the challenges of eking a living from the semiarid land. Added to these difficulties was the need to provide for the widows and fatherless, which the church met by encouraging families to incorporate these women, often as plural wives. (Used by permission of the Historical Department, Church of Jesus Christ of Latter-day Saints)

Manti Temple. It rises majestically above the graves of those pioneers who had sacrificed so much to build it so that their family relationships would endure beyond their deaths. (Photo by Warren Daynes)

Isaac Morley. He was the Mormon leader who founded Manti. His children and those of his plural wives by previous marriages made significant contributions to the town. (Used by permission of the LDS Church Archives)

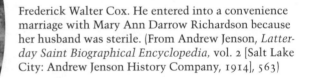

Frederick Walter Cox. He entered into a convenience marriage with Mary Ann Darrow Richardson because her husband was sterile. (From Andrew Jenson, *Latter-day Saint Biographical Encyclopedia*, vol. 2 [Salt Lake City: Andrew Jenson History Company, 1914], 563)

Frederick Walter Cox Jr. His marriage to Lucy Allen in 1857 was pronounced valid by Brigham Young. That the prophet of the church, not a court of law, rendered the judgment reveals that in early Utah marriage was a religious rite. (From Andrew Jenson, *Latter-day Saint Biographical Encyclopedia*, vol. 2 [Salt Lake City: Andrew Jenson History Company, 1914], 564)

Anne Eliza Howland

Amanda Polly
Savage

Phineas Wolcott Cook married
Anne Eliza Howland in 1840.
Believing that plural marriage
was divinely inspired, he married Amanda Polly Savage,
whose father also became a polygamist; Catherine McCleve,
whose parents had not yet immigrated to Utah; and Johanna
Christina Poulson, who arrived
in Utah with her two young
children. (Photos courtesy of the
International Society, Daughters
of Utah Pioneers; used by permission of the Phineas Wolcott
Cook Family Organization)

Phineas Wolcott
Cook

Catherine McCleve

Johanna Christina
Poulson

Herman Julius Christensen. Arriving in Manti in 1853, this Danish immigrant married four plural wives in the next seven years. By his death in 1896, he had been divorced from his first wife, four plural wives, and a subsequent monogamous wife. (Photo from author)

Karen Kirstine Poulsen Christensen. Married to Herman Julius Christensen in 1858 at age fourteen, she bore him fifteen children, only four of whom survived to maturity. In 1885, he filed for divorce from her on the grounds of great mental distress. (Photo from author)

Mary Ann Ayers Young and Lieutenant Sylvester Mowry.
In 1854, Mowry tried to seduce Young, who was married, but
his design was thwarted by Brigham Young's warnings and
by Mowry's commanding officer, who sent the lieutenant
out of the territory. (Courtesy of the LDS Church Archives
and the Arizona Historical Society/Tucson, No. 181136)

Howard Egan and Tamson Parshley Egan. Howard killed James
Monroe when he learned that his wife Tamson had borne Monroe's
child. This dramatic incident symbolizes the seriousness with
which the Saints viewed sexual relationships outside of marriage
and Mormon men's responsibility to protect women from seducers.
(Used by permission, Utah State Historical Society, all rights reserved)

Tombstones of Soren Christoffersen and his three wives, Manti Cemetery. The first wife's larger marker may be a tribute to her for helping rear the children by her husband's other wives when her only child died. (Photo by Warren Daynes)

Nelson tombstone, Manti Cemetery. This monument reveals the ambiguity in relationships as families abandoned plural marriage. In the 1870s, Andrew Nelson joined the Presbyterian church and ceased living with Camilla and cohabited only with Sophia. Nevertheless, Camilla continued to be listed on the censuses as married and is included on the family tombstone, although only Sophia is designated as his wife. (Photo by Warren Daynes)

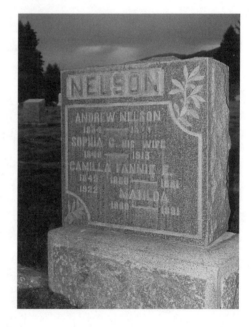

PART 2

I Leviticus: Legal and Ecclesiastical Framework for Marriage

Nevertheless neither is the man without the woman, neither the woman without the man, in the Lord.
—1 Corinthians 11:11

And again, verily I say unto you, if a man marry a wife by my word, which is my law, and by the new and everlasting covenant, and it is sealed unto them by the Holy Spirit of promise, . . . it shall be done unto them in all things whatsoever my servant hath put upon them, in time, and through all eternity; and shall be of full force when they are out of the world; and they shall pass by the angels, and the gods, which are set there, to their exaltation and glory in all things. . . .
—Doctrine and Covenants 132:19

3 Nineteenth-Century Marriage Law in Utah

Twenty-year-old Fred Cox made a momentous decision in the spring of 1857: he would ask Mary Ellen Tuttle to be his wife. He had no wealth to offer his prospective bride—on the 1860 census he listed no real or personal property—but at the height of the reformation in Manti, that was a small consideration. Women were being importuned to marry, especially to become plural wives. Fred was an eligible young man, and several young women had encouraged his attention. He chose young Mary Ellen.[1]

His difficulty was how he should tell Lucy Allen, who had so openly shown her affection for him, that he planned to marry someone else. He concluded he would break the news to her at a church dance on April 20. That night he asked Lucy to walk outside with him. While he hesitated to apprise her of his choice, she told him she was going to Provo to work that summer, unless, she hinted, something happened to keep her in Manti. Before he could use this opening to introduce his subject, Bishop Warren S. Snow approached the couple and stopped to exchange pleasantries. From their former association and their seeking to be alone, the couple appeared to the bishop to be lovers, and he offered to marry them on the spot. Lucy eagerly agreed. Not taking the bishop seriously, Fred submitted. The bishop played his part well and went through the entire ceremony. When he asked Fred if he took Lucy to be his wife, the young man hesitated, but when the question was repeated, he gave the usual answer.

The bishop had made Fred's message to Lucy more difficult, but somehow he communicated enough so that she left for Provo as planned. By late summer, Mary Ellen had agreed to become Fred's wife. As dedicated Latter-day Saints, they wanted to be married in the religious ceremony that would seal them for "time and eternity," a rite generally performed only at the Endowment House in Salt Lake City. For them to be eligible to participate in this ceremony, the bishop had to certify their worthiness. So to the bishop they went.

Bishop Snow seemed perplexed at their request to be married. He had wanted Mary Ellen as his own plural wife but had been thwarted because her father did not want her to enter plural marriage.[2] Fred was unaware of this when he and his prospective bride made their request. The bishop asked the girl if she had carefully weighed her decision to enter plural marriage and queried the young man whether he was financially able to support another wife. Now it was the couple's turn to be perplexed. Mary Ellen assured the bishop that such questions need not be asked, but he countered by affirming that Fred was already married to Lucy Allen and that he himself had performed the marriage. Fred protested, arguing that the ceremony had not been a real wedding and was neither legal nor binding. His protests were for naught. Fred and Mary Ellen enlisted the aid of their parents and even the aid of Lucy's parents, but the bishop was adamant that Fred and Lucy were married. The couple and their parents appealed to a higher authority. While attending the church's semi-annual conference in October, Fred, his father, and Lucy's father sought an interview with Brigham Young. The president of the church listened attentively to their story. After carefully considering the case, he announced to Fred that he was a married man and advised him to go home and make the best of it. On the way home, Fred stopped in Provo to get Lucy and took her home with him to Manti.[3]

Lucy proved the kind of wife who would have confirmed to Brigham Young the sagacity of his decision: she bore her husband twelve children and in 1873 consented to his marrying a second wife. In addition, she ran a boardinghouse to supplement the family's income. Mary Ellen, meanwhile, married Walter Stringham in 1859 and bore fifteen children. She remained true to her first intentions to avoid polygamy, however, and her marriage to Walter remained a monogamous one.[4]

The circumstances under which Fred Cox and Lucy Allen were married were surely unusual, but the story illustrates the most important feature of nineteenth-century Mormon marriage: marriage was considered a religious, not a civil, rite and was governed by ecclesiastical rules.

The president of the church, not a court of law, decided whether the marriage was valid. No civil legislation restricted who could marry or who could perform marriages in Utah until 1887, although the territorial legislature passed a law in 1852 to allow plural wives and their children to inherit from their polygamous husbands and fathers. Because Mormon marriages might be valid only for this life, for eternity only, or for both, the Saints recognized several types of marriage that conferred different rights and responsibilities on husbands and wives, and these were enforced by ecclesiastical, not civil, courts.

Since Mormons held marriage to be sacred rather than secular, the Mormon-dominated Utah legislature saw little need for the civil government to regulate marriage until congressional legislation forced action in the 1880s. The most important early legislation regarding marriage was the incorporation of the church. On February 4, 1851, during debate on the issue, Brigham Young made clear that an important reason for incorporation was to allow plural marriage when he said, "So if the Latter Day Saints wish to have more wives than one to live Holy & raise up Holy seed unto the Lord let them enjoy that privilege."[5] That day the legislature obligingly passed "An Ordinance Incorporating the Church of Jesus Christ of Latter Day Saints," affirming that the "said church holds the constitutional and original right . . . *to solemnize marriage compatible with the revelations of Jesus Christ;* . . . that the pursuit of bliss, and the enjoyment of life, in every capacity of public association and *domestic happiness* . . . may not legally be questioned, . . . inasmuch as the doctrines, principles, practices, or performances, support virtue, and increase morality, and are not inconsistent with, or repugnant to the Constitution of the United States, or of this State, and *are founded in the revelations of the Lord.*"[6]

In essence, the act claims for the church the right to regulate its own marriage practices without interference, as long as those practices are not specifically prohibited by the Constitution of the United States or of Utah. Because neither mentioned marriage, the act left the church free to determine who was married and who was not. The act mandated that all units of the church maintain a record of marriages that occurred in their jurisdictions, but with no provision being made to enforce it, records of marriages that were not also sealings were indifferently kept.[7] A statute dealing with marriage had been introduced into the first territorial legislature, but it had been laid aside on February 28, 1852, "to take up business of more consequence."[8] Although the Morrill Act passed by Congress in 1862 annulled the acts incorporating the church, this did not change the situation in practice. Thus, the most important feature of Utah marriage law was the absence of legislation to regulate marriage until Congress passed the Edmunds-Tucker Act in 1887.[9]

This absence is not surprising, because Mormonism taught that marriage was a religious rite. The struggle between the church and state about who would control marriage has been a long one in the Western world. By the end of the eleventh century, it was generally conceded that jurisdiction over decisions about what constituted a marriage resided with the bishop and his court. In the two centuries that followed, the Roman Catholic church enunciated its beliefs about marriage and increasingly upheld the superiority of church practice over local usage. Articulated in 1140 by the monk Gratian in his definitive *Concordia discordantium canonum*, these beliefs included the idea that the marital bond was indissoluble and that it was created by the free consent of the bride and groom.

Because the church wanted to make the formation of marriage effortless and easy, it followed Roman law, under which "marriage was virtually a formless transaction." The marriage was valid if the man and woman simply exchanged vows of marriage in the present, not future, tense. As long as consent was given in the present tense, the church upheld the validity of the marriage even if there were no witnesses present, no clergy officiating, no specific form followed, or no consent given by parents. Even consummation was not necessary if consent was given in the present tense. Moreover, sexual intercourse after promises given in the future tense also created a valid marriage. Certain impediments could, however, invalidate the marriage. These included a previous commitment either to a living spouse or to a religious life, too close a relationship by blood (consanguinity) or by marriage (affinity), and being impotent or too young. With these exceptions, the church upheld the primacy of present consent between the couple over other considerations. To be sure, the church discouraged the clandestine marriages such consent might foster, and the fourth Lateran Council in 1215 stipulated that couples planning to marry announce their intentions and prohibited priests from officiating in secret ceremonies.[10]

Although the church upheld the validity of secret, informal marriages, marriages usually were performed publicly and contracted in some ritual. This was so not only because the church could punish couples marrying secretly even if it did not invalidate their marriages but also because secular courts retained jurisdiction over property. Marriages without the consent of parents or lord could well result in the loss of an inheritance or succession to feudal lands. Thus, while the church determined what constituted a marriage, it did not control all aspects of it.[11]

Two problems produced inherent tensions in this marriage system. First, allowing secret, informal marriages created difficulties in knowing whether a prospective spouse was already married. Second, jurisdiction over marriage resided mainly in the church, but civil courts asserted their authority over property rights created by marriage and by birth. These inherent tensions helped produce a different set of beliefs about marriage during the Reformation. Although marriage was a divine institution, according to Martin Luther in his *Babylonian Captivity*, it was not a sacrament, it did not impart grace, and it was not necessary for salvation. Other reformers followed Luther's lead, and all reformed churches rejected the Catholic Church's claim that marriage was a sacrament. With that change in belief, control over marriage could be vested in civil rather than religious courts. Reducing the clergy's jurisdiction over moral life, Protestant governments on the Continent began requiring parental consent for minors to marry and mandating the presence of witnesses to validate a marriage.[12] In response, the Catholic Church tightened regulations for marriage at the Council of Trent in 1563, requiring that the traditional exchange of consent take place before witnesses, one of whom was the pastor.[13]

In England, however, the Reformation took a different path in regard to marriage. Because elites found that ecclesiastical courts had adequately served their interests, reformation of the English church did not include abolition of those courts. The Church of England was independent of the Roman Catholic church before the Council of Trent, so its requirement of witnesses and a pastor for a valid marriage had no force. Clandestine marriages flourished; perhaps as many as 20 percent of marriages in England in the mid-eighteenth century were clandestine. Not until 1753, with the passage of the Hardwicke Marriage Act, were such marriages curtailed.[14]

The Hardwicke Act was not passed until long after the American colonies had begun developing their own marriage laws. New England drew on the Reformation's ideas about civil government's control over marriage. Magistrates, not ministers, performed marriages there until 1686, when the Crown established its control over New England after revoking those colonies' charters. In the South, the Church of England was the established church, but without bishops or ecclesiastical courts, civil regulation of marriages was uncontested. A variety of churches proliferated throughout the middle and southern colonies, and the marriages performed by the rites of those churches were recognized.[15] With diverse religious traditions and peoples, the idea that free consent of the couple in the present tense created a valid marriage passed into the common law.

These developments, along with the movement away from government involvement prevalent in early nineteenth-century America, elevated consent of the couple over public control of matrimony. Unlike colonial or contemporary English interpretations of the common law, American nineteenth-century courts generally validated secret and informal marriages.[16] By midcentury in the United States, the opinion of James Kent, the most influential legal commentator of his time, was accepted by all but a minority of courts: "No peculiar ceremonies are requisite by the common law to the valid celebration of the marriage. The consent of the parties is all that is required."[17] This rule was explicitly applied to Utah in 1885, when its supreme court ruled, "The marriage is complete when there is a full, free and mutual consent by the parties capable of contracting, though not followed by cohabitation. . . . Under our law a marriage depends solely upon the mutual consent of the contracting parties. They may enter into the marriage relation secretly, and the fact may be unknown to all save the man and woman. . . . [A] couple may meet on the highway at any time in the day or night and there contract a valid marriage . . . [n]o particular form or ceremony being essential, and no witness being required."[18] Thus, no specific form for solemnizing a marriage was necessary to make it valid, as long as both bride and groom consented to the marriage.[19] Nor were witnesses required. Not until 1888 did the law in Utah mandate that two witnesses sign the marriage certificate. That law also declared that marriages not solemnized by an authorized person were void, thus nullifying common-law marriages.[20]

In the light of these traditions and laws, Fred Cox's case reveals a number of aspects about marriages in early Utah. Reversing increasing civil control, Mormons resacralized marriage and reverted to religious authority to regulate it. When Fred Cox did not believe the wedding ceremony performed by Bishop Snow was binding, he took his case to the president of the church, not to a court of law, and all parties accepted the prophet's judgment. Nevertheless, the judgment rendered was consistent with current common law in the United States that gave primacy to the consent of the couple, not to compliance with a specific form or ceremony.[21] Because both Fred and Lucy had consented to the marriage in the present tense, the presumption was strong that the marriage was valid. Once married, only a divorce could dissolve the union. Although it was long disputed whether in Utah the common law was in force—with the church contending that it was not—both the common law and the church had the same goal of encouraging marriage.[22] Whether Fred Cox's vocal assent to the marriage constituted consent is of course problematic when he had mental reservations, but his consent at the time was not coerced and was in the present tense. Under these circumstances—no positive legislation regarding marriage in Utah, marriage considered a religious act, and an emphasis on consent rather than on the form of marriage—Cox was a definitely a married man.

Contrary to popular belief about them in the nineteenth century, Mormons, like their contemporaries in the Western world, believed in the free consent of parties to a marriage. But freely consenting to a marriage is not the same as freely deciding whether to marry or choosing whom to marry, and the Saints believed that women in particular had a right to choose their marital status as well as their husbands. To counter the erroneous views about coerced marriages in Utah, several Mormon women wrote to the Senate Committee on Education and Labor in 1886: "No Mormon woman, old or young, is compelled to marry at all, still less to enter into polygamy. Every young woman is as free to choose her own destiny as the bird in the air; free to marry from motives of purest affection the man of her choice, or free to live in single blessedness to the day of her death, if she so desires."[23] Mormon women were free to choose their marital status, whether single, monogamous, or polygamous, although there were numerous social and religious reasons to marry.

During the Mormon reformation considerable pressure was put on some women to marry. Orson Hyde and A. P. Rockwood, both general authorities, admonished Manti congregations in 1857 that men should not use their priesthood to get wives. "The rights of woman must be respected," Rockwood warned.[24] Brigham Young had made it clear in 1854 that women should be free to choose their husbands: "When your daughters have grown up, and wish to marry, let them have their choice in a husband, if they know what their choice is. . . . Take this or that man if you want them my girls, I give you good counsel about it, nevertheless you shall have your own agency in the matter, even as I want mine."[25] Although he believed children should have their parents' consent to marry, he did recommend that parents give their daughters the right to choose, as the story of Ann Cook illustrates.

In the fall of 1861, seventeen-year-old Ann Cook showed a preference for William Kilshaw Barton, a man who had been a polygamist but whose first wife had died in the spring of that year. Because she had revealed her preference, William asked Ann if she had any objections to keeping his company, if her father gave his sanction. She replied that she would be glad to do so. William spoke to her father, but he refused to consent. Sometime later, Brigham Young visited Manti and in the presence of many witnesses told Ann and her father that she had the right of choice. Her father then acquiesced, and she married William on October 10, 1864, as his plural wife.[26] Parents' approval was important but did not override a young woman's choice.

Ann showed her preference for the man of her choice but left the initiative to him. Some other women were more direct. By the time Emmeline Woodward Whitney was twenty-four, she had been deserted by her first husband and widowed by her second. Alone and with two young daughters, she wrote "A Letter from a True Friend" to Daniel H. Wells, a prominent church and civic leader with five wives. Reminding him of his friendship with her second husband, Newell Whitney, she asked him to consider her lonely state and "return to her a description of his feelings for her." She then expressed the wish to be "united with a being noble as thyself."[27] She and Wells were married six months later.

Similarly, Nancy Gibbons suggested marriage to John D. Lee. On February 26, 1847, he wrote in his diary that she came to his house and after some conversation said "she wanted I should take charge of her and her effects, that is if I considered her worth taking off." He then asked if she wanted to be married to him, and she replied that she did. The forty-eight-year old woman was subsequently sealed to thirty-five-year-old Lee as his plural wife.[28]

In 1903, seventy-five-year-old Azariah Smith also received a proposal of marriage. A friend invited him to her house so she could introduce him to Sevilla Stoy Mitchell, who was seventy-one. After "some pleasing conversation with her, . . . she proposed being sealed to me for time. . . . She not wishing to put it off . . . and wishing to go and get her things, and come back right away." They were married the next day.[29]

In each of these instances, the woman had been married before, and in two the man already had several wives. Women could expect that older or polygamous men would be willing to marry again, and a few were willing to approach the man directly to bring about the marriage. Orson Pratt intimated that because marriage was crucial to exaltation, women were justified in proposing marriage and reversing the prevailing customs.[30] In contrast, never-married women, such as Lucy Allen and Ann Cook, expressed their preference by their actions but left initiating the marriage proposal to the man, as was customary elsewhere.

The Saints grounded the logic of women's right to choose in the structure of polygamy itself. In plural marriage, men could choose a mate more than once, but each woman had only one husband. In her account of her parents' courtship, Brigham Young's daughter wrote that women "ought to have their choice in the matter for they can choose but one; and they have a right to select that one."[31]

Nevertheless, some women succumbed to the wishes of their parents and entered marriages not of their own choosing. Karen Kirstine Poulsen emigrated from Denmark with her parents in 1853 and suffered through the Walker War and the grasshopper devastations. When Herman Julius Christensen, a church and civic leader in Manti, asked for her as his wife, her parents told her to marry him because he was a wealthy man and could take care of her. Obedient to her parents, she accepted his proposal. She cried the morning he came to take her to Salt Lake for the wedding, but fourteen-year-old Karen Kirstine formally, if reluctantly, consented to become the third wife of a man twenty-three years her senior. Although she always remained somewhat frightened of him, she bore him fifteen children.[32]

Mary Frances Callaway also obeyed her father when she became Daniel D. McArthur's third wife. Her mother died in 1869, leaving her to take care of her father and the six younger children. Her father then married a woman only two years older than Mary Frances. When McArthur asked him for his daughter's hand, Levi Callaway was amenable and told his daughter that she would go to the party that night with McArthur, although she already had a date. She obediently went with McArthur and shortly thereafter, at age seventeen, married him.[33]

Some young women insisted on making their own choices, however, and they married as they liked. When George Peacock's daughter Sarah planned to marry a non-Mormon, he met with her and "gave her Such Council as I thought was my Duty to her as Father[.] I found that She was determined to marry Doct. O. C. Ormsby contrary to my wishes and Council." A second interview produced the same result: nineteen-year-old Sarah married the man of her choice without her father's approval or his presence.[34] Although young women were pressured to marry with their parents' approval, a daughter willing to flout filial and religious duties to wed the man of her choice could do so, albeit at the risk of alienating herself from her parents.

Anna Maria Isaacson insisted on marrying whom she wished but waited until her parents finally gave their consent. She was fifteen when Edwin Whiting, twenty-one, first proposed to her, and she knew "there was no one else for me." Her parents, however, thought she was too young to fall in love, and, according to her, "They didn't like the idea of me going with a young fellow who wasn't tried and tested. Both Mother and Father thought it would be better for me to marry some older man who had already proved himself, had a wife or two and was ready to provide for his families."[35] This favorable parental attitude toward polygamists' personal and economic traits had led Karen Kirstine Poulsen and Mary Frances Callaway to enter plural marriage. At the time, they obeyed their parents and married; however, they had not accepted the proposal of young bachelors. Anna Maria Isaacson had, and she refused offers to enter plural marriage. When she turned eighteen, her parents finally gave their consent, and she married the man of her choice.[36]

Believing the religious aspect of marriage was most crucial, Mormons downplayed the role of romantic love. In 1853, Orson Pratt wrote that love was not "such as is often described in novels, which acts irresistably, forcing all the other powers of the mind into subjection." Charles C. Rich was even more pointed in his criticism of romantic love in 1877: "When a person is love struck, there is no reason in them. We should never be struck very bad."[37] According to the historian Karen Lystra, while romantic love in the nineteenth century was perceived as an uncontrollable force, its most essential feature was the "completely unfettered" revelation of oneself to one's beloved, and only to one's beloved. This intimacy between two lovers set them off from others and "contributed to the displacement of God by the lover as the central symbol of ultimate significance."[38] This nineteenth-century view of romantic love that set the couple apart from the community and tended to displace God was hardly compatible with Mormon beliefs. "Never love your wives one hair's breadth further than they adorn the Gospel," Brigham Young preached. "Never love them so but that you can leave them at a moment's warning without shedding a tear."[39] Love was supposed to be guided by and subordinated to religious purposes.

To be sure, love was crucial to marriage. "No woman should be united in marriage with a man unless she have some love for him," Orson Pratt wrote, but he added, "Any woman who loves righteousness can and does love a man who works righteousness; and she can, by cultivating this love, be happy in his society, as a friend and as a brother; and if she were united to him in marriage, she could love him as a husband; . . . There is not a righteous good woman in the Church of God but what a righteous man loves as a friend and a sister; and if he were lawfully united to her in marriage, he could love her as a wife; and this love, by cultivation and mutual kindness, would grow stronger and stronger, until they were perfect in love."[40] Successful marital love, then, was dependent not on finding one's soul mate but on marrying a righteous person—someone who shared one's beliefs and lived by them—and cultivating love for that person. Such love was not necessarily exclusive or intimate, though close and romantic relationships were certainly not excluded.

Whether a woman's love was romantic or whether a woman or her parents had chosen her husband, she had to consent to the marriage: the matter of consent lay at the heart of the Mormon marriage ceremony that wed couples for time and eternity. The couple joined right hands as they faced the officiator, who first asked the husband if he received the bride as his wife by his "own free will and choice." After an affirmative response, the officiator then turned to the bride, calling her by name, and asked if she gave herself to the groom as his "lawful and wedded wife for time and all eternity," of her "own free will and choice."[41] After both bride and groom had assented that they entered the marriage of their own free will, the officiator pronounced the couple legally and lawfully husband and wife and promised them eternal blessings. The consent of both bride and groom and the officiator's pronouncements constituted the Mormon religious ceremony.

Unlike the nineteenth-century Episcopal ceremony, for example, in which the bride's father or a friend gave the bride to the husband, in the Mormon rite the woman gave herself to the man.[42] If it was a plural marriage, the first wife gave her consent by placing the plural wife's right hand in the right hand of her husband at the beginning of the ceremony. The church permitted a man to take another wife without the first wife's consent if the first wife could give no good reason to refuse her husband permission to enter plural marriage.[43] In any case, the bride gave her free and willing consent, which was no different from the requirements under common law to validate the marriage.

Although free consent was crucial, under the common law no particular form of ceremony was required, nor was public notification of the marriage. The early-nineteenth-century republican ethos combined with social conditions in America to weaken state regulation.[44] As an 1816 Pennsylvania court decision stated, "We have no established church. A certificate of the bishop, therefore is out of the question. We have no law compelling the keeping of a register by all persons who perform the marriage ceremony. Our marriages are celebrated sometimes by clergymen, sometimes by justices of the peace and sometimes before witnesses, without the intervention of clergymen or justices. . . . Many marriages take place in parts of our country but thinly settled. To hold a woman, therefore, to proof of her actual marriage might be productive of great inconvenience, without any advantage."[45] As this judgment indicates, registration of marriages was not compulsory. Americans were averse to state intervention into private affairs, which is what registration of marriages meant to many.[46]

With no law regulating marriage, Utah also had no registration system outside the church. After a sealing ceremony, a scribe was supposed to enter the date of the marriage as well as the names of the witnesses.[47] This record was not public, however. In the 1880s, when the U.S. commissioner of labor compiled statistics on marriage and divorce in America, he could not obtain even the number of marriages performed by church officials. Nor are these records currently available to scholars.[48] Some marriages performed in Manti by local church authorities were recorded in the Manti Ward Record, but others were either not recorded or not preserved.[49] Justices of the peace also performed marriages, but their records were also often indifferently kept.[50]

That such records did not exist or that marriage certificates were not issued did not invalidate marriages under common law—or under church law—as the unwitting Fred Cox learned when Brigham Young pronounced him a married man. Laws about marriage were lenient in mid-nineteenth-century America, giving primacy to the bride's and groom's consent to the marriage. But nowhere outside Utah were the laws lenient enough to allow plural marriage, and such leniency proved to be the rock upon which permissive laws foundered as the century came to a close.

4 The Nature of Mormon Marriages

Unreliable public records made it difficult for many couples to substantiate their marriages, but American courts accepted into common law the rule that a marriage could be presumed from the cohabitation, reputation, and acknowledgment of the couple.[1] On the whole, midcentury law in America encouraged marriage. Because most judges required no particular form of ceremony or a record of it to presume a marriage, they put the weight of the law behind those living as husband and wife. Moreover, both Georgia and Pennsylvania passed laws stating that marriage was encouraged. In Utah, marriage was encouraged not only by continual preaching from the pulpit but also by the lack of legal barriers to it. Even Pennsylvania's encouragement contained a proviso: "All marriages *not forbidden by the law of God* shall be encouraged."[2] In Utah, neither the law nor the law of God was restrictive. Whereas the Episcopal ceremony included the sentence, "If any man can show just cause why they may not lawfully be joined together, let him now speak, or else hereafter for ever hold his peace," the Mormon ceremony omitted such cautions altogether.[3] Utah law listed no "just cause" for preventing a couple from marrying, and Mormon practice placed no restrictions on marriage based on age, existing marriage, or affinity and few based on consanguinity.

Although the Utah legislature enacted no laws legalizing plural marriage, it did pass a measure stating, "No laws nor part of laws shall be read, argued, cited, or adopted in any court, during any trial, except those enacted by the Governor and Legislative Assembly of this Territory, and those passed by the Congress of the United States when applicable; and no report, decision, or doing of any court shall be read, argued, cited, or adopted as precedent in any other trial."[4] Because precedent is the basis for the common law, this measure disallowed the authority of the common law in the territory. Since the common law prohibited bigamy, rejection of the common law at least tacitly made plural marriage legally possible. However, whether the common law was in force was in considerable dispute because of the judicial decisions made by non-Mormon judges.

Except for permitting plural marriage, Mormon practice was generally congruent with contemporary common law in its lack of restrictions on marriage. Following Roman law, under common law the age of discretion, the age at which a valid marriage could be contracted, was twelve for females and fourteen for males. A marriage contracted by an individual under age seven was a complete nullity. Although individuals could contract a marriage between age seven and the age of discretion, they could also disaffirm the marriage at any time before reaching the age of discretion. Such disaffirmation could be either private or public, that is, with or without a judicial decree declaring the marriage invalid.[5] Although under common law parental control continued until the child turned twenty-one, most American judges gave greater weight to the sanctity of marriage than to parental disapproval. Judges in the United States often rendered legislation raising the age for marriage ineffective by treating such laws as merely advisory, not compulsory. In Utah, if any restrictions on age prevailed, they were the common-law ages of discretion, until 1888 when those ages were incorporated into the Act Regulating Marriage. Only in 1897 were the ages raised to fourteen for females and sixteen for males.[6]

The Mormon marriage system similarly gave wide latitude in choice of mates. Brigham Young set the tone for unions among kin when he stated in 1854 that "the children of Adam and Eve married each other; . . . I believe in sisters marrying brothers, and brothers having their sisters for wives. Why? Because we cannot do otherwise. . . . Our spirits are all brothers and sisters, and so are our bodies; . . . for they are of the same flesh, blood, and bones as all the family of the Earth."[7] Not many Mormons chose to marry blood relatives, but a few consanguineous unions have been identified, including one between a brother and his half-sister.

George Darling Watt, one of the first Mormon converts in England, immigrated to Utah in 1851 with his wife, his eight-year-old son, his mother, and his younger half-sister, Jane Brown. Soon after their arrival, Watt's wife died, leaving him to care for their son. Probably while Brown was helping in that endeavor, she and Watt decided they wanted to marry. Watt asked Brigham Young for his consent for the union, citing the biblical example of Abraham marrying his half-sister Sarah as precedent. The church president denied permission for the marriage, which elicited another plea, this time from Jane: "[George] has made me acquainted with your counsel touching our union which alas is unfavorable to the same. What am I to do? My whole affections are placed upon him. His manly bearing, his untiring kindness and unshaken faithfulness as a brother and a friend has won my love over which I have no control to love another."[8] Young's response is unknown, but the *Ordinance Index* does not show that George and Jane were ever sealed. Nevertheless, they did marry in the early 1850s and had three children. Jane's faithfulness to George was shaken, however, after he entered plural marriage in 1853. In 1860, he was living with two wives he had married subsequent to his marriage to Jane, but she did not reside in his household or live near him. Unhappy with plural marriage and the church, Jane joined the Reorganized Church of Jesus Christ of Latter Day Saints in 1864, married a soldier in the Ohio Cavalry Volunteers, and moved with him to Nebraska.[9] From the current evidence, it appears the church did not approve this marriage between a half-brother and a half-sister, though apparently the couple was not punished for it either. The marriage was not successful and ended for reasons unrelated to the close blood relationship between the couple.

More frequent but still rare were uncles who married their nieces. James T. S. Allred and Henry Sudweeks both married their brothers' daughters as plural wives. In both cases, their brothers had died, and the nieces had immigrated to Utah shortly before the marriage. In these cases, neither woman was young: Sudweeks's niece was forty when she married him in 1885, and Allred's was forty-two when they married in 1875.[10] Anne Maria Bertelsen was only twenty-one, however, when she married her mother's brother as a plural wife, which she did in 1858, only a few months after her arrival from Denmark with her fifteen-year-old brother. When her husband died, she became the plural wife of another uncle, her first husband's brother.[11] During the reformation in 1857, Samuel Smith, a church and civic leader in Brigham City, married two of his teenage nieces. Aaron Johnson, high councillor in Nauvoo and bishop in Springville, married five of his brother Lorenzo's daughters, two before leaving Nauvoo and three during the 1850s.[12] It appears that uncle-niece marriages after the 1850s became less common and that nieces who subsequently married uncles were considerably older. Since the validity of a marriage between an uncle and his niece was upheld even in South

Carolina, it is not surprising that Utah also approved such marriages, although such unions seem to have become less frequent over time.

Considerably more prevalent than consanguineous unions were marriages between affines. Men frequently married their sisters-in-law as plural wives. In the Manti subset, eighteen men, or 12 percent, did so. Two also took their wives' nieces as plural wives. Another married his first wife's daughter-in-law when she was widowed. Although the men needed special permission from the church president, seven in the subset, or 4 percent, were sealed to both a mother and her daughter.[13] Marital restrictions based on affinity were being gradually reduced in the United States during the nineteenth century, partly because of the growing belief that marriage united two people, not their two families.[14] By wedding those related by marriage much more frequently than those related by blood, most Mormons showed they shared with other Americans many of the same assumptions about whom it was appropriate to marry, although still tolerating a greater latitude in marriage partners. But Mormons viewed all marital relationships as temporary and pertaining only to this mortal existence unless they were confirmed by sealings to make them effective during the eternities. Believing that in the eternal scheme all are brothers and sisters and that all mortal relationships are temporary if not sealed by the priesthood, Mormons more readily accepted marriages between closer kin than did other Americans, although such marriages, except for sororal polygamy, were not common.

The most glaring lack of restriction, of course, was that an existing marriage did not create an impediment to another marriage. Every state had penalties for bigamy, and the second marriage was considered void, with the bigamous spouse acquiring no property rights.[15] Not only did the Saints allow plural marriage, but they believed it was the ideal form of marriage as well. That the Mormons recognized different forms of marriage, with different rights and responsibilities, is less well known but is an important feature of their marriage system.

Mormons could be married by justices of the peace or by local church officials, just as Fred Cox and Lucy Allen were married by Bishop Snow. Such marriages, which did not differ from those elsewhere in the United States, were called civil marriages, even if they were performed by Mormon clergy. Religious marriages were called sealings, or "celestial marriages," and united the couple for eternity. They consisted of religious covenants made between husband and wife and had to be authorized by the president of the church. Such marriages were reminiscent of the sacramental nature of Catholic marriages.[16]

Civil marriages join the couple for this life; celestial marriages seal the couple for eternity. Unlike ceremonies containing the words "till death us do part," celestial marriages perpetuate the union beyond the grave. Mormon couples, such as Fred and Lucy Cox, that have been married in a civil ceremony are often married again later by someone authorized to perform celestial marriages so that their unions will be eternal. Fred and Lucy were sealed to each other on March 3, 1873, the same day Fred was sealed in plural marriage to Alvira Coolidge.[17] Men could be sealed to many women, whether living or dead, but women could be sealed for eternity to only one man.[18] Eternal marriages could be monogamous as well as polygamous, but plural marriages were religious, not civil, ones.[19]

The importance of marriage is inherent in the Mormon conception of eternity. Mormon theology teaches that the spirits of all humanity were born of God and spiritual consorts in a preexistent state. God wishes his spirit children to become like him, and for that purpose they come to earth, gain mortal bodies, and have the opportunity to prove themselves in their earthly probationary state. Adam and Eve were given the commandment to "multiply and replenish the earth" to provide mortal bodies for spirits waiting to enter the second, or earthly, phase of existence. Those who prove themselves on earth by their righteousness and perform the necessary rituals, including eternal marriage, are rewarded in heaven by "gaining exaltation": they are given a world over which to rule and to people by producing spirits who will then repeat the process.[20] To be worthy of exaltation, a man and a woman must be married for eternity, not merely until death. According to Mormon theology, marriages that seal couples for eternity can be performed only on earth.[21] Mormons are thus encouraged to be sealed in marriage because their exaltation depends on their having a marriage valid for eternity.

Eternal marriage has a dual purpose: first, on this earth, to prepare bodies to receive spirits waiting in the preexistent state and to train them properly so that they will choose righteous ways; second, in heaven, to continue the procreation of spirits for new worlds, thus increasing the dominions and glory of God himself.[22] Because having children is so important in Mormon theology, plural marriage was an advantage—the ability of righteous men to beget children would not be curtailed by the biological limitations of one wife.

How necessary living in plural marriage was to a person's reward in the hereafter was not always clear.[23] Leaders' pronouncements varied over the years that plural marriage was publicly practiced, but the revelation written in 1843 to convince Emma Smith to allow her husband to take plural wives provided the basic framework for understanding the doctrine.

That revelation warned that "if ye abide not that covenant, then are ye damned" (Doctrine and Covenants 132:4). Joseph F. Smith, counselor in the First Presidency, later stated that the revelation as it stood "was not designed to go forth to the church or to the world. It is most probable that had it been then written with a view to its going out as a doctrine of the church, it would have been presented in a somewhat different form."[24] That it was not written for the church membership in general left open the question of whether plural marriage was required of all members. "Some say, 'I would do so, but brother Joseph and brother Brigham have never told me to do it,'" Brigham Young said, acknowledging members' uncertainty about its general applicability if they had not specifically been called to practice it.[25]

Pressure was strongest on church leaders to enter plural marriage, and this pressure increased in the 1880s. In a meeting of the First Presidency, the Twelve Apostles, and stake presidents in 1882, John Taylor told those assembled, "A man obeying a lower law is not qualified to preside over those who keep a higher law." Wilford Woodruff amplified this, saying, "The leading men of Israel who are presiding over Stakes will have to obey the Law of Abraham or they will have to stop."[26] In 1884, the pressure on leaders intensified. In St. George, George Q. Cannon of the First Presidency warned that he "did not feel like holding up his hand to sustain anyone as a presiding officer over any portion of the people who had not entered into the Patriarchial order of Marriage."[27] At the April conference that year, the First Presidency said, "Celestial Marriage . . . was binding on all Latter-day saints, and that no man was entitled to the right of Presiding, without abiding this law. They advised Presidents of Stakes, who have not obeyed this law to do so; or resign their positions as Presidents."[28]

To be sure, leaders of the church were more likely to practice plural marriage, and those who did not were advised to do so. Among the general authorities who were appointed from 1845 to 1888, only fourteen (31.8 percent) were monogamists. With the exception of Anthon H. Lund, who was appointed only a year before the church announced its abandonment of new plural marriages, all those who did not enter plural marriage had relatively short tenure in their positions.[29] Local leaders (stake presidencies and bishoprics) were generally also in plural marriage.[30]

Faithful men outside the leadership were also counseled to take plural wives, and plural marriage was not only the preferred type but also the most honored and most sacred. But whether monogamists sealed in marriage could be exalted—receive the greatest reward in the highest, or celestial, kingdom—was ambiguous. In general, those in plural marriages were told that they would have a greater glory than would monogamists, which implied that those with one wife could be exalted although with lesser glory. In announcing plural marriage to the world in 1852, Orson Pratt said plural marriage was "necessary for our exaltation *to the fulness of the Lord's glory* in the eternal world." In 1878, Joseph F. Smith was more explicit: "It is useless to tell me that there is no blessing attached to obedience to the law, or that a man with only one wife can obtain as great a reward, glory or kingdom as he can with more than one, being equally faithful."[31] Clearly, the general authorities preached that entering plural marriage brought a greater reward.

Several statements from church leaders, however, make it appear that monogamists could not attain exaltation, even at a lesser level. In 1883, Erastus Snow, drawing on Doctrine and Covenants 131, stated that there were many "who are not able to abide this new and everlasting covenant. . . . They may remain in their saved condition [in the Celestial Kingdom] without exaltation, but they enter not into the order of the Gods."[32] In 1873, Brigham Young had warned monogamists that a man who says that he does not want more than one wife "will perhaps be saved in the celestial kingdom; but when he gets there he will not find himself in possession of any wife at all." Drawing on Jesus' parable of the talents, Young compared monogamists to the slothful servant who hid his talent in the earth, and when the master came, he took that one talent and gave it to the servant who had doubled his talents.[33] Earlier, in 1866, Young had stated, "The only men who become Gods, even the Sons of God, are those who enter into polygamy."[34] These pronouncements seemingly indicate that monogamists not only would receive a lesser reward but also could not be exalted.

Nevertheless, these statements are not as inflexible as they at first appear. While the term *new and everlasting covenant* appears to mean plural marriage in this context, it was generally used in its original meaning, as the gospel restored through Joseph Smith. When used in conjunction with marriage, it often included all marriage sealings, not merely polygamous ones. In the speech in which Erastus Snow made his comment about those outside the new and everlasting covenant not being exalted, he also referred to "a new and everlasting covenant, the holy covenant of marriage for time and all eternity, the union of the sexes, the sealing of wives to husbands and husbands to wives."[35] This includes all marriages sealed, not just plural ones. John Taylor used the term in this same way when he referred to a man who "entered into the new and everlasting covenant . . . and by that covenant has been united to his *wife* for time and all eternity and his *wife* to him."[36] The singular form of wife indicates all sealings, not just plural ones, and thus *new and everlasting covenant* encompassed all monogamous as well as polygamous sealings.

In the context of other statements by Brigham Young, his declarations above are also less than absolute. In the same address in which he stated that only polygamists would become gods, he also stated that "if you desire with all your hearts to obtain the blessings which Abraham obtained, you will be polygamists *at least in your faith.*"[37] Moreover, Wilford Woodruff reported in his journal that Young told the Saints in Grantsville that "a Man may Embrace the Law of Celestial Marriage in his heart & not take the Second wife and be justified before the Lord."[38] In short, entering plural marriage might not be essential for exaltation, but believing that it was a righteous principle ordained of God was.

Similarly, belief, not always practice, was essential in some pronouncements warning of damnation. "What will become of those individuals who have this law taught unto them in plainness, if they *reject* it? . . . they will be damned," warned Orson Pratt, drawing on the language of the revelation in Doctrine and Covenants 132. Twenty-two years later, Pratt repeated his warning: "Those who *reject* this principle reject their salvation, they shall be damned, saith the Lord."[39] The word *reject* means to refuse to recognize, credit, grant, or agree to,[40] implying that those who do not believe in plural marriage will be damned, not those who do not practice it. Similarly, Brigham Young admonished the Saints, "Deny [plural marriage] *in your feelings* and I promise that you will be damned."[41] Belief was the central issue, although, of course, faith in the principle would naturally lead to its practice. Orson Pratt averred that the Saints "believe in the principle, and we are *willing* to practice it, because God has spoken from the heavens." The word *willing* indicates that action depends not only on being required to do something but also on the ability to do it.[42] Joseph F. Smith was more emphatic: "I understand the law of celestial marriage to mean that every man in this Church, who has the *ability* to obey and practice it in righteousness and *will not,* shall be damned."[43] *Will not* means more than simply *does not;* it means refusal and indicates willfulness. George Q. Cannon made this point: "I believe there are very excellent, very worthy, very true and very faithful Latter-day Saints of both sexes who have not entered into the practice of plural marriage; and it is not for me to cast reflections upon any of my brethren or sisters about not having obeyed that principle, unless there has been positive disobedience."[44] The crux of the issue was faith in the principle and a willingness to obey it, not that one had entered plural marriage.

In 1880, Cannon had emphasized the importance of obedience when

he stated that no one could enter the celestial kingdom "until he is tested and proved in all things."[45] To deserve the highest reward in eternity,
a person had to prove perfect obedience to all God's commands, just as
Abraham was willing to sacrifice his son Isaac.[46] The ultimate test was
to obey God implicitly in all things he commanded at the time, not necessary to live in plural marriage.

To be sure, a Saint who had faith that plural marriage would bring a
greater eternal reward would want to practice it, but "ability to obey"
was an important qualifier in Smith's statement. As Cannon explained,
"I am perfectly satisfied there are men who will be counted worthy of
that glory who never had a wife; there are men probably in this world now,
who will receive exaltation, who never had a wife at all, or probably had
but one." He cited the example of Elder Lorenzo D. Barnes, "a faithful
man in the Church, a man of zeal, a man of integrity, who did all in his
power to magnify his holy Priesthood" but who died while on his mission to England before he married. Other young men, Cannon averred,
"who die before they have had the opportunity to obey that law . . . will,
doubtless, receive also, inasmuch as they were worthy." To qualify for
exaltation in such a case, one had to achieve the highest degree of worthiness: "It must be perfection before God, and a proof of willingness on
their part, if they had the opportunity."[47]

Those who never were Latter-day Saints could also achieve exaltation. According to George Q. Cannon, "For good Men died without having the Privilege and men would be Judged according to their desires as
well as their acts." Just as all who had no opportunity in this life would
have the chance to accept the gospel in life hereafter, "[s]o with those who
would have received the Patriarchal Order of Marriage if they had a
Chance will be saved in the Celestial Kingdom."[48] Even nineteenth-century Latter-day Saints had limited opportunities to practice plural marriage. Cannon acknowledged that in Utah "the males outnumber the
females; it cannot therefore be a practice without limit among us."[49] The
demographic realities of too few women meant that men willing to practice plural marriage might be unable to.

In short, pronouncements from the pulpit made it clear that entering
plural marriage could bring a higher eternal reward, though monogamists
or single people could achieve exaltation if they believed in plural marriage and were willing to practice it but were denied the opportunity. These
pronouncements, however, were not unambiguous.

It is even more difficult to determine what individual Mormons believed. Those in polygamous relationships were likely to aver that entering plural marriage was necessary for their exaltation. Annie Clark Tan-

ner, a plural wife, wrote, "It was taught at that time that the second wife opened the door of salvation in the Celestial Kingdom not only for herself, but for her husband and his first wife." Joseph E. Taylor, a counselor in the Salt Lake Stake Presidency, interpreted Doctrine and Covenants 131 to mean that exaltation could "only be reached by observing the patriarchal order of marriage."[50] In contrast, some members who had been sealed to one spouse, according to Joseph F. Smith, "supposed that the doctrine of plural marriage was a sort of superfluity, or non-essential, to the salvation or exaltation of mankind." Smith conceded that those who lived up to their covenants made in their monogamous sealing would "receive his reward therefor, and this reward, or blessing, he could not obtain on any other grounds or conditions." What that reward was Smith did not state. The purpose of the address, however, was to make clear that the "law [regarding plural marriage] is in force upon the inhabitants of Zion" and that it applied to every qualified man in the church. Two years later, George Q. Cannon echoed this: "Some men think they can slip around—I have heard such men talk—they think they are going to get into the celestial kingdom without obeying the law of celestial marriage." He, too, refuted that idea.[51] Still, many were reluctant to enter plural marriage, as a number of general authorities acknowledged publicly.[52] Others obeyed the law, without having to live in plural marriage in mortality, by being sealed to another wife after the first wife had died or by having dead women sealed to them. The principle was clearly not a popular doctrine even with many Saints, and church leaders had to give the practice their strongest endorsement for it to expand beyond a small group.

Beyond stressing the eternal significance of marriage, nineteenth-century Mormons also accepted its generally acknowledged purposes: first, to rearrange the relationship between a man and woman and hence their rights and duties to each other; second, to give rights of sexual access; third, to rear children and to transmit material goods and culture from one generation to another; and fourth, to reorder the relationship between the kin groups of the husband and wife as they acquire a common kinship with the children of the couple.[53] Whether monogamous or plural, celestial marriage added a fifth reason—one's eternal salvation—to these.

While most celestial marriages, or sealings, encompassed these five elements, not all did. Some sealings were for eternity only and conferred no earthly rights or obligations. Similar to eternity-only marriages were nominal marriages. Neither appears to have bestowed rights of sexual access on the couple, but wives in nominal marriages used their husbands' surnames and may have received some temporal help. Yet other sealings conferred on the couple all earthly and eternal rights and obligations but with the understanding that these would not take effect until some later time.

In addition to sealings, the church sanctioned second marriages that had no force in eternity if a wife had previously been sealed to a husband. These proxy marriages, like civil marriages, bestowed on the couple all the earthly rights and duties of marriage. In such marriages, however, the man acted as a "proxy" for the husband to whom the wife had earlier been sealed for eternity. Convenience marriages, however, conferred only the right of sexual access. All these various types of marriage are represented in the Manti data set.

Most women who were married for eternity-only were sealed to men who had wives still living. Ann Wickes, for example, married George Taylor in England in 1830, and both were baptized as Latter-day Saints in 1848. They subsequently separated, and she and their children immigrated to Utah in 1854.[54] Two years later, at age fifty-six, Ann was sealed to William Black, who had a wife still living.[55] Ann and William apparently never lived together, and she and an unmarried daughter were listed in the 1860 census as living in the household of Ann's married son. There is no evidence that she and William Black ever cohabited, and when she died, she was buried under the name Ann Taylor.[56]

The original records of the eternity-only marriages have no notations about the nature of the marriage, and unfortunately these records are not currently available for scholarly purposes.[57] In this study, a woman who had passed childbearing age when she was sealed, who did not live in the same household with the man to whom she was sealed, and who was never referred to by his surname is considered sealed for eternity only. Fifteen plural marriages in which the plural wives were sealed to their husbands for eternity only are included in the Manti subset.

Four nominal plural wives are also included in the Manti subset. James Cook, for example, married Hannah Massey Davenport in 1865. She was a fifty-seven-year-old widow, eight years his senior, at the time of the sealing.[58] In the 1870 census, she was listed as Hannah Cook but was living in her daughter Marie's household. After his first wife died, James Cook married Hannah's daughter Marie. In 1879, Marie Cook died.[59] In the 1880 census, James was listed as widowed, and Hannah had reassumed the name Davenport, the surname of her first husband. A short biographical sketch of James Cook written sometime later stated, "Second wife was Anna Davenport, to whom he was sealed but did not live with."[60]

Similarly, Maren Jorgensen was sealed to Morten Mortensen on December 12, 1878, the same day he was sealed to his first wife. Maren was sixty-five years old and twelve years his senior.[61] In 1880, Morten and the two wives to whom he had been sealed all lived in Manti. Maren was living alone, however, and in the census she was listed as Maren Axelsen. Axelsen was Morten's patronymic and the surname he used in immigrating to the United States and in the 1900 and 1910 censuses, although he was listed as Mortensen in the 1880 census.[62]

Although Hannah and Maren were undoubtedly sealed to their husbands for eternity only, they did bear their husbands' names; hence, in this study these marriages are designated as nominal plural marriages. Such marriages apparently did not include the right of sexual access, but what other rights and duties they conferred is unclear. In one case, a widow was sealed to a married man, apparently for eternity only, but later brought a complaint against him in a church court for not supporting her. The man defended himself by saying that "in their marriage contract she promised not to be an expense to him"; his first wife testified that before the sealing, the widow had claimed she wanted the sealing for religious reasons and "would never think of having pleasure with a man at my age." The decision favored the second wife, indicating that, in being sealed to her, the man had accepted a responsibility that he could not shirk.[63] While this form of marriage did not include sexual access, there appears to have been no clear consensus about what responsibilities the husband and wife had for each other.

Another type of sealing was the marriage of a couple with the understanding that the rights and responsibilities of marriage were to be postponed. Some of these marriages were performed for very young couples just before leaving Nauvoo because Mormons feared that it would be a long time before another temple would be built where such rites could be performed. Such a sealing was performed for twelve-year-old Mary Dunn and eleven-year-old Mosiah Hancock. Mosiah wrote in his autobiography that it was done "with the understanding that we were not to live together as husband and wife until we were 16 years of age."[64] As it turned out, they never did so. While both families were at Winter Quarters, Mary came to the Hancock camp and wanted to live with them. Her mother had died, and her father had not only married again but also taken a plural wife. Apparently Mary believed living with her husband's family would be more pleasant, but Mosiah's mother would not allow her to stay because there was no room. Mosiah's father was away in the Mormon Battalion, and life was undoubtedly already difficult for the family. Mosiah later wrote, "[W]ith what joy I hailed my noble, beautiful wife!

But Mary had to go, and oh what sorrow as I saw her depart."[65] Mosiah and Mary were never united after they arrived in Salt Lake City; at age eighteen, Mary married Martin Luther Ensign.[66]

Because celestial marriages transcend this world, it was possible for a person to be married to one spouse for this world and sealed to a different spouse for eternity.[67] The spouse to whom a person was sealed for eternity might not even be living. Isaac Morley's daughter Cordelia, for example, was sealed to Joseph Smith for eternity in Nauvoo eighteen months after he was killed at Carthage. Frederick W. Cox stood as proxy for the sealing to Joseph Smith in the temple ceremony while marrying Cordelia for time, or for the duration of mortal life.[68]

Such marriages for time only—proxy marriages—entailed the same responsibilities and conferred the same rights that civil marriages did. In these marriages, the children bore their biological fathers' names but in the hereafter would belong to the family of their mother and the husband to whom she was sealed for eternity. Mercy Rachel Thompson, who had been in two such marriages, designated this the "proxy method." Her husband for time agreed "to take care of me as long as he lived, and then deliver me up to my first husband in eternity . . . together with all children that we might have."[69] This sometimes affected the way some individuals felt about others in the family. For example, the grandchildren sealed to Brigham Young felt superior to Young's other biological grandchildren who would be in Joseph Smith's family in heaven.[70]

Such marriages could also affect the couple's attitude toward the marriage. Eunice Billings married John Warner in 1849 and was sealed to him for eternity on August 6, 1851. They had four children, the last born after his father was killed by Indians in 1853. Three years later, she became the second wife of George W. Snow. This second marriage produced four children, but by 1870 she had moved from Manti to Provo. The census indicates that she lived in her mother's household and had reassumed her first husband's surname. In the 1880 census, she is again listed as Eunice Warner. Moreover, the census shows her as both married and widowed, appropriately so in her case when she bore the name of her first husband but was recognized by the church and Mormon society as the wife of the second.[71] Eight months after his first wife died, George married Eunice again to regularize their marriage—a common practice in the late 1880s and 1890s. They lived separately, however, and in 1900 George resided with his daughter and her husband in Manti, although the census indicates he was married.[72]

Apparently both considered this a levirate marriage. In biblical times, these were marriages in which a man married his deceased brother's wife to ensure that the deceased would have an heir to carry on his name.[73] For Mormons, these marriages had a slightly different purpose. Discussing a second marriage when the wife had previously been sealed to her first husband, Orson Pratt stated that the second husband accepts "her as a wife for time only, yielding her up with all her posterity in the morning of the first resurrection to her legal and lawful husband."[74] In short, a spiritual brother married a deceased man's wife; he then fathered children who would increase the family belonging to the deceased in the eternities and assisted financially in caring for the family during their mortal lives.

Undoubtedly the rarest type of marriage among Mormons was the "convenience marriage," such as took place between Frederick Cox Sr. and Mary Ann Darrow Richardson. Mary Ann and her husband, Edmund Richardson, as well as their two children, were forced to stay in Salt Lake City during the winter of 1853–54, when their ox died and they could not continue their journey to Oregon. Impressed with the generosity of their neighbors, they soon were baptized into the church and accepted an assignment to help the settlers in Manti. With the importance the Saints placed on having children, however, Mary Ann Richardson worried about her husband's inability to father more children because of his "having become an eunuch."[75] She was also concerned about her exaltation, especially when several had told her she was wrong to stay with her husband and should be sealed to another. Writing to Brigham Young for advice, she expressed her desire to remain with her husband if that course would not hinder her eternal reward. In a letter dated March 5, 1857, Young proposed a novel solution, one of the few possible in that age before the advent of modern reproductive medicine: "If I was imperfect and had a good wife I would call on some good bror. to help me that we might have increase; that a man [her husband] of this character will have a place in the Temple, receive his endowments and in eternity will be as tho nothing had happened to him in time."[76] According to Young, her husband's sterility would not bar him from the most important temple ordinances, and his eternal reward would not be adversely affected. As for having additional children, Mary Ann could be married in a civil ceremony to another man who would father her children. By being sealed for eternity to Edmund, Mary Ann as well as all her children, would belong to him.

The couple eventually accepted the plan, but only reluctantly. Edmund and Mary Ann were sealed for eternity on April 20, 1857, but only after they "each had seen a vision" did they accept President Young's unusual suggestion. After they acceded to the plan, he gave them a paper listing three polygamous men he considered worthy to participate. They chose Frederick Cox. He, too, at first refused to participate in the plan but also became convinced that "the plan was divinely inspired." One of the sons of this union later wrote of his birth: "It took three visions and a religion to reconcile others to my coming."[77] On January 9, 1858, Brigham Young celebrated the marriage of Mary Ann Darrow Richardson and Frederick Cox in a religious ceremony that did not seal the couple. From this union, two sons were born: Charles on October 13, 1858, and Sullivan on January 26, 1861.[78]

Family legend indicates that Brigham Young granted the Richardsons a temporary separation or a civil divorce and that Edmund lived some distance from Manti during his wife's second marriage. He may have spent some time away, but one year after the first son was born, he returned and took his wife to Salt Lake to be sealed again for eternity in the Endowment House. Moreover, as indicated on the 1860 Manti census, he was again reunited with his wife about eight months before the second son was born.[79]

Not long thereafter the Richardsons moved to another town. For about twenty years Cox did not see his sons. When he did, he shook their hands heartily, looked at them and listened to them unceasingly during their visit, but never mentioned the relationship between them.[80]

The second marriage did not bestow the rights and responsibilities that marriage usually confers. Mary Ann retained the Richardson name, lived in the Richardson home, and received her support from Edmund Richardson. Cox received no rights in the children: they were not called by his name, nor did they inherit from him. Because the Cox-Richardson children were cautioned to say nothing about the circumstances of their birth to protect the good name of their mother, it is highly unlikely any public acknowledgment was made of Mary Ann's second marriage.[81] In short, other than the right of sexual access, the marriage ceremony conferred no rights or responsibilities.

This form of marriage was not an isolated instance, although it was undoubtedly a rare one. When Richardson's descendants sought answers about the marriage, the executive assistant of the Genealogical Society of Utah assured them that there were other such marriages and that these were known as "convenience marriages."[82]

As Lawrence Foster argues, calling such marriages polyandrous is misleading because polyandry is incompatible with the patriarchal nature of nineteenth-century Mormon marriages. While Mary Ann's two marriages overlapped, the form of the marriage to each man was different and did not entail the same rights and responsibilities. Marriages for time were perceived as temporary because life on this earth was viewed as ephemeral in the expanse of eternity. Sealings for eternity were thus much more important and took precedence over marriages for time, although they did not necessarily invalidate them.[83]

These examples indicate that nineteenth-century Mormons recognized several forms of marriage that conferred different rights and responsibilities on the husbands and wives. First, civil marriages, those performed by civil or local church authorities, were the same as marriages outside the Mormon community. Second, time-and-eternity marriages added to the usual rights and responsibilities conferred at marriage the pronouncement that the union would endure throughout eternity. Third, proxy marriages also bestowed the usual temporal rights and responsibilities but stipulated that in the hereafter the husband had no rights to either the wife or the children born to their union. Fourth, marriages for eternity only conferred no earthly rights or responsibilities on the couple but dealt only with their union during eternity. Such marriages could be performed for two living persons, for one living and one deceased person, or for two people who were both dead. Fifth, nominal marriages conferred only limited rights on the couple for this life and sealed them for eternity. Sixth, marriages with delayed rights involved ceremonies that sealed the couple for time and eternity, but the couple postponed living together because of the bride's youth. Seventh, convenience marriages conferred rights of sexual access but gave the man no rights to the children and limited responsibility for the woman.

This variety of marriages among Mormons indicates a conception of marriage different from that generally held in nineteenth-century America. Eighteen states defined marriage as a civil contract, while three others described marriage as a personal relationship arising out of a civil contract.[84] English law recognized that Mormon marriages created rights and responsibilities different from those in other marriages, and in *Hyde v. Hyde and Woodmansee* it specifically eschewed acknowledging the first woman a man married as his wife and the others as concubines.[85]

An English convert, John Hyde, had immigrated to Utah and married Lavinia Hawkins according to the rites of the church on November 10, 1853.[86] In 1856, he left Utah for a proselyting mission but soon renounced the church and wrote *Mormonism: Its Leaders and Design*, attacking the church and polygamy.[87] The church excommunicated him. His wife, declared Heber C. Kimball, was "just as free from him as though she never had belonged to him"; she needed no formal divorce.[88] In spite of John's letters to Lavinia urging her to abandon her faith and join him, she refused and in 1858 married Joseph Woodmansee.

Hyde returned to England, became a minister of a dissenting chapel at Derby, and eventually petitioned for a divorce. In 1866, Sir James O. Wilde rendered his decision, an ironic one for Hyde, who had opposed polygamy. "Marriage, as understood in Christendom," the judge decided, "may for this purpose be defined as the voluntary union for life of one man and one woman, to the exclusion of all others."[89] In Utah, the judge ruled, marriage meant something wholly different. Although Hyde's marriage had been monogamous, he continued, Mormon marriages created a set of rights and obligations different from those created by "Christian marriages," because Mormon monogamous marriages always had the potential of becoming polygamous ones. English matrimonial law, the decision maintained, was inapplicable to polygamous marriages, because it allowed a woman a judicial separation and permanent support from her husband on the grounds of "personal violence, open concubinage, or debauchery in face of the wife, her degradation in her home from social equality with her husband, and her displacement as the head of his household." If these provisions were applied to polygamous marriages, "the Court would be creating conjugal duties, not enforcing them, and furnishing remedies when there was no offence."[90] In short, the Hyde marriage may have been binding by *lex loci*—the law of the place in which it was contracted—but English matrimonial law did not acknowledge it as a marriage.[91] What made Mormon marriage different, then, was not just plural marriage, which was only its most notable and notorious feature. Mormon marriages added or limited the rights and responsibilities of those marrying, depending on the type of marriage.

One of the responsibilities Mormons believed marriage—whether a sealing or only for time—entailed was to rear the children of that marriage and to provide financially for those children and their mother. Because plural marriage was not legalized by Utah law and the rights of such marriages were not enforceable in courts of law, it was necessary to make statutory provisions for plural wives and their children to inherit. All states have laws stipulating how an estate will be distributed among a decedent's heirs in the absence of a valid will. The Utah legislature passed legislation in 1852 to deal with such intestate estates—estates in which the decedent left no will—but tried to allow plural wives and their children to inherit by mandating, "The homestead occupied by the wife, or any portion of the family of the deceased at the time of his death, shall in all cases be held free to the use of the wife and family of the deceased . . . in the absence of other arrangements by will, [the estate after liquidation of liabilities will] descend in equal shares to his children or their heirs; one share to such heirs through the mother of such children,

... or if he has *more than one wife*, who either died or *survived in law-ful wedlock*, it shall be equally divided between the living and the heirs of those who are dead, . . ."[92] The language in this section appears pur-posely ambiguous. It could mean a man who had two wives in succes-sion with whom he had children, one who had died before he married the second wife, who survived him. Or it could mean more wives than one who were married to him at the time he died.

Like most territories entering the Union after 1850, Utah Territory enacted a homestead provision exempting the dwelling from the claims of creditors and other claimants and ensuring it would be retained by the wife and children after the husband's death. First passed by Texas in 1839, such provisions replaced dower, or the right under common law for a wife to inherit for her use during her lifetime one-third of her husband's real estate.[93] Dower worked against the interests of plural wives because if the first wife inherited one-third of the estate, the proportion that could be allotted to them would be small, certainly significantly smaller than the first wife's. In addition to providing an accepted alternative to dower, this section of the law allowed for the possibility of a decedent's having more than one lawful wife surviving him and enabled each to inherit from him. Because dower could put up a barrier to plural wives' inheriting from their husbands, the territorial legislature specifically abolished dower in 1872.[94]

Because Mormons did not consider children born to plural wives il-legitimate, it is unclear whether the section that followed was also passed to secure the inheritance rights of plural wives and their offspring. It was, however, used by courts to refer to plural families: "Illegitimate children *and their mothers* inherit in like manner [as legitimate children and wives] from the father, whether acknowledged by him or not, provided it shall be made to appear to the satisfaction of the court, that he was the father of such illegitimate child or children."[95] The broad language of the Utah provision was open to abuse, and in 1876 this law was modified so that the illegitimate child inherited only if the father acknowledged the child.[96] Though in advance of such laws elsewhere, the Utah law was in keeping with the trend allowing illegitimate children to inherit from their fathers. In 1858, Wisconsin passed a similar law allowing an illegitimate child to inherit if the father acknowledged he was the father in writing signed before witnesses.[97] Nevertheless, this provision reflected a deep-ly held Mormon belief that a man who sired a child, legitimate or other-wise, was responsible for financially providing for its needs.

These inheritance laws appear to have fulfilled their purpose of en-suring that plural wives inherited from their husbands, but the legacies given to the wives were not always equal. George Peacock died intestate in 1879, leaving three wives and twenty-five children.[98] In the decree of the distribution of the estate, his first wife was listed as widow, while the two plural wives were designated as "mother & guardian" of their respective children. The property appears to have been distributed fairly equally among the three wives, each one receiving the house, lot, and property—the homestead—she had used during their husband's life. While the first wife was given the property "for and during her natural life," the plural wives received their property "for the use of said mother during her natural life and for the support and care of said minors."[99] Such a careful distinction conformed to section 25 of the Utah inheritance law: each plural wife inherited as mother and guardian of children acknowledged by the father.

Whereas a local merchant had been the administrator of the Peacock estate, the estate of Frederick W. Cox Sr. was settled by an "agreement as to the division of the estate" among the five wives in 1882. The legacies left to the five were not equal. Three wives, including the first, had no unmarried children, but the first wife received over a hundred dollars more than either of these two other plural wives. Another plural wife with an unmarried child received a slightly larger amount than the first wife. By the time the estate was settled, two and a half years after the husband's demise, the fifth wife had remarried, and she received no property. Her second husband, however, as guardian of Cox's four minor children, received an amount only slightly smaller than the first wife's portion. In addition, the two sons who had married since their father's death received amounts approximately equal to the portions given to the plural wives with no unmarried children, apparently to provide for these sons in the manner in which older sons had earlier been provided for when they married. The agreement was signed by all five wives and most of Cox's adult children.[100]

Similarly, when Orson Hyde died intestate, an agreement was made in 1881 among "Mary Ann P. Hyde widow of deceased" and the four plural wives who were "guardians of the minor heirs of Orson Hyde." The childless widow received $136.75 in personal property, while the plural wives received three to five times as much. The residue of the estate not specifically assigned to one of the women was to be divided among them.[101] The childless widow, who was the legal wife, apparently agreed to receive the smallest amount because she had no children for whom she needed to provide.

Although John Taylor left a will when he died in 1887, it consisted only of a listing of his wives and children, and the family had to divide the property. In a family meeting, it was decided that each wife and each child would receive an equal share of the property but that the children would give their mothers use of their share of the property until their mothers' deaths. However, since the seventh wife had the youngest family, she was given use of the farm, and a daughter with mental problems was allowed a double share for her support.[102]

When a plural wife had no children through whom she could make a claim on the man's estate, it was necessary for the polygamist to leave a will. Such wills, however, did not necessarily designate plural wives as wives. Although Madison Hambleton called both his wives members of his family in his will, he referred to them separately as "my wife Chelnicie and Heir Bergetta." Five years later, in 1874, Christian Nielsen made a similar distinction in his will between his "beloved wife Maren Nielsen" and his "heir Marie Nielsen."[103]

Polygamists who died testate were not always so punctilious, however, and some did describe their plural wives as wives in their wills. When James Olsen died in 1883, he willed thirty acres and the house close to Manti "to my wife Katharine and her children." The balance of his farm was "to be divided between my 3 wives . . . according to the size of family."[104]

Many estate settlements did not come before the probate courts, particularly in the early years, but were decided by the church courts. For example, when one polygamist died, it was ordered that each of his four wives would receive $600 while each of his fifty-four children would receive $375. The decedent had deeded property to one wife, and she was allowed to also retain that "in consideration of the large number of minor children she has to rear and educate."[105]

Between wills, decisions of the probate and church courts, and agreements among wives, plural wives and their children were able to inherit even though their status had never been regularized in law. To be sure, not all wives were satisfied with receiving less than other wives or with the proportion they had inherited, especially when a child might inherit as much as a wife, but unless a first wife took the case to a territorial court where it would be decided by non-Mormon judges, plural wives could expect to inherit from their husbands.[106] Although not recognized in law, plural wives in practice were acknowledged as wives who had a claim on their husbands' estates. They did not, however, always inherit as much as the first and legal wife; and legally, if not in practice, their position remained tenuous.

This de facto recognition of plural wives changed as Congress stepped up its campaign against polygamy in the 1880s. Polygamy, along with those consanguineous marriages that many considered incestuous, had become symbols of the family crisis in America. Reformers rallied behind legislation requiring marriage licenses, raising the statutory age of marriage, banning marriages between blood relatives, and curtailing plural wives' ability to inherit from their husbands. Even the courts began to soften their support for informal matrimony amid the reformers' fears of free love and "rampant Mormonism." Polygamy, a "prime instigator" of the social climate that produced these reforms, became one of the first targets for change.[107]

During the 1880s, the federal government dismantled the entire system the Mormons put in place in the 1850s to protect plural marriage. Not only were polygamous families excluded from inheriting from intestate estates, but also Congress passed laws regulating marriage and mandating registration of marriages. By enforcing these laws, by taking the selection of judges out of the hands of Mormons, and by attacking the church itself, the federal government was also able to curtail the church's influence over the civil courts and to diminish the ecclesiastical courts' control over family issues.

But until the 1880s, marriage in Utah was essentially regulated by ecclesiastical officials, with some help from custom. Mormons encouraged marriage, not only through the lack of legal barriers but also from the belief in eternal marriage as a requirement for one's exaltation in the next life. The latitude given for kin to intermarry and in the age youths could wed, although wide, was not much greater than that allowed by the common and statutory law elsewhere in midcentury United States—except, of course, that Mormons' interpretation of their law also supported plural marriage. Although Mormons never regularized through law the status of plural families, territorial legislation did provide for the children and their mothers to inherit. Mormon control over marriage was challenged, however, as Americans throughout the United States in the late nineteenth century demanded and got more stringent legislation regarding marriage for themselves and mounted a federal campaign against marital practices among the Mormons. Before that happened, though, the Mormons had developed a marital system that fostered but did not force marriage.

PART 3

Numbers: An Analysis of the Marriage Patterns of Manti Women

. . . the fatherless, and the widow, which are within
thy gates, shall come, and shall eat and be satisfied;
that the Lord thy God may bless thee in all the work
of thine hand which thou doest.

—Deuteronomy 14:29

. . . all things are numbered unto me, for they are mine
and I know them.

—Moses 1:35

5 *The Marriage Market*

The legal system in Utah promoted plural marriage by posing no barriers to it and protecting the inheritance rights of plural families. The ecclesiastical system encouraged such marriages, and its doctrine mandated marriage for one's exaltation in the hereafter and promoted plural marriage in this life. More important, however, this encouragement of marriage provided by the law and the church had a significant impact on the marriage patterns in nineteenth-century Utah, so significant that they may be described as distinctive features of the LDS life course and Mormon family life.

The presence of plural marriage in Utah, along with the general encouragement of marriage, created distinctive marriage patterns through its operation on the marriage market. First, age-specific marriage rates for women in the representative population under study in Utah were high. In the early years, they were remarkably high, indicating that almost all women married and that they married at young ages. Second, because the demand for wives created by plural marriage produced a scarcity of women, the average age of marriage for all women, not just plural wives, was low, and immigrant women married soon after their arrival in Utah. This was particularly the case during the first years of settlement, when the proportion of plural marriages was at its highest. Third, these patterns were created and maintained by plural marriage, even though plural wives did not represent a cross section of Mormon brides. Plural wives came disproportionately from groups of economically disadvantaged women in the frontier economy: women whose fathers were dead or did not reside in Utah as well as women who had been either widowed or divorced. Finally, because the men who married additional wives were generally among the wealthiest, plural marriage helped shift economic resources from such men to poor women, even though men retained control of the resources.

Life in Utah changed as Mormon society moved from the rigors of isolation and the difficulties of making the desert arable to inclusion in the national transportation network, with the arrival of the transcontinental railroad in 1869, and afterward to provisional acceptance in the nation when the Mormons officially announced in 1890 that they would obey congressional marriage laws. Because of these changing circumstances over time, the sixty years under study is divided into three twenty-year periods. The first, from settlement in 1847 to 1869, is usually described as the frontier period. Fairly isolated from American society, the Mormon community could pursue its own policies but also faced the immense challenge of settling a dry land under difficult conditions. The second period, from 1870 to 1890, encompassed the consolidation of settlement in Utah and the eventual capitulation of Mormon society to national monogamic norms. During the last period, from 1890 to 1910, Mormons, having officially given up plural marriage, moved closer to the mainstream.[1]

The women in the Manti data set whose first marriages took place in Utah were assigned to one of these periods according to their birth dates.[2] Women born before January 1, 1852, would have been at least eighteen years old, and hence of marriageable age, by 1870. Because most women born before 1852 married by 1870, they are all included in the first cohort who married during the frontier period.

Those women born between January 1, 1852, and December 31, 1869, are included in the second cohort. Such women were of marriageable age by the time the Manifesto officially ended plural marriage in 1890. Moreover, 1890 serves as a convenient line dividing those who could have married when the marriage system officially encompassed plural marriage and those who married when it did not. Single women born before 1852 but who immigrated to Utah between 1870 and 1889 are also included in the second period; the Mormon marriage market could affect the timing of their marriages only after their immigration to Utah.

Those women born between January 1, 1870, and December 31, 1890, are included in the third cohort. These women married in a basically monogamic system, after the Manifesto was issued. To be sure, over two hundred plural marriages took place after the Manifesto, but many of these new plural marriages were performed outside of Utah or at least one of the wives resided outside Utah. Many of these marriages were performed in Mexico, and the plural families lived there until their expulsion during the Mexican Revolution of 1911–12.[3] Because these new plural marriages were often outside Utah and few in number relative to the entire membership of the Mormon church, such new plural marriages were no longer a normal part of Mormon society or its marriage system. Among those in the Manti data set, no plural marriage took place after 1890.

The age-specific marriage rates, calculated from the marital histories of 1,084 Utah women—269 in the first period, 395 in the second, and 420 in the third—do indicate considerable change over these three time periods, as shown in figure 1.[4] For the early period in Utah, the age-specific marriage rates (derived by dividing the number of marriages for each age group by the number of person-years—the number of women who remained single at each year of age—in each age category) were extraordinarily high.[5] This is clearly seen by comparing these rates to those in Utah for the two later periods and to American women in marriage registration states in 1960.[6] In 1960, the proportion marrying was at a peak for the twentieth century—91.5 to 94.0 percent—while the average age women married was near its nadir.[7]

In every age group, women in the first birth cohort married at much higher rates than did any of the other three groups of women. Marriage rates for the second cohort are considerably lower than for the first, but they are higher than for the third cohort and for women in 1960, with the single exception that women in the third cohort had slightly higher rates for those aged thirty to thirty-four. Although marriage rates declined substantially over time, the third cohort still married at higher rates from ages twenty to thirty-four than did women in 1960, and rates for the latter are abnormally high for the twentieth century. In contrast, women of the third cohort were not so young as women in the other groups were when they married. Overall, marriage rates of the first cohort during the frontier period were very high, those of the second cohort were considerably lower but still high, while those of the third cohort after age twenty were similar to those of women of 1960 and so were still fairly high.

The Utah age-specific rates for the frontier period are so high because nearly every woman had married by age twenty-five, and those immigrants who came at later ages married soon after their arrival.[8] Only one woman from the first birth cohort, a Dane who immigrated at age twenty-seven, never married. These high rates, however, decreased significantly over time. This is partly because the number of women who never married increased. In the frontier period, less than 1 percent of women in the Manti data set remained single, compared with 7 to 8 percent of American women

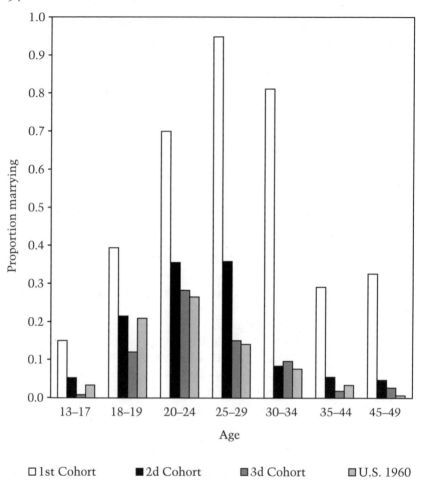

Figure 1. Comparison of Age-Specific Marriage Rates for Women in Manti, Utah, and Marriage Registration States, 1960, for First Marriages. Sources: Manti data set; Irene B. Taeuber and Conrad Taeuber, *People of the United States in the 20th Century,* a Census Monograph (Washington, D.C.: U.S. Government Printing Office, 1971), 318.

in the same birth cohorts who never married. Of those Manti women born between 1852 and 1870, 2 percent remained single, well below the 8 to 11 percent of other American women in similar cohorts who never married. Among the Manti women born between 1870 and 1890, 5 percent never married, a percentage somewhat higher than for women during the frontier period but still far below the 9 to 10 percent of American women in the same birth cohorts who remained single.[9]

Just how many women married young during the frontier period can be seen in the percentage of women married at various ages. At age sixteen, 27 percent were already married; at age twenty, 83 percent had taken marriage vows. By age twenty-four, a mere 3 percent were still single, and that dropped to less than 1 percent by age twenty-eight. By these standards, those in the second cohort stayed single much longer. Only 6 percent of them were married by age sixteen, although 57 percent had wed at age twenty, 88 percent by age twenty-four, and 95 percent by age twenty-eight. Even so, women in the second cohort married when they were young, and most married.

The higher marriage rates during the frontier period shown in figure 1 indicate not only a higher proportion of women marrying but also a lower age at marriage than prevailed during the subsequent periods in Manti. From one cohort to the next, the mean marriage age increased approximately one year. In the frontier period, it was 20.25 years of age, in the middle period 21.07, and in the last period 22.30. The median age at marriage for each period was lower; during the frontier period, it was 18.67 years, while it was 20.25 and 21.58 for the middle and last periods, respectively. In 1960, the median age at which women married was 20.30, approximately the same as in the middle period in Manti, although the marriage rates in Manti for that period are higher because a higher proportion of women married. All these average marriage ages of Utah women are low compared with 23.65 for 1900 and 25.36 for 1990 in the United States in general.[10]

Nevertheless, the overall average ages for the first two periods in Manti obscure important differences between immigrants and other women. Those women who migrated with the Saints from Nauvoo, those women born in Utah, and those women who immigrated to Utah before their fourteenth birthdays—referred to here collectively as Utahns—married considerably younger than did those women who immigrated to the Great Basin when in their teenage years or older—here called immigrants. A considerable number of those in the Utahn category were immigrants from Europe, but they were in Utah when they became of marriageable age and thus were subject to the influences of the Utah marriage market at an early age.[11] The influence of immigrants on the mean age of marriage during the first two periods can be inferred from table 1. In the first period, immigrants constituted 31.3 percent of women who first married in Utah; by the second period, the percentage of such immigrants had dropped to 16.6. Because immigrants accounted for only 5.0 percent of those marrying after 1890 and therefore had small impact on the average age of marriage, the last period is excluded from this table.

Table 1. Utahns' and Immigrants' Mean Age at First Marriage in Utah, 1848–90

Cohort	Overall Mean	Utahns	Immigrants
Born before 1852	20.28	18.07	25.12
Born 1852–70 or immigrated 1870–87	21.07	20.46	24.22

Source: Manti data set.

Almost one-third of those marrying during the frontier period were immigrants, and they married on average at age 25.12—seven years later than did those women who were in Utah from their early teens. By the second twenty-year period, while the number of immigrants decreased by a third, the average age of Utahns at marriage increased two years, to 20.46, and the mean age declined almost a year for immigrant women, to 24.22. Clearly, the considerably older age at which immigrants married substantially increased the overall mean marriage age. Utahn women actually married at younger ages than the average indicates.

These mean ages at marriage are approximately what other scholars studying the nineteenth-century Mormon population have found. Using the large data base collected in the Mormon Historical Demographic Project, Geraldine P. Mineau, Lee L. Bean, and Mark Skolnick found that the mean age at marriage was 20.86 for monogamous Mormon women born between 1800 and 1869. Those born in the last decade of that period, between 1860 and 1869, married when they were slightly younger, on average at age 20.69.[12] These are similar to the averages in the Manti study, though the latter includes both monogamous and plural wives. In a later study, Mineau, Bean, and Douglas L. Anderton found that once-married women born before 1859 along the Mormon Trail married at a mean age of 18.70.[13] This is fairly close to the mean age of 18.07 for the Manti pre-1852 birth cohort, although the Manti data set is lower because it includes not only women who married more than once but also some women whose early, short-lived marriages were omitted from the family group records, which are the basis of the Mormon Historical Demographic Project.

These mean ages at marriage for the Manti women are also comparable to those Larry M. Logue found in his study of St. George, a Mormon town in southern Utah. Basing his calculations on all daughters of St. George residents, he found that women in St. George married at a mean age of 19.40 from 1861 to 1880.[14] These dates overlap ten years for each of the first two periods in the Manti study, but the St. George mean age at marriage lies almost halfway between the Manti mean ages for those two periods. The women in the Manti study thus appear to be fairly typical of women in the nineteenth-century Mormon population.

Compared with other nineteenth-century groups in the United States, Mormon women in general married at younger ages. In Massachusetts, for example, women married at a mean age of 23.6 in 1860, while in Edgefield, South Carolina—where there were many fewer foreign immigrants—white women married for the first time at age twenty. Women in the West married at early ages, though not quite so young as did Mormons. According to Logue's calculations, women in western rural areas who married before 1900 did so at a mean age of 20.5.[15] By the turn of the century, Mormon marriage patterns approached the national norms; however, the median age of 21.6 for Manti women during the last period remained slightly below the median ages 22.0, 21.9, and 21.6 for 1890, 1900, and 1910, respectively, for the coterminous United States, as reported by the U.S. Census Bureau.[16]

Although many Mormon women immigrated from northwestern Europe—in 1870, 67.9 percent of Utah residents twenty-five or older were foreign-born—Utah mean ages at marriage were significantly below those across the Atlantic.[17] Single women who immigrated to Utah from Europe between 1850 and 1887 often married soon after their arrival in Utah, as table 2 indicates. Women entering plural marriage generally wed more quickly than those marrying monogamously, showing the inadequacy of the idea that plural wives were women "left over" after most other women had married.

Single immigrants in the frontier period on average married within a year of their arrival in Utah, while the interval between arrival and marriage increased to two years for the second cohort and to three years for the last cohort. To some extent, this reflects the higher mean age at marriage; a fifteen-year-old immigrant might well marry within a year during the frontier period but was less likely to do so later. Nevertheless, even many older immigrants waited longer to marry than they had during the initial settlement of Utah.

Decreasing age-specific marriage rates, increasing mean age at marriage, and a rising waiting time between arrival of immigrants and their

Table 2. Mean Number of Years between Immigration to Utah and Marriage for Immigrant Women Age Fourteen and Older in the Manti Data Set, 1850–1910

	1850–69	1870–87	1888–1910
Monogamous wives	1.01	2.06	3.12
Plural wives	0.85	1.67	—
Overall average	0.94	1.94	3.12

Source: Manti data set.

marriage are all consistent with patterns elsewhere on the frontier as it developed into a well-settled area.[18] Yet the Utah patterns cannot be entirely explained by the economic development of a frontier region into a well-settled agrarian economy. Although basically the same legal and ecclesiastical framework existed from 1850 to about 1885, immigrant women entered plural marriage in diminishing numbers. This is shown in the proportion of single immigrants over fourteen who entered plural marriage. In the first period, almost half of such immigrants (47.6 percent) became plural wives, while in the second period only about one-third (32.8 percent) did so. Even more dramatic is the decrease in the number of immigrant women in a plural marriage at some point in their lives. Women who first married monogamously in Utah but whose husbands then took plural wives are counted with monogamous wives because when they first married the marriage was monogamous. When immigrant women who became first wives in a plural marriage are added to the number of plural wives, those single immigrant women who were ever in a plural marriage increase from 47.6 percent to 67.9 percent in the first period, but rise from 32.8 percent to only 37.5 percent in the second.

For both immigrant and Utahn women, the likelihood of initially marrying as plural wives decreased considerably over the first forty years in Utah. Figure 2 compares the age-specific marriage rates for monogamous and plural wives for the two cohorts. The high marriage rates for plural wives over thirty years of age in the first cohort reflects the number of older immigrants who entered plural marriage in early Utah. In contrast, marriage rates for plural wives in the second cohort were low for every age group. During the second period, the marriage rates for both monogamous and plural wives were considerably lower than during the first period, but the decline for plural wives was much greater.

The absolute number of women whose first marriage was polygamous also declined. In the frontier period, 99, or 36.9 percent, of those marrying for the first time in Utah became plural wives. In the second period, only 41, or 10.6 percent, did so. Clearly, substantially fewer women chose to become plural wives as the century progressed. This is also indicated by the percentage of those women in each cohort who were either a first wife or a plural wife. Of those born before 1852 whose first marriage took place in Utah, 56.7 percent were in a plural marriage at some point during their lifetimes; of those in the second cohort, only 12.2 percent were, a decisive decrease both absolutely and proportionately.

Figures reported by Lee L. Bean, Geraldine P. Mineau, Yung-chang Hsueh, and Douglas L. Anderton indicate that this was generally the case,

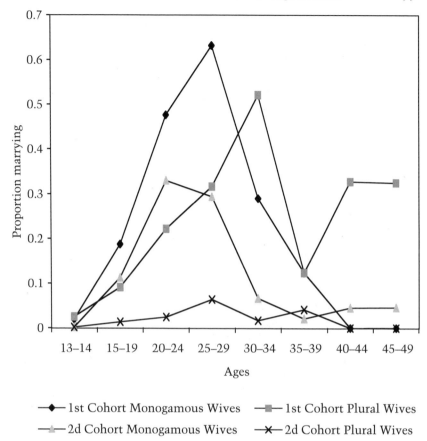

Figure 2. Comparison of Age-Specific Marriage Rates for Monogamous and Plural Wives in Manti Data Set Who First Married in Utah, by Birth Cohorts. Source: Manti data set.

not simply a deviation from the norm by those in the Manti data set. Their data from the Mormon Historical Demography Project indicate that of the 1830–39 birth cohort, 29.0 percent of women married polygamously sometime during their lifetimes. Of those in the 1840–49 birth cohort, 23.5 percent did so, while the percentage dropped to 14.3 for the 1850–59 birth cohort and to 6.3 percent for the 1860–69 cohort.[19] These scholars appear to underestimate the incidence of women entering plural marriage, however, because they were conservative in assigning women to plural marriage categories and because the family group records from which they drew their data are not complete.

Not only was there a decrease in the number of new plural marriages, but also the proportion of Mormons living in polygamous families declined considerably over time. Several polygamists moved to Manti in the late 1870s and 1880s to help construct the temple being built there. Manti thus had more polygamous families in 1880 than it otherwise would have had. Nevertheless, the incidence of plural families in Manti appears to be similar to levels elsewhere. Unfortunately, how large the decline of polygamous marriages is over time in the general Mormon population remains uncertain because most estimates are based on incomplete data. Stanley Ivins's figures have been widely used, but these are based on sources that are incomplete and often erroneous. Even so, he found that plural marriages in 1857 were almost fourteen times as numerous per one thousand Utah Mormons as they were in 1880.[20]

The considerable decline in the incidence of polygamy can be seen by combining studies of polygamy during specific census years. Marie Cornwall, Camela Cartwright, and Laga Van Beek, in studying three wards in Salt Lake Valley, found that 44 percent of the women in the 1860 census were in polygamous marriages, the same percentage for Manti women in 1860. In 1870, about 28 percent of households were polygamous in Sugar House Ward, located in Salt Lake County. That same year Manti's percentage was similar, at 30 percent.[21] For a later census year, the best estimates currently available were made by Lowell "Ben" Bennion based on the 1880 census. He found that when the Utah 1880 census was taken, the percentage of husbands, wives, and children living in plural families differed from one locale to another. (He also included widowed sister wives living in the same town in his calculations.) It was as high as 66.6 percent in Orderville and as low as 4.6 percent in Panaca.[22]

Calculating incidence by using Bennion's method but having greater information about who the polygamists were than can be found in either the census or family group records, I discovered that 25.1 percent of those listed in the 1880 Manti census were living in plural families (see table 3).[23] This includes one nominal plural marriage. Bennion's figures show that 21.8 percent of Latter-day Saints in Davis Stake and 33.0 percent in St. George Stake lived in plural families. When the two stakes are combined, 27.6 percent of men, women, and children lived in plural families in 1880. Dean May's research shows that 24.0 percent of the Kanab, Utah, population were members of polygamous families in 1874. Manti's percentage in plural marriage thus appears to be near average levels elsewhere in 1860, 1870, and 1880.[24]

Moreover, the percentage of the population living in polygamous families shows a significant increase between 1850 and 1860 but a sub-

Table 3. Men, Women, and Children in Polygamous Families and Widows of Polygamists, Manti, Utah, 1850–1900

Census Year	Percentage in Plural Families	Number in Plural Families	Total Number in Census
1850	24.9	89	358
1860	43.1	391	908
1870	36.0	444	1,232
1880	25.1	446	1,774
1900	7.1	170	2,396

Sources: 1850 U.S. Census, Manti, Sanpete County, Utah, Population Schedule; 1860 U.S. Census, Manti, Sanpete County, Utah, Population Schedule; 1870 U.S. Census, Manti, Sanpete County, Utah, Population Schedule; 1880 U.S. Census, Manti, Sanpete County, Utah, Population Schedule; Manti data set.

stantial decline from 1860 to 1880. Both the number and the percentage of men, women, and children in polygamous families increased dramatically during the 1850s, partly reflecting the impact of the Mormon reformation on marriage patterns.[25] Of those listed on the 1860 Manti census, 43.1 percent of the population lived in plural families, but it increased to 56.0 percent if those families in which the fathers later took plural wives are added.[26]

By 1870, the percentage in polygamous families had declined to 36.0, and by 1880, it had decreased still further, to 25.1, a decline of almost half between 1860 and 1880. Several reasons account for this decrease: the number of new plural marriages declined significantly; some of those who had entered plural marriage had died by 1880; children of plural marriages had grown up, married monogamously, and thus were not counted as living in polygamous families; and many immigrants, mostly from outside Utah, had arrived in the town since 1860 who had never practiced polygamy.

However, the pattern changes when numbers rather than percentages are considered. The number of men, women, and children living in plural families greatly increased from 1850 to 1860, grew a little over the next decade, and then stabilized from 1870 to 1880. With the addition of new plural families, even if considerably slowed by the 1870s, and with the prolificacy of polygamous wives, the number in plural families remained near the same level from 1860 to 1880. Unfortunately, the 1890 census was burned, but the greatly reduced percentage and number in plural families by 1900 reflect the effectiveness of the federal government's antipolygamy campaign and the announcement of the 1890 Manifesto. That 6.6 percent still lived in polygamous families (widows were excluded in this calculation) suggests the tenacity with which some adhered to the principle.[27]

The Manti data indicate two other important trends. First, a relatively large percentage (56.7) of women in the frontier period whose first marriage was in Utah experienced plural marriage. Second, the number of new plural marriages decreased greatly by the second twenty-year period, although the number living in plural families remained stable or grew slightly.

The decline in the number of plural marriages was significant but was not uniform over time, as figure 3 shows. Stanley Ivins related the sporadic increases in new plural marriages to "some revivalist activity within the church or with some menace from without." He explained that the peak in 1846 represents those marriages performed in the Nauvoo Temple immediately before the Saints began their exodus west. The church's announcement in 1852 that polygamy was an essential tenet of the church resulted in considerably more plural marriages that year. By far the highest peak occurred in 1856 and 1857 as a result of the Mormon reformation. The number of plural marriages increased again in 1862 in response to the Morrill Anti-Bigamy Act making polygamy illegal. The

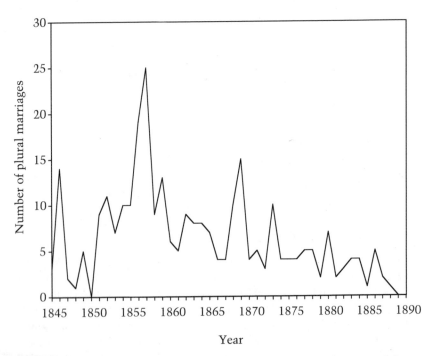

Figure 3. Number of Plural Marriages Performed Each Year in the Manti Subset, 1845–90. Source: Manti subset.

next increase occurred in 1868 and 1869 and, according to Ivins, "coincided with the inauguration of a boycott against the gentile merchants and the organization of an anti-Mormon political party." The last peak of new plural marriages, according to Ivins's figures, came in the mid-1880s in reaction to the federal government's antipolygamy campaign.[28]

Ivins's figures for increases and decreases in plural marriages after 1870 differ from those in the Manti subset. This may be because one major source of his data, *Pioneers and Prominent Men of Utah,* does not include all Utah pioneers, defined in the book as men who immigrated to Utah between July 24, 1847, and December 30, 1868. Some were overlooked, and some did not pay the fee necessary for inclusion. Among those who arrived after 1869, the book lists only prominent ecclesiastical and governmental leaders. For the later period, it is therefore even less inclusive and is biased toward elites, who were more likely to enter plural marriage than were ordinary Mormons.[29]

Nevertheless, Ivins's explanation fits the increases in plural marriages before 1870 in the Manti subset. The small but significant rise in the Manti data for 1873 might be attributed to the establishment of an anti-Mormon secret society called the Gentile League of Utah in 1872 and to Ann Eliza Webb's notorious divorce case against Brigham Young in 1873.[30] The smaller rise in 1880 may be a reaction against the Supreme Court's upholding the constitutionality of the antibigamy laws in the *Reynolds* case the previous year.[31] To explain the peaks in the number of plural marriages in this way, however, points to the weakness in Ivins's interpretation: in Mormonism's turbulent history either preaching or persecution may explain almost any increase in plural marriages.

To explain variations in proportions marrying, according to Ruth B. Dixon, one needs to determine the desirability of marriage, the feasibility of marriage, and the availability of mates in the society under study.[32] Ivins's argument addresses the first of these three factors, the desirability of marriage. Plural marriage became more desirable, in his view, when the church was undergoing revivals or outside threats. Why individual women would respond to a boycott against gentile merchants and the organization of an anti-Mormon political party by entering plural marriage is a puzzle, however. Ivins's contention that Mormons responded to preaching from the pulpit is more persuasive. Certainly the number of plural marriages increased in response to the revivals that characterized the Mormon reformation and to the preaching in the 1880s that made some believe "the second wife opened the door of salvation in the Celestial Kingdom not only for herself, but for her husband and his first wife." One's salvation was a positive inducement to enter plural marriage that increased its desirability, and encouragement from the pulpit was particularly intense during the reformation and the 1880s.[33]

The feasibility of plural marriage—expectations of the society regarding economic and residential independence—may have been a factor in the 1850s, although not enough to explain the variations in the numbers. During the early frontier period when housing was rudimentary for almost everyone, men marrying additional wives were not expected to provide separate rooms for them, at least in the areas outside Salt Lake City threatened by Indians.[34] In 1856, many in Manti still lived in the crowded fort, where space was at a premium and already established families often shared their quarters with others. Moreover, land had not yet been surveyed by the federal government. While church officials distributed plots of land, most men farmed only small plots.

Since there were fairly low expectations about financial support and residential independence, poverty was not a hindrance to marrying an additional wife. As the economy matured, however, wives expected greater financial support, if not always separate houses. As Apostle George Albert Smith noted in 1867, "[T]he majority prefer to buy everything that is imported. Our young men are afraid to get married because they cannot afford to buy all these trimmings." In 1877, Apostle Charles C. Rich tried to counter these rising expectations: "Some people have extraordinary notions concerning marriage; they think they must have everything to start with; they don't want to marry unless they can have a carriage, horses, and servants, and many things besides; these are extravagant notions. I have heard it taught by the Presidency that young people should marry, and to commence they should have a straw bed; they should have at least a bed tick, and fill it with straw, and commence any way."[35] Rich's counsel reveals that the church encouraged marriage by attempting to keep initial economic expectations low and that Saints increasingly demanded more material comforts to begin their married life. Although the feasibility of plural marriages because of rising economic expectations seems to have declined over time and can help account for the long-term decline in the number of new marriages, it does not explain short-term fluctuations.

Availability of marriage partners, however, is an important factor. As already noted, about half of single immigrant women during the early period entered plural marriage. It is not surprising, then, that more immigrants coming into the Utah mountain valleys would influence the number of new plural marriages. Figure 4 compares the number of new plural marriages in the Manti subset with the number of foreign immigrants from 1845 to 1890.[36] After 1852, the lines move roughly together,

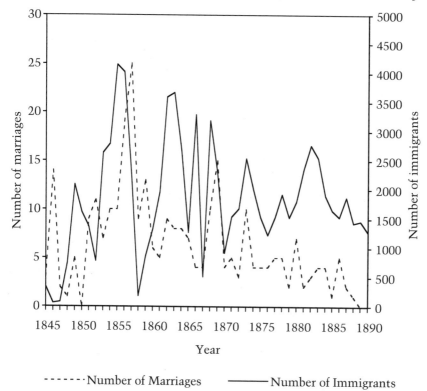

Figure 4. Comparison of Number of New Marriages in Manti Subset with the Number of Foreign Immigrants, 1845–90. Sources: Manti subset; number of foreign immigrants calculated from Conway B. Sonne, *Saints on the Seas: A Maritime History of Mormon Migration, 1830–1890* (Salt Lake City: University of Utah Press, 1983), 148–58.

although the number of plural marriages decreases over time in relation to the number of immigrants. This is what one would expect given the decreasing percentage of immigrant women who became plural wives. The two lines both rise to peaks in 1862–63 and 1873, and both decline in 1858 and 1870.[37]

More significant, however, is the repeated pattern of increases in marriages lagging a year or so behind increases in immigration, just as one would expect if immigration was fueling the pace of new plural marriages. The number of foreign immigrants rises to its highest point in 1855 and 1856, while the number of plural marriages begins a steep ascent in 1856 and peaks in 1857. Similarly, the number of immigrants rises in 1868, and the number of marriages peaks a year later. After 1870, the lag time increases slightly. The rise in the number of immigrants in 1878 is followed by a rise in new plural marriages in 1880, while the 1882 peak in immigration is followed by a slight rise in plural marriages in 1883 and 1884. This is also expected because later immigrant women married on average two years after their arrival in Utah.

The lines do diverge at various points, however, most notably in 1846, 1852, 1858, and 1866. Although a rise in plural marriages occurred in 1852 when the number of immigrants decreased, it followed a period of appreciable in-migration. The immigration figures in the graph represent the number landing in the United States, not the number arriving in Utah. In 1852, over four thousand people arrived in Utah as the Saints finally abandoned their settlements along the Missouri River, a considerably larger number than had come from those settlements in previous years.[38] Even though a large number of immigrants entered Utah in 1852, relatively few of them came from foreign countries. In contrast, the 1866 peak in immigration coincided with a decrease in the number of new plural marriages, though the number of such marriages increased sharply two years later and then peaked in 1869, following another large increase in immigration. The sudden rise in the number of plural marriages in 1846 was an anomaly. Foreign immigration had almost ceased because overseas Saints were counseled not to emigrate until the Mormons established a new Zion after abandoning Nauvoo. The number of marriages increased, however, because the Saints were leaving the temple they had built, at least in part, for performing such marriages. The Saints in Nauvoo had only three months after the temple was completed in December 1845 to perform marriages before rites in the temple ceased in February 1846, as they left Illinois for the West.

The rate of immigration thus appears to be a crucial component in determining variations in the numbers of new plural marriages. Certainly revivals, especially the Mormon reformation, increased the appeal of plural marriage, but the number of new polygamous marriages was also dependent on the quantity of available single women who could become plural wives. Because Utahn women married at fairly young ages and immigrant women married soon after their arrival, an influx of additional single women was necessary to provide opportunities for men to marry, especially during the frontier period. Fluctuations in the number entering plural marriage thus were decisively affected by immigration rates.

The large number of women entering plural marriage in the frontier period, particularly in 1856 and 1857, adversely affected the availability of mates for men by creating a scarcity of marriageable women.[39] It also had an impact on the age at which women married. Finding few women at the usual ages for marriage, men sought wives among increasingly younger women, thus intensifying the decline in women's mean age at marriage. As figure 5 shows, the mean marriage age for both monogamous and plural wives declined rapidly at first and bottomed out during the Mormon reformation period in 1856–57 and its aftermath.[40] For monogamous wives it reached its lowest point of 16.49 years in 1857, while for plural wives the lowest mean age was 16.42 in 1860. From 1860 through 1890, the average age at which monogamous women married rose over one year each decade. Between 1860 and 1870, it soared from 16.59 to 18.68 years; by 1880, it had risen to 19.97; and by 1890, the mean age at marriage was 21.10 years. After 1887, fewer plural marriages were performed—in the Manti subset only one occurred after that—and in the following five years, the mean age at marriage for monogamous wives rose over one year, from 20.36 in 1887 to 21.43 in 1892.

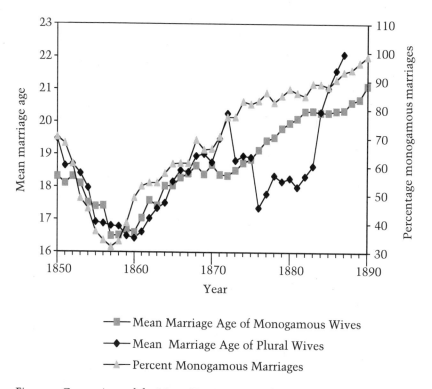

Figure 5. Comparison of the Mean Marriage Ages of First-Married Monogamous and Plural Wives and the Percentage of Monogamous Marriages among All First Marriages for Manti Women, 1850–90, Five-Year Moving Averages. Source: Manti data set and subset.

From 1870 to 1885, the mean age at marriage for plural wives deviated from that for monogamous wives, but the number of new plural
wives became too small to show any overall trends. During the first two
decades, however, when marriage rates were high and many women were
in plural marriages, the mean ages for monogamous wives paralleled those
for plural wives.

That plural marriage had an impact on marriage age for monogamous
women can also be seen in figure 5. The two lines for mean age of monogamous wives and percentage of monogamous marriages move together, both dropping rapidly to their lowest point about the time of the
Mormon reformation and then slowly rising until 1890. Monogamous and
plural wives were both part of the same marriage market. Because the
demand for wives was high, the mean marriage age for all women was
suppressed; and it was suppressed to the greatest degree when the greatest percentage of first marriages were plural ones. Plural marriage thus
significantly affected the age at marriage for monogamous women, not
just for plural wives.

This interpretation differs considerably from that of Bean, Mineau,
and Anderton. They indicate that the lower age of marriage during initial settlement was stimulated by greater economic opportunities on the
frontier.[41] Greater economic opportunities undoubtedly had some impact
on the age at marriage, but how great that impact was remains more problematic. In spite of the availability of land, young men were by no means
assured of economic prosperity. Of the eight men in the 1860 Manti census who had married since the end of 1856, half owned no real estate, and
three of these also had no personal property. With hard work, however,
most could look forward to acquiring some land. Thomas Boyington's
case is illustrative. When he arrived in Utah in 1856 at the age of twenty-
seven, he had few economic assets. Four years later, he was listed in the
1860 census as a single laborer with neither real nor personal wealth. In
1865, he married, and the 1870 census indicates that he had acquired real
estate worth $275 and personal wealth worth $200.[42] The likelihood of
acquiring land undoubtedly affected marriage decisions. It is unlikely,
however, to have caused the precipitous decline of women's age at first
marriage until the reformation and the rise thereafter. In any case, the
feasibility of marriage came as much from low expectations about the
couple's initial economic well-being as from enhanced economic opportunities on the frontier.

The effect the reformation and its aftermath had on the scarcity of
women is as remarkable as its impact on women's ages at marriage. That
dearth of single women is illustrated in the 1860 Manti census. Only two

women over sixteen years old had never been to the marriage altar; they were both eighteen. Slightly more than half of women between the ages of fourteen and twenty were already married, and 77.3 percent of these young women married as plural wives. The full impact of the Mormon reformation on the marriage market may be seen by comparing the proportion of young women who had been married and those who had never married over the four censuses from 1850 to 1880. As figure 6 shows, in 1860 over half of women between fourteen and twenty, inclusive, were married, almost twice the percentage in 1850 and 1870 and almost four times that in 1880. Moreover, although the population of Manti increased two and a half times from 1851 to 1860, from 358 to 908, a greater proportion of the women in 1860 were plural wives. In 1860, 41.5 percent of women fourteen to twenty (three-quarters of married women under

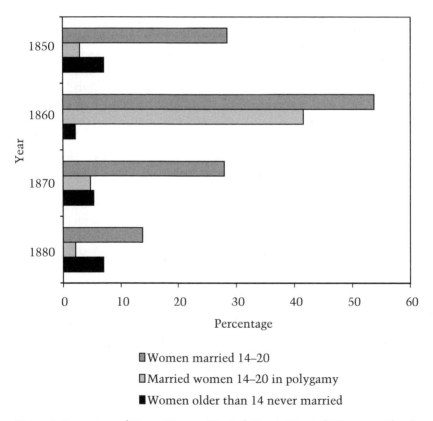

Figure 6. Percentage of Young Women Married, Young Married Women as Plural Wives, and Women Never Married in Manti, 1850–80. Sources: 1850–80 U.S. Census, Manti, Sanpete County, Utah, Population Schedules; Manti data set.

twenty-one) had experienced plural marriage, whereas in no other census did the proportion reach as high as 5 percent. Concomitantly, the proportion of those fourteen and over who had never married was considerably smaller in 1860 than for the other years. In the twenty years after 1860, the population almost doubled, reaching 1,774 in 1880, but the number of those women fourteen and older who had not yet married grew sevenfold.[43]

In short, the number of plural marriages in Manti during the late 1850s was high. This is true even though the town was not a center of the reformation movement, nor have historians singled it out as particularly affected by those revivals.[44] After the 1850s, the proportion of women entering plural marriage was never so high, and the average age at marriage was never so low. Nevertheless, the demand for plural wives continued to create a scarcity of marriageable women until the 1880s, thus depressing the age at marriage for Utah women below that observed elsewhere in the United States in the mid-nineteenth century.

The scarcity of marriageable women is shown by the sex ratio—number of males per one hundred females—of all men and women as well as unmarried men to unmarried women for the ages when most married from 1850 to 1880. Again reflecting the impact of the reformation on the Manti marriage market, the sex ratio for single men and women at those ages when Utahns first married—from fifteen to twenty-nine—was significantly higher in 1860 than in other census years. For those ages, the sex ratio of those unmarried in 1850 was 205 but jumped to 284 in 1860. It then decreased rapidly to 136 in 1870 and 116 in 1880—much closer than in previous censuses to a balanced sex ratio by the last available manuscript census in the nineteenth century. The relatively low sex ratio for the 1880 census reflects not only that women were older when they married but also that the young men frequently left the community to find work freighting, mining, or constructing railroads.[45] The higher percentage of young married women in 1860 resulted in almost three unmarried men for each unmarried woman at the age when most would marry.

The scarcity of marriageable women had a direct effect on men hoping to marry. For example, after a long illness and a divorce precipitated by his seizures, Azariah Smith finally recovered his health enough to consider marrying again. In 1869, the forty-one-year-old Smith bemoaned his situation: "I wish I had a wife and a home of my own." Finding a wife in Manti was not simple, and the following spring he wrote about his difficulties. "I attended Sun School and metings," he recorded in his journal. "I would get me a wife if there was any to be had, but there is a poor chance." Time and patience brought no improvements. "I attended S. School and meting, and again in the evening," he wrote the next month. "I have looked after the women some, but they are looked after so much that there is a poor chance for me." Time and a trip to Salt Lake City over a year later brought success: there he met a Danish widow eleven years his senior. After a short courtship, he married her. It was not a perfect match, however. About two months after the wedding, he penned: "[W]e enjoy life verry well together, as I love her, and she loves me," but he lamented that "it is somewhat disagreable to not understand each others language better."[46] If there had not been a scarcity of marriageable women, Smith probably would not have married a recent immigrant who was considerably older than he and whose language he did not understand.

Not all bachelors found wives. A few, like Ole Petersen, Marcus Troelsen, and Hans Ottosen who immigrated from Denmark in the 1850s, lived in Manti over twenty years and remained single until their deaths. Ira Bemus, a bachelor, left the territory for California.[47] But most men married at least once, and they married at fairly young ages. Men born before 1852 married on average at 24.3, while those born in the next generation married on average seven months later. These are at the low end of mean ages for men elsewhere at the time in the United States, which ranged from 24.8 to 26.4.[48] Moreover, over 80 percent of men in both Utah cohorts were married by the time they reached twenty-eight.

Of men born before 1852—the same cohort in which half of women's first marriages were plural ones—only 3.6 percent of those who were alive and had stayed in Utah until age fifty remained bachelors. That percentage rises to only 6.0 percent if those who had left Utah or died are also included. For men in the second cohort—marrying when only 13.0 percent of women's first marriages were plural—an even smaller percentage of men never married: 2.4 percent of those remaining by age fifty and 2.9 percent overall. Among American men born between 1835 and 1864, over 8.0 percent never wed, while in northwestern Europe, the birth place of many immigrants to Utah, about 20.0 percent remained single.[49] The percentages of Utah men who never married are thus remarkably low, compared with the percentages for men in geographic areas where Utah men originated and for men living in a polygamous society.

For so many to marry, however, men had to seek brides who were somewhat younger or older. In the nineteenth century, most men selected wives about two and a half years younger, except in the western rural areas where there was an actual shortage of women.[50] Over two-thirds of Manti men in the first cohort, however, married women three or more years younger, and almost half married brides five or more years younger. Another 8 percent married wives two or more years older. This is similar to the age difference between husbands and wives in St. George, where grooms were typically four years older than their brides. Men who were born later, between 1852 and 1869, and who married when fewer women's marriages were plural were less likely to be much older than their wives. About 45 percent of men in the second cohort married women in the preferred age group—one year older to two years younger—compared with only 25 percent of the first cohort who did so.[51]

One source of wives, then, was younger women arriving at marriageable age. With fertility high in Utah, each successive age group would have been larger than older age categories. Men willing to marry women five or more years younger would thus be seeking wives in an age group with larger numbers of women than in their own age cohort. For example, among Manti's small population in 1860 were seven twenty-year-old males but fourteen fifteen-year-old females. Although three of these women were already married, there were still more single fifteen-year-old women than single twenty-year-old men. The larger population of younger women provided opportunities for men, both single and married, to wed.

Not surprising, many women preferred to marry younger, single men, and because keeping young Mormon men within the fold was an important goal, marriages to faithful bachelors was encouraged. In 1862, a young woman wrote Brigham Young asking his advice about whether she should marry an older man as his plural wife or a younger bachelor. He advised her to marry the younger man.[52] One church leader even protested when young women were counseled to marry older men. In 1852, J. D. Chase spoke before the Manti congregation, "showing the blessing of a young woman taking an old man for her companion in time and in eternity." He was, however, countered three weeks later before the same congregation by Brother Billings, who "said there were some thing taught here among some of the brethren and sisters—that parents must counsil their daughts to be sealed to old men—said it was all of the Devil."[53] While plural marriage was the Saints' preferred marriage arrangement, the highest priority was for all worthy men and women to marry.

A second source of wives was the slight preponderance of women. If no plural marriages had taken place among Manti residents, there would have been a small surplus of women after 1850.[54] The preponderance of men in 1850 (sex ratio of 107) was typical in Utah during the initial phases of colonization. Church leaders called men with a variety of skills needed for the first stages of pioneering to settle in new areas.[55] After 1850, women in the prime marrying ages of fifteen to twenty-nine outnumbered such men in Manti, with the number of men for every one hundred females at 84, 81, and 89 for the next three censuses.[56] Surprisingly, however, the sex ratio reached its nadir in 1870, not in 1860, when proportionately more marriages were plural ones. In 1860, with the sex ratio at 96 for all men and women fifteen years of age or older (not just those in prime marrying ages), the situation for women was not overly adverse.

The marriage market reached beyond Manti's boundaries, as Azariah Smith's story shows, and Utah's ratios were not as disadvantageous to women as were Manti's. Only in 1860, with a sex ratio of 93, was Utah's ratio for those fifteen to twenty-nine biased against women. In 1870, it was almost equal, with a sex ratio of 99. In 1851, when the first Utah census was taken, the ratio was 124, and by 1880 it had again moved above equal numbers of the sexes, to 105 men for every 100 women. The sex ratios for all men and women in Utah, not just those fifteen to nineteen, also indicate that men generally outnumbered women during the nineteenth century. For every 100 females in 1850, there were 113 males; but in 1860 and 1870, the sex ratio had declined to an almost equal number of men and women, 101 and 99, respectively. By 1880, the sex ratio had climbed slightly, to 107; and by 1890, at 112, it had almost reached its 1850 level again.[57]

It is unclear, though, how many non-Mormon men, such as soldiers, merchants, and miners, were included in each Utah census. Dean May has calculated that non-Mormons accounted for 12 percent of Utah's population in 1860 and 21 percent in 1880.[58] Because non-Mormon men undoubtedly outnumbered non-Mormon women in nineteenth-century Utah, the preponderance of men, as shown in the census, is unlikely to reflect the sex ratio in the Mormon population.

In any case, Mormon women concerned about their exaltation would choose not only a Mormon husband but also one who would be considered worthy to receive his endowment and be sealed to a wife—or wives. Those not considered worthy could neither receive their endowments nor be sealed for eternity. During the 1850s, not every one sealed had previously received his or her endowment; after that time, the ritual of the endowment routinely preceded the sealing ceremony. To be worthy to participate in either, a person had to be a member in good standing in the church.[59] A woman who wanted to be married for eternity had to choose a man who was worthy to be endowed. The ratio of "worthy" men to "worthy" women is more important in explaining plural marriage than is the sex ratio in the general population. A woman concerned about her exaltation would want to be sealed to a man for eternity.

In every year sampled from the Endowment House records listing living persons who had received their endowments, women outnumbered men. During the year preceding May 5, 1856, only 82 men were endowed for every 100 women. Four years later, from August 20, 1859, to August 15, 1860, the number of men endowed for every 100 women dropped to 76. Ten years later (June 7, 1869, to May 30, 1870), it had dropped even further, to 73. A decade later, by the year ending June 3, 1880, it had risen to 83 but fell again to the nadir of 73 in the last full year endowments were given in the Endowment House.[60] Clearly, throughout the period the Endowment House was in use, fewer men than women were deemed worthy to receive their endowments, or at least fewer males chose to do so, and thus fewer men than women participated in the sealing ceremony.[61]

In conclusion, the 1850s stand out as the decade when plural marriage took firm root in Utah. Of all new plural marriages in the Manti subset, 44 percent were in the 1850s. Both the percentage of new plural marriages and the number of such marriages declined each decade thereafter. Nevertheless, the number of men, women, and children living in polygamous families remained essentially stable from 1860 to 1880, even as their percentage of the town's population declined over each decade.

With 72 percent of the plural marriages occurring from 1847 to 1869, it is not surprising that women marrying in the frontier period were much more likely to be in plural marriages than those who wed after 1869. Over one-third of those marrying for the first time during the earlier period became plural wives, and slightly more than half of women born before 1852 and married first in Utah were in polygamous marriages at some point in their lives. In contrast, only about one-tenth of those marrying from 1870 to 1890 became plural wives, and the proportion who were ever in a polygamous marriage was only slightly higher.

The relatively high number of plural marriages in the frontier period could not have occurred without the influx of immigrants from outside Utah. Almost half of immigrant women who first married in Utah from 1847 to 1869 became plural wives. The high percentage of plural marriages during the frontier period pushed down the average age at which women married. When the percentage of plural marriages was at its greatest, the average marriage age of young women was at its lowest. The scarcity of marriageable women resulting from so many polygamous marriages in the 1850s meant that men then sought wives among increasingly younger women.

The Mormon marriage market in Utah from its origins to 1890 was significantly influenced by the opportunity for plural marriage. Marriage for women was almost universal, and the marriage age was low, as is typical among polygynous societies.[62] Moreover, because of plural marriage, single women immigrating to Utah found opportunities to marry soon after their arrival. Finding wives among much younger or older women, Utah men also married earlier and in larger proportions than elsewhere in the United States. Although Mormon women slightly outnumbered Mormon men, particularly in the prime marrying ages, plural marriage created a scarcity of marriageable women. Plural marriage thus dramatically transformed the Utah marriage market for all living in Utah, not just for those who entered plural marriage. Moreover, the desirability of marriage—manifesting itself in the high incidence of marriage and in the high, if declining, number of plural marriages—and the feasibility of marriage were as important as the availability of mates in determining the high marriage rates.

That women were scarce worked to improve women's position in Mormon society. Especially during the early years in Utah, doctrine and rhetoric emphasized the patriarchal nature of the family and the superiority of men. Just a few months before the first Saints left for the West, Brigham Young in Winter Quarters told his family meeting, "The man is the head & God of the woman." Erastus Snow made the same point in 1857 when he declared that women should "reverence her husband as her lord; for he is her lord."[63] In such a climate and with even a slight preponderance of women, the position of women could easily have degenerated. In practice, however, with the desirability of marriage so high, with so many of the Mormon elites taking plural wives and thus raising women's status, and with plural marriage creating a scarcity of women, the position of women was raised simply by their being in so much demand.

6 Women Who Became Plural Wives

The Mormon church's success in encouraging plural marriage depended to some degree on such marriages also fulfilling the individual's needs. Unquestionably, those who entered plural marriage believed that it was mandated by God. In a diary entry about women living in polygamy, Eliza Partridge Lyman wrote that "nothing but a firm desire to keep the commandment of the Lord could have induced a girl to marry in that way." Similarly, Sarah D. Rich, writing about why she permitted her husband to marry additional wives, averred that "this I could not have done if I had not believed it to be one principle of His Gospel, once again restored to the earth, that those holding the Priesthood of Heaven might, by obeying this Order attain to a higher glory in the eternal world."[1] The divinity of plural marriage was often preached from the pulpits—from 1860 to 1889, plural marriage was the fifth most popular topic at church conferences—and it was canonized as scripture and embedded in church doctrines about salvation.[2] Without that doctrinal foundation, few, if any, would have entered into plural marriages.

But plurality was not practiced by all who believed in it. Many of those who did enter plural marriage probably had additional motivations, such as status, love, and financial considerations.[3] Economic reasons appear to have been important to many women marrying as plural wives. Almost half of plural wives in the Manti subset entered plural marriage in the difficult years from 1844 to 1859, years that spanned the exodus from Nauvoo and the initial settlement of a dry land infested by insects and inhabited by sometimes hostile Indians. In 1853, before the Walker War came to an end, the Saints in Manti had to live with reduced provisions because of the "grasshopper war." During the next two summers, grasshoppers again returned to devour the crops. In 1855, the grasshoppers were accompanied by a drought, followed by a severe winter. The next summer crops were again scanty, and the snow was deep during the winter of 1856.[4]

While the Saints were experiencing these difficulties, the largest number of nineteenth-century immigrants coming in a two-year period arrived in the mountain valleys.[5] The record influx of immigrants into the already strained economy undoubtedly exacerbated the financial problems of the Saints. Not only were there many new immigrants, but many of them were impoverished as well. Nearly two thousand of those who arrived in 1856 were too poor to buy wagons and the animals to pull them in order to cross the plains. Many of the indigent pulled handcarts, which contained all their belongings and some provisions, from Iowa to Utah.[6]

In the wake of these agricultural disasters and record immigration, church leaders began the reformation to renew members' commitment to Mormon religious ideals. During the October 1855 General Conference, a system of home missions was instituted to awaken the Saints from their spiritual slumber. When that failed to have the desired effect, a second phase began in March 1856 in which church leaders preached repentance and rededication. In the October conference that year, as the historian Thomas Alexander has pointed out, "the calls for reformation became increasingly intense and personal," with appeals for greater commitment and pressure to enter plural marriage. By spring of 1857, the third phase of the reformation, inaugurated by Wilford Woodruff in December 1856 and "characterized by love and concern," began to supplant the second and harsher phase. In Manti, the second, harsher phase of the reformation lasted seven months, from October 1856 to April 1857.[7]

The increase in immigration during the middle of the decade was accompanied by an upturn in the number of new plural marriages. During the harsh phase of reformation, however, the number of new plural marriages increased dramatically over their already high levels, as can be seen in table 4. As large numbers of immigrants arrived in Utah, the incidence of plural marriage more than doubled—from four marriages to nine—but when the millennialist fervor of the reformation revivals was superimposed on record immigration and economic problems, the number of women entering plural marriages almost tripled—from nine marriages to twenty-six. The number of plural marriages, however, dropped back to the original level—four marriages—when the pressure-laden revivals ended and the economic situation improved with the abundant harvest during the summer of 1857. Although the numbers in table 4 are

Table 4. Plural Marriages in Manti Subset, by Seven-Month Periods, January 1855 to November 1857

Period	Number of Plural Marriages	Percent Change
January 1855–July 1855	4	
August 1855–February 1856	9	+125
March 1856–September 1856	9	0
October 1856–April 1857	26	+189
May 1857–November 1857	4	−85

Source: Manti subset.

small, Ivins's study supports the finding that the number of plural marriages increased dramatically during the second phase of the reformation.[8] It appears that religious motivations were crucial for many women who become plural wives during the reformation; nevertheless, the increased number of immigrants and the depressed economic situation were also important factors in the overall increase in plural marriages.

A comparison of this Mormon marriage pattern during the mid-1850s with that of early modern England during hard economic times reveals how differently the two societies reacted to economic downturns. In England, not only were all marriages monogamous, but also all couples were expected to have sufficient resources to be independent, both economically and residentially, when they married. Plentiful harvests encouraged marriages, while hard times prompted their postponement. Because fertility was linked to marriage, fewer marriages during hard times helped keep the population in balance with economic resources.[9]

In Utah, however, the situation was the opposite. During the difficult economic times in the 1850s, church leaders encouraged young women to enter plural marriage, which meant they usually married older, economically secure men. Young women thus did not need to postpone their marriages until better times when young men could secure sufficient resources to set up independent households.[10] Nor did social custom prescribe that a polygamous husband had to supply his plural wives with independent households. The plural wife might already be living in the household as a servant or a dependent before the marriage. Hard economic times therefore did not postpone marriage for women in Utah as it had in early modern England. Rather, it appears to have encouraged women to select economically secure—and hence already married—men. There was consequently no check on population growth caused by a decreased number of marriages. On the contrary, fertility rates in Utah, which were always above national norms, were at their highest during the 1850s, in spite of the agricultural disasters.[11] Not only were Mormons fulfilling the divine command to prepare bodies for waiting spirits, but also they were ensuring a growing church membership through natural increase and an expanding population that could continue to spread throughout the territory and augment Mormon control of the area.

In the unstable frontier economy of early Utah, however, widowed, divorced, and fatherless women were at a disadvantage. Making the desert blossom as a rose required the hard physical work of grubbing out sagebrush, plowing hardened ground, digging canals for irrigation, planting and nurturing crops in the semiarid climate, and building fences to keep livestock out. To make new areas habitable required building roads, erecting houses, and often making the adobes necessary for constructing buildings. This was considered men's work. Like other Mormon women, plural wives had come from societies with clearly delineated gender roles and generally preferred "women's work"—cooking meals, baking bread, sewing dresses and shirts, knitting stockings, laundering linens and clothing, cleaning house, planting and caring for gardens, tending fowls and other barnyard animals, and nurturing children—tasks that were all the more difficult in rudimentary shelters without the amenities of the more settled areas. Patty Sessions's diary entry on the day she married John Parry illustrates the perceived need for men's help: "I feel to thank the Lord that I have some one to cut my wood for me."[12]

Women's work required stamina more than strength. Running a farm—and most families during the initial settlement were farm families, at least to some extent—required both men's and women's work. Single women were at a considerable disadvantage in an economy where the products of women's work brought little remuneration.[13] This undoubtedly motivated some single women, particularly those without a man in the family to perform the men's work, to become plural wives. Such women—widowed, divorced, and fatherless women—account for the majority of plural wives in the Manti subset (see figure 7). Those women thirty years old or over and whose family status is unknown most likely were divorced or widowed or their fathers were dead or not in Utah.[14] When such women are added to those widowed, divorced, and fatherless, such women were responsible for two-thirds of all the new plural marriages. They also constitute a majority of the new plural wives in each quinquennium. Not surprising, the proportion of women who had fathers in Utah and became plural wives reached its highest point from 1855 through 1859, the five-year period encompassing the reformation, when all Latter-day Saints were under pressure to enter plural marriage.

To understand how these economic pressures affected women's

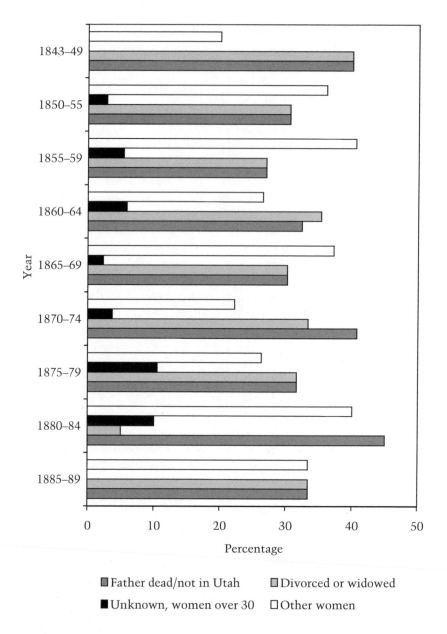

Figure 7. Percentage of Plural Marriages by Wives' Previous Family Status, 1843–89. Source: Manti subset.

decisions, consider the case of Sophia Klauen Petersen. She emigrated from Denmark at age thirty-one with five children. After she had paid for the family's journey to Utah, she had only one rigsdaler.[15] She and her children pulled a handcart across the plains in the Willie Company, but the company left late in the season and was caught by snow in the mountains. Sixty-eight of the 437 in the company died before help arrived. Men were considerably more likely to die of cold and starvation than were women: 24.9 percent of the men died, while only 8.5 percent of women succumbed to the cold and starvation.[16] As soon as the Petersen family arrived in Utah, it was asked to go to Manti. There the destitute family moved in with the Smiths, and less than three months later the impoverished Sophia became the second wife of the man in whose household she was living.[17]

Like Sophia Petersen, Elizabeth Haydock, a fifty-five-year-old widow, could not afford to buy a wagon and the animals to pull it so she traveled to Utah with a handcart company. She was with the ill-fated Martin Handcart Company, which left even later than the Willie Company did. Of the 576 people in that company, over 103 died before rescue teams arrived. Elizabeth and her daughter survived, but Elizabeth lost an eye through exposure to the cold. A year after her arrival, she became the third wife of the bishop of Manti.[18] In the same handcart company, Anne Larsen lost her husband and two children before help arrived. She, too, became the plural wife of a Manti resident a year later. Thirteen years later, her daughter married as a plural wife at age nineteen.[19]

When forty-seven-year-old Mette Christina Christiansen married Niels Peter Domgaard in October 1859, she had already been suffering with dropsy—congestive heart failure—for about eight months. She died of that disease only five months after she became a plural wife. Her husband and her sister-wife could provide not only hot food, shelter, clean linen, and companionship during her waning months but also, because Niels's first wife was a nurse, medical care as her life ebbed away.[20]

Single women without families also were often destitute after their journey to Utah and needed assistance. Maren Andersen joined the Mormon church against her parents' bitter opposition. Although a childhood illness had left her with "an impaired left side," she moved from her parents' home, worked as a seamstress for two years, and by frugal living was able to pay for her passage to Utah. At age twenty-nine, she arrived in Utah with no family or acquaintances and little money. The Jens Hansen family in Manti invited her to stay with them "until other arrangements could be made." Such arrangements were made about a year later when she became Hansen's second wife.[21]

It was not uncommon for a single woman to live or work as a servant in a household and then become a plural wife of the husband. Cecelia
Marie Jorgensen came to work for Hans Jensen Hals in Manti for five
weeks, after which he married her as his third wife. Emma Batchelor
signed a paper saying that she would serve for a year in Brother Kippen's
home, "and the implication was that at the end of that time she would
become his plural wife." In her case, however, she did not like the man
and his wife well enough to join their family. Instead, she became the
plural wife of a man to whom she was first attracted at church.[22]

As the Utah economy matured, women found it easier to earn a living without a man's help, so the economic advantages of plural marriage
decreased. As hard work resulted in surpluses that could be traded for a
variety of goods and services, some women became seamstresses, though
they were generally poorly paid, or milliners. As more women received
further education, particularly after the 1870s, they became telegraph
operators, writers, and medical doctors. New converts immigrating to
Utah with little education or knowledge of English, however, were still
at a disadvantage in the territory's changing economy; and marriage to a
countryman, whether he was single or married, could help ease the ad-
justment to their newly chosen life in Mormondom. Moreover, strong
encouragement to marry continued unabated from the pulpits, and increased economic opportunities did little to change gender roles of most
women in rural communities.[23] Having a man to do men's work remained
important after 1870, although not as necessary as in the struggling frontier days.

Besides providing some economic security, marriage, especially plural marriage, instantly established numerous kinship ties. Unlike in Sub-
limity, Oregon, where many people migrated with kin and neighbors,
many Latter-day Saints had strained or severed ties with their families
when they converted to Mormonism and left for Utah.[24] Cohesive communities, forged by common persecution and a common faith, filled
many of the needs generally supplied by kin, but ties of marriage secured
a woman's place within a family. Because family responsibilities override almost all other moral obligations, marriage created a woman's right
to aid. In Mormondom, as in most nineteenth-century societies, men held
significantly more economic resources than women, and through marriage a woman had a right to some of those resources. "Women have claim
on their husbands for their maintenance, until their husbands are tak-
en," declared Doctrine and Covenants 83:2, giving religious sanctions to
already strong family obligations. Among the general authorities of the

church, uniting one's family with those of other church leaders may have
been an important consideration in choosing plural wives,[25] but such
dynasticism was much less significant for ordinary Mormons. General
authorities, however, also married widows and impoverished women.

Because of the financial problems posed by the lack of a male provider, the types of women who became plural wives suggest that economic considerations, in combination with religious motivations, were a significant factor in many women's decisions to become plural wives. As
illustrated in figure 8, women without fathers in Utah were more likely
than other never-married women to enter a plural marriage. (The wom-
en included in the figure were only those whose first marriages were
performed in Utah and who spent some of their married lives in Manti;
women who remarried are discussed in chapter 9.)

Although plural wives accounted for only about one-fifth of those
women marrying for the first time in Utah between 1848 and 1887, 38.7

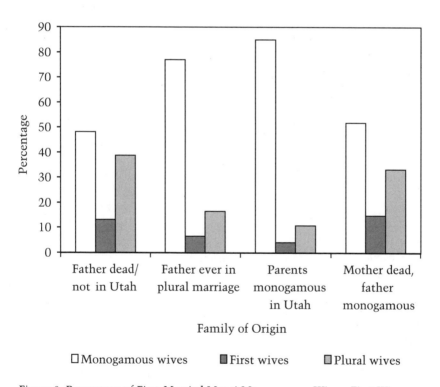

Figure 8. Percentage of First-Married Manti Monogamous Wives, First Wives,
and Plural Wives from Various Family Types, 1848–87. Source: Manti data set.

percent of those women whose fathers were dead or not in Utah became plural wives. When first wives are added, 51.8 percent of fatherless women were in plural marriages. Immigrants accounted for 62.7 percent of fatherless women, many of whom had left their families behind in Europe. Of fatherless immigrants, 45.0 percent first married as plural wives; 65.3 percent became either first or plural wives.

Although the population of Utah was much smaller in the frontier period than in the middle period, women whose fathers were dead or not in Utah were concentrated among those women who first married before 1870. Three-fourths of Utahn women who were fatherless married in the frontier period. Crossing the plains was more perilous in the early years than it later became, and several fathers died before they could complete the journey. Moreover, women were less likely to immigrate to Utah without fathers after the frontier period: two-thirds of the fatherless women immigrated during the early period. Of immigrants and Utahn fatherless women, 69.5 percent married in the frontier period; of these, 43.0 percent became plural wives, while 63.6 percent became either first or plural wives.

For women who were alone or whose families lost the breadwinner along the trail to Utah, entering a plural marriage with an older, established man could provide economic security. Approximately half (53.1 percent) of married women in Manti whose first marriages were as plural wives did not have fathers living in Utah at the time of their marriages (see figure 9), suggesting that economic considerations were important for women in the formation of many plural marriages. Writing about polygamy in general, the economist Gary Becker argues, "Women are better off than if polygyny were forbidden," especially in societies that value many children.[26]

Vicky Burgess-Olson's work also points to the importance of economic motivations. In her study based on records written by polygamous wives, she found that 8.3 percent of first wives, 17.9 percent of middle wives, and 37.5 percent of last/youngest wives gave economic reasons for entering plural marriages. For last/youngest wives, it was the single most important reason. For all wives, at 21.1 percent, economic reasons ranked only slightly below dedication to the principle of plural marriage (26.3 percent) and pressure from a third party (22.4 percent). The women included in her study, however, were all literate and disproportionately from the United States, underrepresenting immigrant women, so her findings undoubtedly do not fully measure the importance of economic considerations.[27] Nevertheless, women, including fatherless women, made various marital choices, and the majority of fatherless women did marry first as monogamous wives.

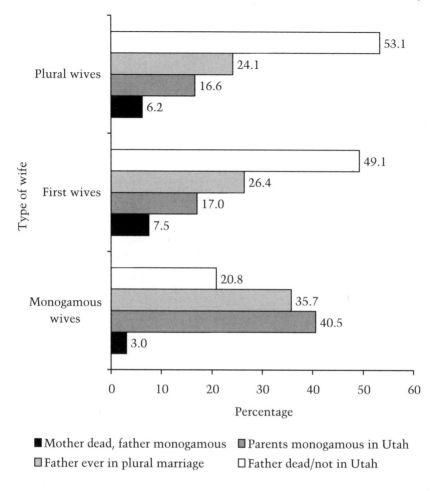

Figure 9. Percentage of Plural, First, and Monogamous Wives from Various Family Types. Source: Manti data set.

Women whose fathers had practiced plural marriage accounted for almost one-fourth (24.1 percent) of those who first married as plural wives, as figure 9 shows.[28] Such women were accustomed to its practice, and many were imbued with the idea that it was the highest form of marriage.[29] Nevertheless, more than three times as many daughters of polygamists became monogamous wives as became either first or plural wives (see figure 8).

Marriageable women whose fathers were monogamous but whose mothers had died were few in number, and the majority became monogamous wives. Nevertheless, a disproportionate number became plural wives. This was particularly the case when the father remarried. The marriage of an older daughter removed her from a household where she might be in conflict with her stepmother.[30] That was accomplished expeditiously through plural marriage: the demand for plural wives appears to have been greater than the supply, and plural marriages could take place without lengthy courtships.[31]

The women least likely to enter plural marriage were those whose parents were monogamous and both living, although such women still constituted 16.6 percent of plural wives. Nevertheless, monogamous parents tended to produce monogamous daughters. Of the 24 exceptions to this in the Manti subset, 6 were women whose families had experienced the trials of Nauvoo and Winter Quarters, 5 came from families that had immigrated within eighteen months of the marriage, 3 were from families that listed no wealth on the census or tax assessment rolls near the date of the marriage, and 1 had borne an illegitimate child. In many monogamous families, however, particularly those who immigrated after the 1850s, no members ever entered plural marriage.

As figure 9 suggests, while the family backgrounds of plural wives differed somewhat from those of monogamous wives, women who were first wives in plural marriages came from families remarkably similar to those of plural wives. Most women who became first wives had married their husbands before immigrating to Utah; however, fifty-six first wives who resided in Manti did marry in Utah. Among these first wives, 49.1 percent had fathers who were dead or not in Utah, a percentage only slightly lower than that for plural wives. Those whose fathers were polygamists constituted 26.4 percent of first wives, while daughters of monogamous parents made up 17.0 percent—within four percentage points of plural wives in each category. Overall, then, plural and first wives who married in Utah came from family situations much more similar to each other than to those of monogamous wives. First wives who had lived without male support appear to have been more willing to help similar women by allowing their husbands to marry those women as plural wives.

Thus, neither first nor plural wives were representative of all Mormon brides. Fatherless women were disproportionately in polygamous marriages. Moreover, about 30 percent of plural wives had been previously widowed or divorced. Among marriages other than the first contracted by Manti women, slightly over half were plural ones.[32] In short, women who were fatherless or who had previously been married—women who were, in other words, largely dependent on their own financial resources—constituted two-thirds of plural wives in the Manti subset.

It is not surprising a church that believed marriage was necessary for exaltation but had limited financial resources found a solution for helping the fatherless and widows by fostering their marriage. Nor is it surprising little is written to indicate that this was the case. The church's extensive missionary program was often accused of being a recruitment program for plural wives. This was not so: almost as many single men as single women immigrated to Utah.[33] Nor did most single female converts become plural wives.

It does appear, however, that the church, with its strong advocacy of separate gender roles, gave different types of financial assistance to women than to men. For poor, immigrant men, it provided jobs on public projects, including work on temples and the Tabernacle.[34] It helped single women by providing them ample opportunities to marry, including as plural wives.

One plural wife indicated that this was what she thought the church intended: "Utah in those days was full of girls and women who had come from the European countries and from the Eastern states [as converts]. Brigham Young used to say to the men: 'Marry these girls and give them a home and provide for and protect them. Let them be wives and mothers.' So all men who could looked upon it as a duty."[35] John Taylor, president of the church, specifically preached that widows should be taken care of through marriage: "[I]f a man has a brother dead who has left a widow, let the woman left in that kind of a position be just as well off as a woman who has a husband. . . . If a woman is left by her husband, let her have somebody to take care of her; if not her husband's brother, then his next of kin. . . . We ought to look after the welfare and interest of all."[36] The brother who married a widow, however, was more often a brother in the gospel rather than a kinsman.

When it was a religious responsibility to take care of the widows and the fatherless and when it was to such women's economic advantage to marry, the high percentage of plural wives belonging to those categories is not surprising. Mormon women undoubtedly believed in the principle of plural marriage, but women who needed economic help disproportionately practiced it.

7 *Economics and Plural Marriage*

The men who became polygamists, of course, needed attributes that could fulfill the religious and economic needs of those marrying as plural wives. For the most part, polygamists were wealthier than other men, and those with a higher church rank were more likely to have plural wives. Wealthier men could more easily provide for additional wives and would certainly be more attractive to economically disadvantaged women, and those of higher church rank were considered more likely to attain exaltation in the next life and thus provide women with the eternal spouses they needed for their own exaltation.

Church rank and wealth were positively correlated: those at the highest levels of the church hierarchy were ten times wealthier than other Mormons.[1] In her study of men from the 1821–30 birth cohort residing in Utah in 1851, Linda Mealy found that wealth was more important when the men were seeking their first wives but that church rank was more influential at the time they remarried or entered polygyny. That is, church rank was more important than wealth in predicting a plural marriage. Mealy also found that a man was significantly more likely to remarry or enter plural marriage in the five years subsequent to his increase in church rank than in the five years preceding it.[2] This is not surprising because many men entered plural marriage after a church official had asked them to do so. Apparently a man's entering plural marriage was not a prerequisite for advancement in church rank but was a responsibility accompanying the increase in rank, although some never took on the additional responsibility of plural wives.[3]

Although no members of the church's top leadership resided in Manti in 1860, Manti was in many ways a microcosm of the larger Mormon society. The thirteen men who held or had held top church leadership positions in Manti—stake presidency, bishopric, high council, and president of the Danish Meeting—and who appeared in the 1860 Manti census had an average of 3.40 wives.[4] In this calculation, all the polygamous wives—first and plural wives—the men had married were included, even if by 1860 the wives had died or had been divorced. The other twenty-eight men listed on the 1860 census who had entered plural marriage by 1860 had an average of 2.07 wives. With one exception, all of these men had married only one additional wife. The exception, Hans Jensen Hals who had married four wives, soon was called as a counselor to the bishop in Manti and later became a bishop.

A majority of Manti polygamists had only two wives at a time, although many had several wives over their lifetimes. The percentage of polygamists with five or more wives during their lives was 13.3 percent, while 16.7 percent had four wives, 32.7 percent had three wives, and 37.3—slightly over one-third—had just two wives. Some of these wives, however, lived only in monogamy. A few were first wives who died before their husbands had much opportunity to take a plural wife. Nathan Lewis's first wife, for example, died in Kirtland in 1836 or 1837 before plural marriage was practiced by the general membership of the church. Daniel Allen's wife died soon after leaving Nauvoo in May 1846, and Elisha Edwards's first wife, Mariah, died in 1847 at Winter Quarters. After leaving Denmark, Henning Madsen's wife of nineteen years died in Echo Canyon only five days before the family arrived in Salt Lake City.[5] Other first wives did not live long after their arrival in Utah. Johannes and Anna Barbara Alder journeyed from Switzerland to the latter-day Zion in 1860, where Anna died two years later. In 1864, Adam Craik Smyth married Emily Brown in Manchester, England. The couple then immigrated to Utah, where Emily died in 1866, ten days after giving birth.[6] The church attracted a few men whose wives remained unconverted. Leaving their unbelieving wives behind, they remarried after arriving in Utah. Soren Christoffersen was baptized in 1851, and he and two sons sailed from Denmark in 1855. His wife, Ane, died in Denmark in 1858, and the next year Christoffersen remarried in Utah and then took a plural wife eleven months after his remarriage.[7] Some wives had little or no opportunity to enter plural marriage, although their husbands did become polygamists.

Polygamists' total number of wives was greater than the number of their plural wives. Only 11.3 percent had five or more wives in polygamy, and the same percentage had four polygamous wives. Those with three wives amounted to one-fifth (20.7 percent) of all polygamists, but those with only two wives living in plural marriage accounted for 56.7 percent, a substantially higher proportion than polygamists who had only two wives during their lifetimes.

Nevertheless, because of deaths and divorces, half of polygamists who had three or more polygamous wives were not living with all those wives at one time. Johannes Alder married Mary Staheli after the death of his wife Anna Barbara; however, ten days after he married another wife, Matilda Sophia Schramm, Mary sued for divorce. Whether the marriage had been an unhappy one, prompting Johannes to take a second wife, or whether plural marriage precipitated the divorce is unclear, although Mary did permit her subsequent husband to take a plural wife. After eight years of living monogamously with Matilda, Johannes married Anna Margaretha Josephine Krause. He lived with both wives for three years, and then Matilda died. While Johannes had three polygamous wives, he had only two wives simultaneously and lived in plural marriage only three years.[8] While the stories of other polygamous men are diverse, almost two-thirds (66.0 percent) chose not to have more than two wives at a time. Approximately one-fifth (21.3 percent) had three wives, while 8.0 percent had four. Only 4.7 percent had five or more wives at the same time.

These percentages are almost the same as those calculated by Stanley Ivins, whose data yielded 66.3 percent for those with two wives and 21.2 percent for those with three. His figures diverge slightly more for those with four wives, 6.7 percent, and those with five or more wives, 5.8 percent, although adding these two categories together, the figures are almost the same as the Manti figures. His higher figure for those with five or more wives results from the sources he used. One of these was *Pioneers and Prominent Men of Utah,* in which prominent men—those more likely to have many wives—are overrepresented. Although he does not indicate how he arrived at his figures, they apparently refer to the number of simultaneous wives, not the total number of polygamous wives.[9]

Not only is the number of plural wives Manti polygamists had similar to that among Mormon polygamists generally, but also church rank and wealth were related in Manti, as elsewhere in Utah. The mean wealth in 1860 for the church leadership in Manti was $3,291.92, compared with the mean wealth for all married men at $1,135.71.[10] Also, as elsewhere, wealth and plural marriage in Manti were related.[11] The average wealth for Manti monogamists in 1860 was $719.50, whereas the mean wealth for those who were or had been in plural marriage was $2,029.02—nearly three times greater. When the top thirteen church leaders are excluded, the remaining polygamists still had a mean wealth of $1,442.68, twice as much as the average monogamist. In 1860, 68 percent of polygamists were in the top three deciles of wealthholders in Manti. To be sure, a handful of polygamists possessed wealth far below the average,[12] and a few in the top deciles did not enter plural marriage; but overall, the wealthier the man, the more likely he was in a plural marriage.

In spite of these differences in wealthholding, wealth in Manti was more evenly distributed than it was in the United States as a whole, although it was similar to the distribution in the northern states in 1860. The Gini coefficient for families in Manti was 0.591 in 1860,[13] when divorced women and boarders over twenty were counted as families. If family wealth had been equal, the coefficient would have been 0.0, and if one family had had all the wealth, it would have been 1.0. In contrast, the Gini coefficient for free white males in the United States in 1860 was 0.832.[14] Wealth in the North was more evenly distributed and, excluding Maryland, ranged from 0.54 in New Hampshire to 0.68 in New Jersey. Manti's wealth distribution was similar to Michigan's, whose Gini coefficient was 0.58 in 1860. Manti's median wealth of $700 was also similar to Michigan's median of $800. Both, however, had lower median wealth than most states had. If Maryland is excluded, only Minnesota, with a median wealth of $500, was lower than Manti's. Median wealth levels in other northern states were over $1,000.[15]

Although the median wealth of Manti's polygamists was about the same as that for monogamous families in the northern states, polygamous families were in general larger. While this meant that polygamous families were poorer per capita than families in the northern states, it also meant that plural marriage tended to distribute wealth more equally in Manti. When each family's wealth is divided by the number of members in the family and the population of the town is then ranked in deciles, the Gini coefficient for Manti dropped from 0.591 to 0.462 in 1860.[16]

The extent of the redistribution of wealth is made clearer by comparing two communities settled about the same time as Manti: Zeeland, Michigan, and Silverton, Oregon. Zeeland was chosen because Michigan's wealth distribution was similar to Manti's, and Zeeland's mostly foreign-born population had a high birthrate, as did Utah.[17] Like the Mormons in Manti, the residents of Zeeland belonged to a cohesive religious group, the Seceders from the State Church in the Netherlands. Beginning in 1847, the same year the Mormons arrived in Utah, the Seceders began emigrating from the Netherlands for primarily economic but also religious reasons. The Silverton area in the Willamette Valley was settled during the first large influx of settlers into Oregon in the 1840s. Located about fifteen miles northeast of Salem at the edge of the Waldo Hills, Silverton became a trading center for the surrounding farming area.[18]

The distribution of wealth in Manti, Zeeland, and Silverton is compared for 1860 and 1870 in table 5. When nonnuclear family members over age twenty except parents are counted as families, the Gini coefficient based on family wealth in 1860 was higher in Manti than in Zeeland or Silverton. When each family's wealth was divided by the number of members in the family, however, the Gini coefficient dropped more in Manti—almost twice the decrease in Silverton and four times that in Zeeland. In 1870, the decrease in the Gini coefficient for Manti was less than in 1860, partly because fewer Manti residents lived in plural families. In 1860, 43.1 percent of men, women, and children were in polygamous families, whereas only 36.0 percent were in 1870. Nevertheless, the decrease in the Gini coefficient for Manti still was greater in 1870 than in either of the two other towns.

The significant decrease in the Gini coefficient for Manti indicates that plural marriage fostered the redistribution of wealth. Men have historically held much more wealth than women,[19] and Manti's polygamists held more wealth than did other married men. By contrast, the women

Table 5. Gini Coefficients for Family Wealth and Per Capita Wealth within Families for Manti, Utah; Zeeland, Michigan; and Silverton, Oregon, 1860 and 1870

| | Gini Coefficient | | |
Year and Town	Family Wealth	Per Capita Wealth within Families	Percentage Decrease
1860			
Manti	.591	.463	21.7
Zeeland	.455	.430	5.5
Silverton	.540	.478	11.5
1870			
Manti	.549	.476	13.3
Zeeland	.480	.429	10.6
Silverton	.587	.574	2.2

Sources: 1860 and 1870 U.S. Census, Manti, Sanpete County, Utah, Population Schedules; 1860 and 1870 U.S. Census, Zeeland, Ottawa County, Michigan, Population Schedules; 1860 and 1870 U.S. Census, Silverton, Marion County, Oregon, Population Schedules.

who became plural wives were disproportionately from among the economically disadvantaged. Even though the economic resources stayed under control of wealthier men, plural marriage helped give poorer women access to those resources.

Had plural marriage been confined to the church leadership, the degree to which resources were redistributed would have been small. In 1860 Manti, however, 37 of the 129 married men (28.7 percent) had more than one wife living. Four additional men had formerly been polygamists, although their second wives had either died or been divorced by 1860.[20] With a fairly large minority of the wealthier married men taking additional wives during the frontier period, a considerable leveling of resources available to each person could occur. Mormon society was hierarchal, making distinctions among men by the priesthood offices they held and their callings within the church. Moreover, those who lived in Salt Lake County or had resided longer in Utah tended to be wealthier than others. Wealth was thus unevenly distributed: the Gini coefficients for 1850 and 1870 were 0.69 and 0.74, respectively, for all of Utah.[21]

One goal of the early church, however, was to eliminate economic class divisions among its members, and it developed programs to accomplish that goal. In 1831, for example, the bishop of the church was told to "appoint unto this people their portions, every man equal according to his family" (Doctrine and Covenants 51:3). Other programs to mitigate economic divisions followed, including the United Orders, which varied from cooperatives to commonly owned resources. In a pamphlet about the Zion's Co-operative Mercantile Institution in 1875, the First Presidency wrote, "Years ago it was perceived that . . . a condition of affairs existed among us which was favorable to the growth of riches in the hands of a few at the expense of the many. A wealthy class was being rapidly formed in our midst whose interests, in the course of time, were likely to be diverse from those of the rest of the community. The growth of such a class was dangerous to our union; and, of all people, we stand most in need of union and to have our interests identical."[22] Although not generally classified as one of the economic plans to provide greater economic equality, plural marriage probably promoted equality "according to family" as well as most of those programs instituted specifically for that purpose. It is not surprising that the United Orders were instituted to counter growing divergence in wealth at a time when plural marriage was decreasing.

Plural marriage also tended to promote equality among women. As George Q. Cannon pointed out in 1869, "Patriarchal Marriage [has] a tendency to elevate the entire sex, and give all the privilege of being honored matrons and respected wives. There are no refuse among us—no class to be cast out, scorned and condemned; but every woman who chooses can be an honored wife."[23] Plural marriage offered equality by giving every woman an opportunity to be a wife, although, of course, it did so at the risk of curtailing a variety of roles for women. It also risked non-Mormon opprobrium, making it acceptable only in communities dominated by Latter-day Saints.

But the roles for women were prescribed by both traditional gender roles and the nature of economy. Women on the frontier and in rural areas made economic contributions to the family, and plural wives were not exceptions. Few Utah women, and certainly few plural wives, could afford not to work. In the frontier days, women's labor was the traditional, nonpaid work of women. They turned wheat into bread, cream into butter, chicken into meals, and wool into stockings. Though a few women taught school, they were not relieved of women's work. "Sister Hannah and I took in spinning and weaving, and I learned to cut clothes so I could cut the boys suits myself," wrote plural wife Lucy Meserve Smith about the early days in Utah. "I taught school a No. of quarters," she continued, but she and her sister wife also "wove hundreds of yards of cloth such as bed coverleds, diaper, geans, kearsey flannel linsey carpets &c."[24] Those who colonized new areas thirty or forty years later found their circumstances not much different. In 1888, Catharine Romney wrote her parents from Mexico explaining why she did not write more often: "I should write but I can say . . . that it seems as if evry hour is fully occupied. in one way or another. with having sick boys and very sore eyes nearly all summer I have got behind with my sewing hat making etc. so that it is crowding me and baby . . . is not quite a[s] good to be down as most of my babies have been. and the time is well taken up with house work sewing braiding, coloring etc. yesterday I made two cans of lye into soap." Romney's day was full of traditional women's work, although she had the advantage of having stores where she could buy some goods when money was available. Her letters were even more likely to include details of her husband's work, such as building rooms for her and her sister wives, bringing home venison for food, and planting crops. Her husband frowned on females milking the cows, so his young sons did it most of the time.[25] When the culture clearly assigned work by gender, men and women needed each other economically.

Although most women gained economically by becoming plural wives, they did not become middle-class women of leisure. Rather, they exchanged working in someone else's household as a servant for working in their husbands' or their own homes. The improvements they made, however, benefited their families and themselves over the long term. Or it might simply be that there was then a man who had the moral and social obligation to make up the difference between poverty and a modicum of comfort by bringing in the firewood. To redistribute the wealth in the territory when Utah was among the poorest areas gave no one opulence; for the most part, it simply mitigated the worst poverty and shared the burden of struggling for a living in a semiarid land.

This is not to say that some plural wives were not successful in their own right. As the economy matured, some were able to establish themselves in businesses and professions.[26] Plural marriage was more likely to make this a necessity as well as a possibility. In a rural and semisubsistence economy, women and children were producers, enlarging the family's assets. As Utah followed the rest in the nation in becoming a consumer society by the 1870s and 1880s, however, it became more difficult for husbands, particularly polygamists, to provide for increasing numbers of dependent consumers. As children spent longer periods in school, their productivity was delayed into their teenage years or later. With growing financial demands on the family, the strategy of polygamous families was increasingly for wives to become part of the cash economy. For many, it was a necessity.

Plural marriage also created the opportunity for some wives to enter the paid labor market. With at least one wife taking over most of the "women's work" in the home, other wives were freed for different labor. But that labor, even for professional women, was not for self-fulfillment but for others. Ellis Shipp became a successful physician, but her work was for her family and community. In 1877, she wrote from medical school, "I will be able to complete my studies in another year, and be ready to return to my loved ones, prepared for a life of usefulness among the Saints of God. Heaven knows it is not for *self* I have thus absented myself from all that earth holds so dear. 'Tis not for worldly praise I labor early and late, but that I may become a more competent wife and mother and better qualified for all the duties of *woman*, and of a *Saint of God*."[27] However much Mormon women might have liked to have lived as nineteenth-century middle-class women with ample time to look after their homes and their children, the poverty, relative or absolute, precluded that for most wives, monogamous or plural. Work, paid or unpaid, was a necessity. For those women who chose to become plural wives, polygamy appears to have offered economic advantages initially. Whether it continued to do so depended on a several factors, including not only the husband's long-term financial success but also the changing economy and revisions in the law that adversely affected their lives.

Change was one of the few constants. Although the legal and ecclesiastical systems supporting marriage remained essentially stable in Utah from initial settlement in 1847 to the repressive federal government intervention in the 1880s, the picture that emerges from this in-depth study of marriage in Manti is considerable change over time, even before the government raids on polygamous households. Age-specific marriage rates were remarkably high during the first twenty years of settlement but declined in each of the two following twenty-year periods. During the frontier period, immigrant women of marriageable age could expect to marry within about a year after their arrival. Those arriving later could expect to wait increasingly longer periods before marriage. Mean age at marriage reached its lowest point during the revivals of the reformation and immediately thereafter, when economic conditions, the influx of many immigrants, and church leaders combined to promote plural marriages. In spite of similar, though perhaps less insistent, exhortations from church leaders thereafter, the mean age at which women married rose steadily from 1860 until after the turn of the century, showing a short, slight acceleration after 1887, when federal prosecutions effectively curtailed new plural marriages in Manti.

The legal and ecclesiastical systems the Saints put in place had a continuing impact on marriage patterns in Utah. This system provided the framework that made plural marriage possible; the financial needs of economically disadvantaged women made some plural marriages probable. It is also clear that the legal framework imposed by the federal government had the opposite impact on marriage patterns by making plural marriage less likely to meet the material needs of disadvantaged women and by making large fines and imprisonment of polygamous men probable.

Even during the period when plural marriage was encouraged by the church, however, marriage patterns altered as society and the economy changed. As fewer women became plural wives, marriage rates declined and the mean age at marriage rose. To some extent, this reflected changes in the number of women whose fathers were dead or not in Utah. Such women made up almost one-third of those who married as plural wives, but the number of fatherless women decreased after 1870. The hardships that cost lives in Winter Quarters and during the crossing of the plains became substantially less as Utah became settled and stable. In addition, fewer never-married immigrants traveled to Utah alone after the frontier period. In short, the economic motivations giving impetus to plural marriage declined over time.

Nevertheless, enough women continued to enter plural marriage until the 1880s that the entire marriage market was affected. The general encouragement of marriage and the high demand for wives held down the mean age at marriage for all women, not simply for plural wives, and ensured that almost all women would marry.

PART 4

II Leviticus: Legal and Ecclesiastical Framework for Divorce

They say unto him, Why did Moses then command to
give a writing of divorcement, and to put her away?
He saith unto them, Moses because of the hardness of
your hearts suffered you to put away your wives: but
from the beginning it was not so.

—Matthew 19:7–8

For the unbelieving husband is sanctified by the
wife, and the unbelieving wife is sanctified by the
husband . . .
But if the unbelieving depart, let him depart. A brother
or a sister is not under bondage in such cases . . .

—1 Corinthians 7:14–15

8 Civil and Ecclesiastical Divorce

On April 19, 1873, the following petition for a divorce was
produced in the Sanpete County Probate Court:

> Ophir City, East Cannon
> March 7 1873
>
> This is to certify that George C. Johnston and E. M. Johnston this day
> and date has dissolved companionship and are both free from each other
> hereafter.
>
> Signed in the Presence of   G. C. Johnston
> J. H. Taylor   Emily M. Johnston
> Martha A. Taylor[1]

Emily's brother, Joseph H. Taylor, and his wife, Martha, testified that this
document was signed in their presence. They further stated that George
and Emily had agreed that Emily would have custody of the two children
and would receive real and personal property valued at $243. Thereupon
the court granted a divorce, allowing them the liberty "to marry with
whomsoever they may" and giving custody of the four-year-old daughter and two-year-old son to Emily. It also awarded her the property that
she and her husband had agreed she would have: a Manti city lot and
house valued at $100, land and water rights at Six Mile Creek valued at
$13, a horse valued at $80, as well as a stove and household furniture
valued at $50.[2]

Such a divorce—no lawyers, no grounds stated, no waiting period for
the divorce to become final, and evidence of cooperation to obtain the divorce—was unusual in nineteenth-century America but not in Utah.[3] Most

couples, or at least one party to the divorce, did come to the court, but otherwise this divorce decree was not an anomaly in Sanpete County.[4]

But the story does not end here, as accounts of divorce based solely on court records do. This quick divorce did not end their relationship. About five weeks after the divorce, on May 30, 1873, Emily bore a son. Twenty-eight months later, she bore George Johnston another son, and thereafter the couple had four additional children. A twenty-eight-month interval between children was about average for Mormons of Emily's birth cohort, and it is actually shorter than the thirty-two month interval between her two previous children.[5] Obviously, the separation had not been long.

No second marriage date for the couple has been found, but this is not unusual for Utah at that period, and a civil remarriage undoubtedly occurred. Nevertheless, their religious marriage most likely had remained intact. Emily and George had been married in the Endowment House in Salt Lake City on November 9, 1867, according to the law of the church that sealed them for time and eternity.[6] Their divorce had been a civil one and did not void the religious marriage covenants they had made. They may well have obtained a church divorce also, though that is unlikely, but it is impossible to check this because records of church divorces (cancellations of sealings) are not currently available to scholars.

Both civil courts and the Church of Jesus Christ of Latter-day Saints exercised jurisdiction over divorces until 1899, when *Norton v. Tufts* declared that ecclesiastical divorces granted by the LDS Church were civilly invalid.[7] This overlapping jurisdiction for divorce posed few problems until the 1870s, because before then Mormons not only controlled church divorces but also, through their control of the territorial legislature, passed the laws that governed civil divorces. Mormon theology holds marriage sacred and provides little justification for divorce. Nevertheless, in what is probably the most obvious example of religion's accommodation to the reality of family life, Mormons instituted systems of divorce that were simple, nonlegalistic, and participant-run. Although the church had mechanisms to try solving marital conflicts and to support established family units, it acknowledged that irreconcilable couples were better off apart. Divorced, each could then marry a compatible partner. If the couple merely separated without the right to remarry, probably neither would have had more children, which was one of the main purposes of marriage according to Mormon doctrine. The primary purpose of Mormon divorce was not to break up families but to encourage the remarriage of those who were already estranged from their spouses.

While divorce provided an escape from an unhappy marriage for all couples, it was particularly important for those in plural marriage. The stress of living in a plural marriage could be great, especially for people whose culture and outlook had recently been monogamous. It is questionable whether plural marriage could have been instituted in such a society without the safety valve of divorce. Divorce from a polygamous husband did not necessarily mean a rejection of plural marriage, however. Plural marriage permitted many divorced and widowed women who wished to remarry an opportunity to do so, and some women were in more than one plural marriage.

Plural marriage and divorce were connected almost from the beginning. In 1842, a pamphlet called *The Peace Maker* appeared in Nauvoo. It contained a biblical and social justification for both polygamy and divorce. Udney Hay Jacob was listed as the author, but Joseph Smith was named as the printer on the title page. When members of the church reacted unfavorably to the pamphlet, however, Joseph Smith dissociated himself from its printing.[8] Nevertheless, some of the pamphlet's ideas surfaced in Utah, although in modified form. Jacob argued that divorce should be permitted only on the grounds of fornication, which he then defined: "But the alienation of the mind or affections from her husband constitutes fornication in a married woman."[9] According to Jacob, when a wife's feelings were so alienated, her husband could write her a bill of divorce "according to the strict letter of the law of God as given by Moses," and she was then free to remarry. "The bill thus registered becomes a matter of record and signifies a freedom from her former husband." This was the type of divorce authorized by the scriptures, he claimed, and legislative bodies and courts that granted divorces had tyrannically assumed that power.[10] Just as Mormons changed the jurisdiction of many marriages from the civil to the ecclesiastical realm, they also transferred power over many divorces to church officials.

Divorce was first instituted through the ecclesiastical courts in Utah, but in 1852 the Utah territorial legislature passed a law regulating civil divorce.[11] Although alienation of feeling was frequently cited in divorce petitions, the law did not name that as one of the grounds for divorce. It did name some commonly recognized grounds for divorce and added an omnibus clause, which several states, including Connecticut and North Carolina, had passed in the second quarter of the nineteenth century.[12] The Utah Act in Relation to Bills of Divorce, approved on March 6, 1852, enumerated the grounds for divorce:

> the court may decree a divorce from the bonds of matrimony against the husband; for any of the following causes, to wit: Impotency of the defendant at the time of marriage; adultery committed by defendant subse-

quent to marriage; willful desertion of his wife by the defendant, or absenting himself without a reasonable cause for more than one year; habitual drunkenness of defendant subsequent to marriage; conviction of defendant for felonies subsequent to marriage; inhuman treatment so as to endanger the life of the defendant's wife; *when it shall be made to appear to the satisfaction and conviction of the court, that the parties cannot live in peace and union together, and that their welfare requires a separation.*[13]

Because of the similarity of the language, the omnibus clause of Utah's 1852 divorce law (the last clause) appears to have been modeled on Iowa's 1846 statute, which permitted divorce "when it shall be made fully apparent that the parties cannot live in peace and happiness together and that their welfare requires a separation."[14] Whatever change of nuance the Utah legislature intended by substituting the word *union* for *happiness* appears to have escaped ordinary Mormons. Many divorce petitions appearing in the Sanpete County Probate Court Record stated that the couple could not live together in "peace and happiness."[15] Echoing *The Peace Maker*, some petitions for divorce declared that "their feelings are so entirely alienated that they cannot live together in peace and happiness as husband and wife" or, similarly, that the husband and wife had "for sometime been estranged in their feelings and cannot live together in peace and happiness as husband and wife."[16] Alienation of feelings appears to have been inextricably intertwined with, if not the same as, the inability to live in peace and happiness.

Although many divorce petitions contained the essence but not always the wording of *The Peace Maker*, they did not conform to the idea that it was alienation of the wife's feelings alone that was important. Many were mutual petitions for divorce based on alienation of feelings from each other. A man could also petition for divorce stating that his feelings were alienated from his wife, and the court still granted the divorce.[17] The section of the law enumerating the grounds for divorce was written in feminine terms, indicating the primacy of women's concerns when the law was framed, but the subsequent section of the law granted men equal privileges in obtaining divorces under the law.[18]

To be sure, more women than men filed petitions for divorce. Of those divorces from 1852 to 1884 in Sanpete County that were not by mutual petition and in which the sex of the plaintiff can be determined, 60 percent (77) were granted at the request of the wife.[19] This was slightly lower than the 69 percent of divorce decrees granted to wives in Connecticut, Maine, and Massachusetts from 1850 to 1880.[20] In the United States from 1867 to 1886, 66 percent were granted to wives.[21] The Sanpete County percentage is potentially biased downward, however, because some divorce petitions may have been by mutual consent even though the record did not specifically indicate this (cases brought by mutual consent listed the husbands' names first). Moreover, the figures for Sanpete County are incomplete because they include only those divorces brought before the civil court, not church divorces. Nevertheless, it appears women in Utah sought dissolution of their marriages more often than did men, just as elsewhere in the United States.

Of the divorces sought in Sanpete County between 1852 and 1884, 26 percent (49) were by mutual petitions. These often stated that the peace and happiness of the individuals could best be served by a divorce. Although these couples did bring their suits to the civil courts and thus acknowledged those courts' jurisdiction over divorce, which *The Peace Maker* did not, their petitions implied that they had written their own bills of divorce and were asking the court to ratify the decision. These were mutual petitions, it should be stressed, by both husband and wife, not the husband's giving his wife a bill of divorce as prescribed by *The Peace Maker.* The petition quoted at the beginning of this chapter is the most obvious example of this kind of self-divorce with court ratification.

Other petitions implied the same, although they used more conventional language. Such was the petition of Joseph A. and Annie D. Smith on May 24, 1878, who claimed they "cannot live together in peace and happiness as husband and wife, that they have mutually agreed on terms of separation and alimony." The court granted the divorce and "ratified" their agreement about the division of children and property.[22] This broad application of the law differed considerably from its application in Iowa. There the court, not the husband and wife, decided whether they could live in peace and happiness. For example, the court would grant a divorce if the husband used harsh language in speaking to his wife and gave the impression of adultery.[23] In California, a husband's charge that his wife was prostituting herself was deemed extreme cruelty. As public opinion increasingly embraced the ideal of mutual affection and intimacy between married couples, the law was interpreted more liberally, particularly in the western states.[24]

But for a husband and wife to decide that they could no longer live happily together and to be granted a divorce based on their mutual petition was decidedly unusual. Because the Sanpete County Probate Court always granted mutual petitions for divorce for which there is an extant record—no petition for dissolution of marriage was ever denied, although it was sometimes delayed—couples could be assured that their agreement to dissolve the marriage would be confirmed by the court. This was certainly not the case elsewhere: in the United States as a whole, only 67.8 percent of divorce petitions were granted.[25]

In many states, a mutual agreement to divorce would have been collusion, which would have barred the divorce.[26] No-fault divorce was still a hundred years away, and most jurisdictions treated divorce much as it had developed in the Reformation. It was perceived as an adversarial process in which one party had to be found guilty of a matrimonial offense, such as adultery or desertion. Divorce was both a punishment of that offense and relief for the victim (the innocent spouse).[27] If a spouse in any way conspired with the other to create grounds of divorce—such as arranging to be caught *in flagrante delicto* so that adultery could be alleged—it was collusion, and he or she was no longer the innocent victim and hence deserving of a divorce.[28]

In Utah, however, couples were encouraged to reach their own agreements about divorce. In 1869, when the Attwood divorce case was called up, the "Parties requested leave of the Court to retire that they might try and effect a compromise." The court granted the request, and the next day the "Plaintiff [the husband] gave notice that a compromise had been agreed upon to the effect that the bonds of matrimony now existing between him and Defendant was to be dissolved, that their only child . . . should remain in charge of its mother until ten years old." After hearing testimony that "the future peace and happiness of the parties demanded a dissolution of the bonds of matrimony," the court ratified the couple's decision.[29] Amicable, not adversarial, divorces were encouraged in Utah.

Despite the Utah law's leniency regarding grounds for dissolution of marriage, Mormons do not seem to have abused the law.[30] Most cases probably did not even go to court until after the church had used various means to mediate the marital conflicts and reconcile the couple. Teachers, who were assigned to visit church members regularly, tried to resolve conflicts, including domestic ones. If they were unsuccessful, the dispute usually went to a bishop's court. Cases not resolved by the bishopric could then be taken before the stake high council, a body of twelve men, and the stake presidency. In 1878, for example, a plural wife filed a case before the Weber Stake High Council, and the stake presidency met with the husband and wife and effected a reconciliation. The husband later described the agreement: "[My wife] wanted a house built on the farm. I left it to the President and his councillors, and was willing to do what they said about it. They came to the conclusion that I should build her a house of four rooms on the farm, and make her as comfortable as I could. I am willing to carry this out, as well as possible."[31] In a similar case, a bishop heard a wife's complaints in a meeting she and her husband had jointly requested. The wife made various charges against her husband, who refuted the most serious of them. He expressed his willingness "to do what was just and right," and the bishop decided that the husband should "turn over the best house of the two for his wife's use, and as soon as possible get the present occupant to move to another place; that he allow her $6 per week and find her in sufficient flour and fuel; that he let her have the sewing machine, cooking stove, and an equal share of the furniture, and that the fruit of the orchard be fairly divided."[32] The bishop then appointed a man to see that the "weekly payments be made as far as could be conscientiously done." Despite the efforts, the reconciliation failed, and divorce proceedings began in the probate court six months later.[33]

Although church doctrine and institutions sometimes failed to reconcile a couple, the pressures to stay with a spouse appear to have been strong. It was not only the Johnstons, whose divorce is detailed at the beginning of this chapter, who were reconciled after the probate court dissolved their marriage but also at least five other couples from Manti. Of the forty-five Manti couples whose divorces appeared in the probate court from 1852 to 1887, 13.3 percent of the couples were reconciled after their divorces were granted. The policy of granting divorces the same day they first came before the court was a problem, although probably most couples' cases had already been adjudicated before ecclesiastical courts. Nevertheless, some couples divorced in haste and repented at leisure.

While the use of church courts mitigated against Mormons' misusing the lenient divorce law, it was abused by non-Mormon nonresidents. The 1852 law did not require a petitioner for divorce to be a resident of the Utah Territory if the court was satisfied that the person "wishes to become one."[34] By 1875, certain lawyers in Chicago, Cincinnati, and New York discovered how easy it was to secure divorces for their clients in Utah. Three counties obliged by readily granting divorces to plaintiffs who signed printed forms stating, "Plaintiff wishes to become a resident of Utah . . . but is so situated that he can not at present carry his desire in this respect into effect."[35] Demand for divorce was so great that the attorneys used printed forms for both petitions and decrees. The printed decree, which the attorneys filed with the petition, stated that the "defendant, after having been thus called upon and duly warned to appear and answer said plaintiff's complaint, and appearing and answering not, but making a default therein, the complaint is therefore taken as confessed." Instead of notification of divorce proceedings being delivered to the defendant, publication of notice to the defendant was printed in special editions, which never were circulated in the community. When the defendant did not appear, the judge took this as presumptive proof that the plaintiff's allegations were true and granted the divorce.[36]

The number of divorces in Utah soared from 1875 until 1878, when a revised law was passed requiring a petitioner to be a bona fide resident of a Utah county for a year before commencing divorce proceedings there.[37] The average number of divorces per year in Utah from 1870 to 1874 was 110, but the number reached 295 in 1875, soared to 709 in 1876, went to 914 in 1877, and then dropped to 298 in 1878 as the new divorce law went into effect. From 1879 until 1883, the average number of divorces per year decreased, to 137.[38] Based on the number of Utah divorces in the quinquennia before and after this escalation in nonresident divorces, no more than 140 divorces a year were granted to Utahns from 1875 to 1878. When 140 is subtracted from the number of divorces granted annually during those years, it appears that a minimum of 40.6 percent of all divorces granted from 1867 to 1886 in Utah were for nonresidents. Thus, while Utah courts granted many divorces, a large minority of these were granted to non-Mormons.

The divorce bill of 1878, which changed the residency requirements, also eliminated the omnibus clause, substituting for it the following grounds for divorce: "cruel treatment of plaintiff by the defendant to the extent of causing great bodily injury or great mental distress to plaintiff."[39] This changed language appears not to have appreciably changed the grounds for divorce, particularly at first. On August 29, 1878, J. Petersen filed a petition for divorce stating that the "affections of plaintiff were alienated from defendant and that her conduct to him had caused him great mental distress, that parties had entered into an agreement in writing as to alimony."[40] The petition was granted, although the grounds for the divorce were strikingly similar to those based on the former omnibus clause.

Nevertheless, most plaintiffs specified what caused the "great mental distress." The court accepted slander as grounds for divorce under this clause. One wife was granted a divorce because her husband "had treated her in a cruel and unbecoming manner charging her without cause with improper conduct with various parties, and calling her opprobrious names . . . thereby causing the plaintiff great mental distress." Similarly, a husband won his suit when he claimed that the "Defendant did call Plaintiff a vile and opprobrious name to wit an adulterer thereby causing him the said plaintiff great mental distress." Another husband was granted a divorce because his wife "did cause great mental distress to plaintiff by calling him a black devil and other bad names, and by saying that she did not love him and that she never should."[41]

The court also accepted the claim that the spouse's inappropriate behavior with members of the opposite sex caused great mental distress. One couple was granted a divorce in 1885 on the grounds of great mental distress because the wife "during the absence of plaintiff at his place of business, would entertain at her home, men of an open and notoriously lewd character, and visit house of public resort and amusement with said men." Another husband was granted a divorce because his wife "conducted herself in such an indecent and unwifely manner with a certain transient man known by . . . 'Scottie' as to cause the plaintiff great mental distress." Wives were granted divorces on similar complaints, as was a wife who claimed in 1883 that the "defendant did conduct himself in such an unbecoming manner with one C . . . N . . . that it caused plaintiff great mental distress." In 1879, another woman won her divorce on the grounds of "great mental distress" caused by her husband when he brought a "woman not his wife" to the house of the plaintiff in October 1878 and "did lay in same bed with same woman for six or seven nights."[42] Certainly proving that such conduct caused mental distress was easier than proving adultery, even in this last case.

Those in plural marriage were readily granted divorces on the grounds of great mental distress. This applied to not only women but also men.[43] In December 1885, shortly after U.S. deputy marshals made their first raid on Manti to arrest men for unlawful cohabitation,[44] the polygamist Herman Julius Christensen filed for divorce from his wife Karen Kirstine on the grounds of mental distress, although the impetus for the suit was probably to avoid being arrested for polygamy. His petition stated that "Plaintiff cannot live with Defendant in peace and happiness and that her conduct to him causes him great mental distress." She agreed that this was the case in her written answer to the complaint, which she signed with her mark. She had married her husband, twenty-three years her senior, at age fourteen in 1858 and had borne him fifteen children, all but four of whom died in infancy. She later told her descendants that she had always been somewhat afraid of her husband. Because couples could not mutually petition for divorce after 1878, legal fictions such as in this case yielded the same result. The court granted the divorce within less than a month from the time the initial petition was filed.[45]

This divorce proved more lasting than Christensen's first divorce, which was declared void because it had been granted by the probate court. The legality of divorces granted by the probate courts was a matter of some dispute. In *Kenyon v. Kenyon*, decided in 1861, the Utah Supreme Court declared that the territorial legislature had the right to grant probate courts "exclusive control" over divorces. Twelve years later, in *Cast v. Cast*, the court reversed itself and declared that only the district courts had jurisdiction over divorces.[46] However, Congress passed the Poland Act in 1874, which seemed to overrule this decision by confirming the probate courts' jurisdiction over divorce. When the issue came up again in 1881, the Utah Supreme Court reverted to its original position, declaring that the territorial legislature had the power to name which court would deal with divorce and that the real question decided by *Cast v. Cast* was that district courts as well as probate courts had jurisdiction. This position was confirmed in *Amy v. Amy*, but with the proviso that the probate court had records to show it followed the steps prescribed by the statute.[47]

When such records were lacking, the divorce decree was held to be void. Herman Julius Christensen had been granted a divorce from his first wife, Hannah, in 1854 by the Sanpete County Probate Court. When he died in 1897 with an estate worth over $77,000, however, Hannah filed for dower rights and an allowance from the estate, even though she had remarried around 1859.[48] Chief Justice Charles S. Zane, who had previously enforced the Edmunds Act vigorously, wrote the decision for *In re Herman J. Christiansen* when the case came before the Utah Supreme Court.[49] The decision stated that the Utah territorial legislature had no power to give jurisdiction of divorce cases to the probate courts and that the U.S. Congress had no power through the Poland Act of 1874 to validate and confirm decisions previously made by the probate courts. This was especially so in the Christensens' divorce suit, the decision declared, because the record of the divorce did not contain a charge against the wife, did not state what the petition contained, did not report the findings of the court, and did not indicate that a petition had been filed.[50] The Sanpete files for divorce cases before 1869 apparently no longer existed in 1898,[51] and the record contained in the minutes of the court was insufficient.

Nevertheless, it is not altogether clear that a complete record would have altered the decision. Zane argued, "It does not appear from the language of the curative provision [the Poland Act] that congress understood that the judgments and decrees referred to were absolutely void. . . . As we have seen, 'a judgment pronounced by a tribunal having no authority to determine the matter in issue is necessarily and incurably void.'"[52] This decision declared that the probate courts had no jurisdiction over divorce and that Congress had limited power to validate their proceedings.

Although it is unclear whether the case's precedent had any practical effect beyond the case at hand, the decision was a clear repudiation of early Utah civil divorces, which were nonlegalistic and accessible and were granted for incompatibility. Elsewhere in the United States, divorce also became more difficult as reaction set in to the midcentury divorce reforms;[53] Utah followed suit as it was forced to tighten its laws in 1878 to prevent their abuse by nonresidents and as its laws were administered by non-Mormon judges.

While civil divorces became more restrictive, the efficacy of ecclesiastical divorces was increasingly questioned. Which divorce cases were tried in each type of court has been somewhat unclear. Richard Aaron stated that the civil courts dissolved first marriages but that ecclesiastical courts had jurisdiction over polygamous marriages, a division he conceded was not always maintained.[54] Edwin Firmage and Richard Mangrum maintained, "Expediency required that members look to the civil courts and the liberal divorce statutes to legitimize divorces to nonmembers (or to confirm church divorces to avoid subsequent polygamy prosecution), but the church regularly enforced the 'exclusive jurisdiction' rule in other domestic cases."[55] According to Firmage and Mangrum, civil courts were used when one spouse was a non-Mormon until 1875 but after that were also used to confirm ecclesiastical divorce decisions.[56]

Divorces in Sanpete County have a more complex pattern. It appears that from 1852 until 1870, probate courts dissolved civil marriages, while church courts handled divorces involving temple marriages, or sealings. No couple identified in the *Ordinance Index* as having been sealed was granted a divorce by the Sanpete Probate Court before 1870.[57] Mormon couples whose marriages were performed by Mormon officials but who were not sealed filed for divorce through the probate court rather than through the church courts. For example, German Buchanan and Emily Lemaster, both Latter-day Saints, were married in 1855 by Welcome Chapman, the stake president of Sanpete, and were divorced in 1857 by the probate court.[58]

In 1870, the pattern began changing. In December of that year, a couple that had been sealed sought and obtained a divorce in the probate court; however, the couple had had a civil marriage before the sealing ceremony was performed.[59] Subsequently, other couples who had been sealed sought divorces in the civil court, including some first wives of polygamists who had had civil marriages before being sealed to their husbands.[60] By the mid-1870s, women who had married as plural wives but had become the first wife through divorce or the death of previous wives began to seek divorces in the probate courts. Later, the Utah Supreme Court would rule that such women were not legally wives, but those women considered themselves to be such and sought civil divorces.[61] Many of these divorces, however, were probably confirmations of decrees already obtained in ecclesiastical courts, as Firmage and Mangrum have suggested.[62]

Before 1870, couples, even monogamous ones, whose marriages had also been sealings applied for divorces through the church. Such was the case for Camilla Augusta Taylor and Azariah Smith. Their history illustrates not only the nature of church divorces but also the church's role in their marital affairs. Smith had been a member of the Mormon Battalion, had stayed in California to work after he was mustered out of the army, and had been at Sutter's Mill when gold was first discovered in 1848.[63] After gathering five hundred dollars in gold, he returned to Salt Lake City and married Camilla Augusta Taylor in 1849. Unfortunately, during his stint in the army, he received a blow on the head, which caused "fits" that plagued him for the next twenty years.

These seizures apparently were difficult for his wife to handle. In 1853, she was tried before the Manti High Council for, according to Smith's journal, "unchristianlike conduct. And it was brought against her, and proved; being also acknowledged to, that she had, had to do with Harvy Moss not long since in our own house." She was disfellowshipped (a punishment short of excommunication), and the couple was advised not to live together until "Brigham comes to straiten it." When Brigham Young arrived two weeks later, he asked Smith if he wished to live with his wife again. Smith replied that he did not "as things stood." Brigham Young advised him "to let her be and get me a good wife."[64]

Smith did not marry again, and eighteen months later the president of the church returned to Manti. Smith wrote in his journal that Brigham Young told him, "Augusta had done very well, and that it was our privelege to live togather again if it was our wish."[65] An innocent spouse was not allowed to have sexual intercourse with an adulterous one until the transgressor had repented and been rebaptized. According to the law, cohabitation by a husband or wife with an adulterous spouse, knowing or believing the spouse was guilty of adultery, was conclusive evidence of condonation and barred divorce on those grounds.[66]

The reconciliation effected by Brigham Young did not last long, however. Within three months, Smith wrote the president for advice. The reply was "that if we could not live togather in peace the quicker we had a seperation the better. Also sending a Scedule of a divorce for us to sign." At first Smith's wife was reluctant to sign the divorce papers, but finally on the advice of Welcome Chapman, the stake president in Manti, she did so.[67]

The divorce they signed was the standard one used in the church, probably as early as 1852 and as late as 1887. As Smith wrote it in his journal, it read:

Know all men by these presents, that we the undersigned Azariah Smith and Camillia A. Smith his wife (before her marriage to him Camillia A. Taylor) do hereby mutually Covenant, Promise and Agree to Dissolve all the relations which hitherto existed between us as Husband and wife, and to keep ourselves seperate and apart from each other from this time forth. In witness Whereof, We have hereunto set our hands at Manti Utah Territory, this 18th day of February A. D. 1855.
Signed in the presence of

George Peacock	Azariah Smith
James Wareham	Camillia A. Smith[68]

On the advice of President Chapman, Smith gave his former wife a cow, presumably as a divorce settlement. Being afflicted with seizures, he probably had little other property to give her. He listed no real or personal property in the 1860 census.[69]

This account reveals several important points about church divorces. First, although the case was not tried before an ecclesiastical court, church leaders were involved at almost every stage, from punishing the wife for adultery, to reconciling the couple, to awarding the alimony. In addition, the president of the church gave the couple permission to divorce. Second, although the president of the church permitted the divorce, it was not awarded by the church: it was an agreement between the couple to dissolve their marriage. It was similar to the Mosaic law, which allowed a man to give his wife a writ of divorce,[70] with the important difference that both husband and wife mutually freed each other. Third, George Peacock, who was the probate judge for Sanpete County, signed as a witness but not in his capacity as a judge. No record of this divorce appeared in the probate court record. Fourth, the divorce was then recorded by the church. Decrees of divorce were made out in triplicate. The original was kept by the church for record, and the other two copies were given to the man and woman.[71] Although no civil court played a role in these proceedings, in the eyes of the church and Mormon society, the divorce was valid, and Camilla Augusta Taylor Smith soon remarried.

This divorce was apparently only for time and was not a cancellation of the sealing. The church, however, granted both types. A divorce for only this world allowed both man and woman to remarry, but a woman could marry for this world only. A divorce for time and eternity—a cancellation of the sealing—completely freed the husband and wife from each other, and the woman could be sealed to another man for eternity.[72] In 1854, the former type cost ten dollars, while the latter cost fifty, a large amount at a time when money was scarce.[73]

The grounds on which one could obtain both types of church divorces were the same. A man could obtain a divorce on the grounds of murder, adultery, infanticide, feticide, or "incompatibility of temper rendering it impossible to live together harmoniously." In addition to these causes, a woman could obtain a divorce for the following: "for impotency existing at the time of marriage or contracted subsequent thereto, cruel treatment, refusal or neglect to support her and her children, or repeated injuries of any kind till her love is turned to loathing."[74] These grounds were not appreciably different from those listed in the 1852 civil divorce law. The most notable changes—specifying infanticide and feticide as well as allowing divorce for impotency subsequent to the marriage—indicate the importance Mormons placed on having children within a marriage.

In practice, a woman who insisted on a divorce could obtain one. For example, one bishop, in recommending that the president of the church grant a divorce, wrote, "We consider in our opinion that it would not be wise to compel [MH] although her grounds are not just, to continue to be the wife of [CH] inasmuch as she claims that she does not now nor never did have any affections for him."[75] This was also Brigham Young's position. His clerk stated, "As a rule, the Prest. never refuses to grant a bill on the application of the wife, and NEVER when she INSISTS on it." Although Brigham Young preached against divorce, he was fairly liberal in granting women permission to divorce.[76]

Brigham Young was so tired of hearing complaints about plural marriage that on September 21, 1856, he announced that in two weeks he would set at liberty all women who did not wish to stay with their husbands. This was not a new policy to liberally grant divorces, and the conditions for divorce he announced two weeks later were similar to those both before and after that time: women would have to "give good & sufficient reasons & then marry men that will not have but one wife."[77] The purpose of his September 21 sermon was not to announce divorce policy but to offer polygamous wives stark alternatives. They could either be released from their polygamous marriages or they should quit whining. "I want to . . . do something to get rid of the whiners," he said. Every women who stayed with her husband should "comply with the law of God, and that too without any murmuring and whining. You must fulfil the law of God in every respect, and round up your shoulders to walk up to the mark without any grunting."[78] This sermon was preached during the reformation, just as the harsh phase was beginning. This was also the time when many more women entered plural marriage than in any other period. In typical hyperbolic fashion, Brigham Young was telling women they were not fulfilling the laws of God when they entered plural marriage and then whined about it.

Because men were permitted to take other wives, he preferred not to grant men divorces. On one occasion when a polygamist applied for a divorce, Young said that a man married a wife for better or worse and had no right to misuse her; he knew of no law to give a man in plural marriage a divorce. Apostle George A. Smith replied, "Pres. Young, it is with you as it was with Moses. There is no law authorizing divorce, but through the hardness of the hearts of the people you are obliged to permit it." A clearer statement of the church's accommodation to the realities of family life could hardly be found. The polygamist was granted the divorce.[79] It thus appears that men as well as women who insisted on divorces received permission for them.

Most of the divorces Brigham Young granted were probably not cancellations of sealings but only freed couples from each other in this life so they could remarry on earth. He stated:

> If you want a bill of divorce give me ten dollars, so that I can put it down in the book that such a man and such a woman have dissolved partnership. Do you think you have done so when you have obtained a bill of divorce? No, nor ever can if you are faithful to the covenants you have made. It takes a higher power than a bill of divorce to take a woman from a man who is a good man and honors his Priesthood. . . . You might as well ask me for a piece of blank paper for a divorce, as to have a little writing on it, saying—'We mutually agree to dissolve partnership and keep ourselves apart from each others,' &c. It is all nonsense and folly; there is no such thing in the ordinances of the house of God; you cannot find any such law.[80]

With his sights on eternity, Brigham Young's major concern was those marriages and divorces that affected the afterlife. For a marriage to be valid after death, both husband and wife had to be righteous and worthy of exaltation. If both were righteous, the divorce on earth left intact the eternal relationship. If the mutual agreement to dissolve the marriage came about because one spouse was unrighteous, the eternal bonds already had been broken, and the divorce simply ratified this. In such a case, it was better for the two to be free from each other and to be able to remarry.

In his oft-quoted book *Isn't One Wife Enough?*, Kimball Young stated, "At the outset, however, the whole process of separation, divorce, and possible remarriage was a hit-and-miss affair. . . . Moreover, a certain looseness of action with regard to getting married or splitting up reflected the personal freedom of the frontier. If a couple could not make a go of marriage, one or the other might merely pick up and leave."[81] His book's lack of documentation, however, makes it difficult to check the evidence on which his judgments are based.

It is undoubtedly true that many apostates, no longer believing the church had authority to solemnize marriages, were not overly concerned about obtaining divorces. Believing Mormons, however, do not appear to have been casual about their marital relationships. The mechanisms used to confirm their separations and divorces were, however, extralegal—the legal system in Utah did not secure its exclusive authority over divorce until the 1890s. Since these mechanisms were not necessarily formal ones, their traces are sometimes difficult for scholars to find. But these informal means hardly led to the type of casual relationships Kimball Young claimed existed.

The "certain looseness" Kimball Young mentioned probably referred to the church's recognition of desertion as divorce. In other words, the church accepted de facto divorces as valid. Mary Ann West, who had been sealed as a plural wife in Nauvoo, put it succinctly: "William B. Smith divorced himself from me. I considered he did that when he went away East."[82] After Smith had left the church and his wives, the church leaders permitted West to remarry. The grounds appear to have been the "Pauline Privilege," though the Mormons did not call it such: "For the unbelieving husband is sanctified by the wife. . . . But if the unbelieving depart, let him depart. A brother or a sister is not under bondage in such cases."[83] Desertion by an unbeliever, seemingly unambiguous grounds for divorce in the Bible, was apparently considered the same as a divorce itself by church leaders. For example, Elizabeth Coolidge's husband, to whom she was sealed in Nauvoo, did not leave Iowa to go west to Utah with her and the other Saints. She wrote Brigham Young about the matter, and he replied:

> November 23, 1853
> Sister Elisabeth Coolidge,
>   Your letter of the 16th Inst is before me and I write again that you are at full liberty to marry again as soon as you choose and that you are perfectly free from all marriage obligations or ties to Brother Coolidge.
>
> In marrying again please try to get a saint who will take good care of you.
>   from your Brother in the Gospel
>   Signed Brigham Young[84]

According to the president of the church, her husband's apostasy and desertion were sufficient grounds for her to remarry without further formalities.

The church also apparently applied this principle to civil marriages. When Ane Larsen arrived with her children in Utah in 1874, she expected her husband to emigrate from Denmark the next year. He did not, and in 1876 she married as a plural wife.[85] Although she lived in Sanpete County, no divorce was recorded in the Sanpete County Probate Court for her. While it is difficult to prove that no divorce took place in any jurisdiction of Denmark or the United States, this may be an example of desertion treated as divorce. The church president's permission to be sealed to another husband ratified the de facto divorce.

This principle seemingly also applied to "constructive" desertion, in which one spouse made life so miserable for the other that he or she left. This seems to be the case with Mary Ann West before she went to Nauvoo: "I was married in England to a man by the name of Sheffield, he did not treat me well, and so I left him before I came to America. I was not divorced from him; never have been divorced from Mr. Sheffield; left him because he drank too much, and did not treat me right."[86] Her husband's abusive behavior was such that she left him, and the church permitted her to remarry.[87]

Members of the church treated such de facto divorces as binding as de jure dissolutions. Sometime before the Saints' departure from Nauvoo, Charles Jackson left his wife, Harriet, and returned to Ohio. Deserted by her husband, she became Isaac Morley's plural wife not long before they left for the West. While they were camped in Iowa, however, Jackson returned. Harriet considered her second marriage binding, and Jackson left for Ohio again and soon remarried.[88]

Firmage and Mangrum claim that a marriage was also automatically dissolved as a result of adultery, the other cause for divorce specifically mentioned in the Bible. In one court case, a bishop explained, "According to the laws of God and the Church, she ceased to be his wife as soon as she had committed adultery." Because her husband had had sexual intercourse with her after her transgression and she hence had ceased to be his wife, the husband "also was guilty of the same crime."[89] The church condemned the innocent spouse for continuing to have sexual intercourse with an adulterous spouse until the transgressor had repented and had been forgiven by the church, as the above account of Azariah Smith and his wife indicates, but husbands like Smith also did resume living with their wives when the period of penance was completed. "If either party have been guilty of adultery, then divorce *may be* justifiable," Apostle Orson Hyde claimed.[90] Adultery was sufficient grounds for divorce, but divorce was not the inevitable result.

Another circumstance not requiring a formal divorce proceeding was, stated Brigham Young, "if the woman Preferred—another man higher in authority & he is willing to take her. & her husband gives her up—there is no Bill of divorce required, in the case it is right in the sight of God."[91]

Although this rarely happened, it may have occurred in the case of Zina Diantha Huntington. She married Henry Jacobs in 1841 but was sealed to Joseph Smith soon thereafter. After Joseph Smith was assassinated, Brigham Young claimed her as his wife, saying he was the proxy husband for Joseph Smith. With Jacobs standing as witness to the ceremony, Young and Zina Huntington were married in 1846.[92]

Apostasy was another circumstance in which divorce was readily granted. When John Hyde left the church, Heber C. Kimball announced from the pulpit, "He has taken a course by which he has lost his family and forfeited his Priesthood. . . . The limb is cut off, but the Priesthood takes the fruit that was attached to the limb and saves it, if it will be saved. . . . His wife is not cut off from this Church, but she is free from him; she is just as free from him as though she never had belonged to him. The limb she was connected to is cut off, and she must again be grafted into the tree, if she wishes to be saved. . . ."[93] Because a woman was sealed to only one man at a time, she was freed from an apostate husband so that she could be sealed to a worthy man. All that was necessary was permission from the leaders of the church; no special documents or proceedings were required.

President John Taylor related a similar circumstance, although the divorce was more private. A man who had left the church visited Taylor's office with his two wives, and the wives requested that they be granted a divorce.

> I asked [the wives] why they desired to be divorced, and they answered that their husband had apostatized from the Church, and to all appearance would remain in that condition. The husband expressed his sorrow at having to part with his wives, . . . But I explained to him the position that his wives occupied. . . . [W]hen we appear behind the veil, we shall have to pass by the angels and the Gods, and this can only be done by the righteous and the pure. . . . I said further, you are the head of this family, and as such you ought to take the lead; but can you lead your wives past the angels and the Gods? No, (I said) you cannot do it, for unless you change your course you will not be there; you have trifled with the things of God, . . . The result was, he and they parted by signing the divorce.[94]

By the 1880s, divorce for apostasy had become more circumspect. The wives had patiently waited a number of years to see if their husband would rejoin the church. When it became clear that he would not, they sought a divorce in the President's Office; it was not declared from the pulpit as John Hyde's was. Moreover, all three signed the divorce, unlike the unilateral decree given Hyde's wife. But the grounds—apostasy—and the result—divorce—were the same.

Divorces granted by the church were, however, of doubtful validity in civil courts of law. The church recognized this in the 1870s when it encouraged couples to seek divorces in both jurisdictions. In 1899, the Utah Supreme Court settled the issue in *Norton v. Tufts* by declaring that divorces granted by the church did not dissolve marriages. Even if both parties remarried, a woman could claim dower rights in the first husband's estate if their divorce was one recorded only by the church. This decision was confirmed by *Hilton v. Roylance* in 1902, which stated succinctly that "while the church could solemnize a marriage, it had no power to dissolve it."[95] The law finally established its hegemony over divorce and relegated the church's power over dissolution of marriages solely to the afterlife.

In conclusion, although the church encouraged reconciliation between couples and discouraged divorce, it did permit the dissolution of marriages on a variety of grounds. The Mormon-dominated legislature passed a lenient divorce law in 1852, so lenient that loopholes in the law had to be closed in 1878. The law, however, would have affected only divorces involving civil marriages until 1870 because before that the church retained sole jurisdiction over both plural and monogamous sealings. Particularly after 1875, couples whose marriages were also sealings secured divorces by obtaining them from both civil and ecclesiastical jurisdictions. In addition to divorces granted by those jurisdictions, the church recognized de facto divorces created when one spouse deserted the other or when one spouse caused the other to leave because of abuse. Moreover, it also considered a former marriage dissolved when a wife, dissatisfied with her former husband, was sealed to a man higher in authority. The church's leniency, however, was not looseness. Any remarriage without a civil divorce or the church's sanction would have been considered adultery, and adultery required a period of repentance and penance before the transgressor could again be admitted to full membership in the church. Although the church readily granted divorces when a person wished to be free from a nonmember or apostate spouse or would not be reconciled to a spouse after mediation by church leaders, church members were not free simply to separate and remarry other spouses at will. Church and social sanctions were too strong for such permissive behavior.

9 Incidence of Divorce and Remarriage

The church wanted its members to be married to other Latter-day Saints. Lenient divorce laws fostered members' marriages to Saints by permitting them to easily dissolve their marriages with nonbelievers or apostates. Leniency in granting divorces also allowed those unhappy in plural marriages to escape from them. Plural marriage made it possible for women to find other mates easily, either directly by their entering plural marriage or indirectly by creating a shortage of marriageable women so divorced women could marry single men seeking a wife. Lenient divorce laws did mean that the number of divorces was greater in Utah than in most states in the nineteenth century, although western states in general tended to have higher rates of divorce than did eastern ones. Nevertheless, the number of divorces even from plural marriages was moderate, especially by today's standards.

Unfortunately, ascertaining the number who sought divorces in both civil and ecclesiastical jurisdictions cannot be accomplished without full access to church records. It does appear, however, that the church granted slightly fewer than 1,900 divorces from 1847 to 1886. The Campbells, who did have access to the records in the 1970s, indicated that Brigham Young granted 1,645 divorces during his presidency (1847–1877).[1] When Carroll Wright, the U.S. commissioner of labor, wrote his report on marriage and divorce in the late 1880s, the church reported that from 1877 to 1886, the number of divorces had decreased to 266.[2] Because the two sets of figures overlap by eight months, the total divorces granted would be slightly fewer than the sum of 1,911.

While the population in Utah grew immensely over the period—from 1870 to 1880 alone it grew 65 percent—the average number of church divorces a year declined considerably. From 1847 to 1866, the average number of divorces granted by the church per year was 57.6; from 1867 to 1876, it declined slightly, to 49.3 per year; and from 1877 to 1886, it dipped to 26.6 per year. The number granted in the last decade was 54 percent less than that granted in the first two decades. To some extent, the decline represented the shifting of divorces from ecclesiastical to civil courts as the validity of church divorces came into question. Nevertheless, the magnitude of the decline suggests that it was more than the result of such a shift because many couples undoubtedly sought divorces in both jurisdictions after 1875.

From 1867 to 1886, the church granted 759 divorces, while the civil courts granted about 2,420 to Utah residents.[3] Using only the civil divorces, Wright found that in 1870 Utah's ratio of one divorce for every 185 married couples gave it the second highest divorce rate in the nation. Only Wyoming had a higher rate, one divorce for every 123 couples. If the average number of ecclesiastical divorces per year is added, however, Utah had the most divorces per estimated married couples of any state or territory. By 1880, Utah's ratio had risen to one divorce for every 219 married couples, and nine states or territories had ratios lower than Utah's. With the addition of half the average number of ecclesiastical divorces—assuming that by 1880 half would have sought divorces in both jurisdictions—seven states and territories still had higher rates than did Utah. Nevertheless, Utah had more than twice as many divorces per estimated married couples as the national average.[4]

All these calculations assume, however, that Utah had the same number of married couples relative to its population that other states had.[5] Given the presence of polygamy, the high proportion of married women, and Utah's low age at marriage, Wright's estimates of the number of married couples in Utah are probably low. If Utah had more married couples than Wright estimated, there would have been fewer divorces in relation to number of couples than his figures indicated. Still, it appears that Mormons valued happy marriages over long-lived ones and granted divorces accordingly.

Even if the total number of divorces were known, there would be considerable difficulty obtaining a measure of divorce in Utah that is comparable to measures elsewhere. Wright eschewed comparing the number of divorces to the number of people in the population under study, though this is a common method.[6] It takes into account neither the age structure of the population nor the proportion married. If questions of comparability for Utah arise from ratios of divorces to estimated married couples, comparability of figures based on numbers of divorces per thousand people is even more questionable. Nevertheless, such figures support other conclusions about divorce in Utah. Using Wright's work, Geraldine Mineau calculated the number of divorces in Utah per 100,000 population and compared it to that figure for the United States. She concluded, "For 1870 and 1880 the Utah rate was two to three times higher than the U.S. rate; by 1890 and 1900 the difference had greatly decreased."[7] Nevertheless, her figures indicate the divorce rate in Utah remained higher than that of the United States at the turn of the century. These figures, however, do not include church divorces.

Considering the problems with the various measures of divorce rates, Phillip Kunz calculated the percentage of Mormon divorces for the number of known marriages. Using family group records for those who were married between 1844 and 1890, he found that 9.0 percent of polygamists were divorced, while less than 3.0 percent of their wives were. This was still considerably higher than the 0.9 percent of monogamists in Utah during the same period whose family group records indicated that a divorce had taken place. He conceded, however, that the relatives who submitted the family group records might not be aware of or list all divorces.[8]

The Manti data set indicates that this was the case. Those divorced were less likely to have family group records. Although the section on the records listing other spouses sometimes indicates a divorce, this section is not vital to the central purpose of the family group records—to ensure that the family is sealed—and hence has a higher incidence of omissions and errors than other parts of these records.

This investigation revealed a considerably higher incidence of divorce than did Kunz's. Because of the different types of divorces and the unavailability of church records, the following guidelines were used for determining whether those in the Manti subset had divorced. All divorces found in court records and those listed on family group records were counted. In addition, it was assumed that a couple had divorced if the records showed a subsequent marriage for the wife during the lifetime of her former husband. Also counted as divorced was one woman who, according to a letter, left her husband and who was not listed with that husband or in his community on subsequent censuses.[9] Women merely separated from their husbands were not considered divorced.

Excluding eternity-only and nominal plural marriages, there were 83 divorces among the 465 plural marriages in the Manti plural marriage subset. That is, 17.8 percent of these plural marriages ended in divorce. The percentage remains about the same when individual women rather than numbers of marriages are the basis for calculation: 77 (or 18.2 percent) of the 423 women were divorced.[10]

When a distinction is made between the first and subsequent wives in a plural marriage, these divorces were not distributed equally. Only 15.7 percent of the divorces were obtained by women who were the first wives in plural marriages. In all, 8.0 percent of the 163 first wives were granted a divorce. These percentages are considerably smaller than those for plural wives. Not only did plural wives obtain most of the divorces, but also one-fourth (24.6 percent) of plural wives divorced. Among men, the percentage is higher still, although, of course, a man increased his chance for a divorce with each additional wife. Of the 151 polygamous men in the Manti subset, 35.1 percent—slightly over one-third—were divorced one or more times.[11] Nevertheless, compared with today's rate of just under half of all marriages ending in divorce, those rates for polygamous marriages are low.[12]

These figures suggest some difficulties presented by plural marriage and indicate the relative ease in obtaining divorces in Utah. The church did not approve of divorce, but leaders referred to Matthew 19:8 about why divorce was permitted: "Moses because of the hardness of your hearts suffered you to put away your wives."[13] In practice, the church showed that it believed dissolving a marriage was preferable to spouses' living together and begetting children when, in the parlance of the day, their feelings were so alienated they could not live together in peace and happiness.

Still, this ground was not the only reason for approving divorces; at least 17 of the divorces (20.5 percent) can be attributed to apostasy and the results of the government raids and the Manifesto. Seven of the divorces were caused directly or indirectly by the husband's apostasy from the church. Because Mormons considered being sealed for eternity to a worthy spouse essential for exaltation in the next world, church leaders not only permitted women sealed to men who left the church to obtain divorces but encouraged them to do so.[14] In these cases, divorce was not the lesser of two evils; it was a positive good.

Among the wives of the four Manti men who apostatized or were excommunicated, six divorced their husbands, one separated from her spouse, and three left the church themselves.[15] For example, when Andrew Nelson became a Presbyterian, his first wife divorced him, while his two remaining plural wives also joined the Presbyterian church. He continued to live with the younger of these wives, who were sisters. He deeded property to the older sister and apparently no longer lived conjugally with her, although she reported in the 1900 census that she was married and had been so for forty-one years.[16]

Church leaders also recommended divorce for actions other than apostasy. When one man killed his adulterous first wife's lover, church authorities recommended that his plural wife dissolve her marriage to him, which she did.[17] Lucinda Dalton is an example of women who dissolved their marriages because of their concern for their eternal welfare. Because sealings are for eternity, not merely for this life, she became concerned about her husband's worthiness after his death. She wrote to her stake president for advice: "now the brethren say he was unworthy, (though I know not who appointed them to judge him,) they urge that I stand in a very insecure position, and that for my children's sake, as well as my own, I ought to marry again. . . . Here is the thought that appalls me. My feelings as a mother are far keener and deeper than my feelings as a wife. I am the mother of six children; four still living, and two gone before; and I would not forfeit my claim to them as their mother, for the sake of the best man in God's kingdom."[18] She then wrote about her deceased husband to John Taylor, the president of the church, who replied: "From all that I can learn concerning his life, in addition to what you yourself have written to me, I consider your future unsafe in his hands." He assured her that if she wished to have her sealing to her deceased husband canceled, he would grant it.[19] Concerned for her own and her children's eternal salvation, she made the request within a month after receiving this letter.[20]

Although almost 10 percent (eight cases) of the divorces may be attributed to either the government raids or the Manifesto, most polygamists continued to live either with their wives or away from them while giving them some financial support after the raids began. A few, however, like Christian Madsen, avoided prison on the charges of unlawful cohabitation and adultery by pleading guilty and promising to obey the law in the future. Upon receiving his promise on October 29, 1888, the court suspended Madsen's sentence "during good behavior." Madsen took the promise seriously, and within a month the same court granted him and his first wife, who was childless, a divorce. Three days later, in a civil ceremony, he married his plural wife, by whom he had had several children.[21]

Another man served two and a half months in prison for unlawful cohabitation, but later, after the Manifesto made church and social support for plural marriage uncertain, his first wife divorced him. On October 27, 1896, Mary Jolly filed for divorce in the Utah Seventh District Court, accusing her husband of adultery with Cena Lauritzen, his plural wife. Although the plural marriage had been solemnized in 1882, Mary's petition accused her husband of committing adultery with Cena "on or about the 11th day of March 1896" and that each action of adultery was committed without her consent. The court granted her petition, even though the judge probably knew the actual circumstances.[22] Although the real reasons for the divorce were hidden under this subterfuge, Mary's bringing the suit based on Joseph's "adultery" after their having lived in plural marriage for fifteen years suggests growing ambivalence toward plural marriage in Mormon society after the Manifesto.

During the early years when plural marriage was first openly practiced, the stresses and strains of the exodus from Nauvoo and the journey to Utah also disrupted nuptial unions. While this was true for monogamous as well as polygamous families, the newly formed plural unions were particularly subject to disruption. Benjamin F. Johnson, for example, had married Flora Gleason in Nauvoo, but by the time they reached Utah she wanted to be released because he had been away during the entire winter when their child was born. She later married Abraham Washburn, the man who had helped her across the plains.[23]

Some other Nauvoo plural marriages did not last even that long. Fanny Myrick, a plural wife of Levi W. Hancock, stayed behind when he went west with the Saints. She moved to St. Louis, married the Danish convert Paul Kofford, and eventually moved to Sanpete County.[24] Thomas Woolsey's plural wife Elizabeth Ann Holdaway also left him soon after the Saints migrated from Nauvoo; she, too, remarried and accompanied her second husband to Utah but soon moved on to California.[25] Because his family was so large and the administrative burdens he carried so great, Brigham Young also faced disruption in his family. His plural wife Mary Ann Clark Powers, still in Iowa in 1851, wrote him in Utah asking to be released from him because of the "bitter cup" she had drunk during her stay at Winter Quarters.[26] In spite of the difficulties during the exodus from Nauvoo and the trek west, the percentage of marriages in the Manti subset ending in divorce during the 1840s was almost the same (24.1 percent, or 7 of 29) as the overall percentage of plural wives who were granted divorces (24.6 percent).

Plural wives who married during the spiritual and emotional excitement of the Mormon reformation were more likely to divorce than were plural wives who married earlier or later. Of the 26 women who became plural wives during 1856 and 1857 when pressure to contract plural marriages was intense, 10 (38.5 percent) were later divorced. This does not include one woman divorced during the government raids. Although the actual divorce dates are uncertain, it appears that 7 of the 10 plural wives who divorced their husbands did so within five years. The relatively high percentage of reformation marriages ending in divorce may be attributed not only to the millennialist fervor of the times but also to the youthfulness of the plural wives. Seven of the 10 divorced plural wives (70 percent) were seventeen years old or younger at the time of marriage, while only 46.2 percent of all plural wives married during that seven-month period were that young. Younger women had ample opportunities to marry, and some caught up in the fervor of the times repented fairly quickly of marriages entered into in haste.

Those married at a young age were generally more likely to seek divorces. Fifty of the 260 plural wives in the Manti subset were seventeen years old or younger when they married. Of these, 23 were granted divorces, though 5 of these are attributable to apostasy or the government raids. Even after subtracting those five, 36 percent of marriages involving these young women ended in divorce compared with 25 percent of all plural marriages in the Manti subset.

After subtracting divorces attributable to apostasy, the government raids, the Manifesto, the disruptions of the trek west, and the youthfulness of some plural wives, about half of the divorces remain unexplained. Studying the records of the St. George Stake, Nels Anderson stated that "the records of the High Council reveal no cases of women wanting to shake off the responsibilities of polygamy because of hardship."[27] But when the average household head in Utah was much poorer than the average American head of household, owning less than half as much in the 1850s and 1860s,[28] it would not be surprising if economic problems were a significant factor in many divorces.

Katherine Winget's account is illustrative. Her husband died in 1854, leaving her a thirty-four-year-old widow with six children under twelve years old. A seventh child was born posthumously. Two years after her husband's death, she married Nathan Stewart as his plural wife. She married him, she later wrote, because "I realized the need of a helpmate, and I thought he would be a father to my children." The marriage did not fulfill her expectations: "[A]s he could not assist me much in a financial way, and we did not agree as well as we ought, I thought it best that we should not live together."[29] His inability to help out financially is understandable: in the 1860 census, he listed no real wealth and only five hundred dollars in personal wealth.[30] The "alienation of feelings," in combination with financial problems, was opposite from a union of "peace and happiness." Although there was apparently no divorce in this case, there was a breakdown of the marriage. How many more breakdowns without divorces took place is difficult to assess.

Some wives did reject the idea of plural marriage after they had entered it, but there were other reasons for leaving it. Even though church doctrine in general discouraged divorces except in cases of apostasy or sexual transgression, church practice permitted them. No ecclesiastical or social sanctions appear to have followed in the wake of a divorce, except when it was the result of a sexual transgression. Moreover, women who were divorced were often sealed within two or three years to another man.[31]

A divorce from a plural marriage did not necessarily signify rejection of that type of marriage. Of the 76 women in the subset who divorced, 29 (38.2 percent) again entered plural marriage. About one quarter of the 29 women married monogamously after their divorces but then later permitted their husbands to take another wife.[32] An additional 4 women were sealed for eternity only following a divorce, and with them the total who were again polygamous wives rises to 43.4 percent. Of the 423 wives in the Manti subset, 35 were in two plural marriages, and 3 married three times as plural wives. That is, 9 percent of polygamous wives in the Manti subset experienced two or more plural marriages, not counting the 4 who were sealed for eternity only after their divorces from their first husbands.

The number of second plural marriages is not surprising, because slightly more than half the women who remarried before 1888, whether because they had been widowed or divorced, married into a plural marriage, as table 6 indicates. In this table, only those women who lived in Manti are included, not all wives in the subset, and the remarriages of women widowed or divorced outside Utah were counted if the remarriage

Table 6. Types of Remarriages for Women in the Manti Data Set, 1846–88, Expressed as a Percentage of All Remarriages

Previous Marriage	Percentage of Each Type of Remarriage (number of marriages in parentheses)			
	Monogamous	First Wife	Plural Wife	Total
Monogamous	17.3	4.5	31.8	53.6
	(31)	(8)	(57)	(96)
Polygamous	20.7	3.9	21.8	46.4
	(37)	(7)	(39)	(83)
Total	38.0	8.4	53.6	100.0
	(68)	(15)	(96)	(179)

Source: Manti data set.

took place in the Utah Territory. Because some women remarried more than once, the table includes 179 remarriages for 160 women. Most young widowed and divorced women did remarry. During the first forty years of settlement, only 35 of the 195 widowed or divorced women forty-five years or younger in the Manti data set have no record of remarriage, although the actual number may be less because the marital histories of the majority of these 35 may not be complete. In the frontier period, only 9 women under age forty-five did not remarry. Older women tended to remarry less frequently: 40 percent of the 35 women who did not remarry were forty to forty-five years old when they became single again. But most women of childbearing age who had been widowed or divorced did remarry.

As table 6 shows, although slightly more than half of the previous marriages had been monogamous, just over half of the remarriages were polygamous. Of the 83 former polygamous wives, however, 53 percent (37 monogamous and 7 first wives) remarried monogamously. Many of these were younger plural wives who had divorced their polygamous husbands. Two of these women married into monogamy, found their marriages unsatisfactory, and married again as plural wives. Conversely, another woman found a satisfactory marriage in monogamy only after one monogamous and two polygamous marriages had ended in divorce.

Almost as many former polygamous wives remarried into plurality as those who did not, and a majority of polygamous wives who remarried experienced another plural marriage during their lifetimes. Moreover, 59 percent (57 of 96) of those whose first marriages had been monogamous remarried as plural wives. A number of these were widows who immigrated to Utah. Also included were women entering proxy marriages. Such marriages not only were to provide their deceased husbands with additional children in the eternities but also could help supply a woman's economic needs in this world. Plural marriage also offered a woman whose husband had apostatized an eternal mate and a present provider.[33]

Life was difficult particularly in the early years in Utah, and women who found themselves alone, such as Katherine Winget, sought helpmates. Another widow, Ellen Fowler, entered plural marriage after she and her children suffered the financial hardships that often accompanied widowhood.[34] Her daughter later wrote, "After Father's death Mother had to work very hard at sewing, gleaning wheat and teaching school three months of the school year. Still we suffered for want of food and with the cold."[35] Under such circumstances, it is not surprising widows hoped that becoming plural wives would improve their lot. While the church could provide some help, it was often ad hoc, and the level of poverty among its members meant that the church's meager resources were often insufficient.[36] Plural marriage offered a more permanent solution, if the man was wealthy enough to help an additional family.

While plural marriages might alleviate widows' financial difficulties, they also were a means by which the church could see that the widows and fatherless were cared for. Moreover, plural marriage, by providing more opportunities for remarriage than would have otherwise existed, made it possible for young widows to continue to bear children. While widows over forty rarely married, those under forty usually did, especially before 1880.[37]

The same could be said of women who were divorced. As early as the seventeenth century, thinkers and politicians recognized the link between divorce and the population.[38] An estranged couple's separation meant years of barrenness. This certainly would have been true of those women whose husbands stayed behind when they immigrated to Utah or whose husbands deserted them and the church. The lenient divorce laws and plural marriage practiced in Utah provided an escape for such women from their fruitless marriages and permitted them to form new unions. The number of women whose second marriages were polygamous testifies to the benefits of this type of marriage, which allowed women to remarry when they otherwise would have remained single.

Although Mormons preached against divorce, permitting divorces for the unhappily married and the deserted naturally followed from the nineteenth-century Mormon view of marriage. Sealings for the dead were introduced as early as the Nauvoo years, and the idea that to be saved one had to be sealed in this life to a person worthy of exaltation in the next soon prevailed. For persons married to non-Mormons, apostates, or those whose worthiness was questionable, divorce was necessary for them to avail themselves of exaltation. Moreover, Mormons preached that couples should not have children when their feelings were alienated, but one of the main purposes of marriage was having children. Happy marriages wherein both husband and wife were righteous members of the church were deemed more important than the longevity of individual marriages, especially when they were dysfunctional ones.

In this context, divorce was available, not to create single persons but to free Mormons so that they could find more suitable mates. For women, at least part of the supply of suitable mates was provided through plural marriage. Divorce and plural marriage were thus two sides of the same doctrine of eternal marriage.

Just as the permissiveness of the law in Utah encouraged marriage, lenient divorce laws encouraged remarriage. But while the church could formulate its own doctrine, it could not always control the laws. As Congress and the courts increasingly limited the church's control over divorce, as the number of plural marriages in Mormondom declined, and as the number of immigrants to Utah shrank, the importance of divorce within the Mormon marriage system also declined. Divorce, unlike plural marriage, did not dwindle, but it succumbed to the conservative reaction that swept the country at the turn of the century. Accessible divorce, like plural marriage, gave way both in law and in practice to the support of binding monogamous family units.

PART 5

Acts and Judges: The Mormon Marriage System and Its Demise

Verily, verily, I say unto you, that when I give a commandment to any of the sons of men to do a work unto my name, and those sons of men go with all their might and with all they have to perform that work, and cease not their diligence, and their enemies come upon them and hinder them from performing that work, behold, it behooveth me to require that work no more at the hands of those sons of men, but to accept of their offerings.

—Doctrine and Covenants 124:49

We believe in being subject to kings, presidents, rulers, and magistrates, in obeying, honoring, and sustaining the law.

—Articles of Faith

10   The Decline of Plural Marriage

The nineteenth-century Mormon marriage system could not survive in the face of a determined American public operating through the power of the federal government. The Edmunds Act put an incredible strain on polygamous families whose husband-father was in hiding or in prison. Communities, too, lost leaders, many of whom practiced plural marriage. Then in 1887 the Edmunds-Tucker Act created new marriage and inheritance laws for the territory, gravely undermining the Mormon system. The power of Mormons to govern themselves was further eroded by the disfranchisement of all polygamists and all women. Superimposed on this was the confiscation of large amounts of church property and a threat to take the temples themselves. Mormons were not passive in the face of this legislative onslaught. They passed laws in the Utah territorial legislature in an attempt to mitigate the effects of the federal laws.

Significant as these were, not all changes that occurred as the century waned were forced on the Mormons. Attitudes, too, were changing, particularly among the young. When polygamy was first practiced, polygamous wives adapted in a number of ways. Some strengthened their bonds with other women as those with their husbands loosened; others valued the independence that the husbands' frequent absences fostered; still others emphasized the mother-child bonds rather than the relationship between husband and wife. In its own way, each of these means of adapting was, in Joan Iversen's words, an "assault on the ideology of romantic love."[1] Increasingly, however, young women rejected plural marriage in favor of romantic love. This rejection was prevalent enough among young women that a writer in a Mormon women's magazine, the *Woman's Exponent*, acknowledged, "I know that some of my young sisters would rather marry a young man with bad habits than one who is religious for fear he (the religious one) would some time take another wife."[2] The young women addressed here not only rejected becoming plural wives but also tried to forestall becoming first wives by selecting as husbands men unqualified to participate in the sealing ceremony.

While it is unclear how widespread such an attitude was, it is certain that fewer women, both absolutely and relatively, entered plural marriage in the last twenty years it was sanctioned by the church.[3] By then, women had greater educational and economic opportunities. The geographic isolation of Utah had been overcome by the completion of the transcontinental railroad in 1869, and the cultural isolation of Manti had been broken by the establishment of a Presbyterian mission school in 1877. Adapting to these changes, women, beginning with the 1860 birth cohort, also started to curtail their fertility.[4]

Such changes led such scholars as Klaus Hansen and Stanley S. Ivins to believe that the demise of polygamy was inevitable, even had there been no antipolygamy campaign by the federal government.[5] Decline, however dramatic, is not demise. Even after the Manifesto, couples importuned the church president for permission to enter plural marriage, and some church leaders initially circumvented the law of the land and the officially stated rule of the church prohibiting plural marriage.[6] Moreover, as Jan Shipps makes clear, the importance of plural marriage was not determined by the number who practiced it: "Identity [as Latter-day Saints] was maintained corporately, not individually, which explains why all the citizens of the kingdom—those who were involved in plural marriage and those who were not—were willing to defend to the last possible moment the practice of polygamy that kept them set apart."[7] Belief in the divine origin of plural marriage united Mormons in a way that transcended differences in practice, and it set them apart from other Americans. The decline in new marriages also obscures the large number of plural families still intact when the government raids began. While the decline of new plural marriages undoubtedly made accepting the Manifesto easier—or even a relief—for the younger generations, the institution was still vigorous during the raids in the 1880s and took a long time to die even after the Manifesto.

A means to end polygamy that was fair and just to all was never found. Congress claimed the right to create the matrimonial laws under which people in the territories would be governed. In 1882, Congress passed the Edmunds Act, making prosecution of polygamists easier.

After U.S. marshals first arrived in Manti on November 29, 1885, to search for polygamists, Manti men used several means for staying out of the marshals' hands. Communities at entry points into the Sanpete Valley established the Kolob Guard to look out for the marshals. When polygamists learned the marshals were on their way, they went to stay with relatives or hid in hastily constructed cellars or in the mountains.[8] Some moved one of their wives to another state or to Canada, while others, such as Francis Wall, took their wives to live in Mormon colonies in Mexico.[9] William Braithwaite's second wife went to stay with her parents in a neighboring county, a ploy that did not prevent his being charged on October 2, 1888, with unlawful cohabitation, to which he pleaded guilty. He was fortunate, however, because the judge was supposed to hand down his sentence on November 17, but court was not in session that day. He served no time in prison.[10] Jens C. A. Weibye was not so fortunate. To avoid the marshals, he went on a proselyting mission to Denmark. When he returned, however, he was arrested for cohabiting with his four wives. Weibye pleaded guilty to the charge of unlawful cohabitation and served five months in prison.[11] Some, such as Eric Ludvigsen who was indicted for unlawful cohabitation, promised to obey the law in the future and received a pardon from the president of the United States.[12]

Between 1884 and 1895, over a thousand men were convicted of a crime relating to plural marriage. Not all those convicted served time in prison, however, and the reasons are not always clear why some were imprisoned while others were not.[13] For a few, the reason is stated in the record. Some, such as John Buchanan and William Braithwaite, had their sentencing date postponed and never served time.[14] Isaac Morley's case was dismissed because it had been ignored by the grand jury. Although John D. T. McAllister continued to provide for his wives, he was found not guilty of unlawful cohabitation. Isaac J. Riddle was fined a hundred dollars but was not imprisoned. He believed it was because he had cooperated with the court: he had written the deputy a letter stating that he, Riddle, would be available for trial whenever he was wanted.[15] Whatever the reasons, the courts were lenient with these men. Those cases where polygamists promised to obey the law in the future were clearer cut; their sentences were suspended "during good behavior."[16]

While the Edmunds Act of 1882 punished polygamists, the Edmunds-Tucker Act of 1887 effected changes that corroded economic equity within plural families. Regarding inheritance, the Edmunds Act of 1882 contained a clause that made children of polygamous marriages born before January 1, 1883, legitimate.[17] This was a well-meaning clause meant to protect innocent children, but it implied that such children born after that date should be treated differently. The next year, the Utah legislature reacted by passing a statute reiterating that illegitimate children when acknowledged by the father were to be his heirs. It also contained a new clause: "The issue of *all marriages null in law*, or dissolved by divorce, are legitimate."[18] Since polygamous marriages were null or void under common law, this wording would make the children of such marriages legitimate. Legitimating children born of marriages not recognized by law put Utah outside the mainstream of other states, forty of which had passed legislation by 1900 legitimizing children of annulled marriages or of unions formed after the child's birth.[19] Congress responded to the Utah legislation in the Edmunds-Tucker Act of 1887 by annulling all territorial laws that allowed illegitimate children to inherit from their fathers. This law was not ex post facto, however, because it stipulated that such children born within twelve months of the act's passage would not be affected.[20]

The ability of polygamous children to inherit was further eroded by the non-Mormon Utah Supreme Court in *Chapman v. Handley* in 1890. The Morrill Anti-Bigamy Act of 1862 had annulled all Utah laws that "establish, support, maintain, shield, or countenance polygamy," and the court ruled that because this applied to the 1852 law allowing illegitimate children to inherit, offspring of plural marriages could not inherit from their fathers.[21] Fortunately for such children, a similar ruling in *Cope v. Cope* was appealed to the U.S. Supreme Court and was overturned by its decision in 1891 that allowed the 1852 law to continue in force.[22]

Almost immediately thereafter, another case regarding the rights of plural wives' progeny to inherit came before the Utah Supreme Court, this time involving the children of Orson Pratt, the apostle who in 1852 publicly announced the practice of plural marriage and was one of its staunchest defenders. In 1881, Pratt had died intestate, leaving considerable property. The polygamous children, headed by Milando Merrill Pratt, a believing Mormon, were appealing the district court's denial of their share of the estate. The defendants were led by the first wife's son, Arthur Pratt, who had been excommunicated for apostasy in 1874 and subsequently became a U.S. deputy marshal during the government raids and the warden of the Utah territorial penitentiary during 1888 and 1889, when many polygamists were serving their terms for unlawful cohabitation. The case was not only an intrafamily fight about the father's property but also, to some extent, a contest between those who believed in Mormonism and those who did not. The facts of the case did not differ significantly from those in *Cope v. Cope*, and the court, basing its ruling on that decision, decreed that all children acknowledged by the father or "proved to be such by satisfactory evidence" should share in the distribution of the estate.[23] The precedent set by *Cope v. Cope* thus reinstated inheritance rights for many polygamous children.

When Utah became a state in 1896 and regained control over legislation on domestic matters, the legislature passed laws entitling children of polygamous marriages to inherit and declaring legitimate all children of LDS polygamous marriages who were born on or before January 4, 1896. It also allowed inheritance cases adversely decided to be tried again, but the Utah Supreme Court struck down this provision as unwarranted legislative control of the judiciary.[24] The section legitimating all polygamous children born on or before January 4, 1896, however, did remain in force and was upheld by the Utah Supreme Court in *Rohwer v. District Court.*[25] The language of the law, indicated the court in that case, "is that such a child is legitimate for *all*, and not only for *some*, purposes." Because such a child was considered legitimate in every sense, the father of a polygamous son was able to inherit that deceased child's property. By 1912, the court was willing to concede: "Neither in the eyes of the law nor in the eyes of society were the children [of Mormon plural marriages] born as the result of mere lust or meretricious relations. . . . The social standing of such children was practically the same as that of other children born in lawful wedlock. . . . Besides, every Latter Day Saint, or so-called 'Mormon,' who believed in plural marriages, regarded that relation as sacred and as binding as we who believe in monogamy hold that relation sacred and binding."[26] The court could be gracious about children of plural marriages because it also diminished the number of children protected by the law.

According to the court opinion, the laws of the state limited inheritance rights to children born before 1896. According to the majority opinion, the clause reenacted by the state legislature stating "the issue of all marriages null in law . . . are legitimate" applied to plural marriages. "All plural marriages were necessarily void in law" because the Utah Constitution forever prohibited plural marriages, and statutory law made them void. Because the law prohibited polygamous marriages, the court declared, the clause legitimating children of marriages null in law covered only children born before statehood.[27]

Overall, Utah law protected the inheritance of most children born in plural marriage during the territorial period. The interests of those children conceived after 1895 by polygamous parents, however, inherited nothing if the father wrote no will.

The rights of plural wives to inherit had never been secure under Utah laws. By establishing the right of dower, the Edmunds-Tucker Act put up even greater barriers to inheritance by plural wives. The act, by stipulating that the widow inherit one-third of all unmortgaged lands belonging to her husband unless she "lawfully released her right," left only two-thirds of what was often a small estate to be shared by all children and all plural wives (if those women were fortunate).[28] Because the bar to dower was a statutory one, a law had to be passed to stipulate the requirements necessary to override the dower. In 1888, the territorial legislature tried to mitigate the effect of the Edmunds-Tucker Act by passing a statute to facilitate the release of dower. It provided that any conveyance of real property by deed properly signed by the wife as well as by the husband also transferred all right of dower she had in the property. In addition, any property so conveyed since March 2, 1887—one day before the Edmunds-Tucker Act took effect—would be considered an effectual release of dower rights. No separate release of dower needed to be signed, nor did the wife need to be examined separately from her husband by an officer of the court to determine whether her release of the dower was voluntary. She did, however, have to acknowledge before an authorized officer that she had signed the deed.[29]

But a legal wife might renounce the provision made for her in her husband's will and take her dower right as her inheritance. Instituting dower put all plural wives' inheritance at the mercy of the first wife, even if the husband left a will. The first wife could claim for her lifetime one-third of the lands her husband had owned during their marriage, leaving the remaining two-thirds to be distributed to his plural wives and all his children.[30] Moreover, the Edmunds-Tucker Act stipulated that county probate judges were no longer to be selected by the Utah legislative assembly but were to be appointed by the president of the United States with the advice and consent of the Senate.[31] In short, Mormon probate judges sympathetic to plural wives were to be replaced. The protection Mormons had tried to provide legally for plural wives' inheritance was thus abolished.

To secure their plural wives' economic well-being, some polygamists conveyed real property to their wives.[32] For example, Fred Cox's property was all in his name in 1887, but by 1888 he had transferred the title of the house each wife occupied to her. By 1890, he had transferred even more property to each wife so that each was assessed more in taxes than he was. Similarly, Soren C. Hansen (Christoffersen) held all his property in his own name in 1887. By 1888, he had transferred to his plural wife Anna the title of the house in which she lived. She was the only wife who had living children. By 1890, he had transferred additional property to her, and she was assessed taxes under "Mrs A. B. Steck," her maiden name.

He had also conveyed property to his other plural wife, and she, too, was assessed under her maiden name. Similarly, by 1888, William Bench had divided his property between his two wives, whereas previously all the property had been in his name.[33] Although some polygamists kept their property in their own names and others transferred property only later, the concern for providing for polygamous families is evident both in territorial law and in the actions of many in plural marriage.

After statehood, when the Mormons regained considerable power, the law did not continue to evince that concern, however. In 1896, the first state legislature provided for the right of dower, endowing "a widow" with a third of all the lands her husband had owned during their marriage, but no vagueness of language provided for plural wives. Although the first state legislature legitimated children already born of polygamous marriages, ensuring they could inherit, no similar right was bestowed on their mothers.[34] To inherit from her husband, a plural wife had to depend on his willingness to provide for her in his will and his first wife's willingness not to petition to take her dower instead of the legacy left in the will.

Not until 1898 did the Utah legislature pass a law declaring that "[t]here shall be neither dower nor curtesy in this state." The distinction made no real difference, however, because it gave the widow a right to one-third of the real property her husband owned during their marriage if she had not relinquished her right to it and because she was given that property in fee simple; that is, she could sell it or devise it by will, unlike her dower rights by which she had only the use of the property during her lifetime. Despite the act stating that there was to be no dower in the state, the Utah Supreme Court reconciled that declaration with the widow's right to one-third of her husband's real estate by ruling in 1906 that while the legislature had abolished the term, it had in fact retained and enlarged the right of dower.[35]

Even more significant than the widow's right to dower were the judicial decisions that continued to limit a plural wife's right to inherit from her husband's estate. In 1901, Alonzo H. Raleigh died leaving a will to provide for his family, including property for his plural wife Emily Raleigh.[36] He did not, however, devise to her the house in which she had lived since her marriage in 1857. She had not contested the will but had accepted the decree of distribution giving her an equitable share of the property. Only a legal wife could have renounced her rights under the terms of the will and, with any likelihood of success, asked the court to give her the home in which she had lived. That option not being open to her as a plural wife, Emily Raleigh brought suit, claiming that her husband had verbally given the property to her and that she held title by adverse possession, the right to property based on possessing it long enough to become recognized as the legal owner. The court denied her suit.

Her husband, the decision stated, had shown his continual control over the property during his lifetime. The court went further, however, to declare that "when she consented to become a plural wife, she did so at her peril, in so far as the law of inheritance is concerned, and, thereby failing to acquire the status of a lawful wife, . . . thenceforth she was without the pale of the law of inheritance as to any property which her husband had acquired or might thereafter acquire. As to all such property she could but depend for justice upon the will of him in whom she had thus confided." In short, a plural wife did "not acquire the status of a lawful wife" and therfore had no right to an inheritance from her husband's estate and certainly no dower or homestead right in her husband's property. A plural wife might, however, accept a gift of property from her husband or even acquire title to real estate by adverse possession founded on a gift, just as any stranger might.[37] In law, the right of a plural wife to inherit from her husband was no greater than that of any person outside the family.

Moreover, common law was invoked to make it difficult for a plural wife to become a legal wife after the death of the first wife. In *Riddle v. Riddle,* decided in 1903, the Utah Supreme Court declared that common law had governed marriage in the territory until passage of the Edmunds-Tucker Act in 1887.[38] Relying on the English case *Hyde v. Hyde,* the court declared that any marriage was void in which the couple did not mutually agree to live with each other to the exclusion of others. A woman entering a marriage as a plural wife therefore could not become a legal wife after the death of the first wife *if* the husband continued to cohabit with other wives. Nor was a marriage performed by a justice of the peace valid when entered into by the husband to disqualify the wife from testifying against him in court. In short, neither by common law nor by a marriage performed by the justice of the peace was Isaac Riddle legally the husband of any of his three plural wives. In an ironic twist, particularly since financial support of a plural wife had constituted evidence of cohabitation that might put a polygamist behind bars, the court stated its opinion that Riddle was "morally bound, not only, if able to do so, to support his plural wives but also to support and educate the children of the plural wives begotten by him." But, the decision conceded, "secular courts are powerless to enforce any but legal obligations," and clearly husbands had no legal responsibility to support their plural wives.[39] Although the moral law professed by the court had changed, the legal position of plural wives had not: they still existed beyond the pale of the law.

The ability of a plural wife to inherit therefore did not change upon the death of the legal wife. Bertha Goss became John Beck's plural wife in 1885, but the marriage was not made public knowledge because he might have been prosecuted for unlawful cohabitation. After the death of his first wife in 1894, Bertha wanted to become his legal wife but objected to obtaining a marriage license, fearing that it would bring the legitimacy of her children into question. So she and John went to Nevada, where common-law marriages were recognized as valid, and there consented in the present tense to be husband and wife, a legal marriage under common law. After their return to Utah, however, John sold property as a "widower," declared his intention to treat all his plural wives alike, and during his last illness lived with his plural wife Matilda.

The Utah Supreme Court refused to grant Bertha a dower right in property her husband had sold during their marriage. When a woman became a plural wife and continued without any apparent change in their relationship to live with her husband after the legal wife's death, the decision declared, "there is a presumption of law that their living together as husband and wife continued to be unlawful." Also, her deceased husband's statements that Bertha was not his legal wife disproved a common-law marriage. Bertha was thus not John's legal wife and hence not entitled to a widow's dower right.[40] These court decisions and the statutes passed after statehood worked against the tenuous rights a plural wife had in her husband's estate; the only right she had to inherit was the same as any stranger's right to receive a legacy through her husband's will.[41] Fortunately, these rulings were not applied ex post facto to the many plural wives who had assumed the position of legal wife upon the first wife's demise.

The Edmunds-Tucker Act, which applied to all territories, not only significantly altered inheritance laws but also was the first legislation that specifically regulated marriage in Utah. Section 9 required that every marriage ceremony be "certified by a certificate" stating the full names of the bride and groom as well as every person participating in the ceremony. The certificate had to be signed by the parties to the ceremony, "whether either or both or more of the parties to such ceremony be lawfully competent to be the subject of such marriage or ceremony or not." This last clause clearly was aimed at polygamists and their wives because few others would not be "lawfully competent" to marry under the laws that applied to Utah. Moreover, the law mandated that the certificate be filed in the office of the probate court, "immediately recorded," and subject to inspection. This brought Utah in line with most other territories and states, which by 1889 required that a written return of a marriage ceremony be given to a public official.[42] An important purpose was to provide a means by which to separate legally acknowledged marriages from irregular ones.

Section 4 of the same act banned unions of persons "within and not including the fourth degree of consanguinity"; that is, a person could not marry any blood relative closer than a first cousin. Congress, however, made no mention of affinal relationships. In permitting marriages between first cousins, the law was less restrictive than the laws of most western states, which prohibited such marriages, but was like them in permitting marriages between those related only by marriage.[43] The section further stated that any person who "shall marry or cohabit with, or have sexual intercourse with such other so related person" was guilty of incest and, upon conviction, would be imprisoned for no less than three years but no more than fifteen. Moreover, the act annulled the incorporation of the church; the validity incorporation had given to plural marriages was thus abolished.[44] In short, in 1887, Congress passed legislation to correct three practices in Utah abhorrent to late-nineteenth-century family reformers: no public record of marriages, consanguineous unions, and plural marriage.

In other respects, marriage in Utah remained unregulated, however, until the territorial legislature passed its first act regarding marriage on March 8, 1888. The act reiterated the ban on unions between persons whose consanguineous relationship was closer than first cousin. It also incorporated many of the restrictions adopted by other states near the end of the century, prohibiting marriages, in the words of the law, "with an idiot or lunatic," "between a negro and a white person," and "between a mongolian and a white person." The law also prohibited and declared void marriages not solemnized by an authorized person and, more significant, when a husband or wife from whom the person had not been divorced was still living.[45]

In 1887 and 1888, then, plural marriages ceased to have the benefit of even the ambiguous legal position that had prevailed in Utah. Henceforth, plural marriages did not have even the shadow of legality to support them; the law simply declared such marriages void.

In addition, Utah law required two or more witnesses to a marriage, stipulated penalties for those solemnizing a marriage without a license issued by the clerk of the probate court, and provided for the registration of marriages.[46] Thus, in 1887 and 1888, the permissiveness of the old regime in Utah was abruptly replaced by regulations advocated by the late-nineteenth-century family reformers. The determination to uphold monogamy overrode the earlier commitment in America to making

marriage simple and sustaining the sanctity of marriage against competing obligations.

But even the more liberal view of marriage was interpreted to the
disadvantage of Mormons. Heretofore, common law had presumed a
marriage by the couple's cohabitation, reputation, and acknowledgment.
But this broad interpretation of marriage worked against, not for, polygamists when the government prosecuted them under the Edmunds Law
in the 1880s for unlawful cohabitation. To convict the defendant, the
prosecution did not need to produce an eyewitness to, or record of, the
marriage ceremony. Admission by the defendant that the marriage had
taken place constituted sufficient proof of the marriage.[47]

In addition, the courts could convict a man of unlawful cohabitation
if he was reputed to be the husband of and cohabited with more than one
wife. The courts, however, interpreted "cohabitation" loosely. Sexual
intercourse did not need to be proved.[48] Establishing that the couple exchanged acts of kindness and attention over a period of years, even though
they did not live in the same house, was sufficient to convict a man of
unlawful cohabitation. Apostle Lorenzo Snow found that his living solely
with his youngest wife, Minnie, did not prevent his conviction. One
witness testified at his trial that he had seen Snow visiting the house of
his wife Sarah, sitting with her at the theater, and riding with her in a
carriage. These acts, along with his financial support of Sarah and their
reputation in the community as husband and wife, were sufficient to find
the apostle guilty of unlawfully cohabiting with Minnie.[49]

The presumption of a common-law marriage based on acknowledgments, reputation, and cohabitation was used successfully to convict
polygamists, even as it was ceasing to be sufficient to establish a lawful
marriage. Still, evidence was generally lacking to prove the greater crime
of polygamy—only twelve were imprisoned for that crime between 1884
and 1895—and the penalties for unlawful cohabitation were much less
severe.[50]

With the authority of both common and statutory law, the federal
government was successful in using the courts to weaken the power of
the Mormon hierarchy. Most Mormon leaders were polygamists, and like
other men in plural marriage, they often served prison sentences or went
into hiding to escape capture by the marshals. The Edmunds-Tucker Act
struck a further blow at the Mormons' ability to define and regulate their
own marriage system. Section 24 disfranchised not only polygamists but
also all Mormons who could not in good conscience swear an oath saying they would not "directly or indirectly, aid or abet, counsel or advise"
others to enter plural marriage. Moreover, the act disfranchised all wom-

en.[51] The passage and enforcement of the Edmunds Act and the Edmunds-Tucker Act not only revolutionized the marriage system the Mormons had put in place in the 1850s but also undermined the power of the church that had sustained that system.

Although church leaders criticized polygamists who avoided punishment by promising to obey the law in the future, they gave little guidance after the Manifesto was issued about what that statement meant for those already in plural marriage.[52] They did say men had an obligation to support their wives, but in 1891 the president of the church testified before the master in chancery that the Manifesto meant cohabitation with plural wives should cease.[53] In practice, each family decided for itself how to react to the new situation.

Many men continued to cohabit with all their wives; others ceased living with all but one wife. The 1900 Manti census provides some indication of the extent of continuing cohabitation. Of the twenty men remaining in Manti in 1900 who had at least two wives still living, seven (35 percent) clearly continued to cohabit with their wives beyond 1891. After that date, five had children by wives with whom they were not residing, and two lived in the same household with all their wives. Another three were at least technically cohabiting: they were living with and having children by their plural wives while their legal wives lived in separate households.[54] The other men may also have been cohabiting with more than one wife, but because those women were all over forty years of age, the lack of births provides no evidence about the relationships. Many younger men had taken their wives out of the state or out of the country, where they felt safer from the law, and the wives were therefore no longer residents of Manti.

The census taker in 1900, however, asked the marital status of each person. All wives residing with their husbands naturally listed themselves as married, even when all wives were residing in the same household. Of the other wives, three-quarters said they were married. Among the three who were enumerated as single, one listed herself as married on the 1910 census. The two others were living next door to their husbands and so perhaps wished to obscure their marital status. The remaining two women lived in other towns and listed themselves as widowed.

The ambiguity of a polygamous wife's status is illustrated by the records of Johanne Breinholt, who was a legal wife. She became an independent though still married woman in 1891 when her husband and his plural wife moved to Mexico and she preferred to stay in Utah. "This is a sad parting," her husband lamented.[55] The uncertainty of her status is reflected in the next two censuses. In 1900, she listed herself as widowed, but in 1910, after her husband returned with his plural wife from Mexico, she was listed as married, with her "own income." She had acquired a farm that had no mortgage, which she probably ran with the help of her twenty-six-year-old son, who was listed as a farmer.[56]

Whatever their sexual and economic relationships with their spouses, almost all these women thought of themselves as married. While some men took advantage of the Manifesto to free themselves from the economic burden of other wives, they were, according to Carmon Hardy, "gratefully few."[57] The 1900 census provides some evidence for that statement. Of the twenty wives not residing with their husbands, fifteen (75 percent) are listed as owning their houses free of mortgage. One other plural wife, although living in the same household as her husband, also owned her house free of debt. (He, incidentally, rented his farm.) Two other plural wives, who resided in their husband's household, had taxable property. Two wives rented their homes, although one owned her house by 1910. The second renter, aged sixty-five who listed herself as widowed and a weaver, may not have received economic help from her husband, who was one of the few men whose house was mortgaged.

For two wives, the columns for whether the house was owned or rented and whether it was mortgaged or free are left blank. One, however, acquired a house free of mortgage by the next census. The other probably moved back into the household with her husband and his first wife during the next decade. Her husband's occupation was given as laborer, and although he was listed as owning his house, it was undoubtedly a humble one. His taxable assets in 1900 were listed as $196, considerably less than the two plural wives who did not own houses but had taxable property; one had property valued at $371, and the other, still with young children, had $830 worth of property.[58] One wife, Ann Davis Hailstone McAllister, lived in Logan, Utah, with her married son by her second marriage. She had married John D. T. McAllister as her third husband in 1871 at age fifty, a marriage that was probably contracted more for her eternal salvation than for temporal assistance. In the 1900 census, she was listed as Ann D. McAlister (*sic*) but as married for sixty-one years—calculated from the date of her first marriage. The nature of the marriage in 1900 is thus unclear.[59] Nevertheless, even including Ann McAllister, 85 percent of the wives possessed houses (89 percent if she is not included), while two who did not own property were married to men whose own financial straits did not permit them to provide for their wives.[60]

Whether the property came from family funds, to which wives had contributed, or from the earnings of the women themselves, the census does not say. It probably came from both, although some, like Johanne

Breinholt and Inger Marie Schougaard, were clearly self-supporting.
Schougaard had been a plural wife for only four years when the Manifesto was issued. After 1892, her husband lived with his first wife in another town, while Schougaard took care of herself and her son by becoming
"a dealer in groceries and notions and owner of restaurant and ice cream
parlor." By 1898, a short biography of her noted, "Being left with nothing, she has by energy and perseverance worked up a good trade and purchased the building in which she lives and does business."[61] It is not clear
whether the "nothing" she started with was akin to that with which
nineteenth-century self-made men commenced, almost all of whom started with some family resources.[62] Nevertheless, while subsequent censuses listed her as married, she was actually an independent woman.

Overall, then, the wives not residing with their husbands after 1890
did not believe the Manifesto had changed their marital status, and most
of them probably continued to receive some financial support. After the
Manifesto, plural families' status grew increasingly ambiguous, however. One child born after the Manifesto said that his family was persecut-
ed because of polygamy and that fellow Mormons in the community
called the children bastards.[63]

Instead of being among the elite as in former times, polygamous families became anomalous as their numbers declined. In 1899, the church
compiled a report indicating that in 1890 there had been 2,451 polygamous families. Of these, 750 had been broken by death and 95 by divorce.
Another 63 families had left the United States. That left 1,543 polygamous families. By May 1902, the number had dropped still further, to
897.[64] Whether polygamous families living separately, such as the Schou-
gaards, were included in these figures is unclear, and almost certainly no
post-Manifesto marriages were included in the count. Nevertheless, the
number of openly plural families declined rapidly, and the few remaining families became marginalized.

The decline of plural marriage was only one of the changes in the late
nineteenth century and early twentieth. Mormons and their leaders increasingly made a distinction between the temporal and religious spheres,
a distinction that produced a new worldview that could accommodate
the changes wrought by the Manifesto.[65] The attempts to establish communal economic enterprises to fulfill the law of consecration and stew-
ardship were abandoned, and the law of tithing was emphasized. The
church's political party, too, was disbanded, and Mormons became Dem-
ocrats and Republicans. Whereas formerly belief in and practice of plural marriage had provided boundaries that established Mormon identity,
after the Manifesto adherence to the Word of Wisdom—abstention from

alcohol, coffee, tea, and tobacco—increasingly played that role. Instead of expanding families through plural marriage and adoption into the families of church leaders, family trees were extended back in time as the emphasis changed to identifying one's own ancestors and sealing this chain of ancestors together through vicarious temple ordinances. Thomas Alexander has aptly named his history of the period from 1890 through 1930 *Mormonism in Transition.*[66]

Although church leaders issued the Manifesto only after many polygamists had gone to prison, the federal receiver had confiscated most of the church's resources, and Congress had threatened to disfranchise all Mormons, the groundwork had been laid for the Manifesto's acceptance by a changed outlook on the world and a decline in new plural marriages. Nevertheless, the Manifesto did not end either the belief in plural marriage or its practice.[67] Even within the church, a few continued to practice it long after 1890, and it still thrives in such break-off groups as the True and Living Church.

11   The Nineteenth-Century Mormon Marriage System

The rules governing Mormon marriage and divorce were non-legalistic and nontraditional—so much so that the federal government spent enormous sums to enforce its antipolygamy legislation, imprisoned over nine hundred polygamists, disincorporated the Church of Jesus Christ of Latter-day Saints, and seized over a million dollars of church property.[1] Unconventional though the system was in Western society, the basic framework seems to have been fairly well in place by the time the Mormons reached Utah in 1847. Through plural marriage, the church could fulfill its responsibility to the widows, the divorced, and the fatherless and could more equitably distribute wealth.

LDS leaders' injunctions to enter plural marriage were only one of the influences that affected ordinary Mormons' decisions about marriage in the nineteenth century. Individual decisions about marriage were also affected by economic circumstances, concern for status, views about what constitutes marital bliss, as well as belief in plural marriage.[2] All these factors interacted to alter marriage patterns even as the system itself was changing over the last half of the nineteenth century.

That it was a system, that it had rules governing marriage and divorce, needs to be defended in depth because of the historiography of plural marriage. Lawrence Foster's study of the origins of Shaker celibacy, Oneida complex marriage, and Mormon polygamy argues that each community experienced a "'liminal' period when neither the old nor the new standards are in effect." In this liminal period, the leaders of mil lennial movements "must begin to create a new way of life and status relationships at the very same time that they are trying to initiate individuals into those not yet established roles. In short, the desired end point is often unclear, or else is still in the process of being created. Thus, such movements typically go through great confusion and a more severe process of breaking down the old order as they seek to find and develop a new way of life."[3] In the context of his argument, the "great confusion" and "severe process of breaking down the old order" also referred to the changes individual members of the millennial movements went through as they moved from the old order to the new. Once the liminal period was over, however, a new system was in place.

Eugene Campbell and Bruce Campbell, in their article on polygamous divorce, argue that even in Utah "Mormon polygamy developed within a context of normlessness or anomie" and that there was "a lack of regulations in the social structure including the marriage and family system."[4] The concept of anomie was first systematically developed by Emile Durkheim. According to him, humans' desires are unlimited because in humans, unlike animals, desires are not satiated when biological needs are met. Those unlimited desires are held in check only by societal control, which "must play the same role for moral needs which the organism plays for physical needs."[5] During crises or abrupt transitions, however, society loses its ability to regulate human desires. If the degree of anomie is mild, society becomes less rigid and adapts to changing circumstances. Historians and sociologists have used the concept of anomie to elucidate social changes in Western societies as they moved from traditional to industrialized economies.[6]

Robert Remini's characterization of Jacksonian America fits Durkheim's description of an anomic society:

> Starting early in the nineteenth century, the country burst its narrow confines. Within a few decades the nation was converted from an insulated, agrarian society squeezed between ocean and mountains into a dynamic, industrial society sprawled across a three-thousand-mile continent. Gone were the old ties of family, church, and community; gone, too, was the security they provided. . . . For individuals [the "Go ahead" spirit] meant the consuming need to make money. There was a restless, driving desire to be better off, and this was the ambition of all classes of society, none excepted. . . . There was only one way to describe them. Restless, searching, driving. By the time of Jackson's inauguration in 1828 [*sic*] it was the prevailing mood of the country.[7]

The market revolution changed not only the economy but also American society, releasing social restraints especially in newly settled areas.[8]

The anomie inherent in that period accelerated the loosening of the authority of the patriarchal family and its replacement by the middle-class family, with the mother as a central figure in the home and in her children's lives.

Not everyone embraced these emerging new values, however. The relaxed restraints provided the social space in which nonconformers could flourish. Nonconformers, as defined by Robert Merton, are those who challenge the legitimacy of current social norms by appealing to a higher morality as authority for an alternative set of norms.[9] Among those nonconformers who provided alternatives by returning to the Bible, albeit interpreting it differently, were Ann Lee, who established the first Shaker settlement in the United States; John Humphrey Noyes, the founder of the Oneida community; and Joseph Smith. Mormonism, with its claims of divine authority and its doctrine of the Saints' gathering together, provided a refuge for those fleeing from growing American pluralism.[10]

Although the anomie of the Jacksonian period helps account for the initial attraction to Mormonism, Foster's concept of a liminal period better explains the acceptance of plural marriage. The concepts of anomie and liminal period both encompass a period of normlessness. Foster states that during the liminal period, before new standards were initiated, "there was a brief but disruptive interregnum when neither set of standards was operative and the basis of social authority was unclear."[11] By averring that neither old nor new standards of marriage were in place during a liminal period, he explains "apparent discrepancies between belief and practice" during the introduction of plural marriage in Nauvoo, such as when Joseph Smith took as plural wives some women whose husbands were still living.[12] In contrast to the insecurity, sense of disrupted social cohesion, and dependence on only oneself that are inherent in anomie, a sense of communitas and emotional unity, intense egalitarianism, and submission to the authority of leaders characterize the liminal period. These latter traits describe Mormons in Nauvoo much better than the former, as shown by the persecution they collectively endured, their working together to build the church, and the endowment and sealing rituals that spiritually bound them together. Unlike anomie, religion is, according to Durkheim, "something eminently social."[13]

This liminal period, Foster observes, was "brief": by 1852, the problems experienced in the early days of polygamy had been overcome, and, under Brigham Young's leadership, plural marriage may justly be characterized as, in M. R. Werner's words, "Puritan Polygamy." To counter fragmentation in their movements, the Mormons, the Shakers, and the

Oneida Perfectionists developed "a highly authority-conscious and strongly centralized Church-type structure of government."[14]

Bruce Campbell and Eugene Campbell, however, maintain that the period of normlessness continued throughout the practice of plural marriage. They support this argument by citing the Old Testament, noting a discrepancy between regulations and practice, and recounting four examples.

First, they state, "Although the practice of sororal polygamy was frequently used in Mormon polygamy, the code of the Old Testament forbade this practice."[15] Here they refer to the prohibitions on intercourse and marriage contained in chapters 18 and 20 of Leviticus. The problem with these prohibitions, however, is that it is not always clear whether they refer to extramarital relations or marriage.[16] The Mormons imitated the patriarchs in their practice of plural marriage, one of whom—Jacob—married the sisters Leah and Rachel.[17] Nevertheless, the Campbells are correct when they declare, "There is little indication that [the Old Testament] was used as a serious guide to their marriage regulation."[18] The practice of plural marriage was accepted among Mormons because they believed that God had commanded it through his prophet Joseph Smith, and the rules regarding plural marriage appear to have been accepted on that same basis.

Second, the Campbells acknowledge that the Saints had rules regarding marriage but argue that these were not carefully followed. Among these was the rule that the first wife had to give her permission before a husband could take a plural wife. This rule seems to have been generally followed. Although Kimball Young states, "There were . . . many instances where the husband . . . married again without any consultation with the first wife," he gives only two examples. Moreover, he also indicates that "judging from our records there was usually explicit, or at least implicit, consent." Jessie Embry's conclusions are similar; she states that some first wives freely gave their consent or even encouraged their husbands to take another wife, some gave their consent only because they feared the repercussions in the next life for saying no in this one, and "a few" were not consulted. In Vicky Burgess-Olsen's study, 91.7 percent of the first wives indicated they gave their consent to subsequent marriages.[19] In any case, Orson Pratt explained in 1853 that the first wife did not have absolute veto power over her husband's entering plural marriage. If her reasons for objecting were justifiable or the husband was found at fault or in transgression, he could take no further steps toward entering plural marriage. But if her basis for refusing was insufficient, the husband would be justified in marrying again without her consent "if permitted by revelation through the prophet." All plural marriages had to be approved by the president of the church.[20]

Third, the Campbells cite four examples they argue indicate lack of regulation. Two of these concerned women who did not obtain formal divorces before they were sealed to their second husbands.[21] That in certain circumstances formal divorces were not required under the Mormon system has already been discussed in chapter eight. The church president's permission for a woman to remarry was sufficient. Such permission indicated not the lack of regulation but how highly centralized in the person of the prophet that regulation was.

Unintentionally, another of their examples illustrates that centralization. In 1854, when Orson Hyde found that he would be spending the winter in Carson Valley, he wrote to Brigham Young asking either that one of his wives be sent or that he be given permission to marry another wife there. The Campbells write, "Marriage for Hyde seemed to be just a temporary convenience. Such an attitude would not have been honored in a well-established community that had developed strict standards of conjugal behavior."[22] If by "well-established community" the Campbells refer to the nineteenth-century Mormons' contemporaries in America and Europe, they are certainly correct. To be sure, the Mormon system of marriage was unorthodox and nontraditional, but Hyde's letter indicates a high degree of regulation. Hyde was one of the Quorum of the Twelve Apostles, a governing body of the church next in power only to the president of the church and his counselors. Yet even he asked the president for permission to marry again or to have one of his wives sent to him. On this occasion, Brigham Young decided to send one of Hyde's wives.

The last example the Campbells cite is George Stringham. After Stringham married his second wife, the Campbells said he moved from the house of his first wife, leaving her almost destitute, although he returned to live with her fourteen years later. The Campbells conclude, "Apparently there were no powerful social mechanisms to regulate Stringham's behavior."[23] The first wife, however, could have brought her husband before a church court to ensure that she would be treated equitably. But it was the daughter, not the wife, who was distressed by Stringham's behavior. The daughter Sabra, who remained in the Midwest and joined the RLDS Church, wrote her mother three years after her father had married a widow from England, condemning her father for marrying a "young one" (the widow was forty-five when she married Stringham) and polygamy in general. Her letter to her mother indicates that the perception of problems in the marriage lay with the daughter because she writes, "I am glad you are as well satisfied with your lot."[24] Moreover, it is unclear whether the situation was as unfavorable as the Campbells describe. A family history notes that George and his first wife, Polly, resided in a home on Main Street in Salt Lake City, while the second wife lived in "a small home" on Eleventh East, where George "lived with her here from time to time for a number of years."[25] In short, George Stringham's behavior was not as reprehensible or as unregulated as the Campbells assert.

Nevertheless, most scholars have agreed that the living arrangements for plural families were never institutionalized. Housing arrangements, methods of distributing resources, the husband's system for spending time with each family, and the wives' relationships all varied.[26] Less than a year after Orson Pratt first publicly announced the practice of plural marriage, he wrote that there was "no particular rule" about residential patterns for the various wives and their children, although it was "the duty of a man who takes another wife to look after her welfare and happiness, and to provide for her the comforts of life the same as for the first." He further stated that in domestic affairs, a polygamist should not set rules that compelled him "to act invariably in a certain way"; rather, circumstances and wisdom should determine when and how much time he should spend with each branch of his family.[27] The Campbells' statement that "the Mormon system of polygamy was not one of consistent and strong regulation" justifiably applies to the various arrangements for living in plural marriages, not to their being contracted or dissolved.

There were rules governing the establishment and dissolution of plural marriages and even many monogamous marriages administered by the church, or, more precisely, by the president of the church. To be sure, the rules on marriage and divorce were lenient. That was not because these rules "developed within a context of normlessness," as the Campbells maintain,[28] but because the church's policy, like policy elsewhere in mid-nineteenth-century America, was to encourage marriage and to minimize barriers to it.

To be sure, Durkheim considered divorce as "a weakening of matrimonial regulation." His argument, however, is based on the contention that monogamy serves as a restraint on men's unlimited passions. Divorce removes that restraint, increasing anomie and hence suicide. However, he maintained that women, whose "mental life is less developed," do not need marriage, particularly monogamic marriage, to serve as a social regulation to their passions, and his statistics show that in societies where divorces are common, wives commit suicide less frequently than elsewhere.[29] Aside from his erroneous assumptions about women that would not be countenanced today, his discussion shows that women's circumstances are improved when divorce provides a release from unhappy marriages. What applies to monogamous marriages must with much greater force apply to polygamous ones. Durkheim's argues that divorce does not increase anomie for women. Even if one concedes his arguments about men, it is difficult to see how they would apply in a polygamous society. A man's life of passion is not restrained in such a society by his attachment to only one woman when he is allowed by law and encouraged by religion to have more than one wife. Even monogamous men had the potential to become polygamists. It is therefore difficult to see how Durkheim's argument that divorce increases anomie for men by releasing the restraint on their passions pertains to nineteenth-century Mormon society.

But there were restraints on sexual passion in Mormon society. One of the most important was that the church's president had the exclusive power to authorize plural marriages. The revelation on plural marriage declared that "there is never but one on the earth at a time on whom this power and the keys of this priesthood [to seal marriages] are conferred."[30] The president also had to countersign all temple recommends until November 1891. When one woman complained to Brigham Young in 1875 that her husband had not sought her permission to take a plural wife, the president wrote to her bishop indicating he would not approve the man's marriage unless the husband was reconciled with his family. Moreover, a man planning to marry another wife needed the approval of his bishop and stake president as well as the church president. On September 16, 1865, Charles Walker confided to his journal that he had sought and obtained Brigham Young's permission to take another wife, with the proviso that he also obtain the approval of his bishop and stake president.[31] Heber J. Grant stated that while he was a stake president from 1880 to 1882, he denied both applicants who asked for an additional wife. He refused one because of the man's drunkenness, and he said to the other, "What is needed in your family is sufficient brains to take care of one wife and one family, and certainly you cannot get a recommend from me to marry another wife."[32] Whether the man took umbrage at such a pointed refusal, Grant did not say. What is clear, however, is that the church leaders, although encouraging plural marriage, denied permission to some men who were not worthy or not capable of marrying additional wives.

In addition, the church provided guidelines for courtship when a man was already married. One ecclesiastical leader in 1857, when the sealing of plural marriages was at its height, indicated that a man should obtain consent from the prospective wife's parents before asking the woman herself and that he should have permission from Brigham Young to take an additional wife. Moreover, according to Sarah Leavitt, "the Gentile custom of Sparkification was done away so that the passions may not be aroused."[33] With the Saints' distrust of romantic love, it is not surprising that one Mormon declared in the 1850s that flirting was "a gentile word, we never use it," although the behavior itself was not entirely absent.[34] Mary Elizabeth Croshaw, who in 1887 became the fourth wife of George Lionel Farrell, made much the same point: "Married men didn't do any courting of their plural wives. Why, we would have thought it was dishonorable for a mature married man to go sparking like a young man. They just came and asked us, and if we wanted them, we agreed."[35] Most stories confirm this kind of restraint when courting plural wives. Annie Clark Tanner, for example, noted that her husband, "Mr. Tanner insisted that a long courtship in cases of polygamy was entirely improper." Her prospective husband obtained her father's consent before the courtship had progressed very far, and on at least one occasion he took his first wife to visit his future bride.[36] As Kimball Young concluded, most Saints followed the counsel of President John Taylor that "courtship should be short and direct."[37]

Another constraint was penury. Poverty, Durkheim points out, "is a restraint . . . desires have to depend upon resources to some extent."[38] The difficulty of providing economically for additional wives and children surely limited men's desires for marrying more women, particularly as expected living standards increased over the last half of the nineteenth century. The majority of polygamists had only two polygamous wives, and two-thirds had no more than two wives at a time. The number of wives a man could support depended not only on his resources but also on whether his wives were young and fecund, whether the wife brought to the marriage children from other marriages, whether those children were young and dependent or old enough to be producers, whether some of those marriages were for eternity only, whether plural wives died young or divorced their polygamous husband, and whether the man married later in the century when living standards had risen. With only one exception, the Manti polygamists with five or more polygamous wives entered plural marriage in Nauvoo or in the 1850s. That one exception became a polygamist in 1862 and had no more than three wives at one time. Moreover, the number of children born to polygamists could vary considerably, ranging from ten to forty-two among those Manti men with five or more wives.

There was another, more important restraint on men's passions in Mormon polygamous society. To remain in good standing, a Mormon could have a sexual relationship with a woman only if he married her.

Although Durkheim states that divorce weakens the regulation of marriage, he acknowledges that custom allows men "certain privileges" that mitigate the strictness of monogamy.[39] For Durkheim, those "privileges" apparently did not represent a lack of regulation of marriage.

Under the Mormon system, regulation operated differently. Instead of infidelity as an escape hatch, divorce was the safety valve for unhappy marriages, and plural marriage permitted men's passions to be confined within marriage relationships. But outside marriage, the rules for sexual conduct were strict. As George Q. Cannon explained, "We believe in marriage, we have opened the door in that direction, and we say to the sexes marry; but we close the door in the other direction, and say, you shall not commit adultery, you shall not seduce, defile, prostitute or lead astray innocent beings."[40] Sexuality outside of marriage was decried, and extramarital sex could bring especially heavy penalties.

Sexual desire, when properly restrained, was from God, according to Apostle Erastus Snow:

> The lusts and desires of the flesh are not of themselves unmitigated evils. . . . These affections and loves that are planted in us are the nobler qualities that originate from God. They stimulate us to the performance of our duties; to multiplying and replenishing the earth to assume the responsibilities of families, and rear them up for God. They encourage and stimulate the woman to bear her burden and perform the duties of life because of the hope of a glorious future, while it stimulates the husband and father in like manner. Every instinct in us is for a wise purpose in God when properly regulated and restrained, and guided by the Holy Spirit and kept within its proper legitimate bounds.[41]

Both premarital and extramarital relations were condemned in the strongest terms.

Among Mormons, there was not the "double standard" widespread elsewhere in America that countenanced men's sexual dalliances but demanded chastity of women.[42] The double standard in Utah held that men were more guilty of sexual sins than were women. In discussing women in Salt Lake City who had "committed the sin of debauchery," Heber C. Kimball rhetorically asked, "Who is the most to blame?" Although he did not absolve women of all guilt, his answer was, "The man holding the Priesthood of God."[43] Similarly, on October 9, 1869, George Q. Cannon, one of the Twelve Apostles, preached a sermon in which he stated:

> the lower passions of our natures . . . have been implanted in both male and female for a wise purpose, but their immoderate and illegal gratification is a source of evil. . . . Why, women, in their yearning after the

other sex and in their desire for maternity, will do anything to gratify that instinct of their nature and yield to anything and be dishonored even rather than not gratify it; and in consequence of that which has been pronounced upon them *they are not held accountable to the same extent as men are.* Man is strong, he is the head of woman, and God will hold him responsible for the use of the influence he exercises over the opposite sex. . . . *[a woman] is not held accountable to the same degree that men are.*[44]

Consonant with the Mormon belief that having children is a God-like act, these two church leaders averred that sexual desire was not evil except when it led to sexual relations outside of marriage.[45]

Nor were women regarded as the pure and passionless creatures that some of their contemporaries in the northern United States believed females to be.[46] Snow and Cannon acknowledged that women had sexual desires. Cannon claimed, however, that women were less accountable than men for sexual transgressions because after the Fall, God, in placing on Eve the curse that her "desire shall be to thy husband," had placed in women a desire for protection and guidance from men.[47] Men were to be strong, and that strength was to be shown in self-discipline that protected female virtue and unborn children, not in conquests of women.

At times, the church courts appear to have meted out greater punishments to men than to women for sexual transgressions. For example, when one man in St. George confessed to his bishop that he had had "unlawful cohabitation with his wife before marriage," he had to be rebaptized, but his wife did not.[48]

Men, assumed to be the stronger sex, were admonished to protect the chastity of women, and defilers of the innocent were to be "shunned as a pest, or as contagious disease" and considered "among the worst of felons."[49] Just as southerners considered it a point of honor to protect the "purity" of their women, Mormon men believed it was their duty to protect the "virtue" of theirs. Whereas southern men's obligations extended little further than to the females in their families, Mormon leaders tried to protect all Mormon women, particularly against "Gentile" men.[50] This often took the form of dire threats from the Mormon pulpit. Richard Burton wrote that Brigham Young used "purposely violent language, making the terrors of a scolding the punishment in lieu of hanging for a stolen horse or cow."[51] The same could be said of not only Young but also other leaders when what was being stolen was a woman's chastity.

Certainly their rhetoric was well tested when Colonel Edward J. Steptoe and his troops en route west spent the winter of 1854–55 in Salt Lake City. Lieutenant Sylvester Mowry, along with other soldiers, heard the warnings from church leaders. In spite of these warnings and what Mowry termed "their damnable system of espionage—better than that of the old Inquisition or Napoleon's police," the gallant lieutenant planned an intrigue with the prettiest woman he had seen, Brigham Young's daughter-in-law, whose husband was in Britain on a mission. On the verge of succeeding, according to Mowry, a report that he had been "caught in the act" reached the president of the church. The West Point graduate claimed that it was "an infamous lie," and he felt his reputation had been ruined "among those who have the care of the females."[52]

More warnings thundered from the pulpit. Jedediah M. Grant, counselor to Brigham Young, "told [the non-Mormons] of their wickedness, & corruptions, and abominations & strongly warned against attempting any further to traduce & corrupt the wives & daughters of the Latter Day Saints." Young's other counselor, Heber C. Kimball, then followed with the threat that "if He caught any man committing Adultery with one of his daughters He would kill them both."[53] Such violent threats fortunately led to nothing more than some fights between Mormons and the soldiers, while the case against Captain Rufus Ingalls for abducting a minor female was dismissed.[54]

Lieutenant Mowry, however, had to give up his intrigue. His colonel sent him an order to stay in the army camp outside the city, and "Brigham sent me word that if I took her away he would have me killed before I could get out of the Territory. He is a man of his word in little matters of this sort and I concluded I had better not do it."[55] By the end of April, Steptoe had ordered Mowry and Ingalls to lead two separate detachments to California. In this case, the cool head of the colonel and the rhetoric of the church leaders had their effect, though some other soldiers did take women with them when they left.[56]

Threatening rhetoric also had the desired effect on a young non-Mormon miner from Silver Reef about 1875 who was courting a young woman in a nearby Mormon town. The young man was given notice to appear before a bishop's court, which he did, only to scoff and claim that the court had no right to try him. The local justice of the peace was one of the elders, however. Declaring that "it is our duty to protect our women against strangers who would pick the grape and trample the vine," he claimed the elders had a right to know if the young man's intentions were honorable and affirmed that "the bishop's court is good enough for any man who will not lie." Another elder proposed giving the miner an hour to make his decision whether to submit to the court or leave town. "If he stays and you don't shoot him, Bishop, I will," he threatened. To the amusement of the elders, the young miner left for Silver Reef ten minutes later, never to return.[57] Enjoying their success, especially at so little cost, the Mormon elders nevertheless had been earnest about protecting women from unscrupulous men.

The vehement rhetoric was not always successful, of course, but the low incidence of premarital conceptions indicates how seriously Mormons took the proscription against premarital sexual relations. The records used for the Manti data set reveal no prenuptial pregnancies for the frontier period. For the middle period, the records show only 1.8 percent of brides (7) bore children within eight months of their marriage, while from 1890 to 1910, 5.5 percent (23) did so.

Marriage dates can be verified, however, only for the last period. Of the twenty-one couples who had family group records and had a child within eight months of their wedding day, seven records, or one-third, listed a marriage date that obscured that fact. The records therefore probably do not indicate the real level of prenuptial pregnancy for the first two periods.[58]

Nevertheless, even the incidence of 5.5 percent for the last period, from 1890 to 1910, is low. It is below the 9.6 percent of American brides from 1841 through 1880 who bore children within eight and a half months of marriage and considerably lower than the 23.3 percent who did so from 1881 to 1910. For the United States, the period from 1841 to 1880 had the lowest incidence of prenuptial pregnancies except for New England before 1680, when 6.8 percent of women had children within eight and a half months of their wedding day. Likewise, the percentage of women bearing children within six months of marriage was low in Manti. From 1890 to 1910, only 4.0 percent did so, compared with 5.8 percent from 1841 to 1880 and 15.1 percent from 1881 to 1910 elsewhere in the United States.[59] Although prenuptial conceptions were probably increasing in Manti, the overall levels remained remarkably low.[60]

The number of illegitimate births was also low. Over the sixty years encompassed by this study, only eleven illegitimate children were born to Manti women. These were not evenly distributed throughout that time, however. Only one illegitimate child was born in the frontier period, three in the middle period, and seven in the last twenty years. Five of the eleven women who gave birth to illegitimate children eventually married the fathers of their children. Moreover, all the women had married within five years of the birth of the illegitimate child; most did so within three years. Such women were not made pariahs but rather were incorporated into Mormon society.

In contrast, males faced criminal charges if they did not marry the women they seduced. In 1866, at age thirteen, an illiterate Danish immigrant conceived a child, and two young men were brought before the probate court on a seduction charge in 1868. Hans Hansen pleaded guilty "to having intercourse with Maria Larson but denied using coercion."[61] Joseph A. Smith also pleaded guilty. For reasons not made clear in the record, he was deemed to be father of the child. Smith and Hansen were both found guilty of a misdemeanor, and each was fined a hundred dollars plus costs of the court. In addition, Smith was required "to enter into lands with approved security to pay to Maria Larsen for support of child (fifty) Dollars per Annum."[62] The twenty-three-year-old Smith filed claims for the required land and soon left Manti for the Nevada Territory, though not before his father "had a long talk" with him. Larsen stayed in the town and in less than two years became a plural wife.[63]

In 1896, the state made intercourse with a woman between the ages of thirteen and eighteen a felony.[64] Thus, when fifteen-year-old Melinda Jensen conceived a child in 1903, Joseph Hill, the father of her child, received a harsher treatment than had been meted out to the two young men for seduction in 1868. He was sent to prison for carnal knowledge of a female under age. As the incidence of illegitimacy increased and the church's power to impose its standards declined, the community made greater use of prison sentences to enforce sexual mores. Though the numbers remained small, cases of fornication, adultery, and "assault with intent to commit carnal knowledge" increasingly appeared on the court docket, with jail or prison sentences following the convictions. In 1910, a man was sentenced to ninety days in the county jail for fornication, while a man and a woman convicted of adultery in 1911 served ninety days and thirty days, respectively, in the state prison.[65]

Although prison sentences were harsher penalties than the fines and child support required in the early years, they were less severe than the punishment that was sometimes meted out by extralegal means. On Sunday, February 6, 1851, as the Manti worshipers were leaving church, Madison Hambleton drew a pistol and killed twenty-two-year-old Dr. J. M. Vaughn. Hambleton immediately gave himself up to the bishop for judgment. Testimony taken in Manti indicated that while Hambleton had been away, the doctor had become intimate with Hambleton's wife, Chelnecha. How intimate is unclear. In the confined, crowded log cabins of pioneer Manti, the erring couple had found privacy by blowing out the candle, covering up the fire, and retiring to the back of the room.[66] Dr. Vaughn's reputation had already been besmirched by his arrest the previous fall in Salt Lake City for adultery, and in spite of warnings, he had persisted, according to the testimony given, in visiting Chelnecha Hambleton at every chance. Later, she appeared before those assembled for worship, confessed her wrong, and was excommunicated from the church. Her husband went to Salt Lake City, appeared before the Territorial Supreme Court, and was acquitted of wrongdoing in the doctor's death.[67]

Hambleton's action set a precedent Howard Egan found difficult to ignore. When news reached Egan that James Monroe had seduced Tamson, Egan's first wife, and that she had borne Monroe's child, there was a "universal conclusion" that Egan "would have been damned by the community for ever, and could not have lived peaceably" had he not killed his wife's seducer.[68] Egan met the wagon train with which Monroe was traveling west, and the two talked "peaceably some time" before Egan drew his pistol and shot him. It is unclear whether the jury believed the killing was justifiable homicide or whether it was convinced the court had no jurisdiction over the case, but it took only fifteen minutes to return a verdict of not guilty.[69]

Because Egan was a polygamist, Mormons publicized the case widely as a warning to other would-be seducers. Many Americans had wrongly assumed that plural marriage meant promiscuous relationships for women and men, and the Saints wanted to disabuse them of that erroneous notion.[70] The full argument of Egan's attorney, Apostle George A. Smith, was published in the *Deseret News*, which included this pointed warning: "In this territory it is a principle of mountain common law, that no man can seduce the wife of another *without endangering his own life. . . . The man who seduces his neighbor's wife must die, and her nearest relative must kill him.*" The account of the case concluded with the editorial comment that it should "prove a sufficient warning to all unchaste reprobates, that they are not wanted in our community."[71] This case certainly prevented the threats thundered from Mormon pulpits, aimed at Colonel Steptoe's troops and others like them, from appearing empty.

In 1866, Newton Brassfield was less wise than Sylvester Mowry and met Monroe's fate. Ignoring warnings, Brassfield wooed and won the plural wife of Archibald Newell Hill, then on a mission to Europe. Without securing a divorce, church or otherwise, she married Brassfield. The newlyweds then tried to take her children and goods from Hill's house, but the rest of the family resisted the attempt, despite Brassfield's threat to shoot. Charged with larceny and an attempt to kill, Brassfield spent the night in jail and then was released on bail. As he was returning to his boardinghouse the next day in the company of a U.S. marshal, he was shot, and he died within an hour. The unknown assailant proved fleet of foot and escaped his pursuers as well as their pistol shots.[72]

Claiming that the murder could just as well have been perpetrated
by a longtime enemy of Brassfield as by those "directly aggrieved" by
the marriage, an editorial in the church's newspaper deprecated violence
"as a method of righting wrongs" but acknowledged a "strong and general . . . feeling of just indignation." In the church's General Conference
that followed the murder by only a few days, Brigham Young defended
himself against accusations that he had anything to do with the killing,
declaring that he knew nothing more about it than anyone else did. But
as in the Egan case, the church used the occasion as a warning to other
would-be seducers. "Were I absent from my home," Young continued,
"I would rejoice to know that I had friends there to protect and guard
the virtue of my household; and I would thank God for such friends."[73]
Between 1868 and 1877, two other men were killed and two wounded
by fathers or relatives of seduced women, although none of these wom-
en was in plural marriage. In each case, the male relatives were either
acquitted of the crime or escaped from the hands of the law. Although
Mormon newspapers continued to disapprove of taking the law into one's
own hands, they considered it just to acquit "a person who kills a heart-
less seducer."[74]

Most cases of seduction were resolved more peaceably, but at the
heart of these cases lay important Mormon values. First, although seduction as a legal concept was hardly unique to nineteenth-century Mormons, it clearly was consonant with their idea of gender differences. In
the Mormon view as stated by church leaders, women could easily be
persuaded; men would influence them for good or ill, either to protect
them or to ruin them.[75]

Second, and more important, these cases illustrate how seriously the
Saints took their sexual mores. Adultery was not simply one of several
behaviors proscribed by the Ten Commandments; it was "one of the greatest crimes any man can commit in this world. It is next to murder."[76]
Sexual sins were so serious precisely because rules surrounding marriage
were so lenient. As George Q. Cannon, a member of the First Presidency
of the church, explained it, "And as for adultery . . . and fornication, there
are no people on the face of the earth that will be damned with a greater
damnation for that sin than we, if we be guilty of it. Why? Because there
is no necessity for it."[77] The barriers to marriage were minimal. The rules
governing divorce were lenient so that remarriage could take place. But
the rules were absolutely rigid that a marriage take place before a couple
assume the sexual rights that the Saints believed belonged only to the
married state.[78]

Sinners were to be not ostracized, however, but brought back into conformity with the religious community's values. Excommunication was a first step in the process, symbolizing that the transgressors had set themselves outside accepted patterns of the community. Sometimes they were required to make a public confession, though at times the acknowledgment was made only to the church court. By confessing the sin and expressing remorse for it, the sinners reaffirmed the values of the community's mores and their wish to conform again to them. For example, in St. George, Brother G. at first affirmed values inconsistent with Mormonism when he refused to answer whether he had had sexual intercourse with his divorced wife. "I never have nor never will do or say one act that will reflect censure on that lady, Jerusha G.," he replied. In a culture concerned with propriety and avoidance of scandal, his answer would have been admired. In Mormon society, however, where adherence to its central values was expected, his answer elicited the warning that he had a month "to set himself right before the brethren in the ward where he belongs" or be excommunicated from the church. He set himself right by making a public apology;[79] that is, he affirmed the community's sexual mores by accepting and conforming to them.

A final step was usually rebaptism. This second baptism represented "the new birth" through which the sinners became "a new creature," cleansed of sin.[80] In short, they again became full members of the community, upholding its values and its practices. The entire process emphasized the seriousness of the transgression for both the sinners and the community while providing a means for repentant sinners to return to their place in the society.

There were thus rules and regulations governing marriage, divorce, and sexual relationships in nineteenth-century Mormondom. Marriages were to take place only between two freely consenting individuals, and while a man could be married to more than one wife simultaneously with permission from the president of the church and his local leaders, a woman could be sealed to only one husband. A first wife's permission was supposed to be sought before her husband married other wives, but she could veto additional marriages only if she had sound and valid reasons. Moreover, men suffered ecclesiastical punishment for marrying plural wives by the civil law while still living with their wives to whom they had been sealed by the church. The church sanctioned only plural marriages it had authorized.

Divorces, however, were permitted on a variety of grounds, including alienation of the couple's feelings for each other, although women were more readily granted divorces than were men. After a divorce, an individual was free to remarry. The form of the divorce could vary—it might be a divorce granted by a civil court, a mutual agreement to separate permanently signed before church officials, or permission to remarry granted by church leaders—but if former spouses recommenced sexual relations after a divorce, they were liable to charges of sexual misconduct before a church court.[81] If a wife committed adultery, her husband was also considered an adulterer if he resumed a sexual relationship with her before she repented and was received again into fellowship in the church. Only properly married couples could engage in sexual intercourse without experiencing church sanctions. Adultery was punished by excommunication, while premarital sex might result in being disfellowshipped, a curtailment of privileges within the church. Coitus was to be confined strictly to married couples. In short, although the rules permitted fairly wide latitude in marriage and divorce, they were narrow and exacting about sexual relationships.

While these mark the broad parameters of the Mormon system, policy and practice within it were not static. Economic, social, and demographic changes modified practice, and competition from a legal system imposed from outside Mormondom necessitated alterations in policy.

When the system changed in the 1840s from a monogamic one controlled by civil law, to protopolygamy in Nauvoo, finally to a polygamic system governed by ecclesiastical rules in Utah, the shift was not smooth, and church regulations took time to develop. As Apostle Amasa M. Lyman acknowledged in 1866 about the introduction of plural marriage, "We obeyed the best we knew how, and, no doubt, made many crooked paths in our ignorance."[82]

One of these was undoubtedly polyandrous marriages, although few in number. Beyond the ethical problems, they had the potential of creating disaffection among the Saints. That was particularly so of Brigham Young's marrying and living with Zina Huntington Jacobs. While this marriage had the consent—albeit reluctant—of Zina's former husband, the new couple's commencing to live together while her first husband was on a mission caused a stir. Almost immediately, some men in Winter Quarters expressed their concern about serving on missions, fearing they would return home to find their wives sealed to someone else.[83]

That there were no more such marriages apparently allayed their fears. Then during the General Conference in 1853 John Taylor reassured the Saints that the sealing ordinance prevented anyone from depriving them of their families in the eternities. In the same conference, Brigham Young declared that faithful men who died before they could be sealed to their wives could have it done by proxy, their sons standing in their stead. That way these devout men would not be deprived of their eternal blessings by "avaricious" men "crawling round" asking widows to be sealed to them.[84] Confirmation that happy marriages between faithful husbands and wives would be sealed for eternity not only alleviated lingering fears but also helped anchor the devotion of ordinary Saints to the church. In the early period, secrecy caused problems because men did not know if the young women they wished to court were already married to someone else.[85] Geographic isolation in Winter Quarters and Utah allowed greater acknowledgment of plural marriages, and the public announcement of plural marriage in 1852 ended what vestiges of secrecy still remained.

By today's standards, another of the "crooked paths" would be consanguineous marriages. Uncle-niece marriages, never common, occurred more frequently in the early Utah period than later, decreasing from a scant 0.16 percent of all marriages from 1847 to 1869 to only 0.06 percent from 1870 to 1889.[86] Also more common in the late 1840s and 1850s than thereafter was the marriage of girls at young ages, particularly as plural wives. Women tended to marry early on the frontier, to be sure, but the average marriage age in Utah reached its nadir during the period when the number of plural marriages was at its peak. In the context of the Mormon reformation—the dearth of food, the arrival of many penurious immigrants, the impassioned preaching, and the millennialist fervor—young women, a few as young as thirteen, heeded the advice of church leaders, parents, and eager suitors to become plural wives. Although these teens at least formally gave their consent to these marriages, their inexperience meant their judgments were, at the very least, uninformed. The demand for divorces in the wake of the many reformation-induced, ill-advised marriages appears to have convinced church leaders that pressure applied during the revivals could impel people to comply at the moment with outward signs of religious conformity but that they could not produce sudden perfection in the Saints. Although leaders continued to encourage plural marriage, it was never with the intensity of the 1856–57 period. Mormon daughters, along with immigrant women, continued to be a source of plural wives, but their average age at marriage rose as the number of plural marriages decreased.

While federal officials had made their presence felt in Mormondom earlier, it was in the 1860s that the federal government began in earnest to pass laws designed to eliminate polygamy. In 1862, the Morrill Anti-Bigamy Act prohibited polygamy, but Mormon juries refused to indict or convict their fellow religionists under that law. The church did appear to comply by permitting only one civil marriage and calling additional marriages sealings.[87] New plural marriages continued to augment the number of the previous ones, supplying husband-providers for indigent immigrants and fatherless females as well as for the widowed and divorced. In addition, young women whose parents lived in polygamy were more likely to enter plural marriage than those raised in monogamous homes, but most daughters of polygamous marriages became and remained monogamous wives. As the number of immigrants decreased and contact with ideas and influences from outside Mormon culture increased, new plural marriages continued to decline. Moreover, as many Mormons coming of age and newly arriving immigrants failed to enter plural marriage, the percentage of those living in plural families diminished.

By the early 1870s, Mormon control of the courts was undermined by Chief Justice James B. McKean. Excluding Mormons from the grand jury, he was able to get indictments against some polygamists, including Brigham Young, George Q. Cannon, and Daniel H. Wells, under an 1852 Utah statute against lascivious cohabitation. The indictments were quashed by a U.S. Supreme Court ruling that juries had to be empaneled according to territorial laws. To resolve problems about the jurisdictions of the courts, Congress passed the Poland Act in 1874. This stripped Mormon-controlled probate courts of jurisdiction over criminal and civil cases and gave it to the territorial district courts, with their federally appointed judges. In the wake of this intensified judicial campaign, Mormons began having all divorces from legal wives granted by civil rather than church courts. The church thus lost some control over divorces.

Federally appointed judges also continued to contest the church's control over marriage. The first conviction for polygamy under the Morrill Act was obtained when the second wife of George Reynolds furnished evidence against him in 1874 to test the law.[88] His conviction was eventually upheld by the U.S. Supreme Court in 1879 in the important *Reynolds* case. Mormons, however, continued to practice plural marriage and solemnize new ones, hoping, according to Joseph F. Smith, that the decision might be reversed if they did not surrender their constitutional rights too easily.[89]

When the Supreme Court issued the *Miles* decision, stating that a wife could not testify against her husband, thus stifling other convictions under the Morrill Act, Congress passed the Edmunds Act in 1882.[90] This act made securing convictions easier by making unlawful cohabitation a misdemeanor and allowing challenges to jurors who professed a belief in polygamy. It further reduced Mormon power by disfranchising all polygamous men and women and prohibiting polygamists from holding public office. The civil power of most Mormon leaders, many of whom had more than one wife, was thus considerably curtailed. The law accomplished its purposes, and over a thousand convictions were obtained under its provisions.

New plural marriages decreased during the 1870s, and this pattern continued through the 1880s, although brief, minor upsurges in the number of new unions occurred. Prosecutions under the Edmunds Act constituted only one of many reasons the majority of Saints remained monogamous. The law, however, was a significant challenge to the many already existing plural marriages. Polygamists were caught in the conflict between their conviction that their covenants to their wives were sacred and their desire to avoid prosecution and prison. Nevertheless, some followed their own counsel rather than the church's and avoided imprisonment by swearing to abide by the law in the future.

Much of the remaining power the church had over marriage was swept away by the Edmunds-Tucker Act in 1887. No marriage was to take place unless those involved signed a certificate, which was to be filed as a public record, and consanguineous marriages closer than first cousins were made punishable by imprisonment. Dower was reinstated, thus threatening plural wives' inheritance, and Mormons' power to mitigate the effect of this was undercut by the stipulation that judges of probate courts were to be appointed by the president of the United States, with the advice and consent of the Senate.

Change occurred not just for polygamists but also for those marrying monogamously, although they were much less aware of it. After the Edmunds-Tucker Act of 1887, the state, not the church, regulated marriage. This change may have seemed trivial to couples, because they still could be sealed in the time-honored way, but the change was significant. The civil courts henceforth decided what the sealing ceremony meant. In 1902, the Utah Supreme Court held that "the revelation concerning celestial marriages constitutes the only law on the subject of marriage in the Mormon Church; that such law provides but one form of marriage, the same being for time as well as for eternity."[91] No longer could a man marry a wife for eternity only, for the state considered all the church's marriages as effective in this life, with all the property rights inherent in marriage. In addition, the court stated that "the sealing ceremony is a marriage ceremony, which is good at common law; the part referring to eternity, as we have seen, being regarded as simply surplusage."[92] The court thus validated all monogamous marriages the clergy of church had performed. But because consent was the essence of marriage under common law, the court regarded as irrelevant that part of the ceremony relating to eternity, so important to Mormons.

Within sixty years of Utah's settlement, both Utah and its marriage system had been transformed. As the state wrested the power to regulate both marriage and divorce from church control, however, the strict rules concerning sexual behavior remained in place, while increasingly rigid, state-enforced rules governing marriage and divorce replaced lenient ones. By the end of the century, the church was left with authority only to determine whose marriages might be for eternity, whose sealings for eternity might be canceled, and, of course, who would be put under church sanctions for sexual transgressions. That the system could change so greatly while the rise in prenuptial pregnancies and illegitimate births was so moderate may be attributed to the success Mormons had in inculcating the "internal control" that was the central feature of Victorian morality.[93]

The church thus regulated its marriage system throughout much of the nineteenth century: plural marriage did not flourish in a society characterized by a high degree of anomie. But there was a rival system, one enforced by the federal government that had the power not only to punish individual violators of that competing system but also to strike at the very foundations of the church itself. Stripping the church of its control over marriage, Congress through the Edmunds-Tucker Act also dissolved the legal existence of the church and provided for confiscation of all the church's assets in excess of $50,000. With its religious purposes in jeopardy, church leaders sought a way to continue the practice of plural marriage and to carry out its mission of providing salvation for the living and the dead. The church eventually had to sacrifice plural marriage to fulfill that essential mission, but on the convoluted path before reaching that decision, the old system of regulations broke down. It was the period during the shift from the polygamic system to a monogamous one, not when plural marriage was open and acknowledged, that was actually characterized by anomie.

Convinced that plural marriage was divinely ordained, church leaders gave ground slowly and only when no alternative could be found. In 1887 and again in 1888, leaders were counseled to discontinue publicly preaching about plural marriage, although a few, probably from conviction and habit, still did so. In October 1889, President Wilford Woodruff told the press that he had approved no new plural marriages since becoming head of the church. When these measures did not prevent the draconian features of the Edmunds-Tucker Act from being carried out, Woodruff, feeling compelled as well as inspired, issued the ambiguous Manifesto, stating that since the laws prohibiting polygamy had been found constitutional, he would submit to those laws and use his influence with other Saints to do likewise. That announcement relieved some pressure, but in October 1891, while trying to get the government to return church property, he felt he had to go further. He testified in court that the Manifesto applied to polygamists' continuing cohabitation with their wives as well as to new plural marriages anywhere in the world. Additional statements that the church was no longer sanctioning plural marriages were issued at various intervals. More strident than the original Manifesto, the Second Manifesto of 1904 declared that all who entered or performed new plural marriages would be liable to excommunication, and a 1910 letter to stake presidents directed them to enforce that policy. These were followed by still other statements reinforcing the church's position that new polygamous unions were prohibited.[94]

The repeated statements that new plural marriages were no longer sanctioned are an indication of how loathe some were to give up the principle. New plural marriages continued to be contracted after the 1890 Manifesto, but the secrecy surrounding many of these makes it unclear just how much regulation the church maintained. Although most who entered plural marriage before 1898 probably received permission from a general authority of the church, it was often indirect, such as in a form letter "worded so that their real intent would have been unclear to a stranger." When Lorenzo Snow became the president and said that he authorized no new plural marriages, couples still continued to enter polygamous relationships through those local leaders who had been given blanket authority in Mexico, through apostles, or through counselors in the First Presidency. One woman receiving permission from Counselor Joseph F. Smith said the leader gave his approval by speaking in parables. Since the approval was indirect, individuals bore responsibility for entering plural marriage.[95]

Regulations for polygamous marriages became more diffuse, especially when some general authorities were cognizant of the new marriages and others were not. Apostle Matthias F. Cowley, who performed a number of the new marriages, said he had been directed not to divulge to other apostles that he had the authority to solemnize plural marriages.[96] Delegation of such authority further eroded the church's ability to regulate such unions, as did divisions among the general authorities about whether new marriages were countenanced. Public denials that the church had sanctioned these marriages even though evidence abounded that they had taken place also made obstructing unauthorized marriages difficult.

Even more difficult for the church was the question of polygamists' continued cohabitation with the wives they had married before the Manifesto. As late as April 1891, George Q. Cannon hoped that the Manifesto's sacrifice of new marriages would suffice and that "some favorable action will be taken in regard to existing relations."[97] After the church president felt compelled to state that the Manifesto covered continuing cohabitation as well, many, including the majority of the apostles, continued to live with and have children by their wives. Although leaders counseled that men should financially support their wives and children, individuals made their own decisions about whether to continue cohabiting.[98]

Decentralizing authority to approve and solemnize plural unions as well as reliance on individuals to make their own decisions about additional marriages and continuing cohabitation severely undermined the church's regulation of marriage. Because of their beliefs in the principle and the persecution Mormons had endured to maintain it, attempts to preserve it were perhaps to be expected, but they did result in anomie. An unintended consequence, the climate of anomie was conducive to the formation and growth of so-called fundamentalist groups that claimed a mantle of righteousness for adhering to the old ways.

Estimates of those in families practicing polygamy at the end of the twentieth century vary from 20,000 to 100,000, but the most generally accepted figures are 30,000 to 35,000 in the United States. The largest group, the Fundamentalist Church based mainly in Colorado City/Hildale on the Utah-Arizona border, has 8,000 to 12,000 members. The Fundamentalist Church, along with the Apostolic United Brethren centered just south of Salt Lake City, claim that in 1886 John Taylor gave their founders not only the authority but also the injunction to continue to perform plural marriages and to live the principle. Some other groups avow that their authority is of more recent divine origin. Among these are the True and Living Church founded in 1994 in Manti and the Latter-day Church of Christ, often called the Kingston clan, centered along the Wasatch Front in Utah but with holdings in other western states. Reputedly the most affluent and secretive of the modern-day polygamous groups, the Kingston clan emphasizes the purity of the Kingston blood line, and hence men frequently marry their half-sisters and nieces. But many polygamists are independents or in unorganized groups of families.[99]

Although it is difficult to generalize because of the diversity of the groups practicing polygamy, there appear to be some significant differences between polygamists today and those in the nineteenth century. Even though some polygamists today are wealthy and can comfortably afford to support their large families, many depend on welfare payments and food stamps to support their numerous progeny. In 1998, the *Salt Lake Tribune* reported that Colorado City/Hildale, the home of about 5,000 members of the Fundamentalist Church, ranked among the top ten towns with a population greater than 2,000 in the Intermountain West dependent on Medicaid, which furnishes medical care for the poor, and the WIC (Women, Infants, and Children) program, which provides food for indigent women and their children. In addition, a third of the town's residents feed their families with the help of U.S. Department of Agriculture food stamps. In 1999, Utah's Office of Recovery Service sued the polygamist Thomas Green to recoup $74,512 in welfare payments paid to support eighteen of his children.[100] Dependence on government welfare turns one important purpose of nineteenth-century polygamy on its head: whereas early Mormons helped support disadvantaged women through plural marriage, many today need help from the government to support their large families.

Early Saints entered plural marriage for religious reasons, just as today's polygamists do. Beyond that, daughters of polygamists now, as in early Utah, are encouraged to become plural wives, but among some modern groups, such as the Fundamentalist Church and the Kingston group, marriages are often arranged by the leaders or parents.[101] In the nineteenth century, church leaders suggested polygamists marry certain women, but they were usually mature women, not teenagers. Moreover, most polygamists' daughters were monogamous then.

The majority of plural wives in pioneer days were found among the fatherless, the widowed, and the divorced, groups with compelling economic reasons to marry in a male-dominated frontier society. Although no comparable studies have been done on modern polygamists, Janet Bennion, who studied women in the Apostolic United Brethren, concluded that "many people, primarily female converts, . . . entered the group for the sole reason of finding economic stability and marriage."[102] It appears economic reasons have influenced both eras. In pioneer Utah, however, marriage was one of the best among the few available options, whereas in the twentieth century, economic opportunities for women greatly expanded.

Whether all contemporary polygamous groups allow divorce is unclear, but among some that do, the rate is higher than that in the territorial period. In a group in Pinedale, Montana, 35 percent divorce, somewhat lower than the nearly 50 percent rate in the United States generally, but higher than the less than 20 percent for Manti polygamous marriages. Another study of modern polygamists showed that half of polygamous men divorce, while only a third of nineteenth-century Manti polygamists did so.[103] Greater social acceptance of divorce today is undoubtedly one reason for the higher rate among contemporary polygamists. Expanded opportunities for women in modern industrialized society constitute another.

In the mid-1850s, the average age at which women first married was sixteen, but the age rose thereafter as the number of plural marriages declined. This pattern is remarkably similar to the one in Colorado City/Hildale a century later. In the 1950s, the average age at marriage among fundamentalist women was sixteen, but as the local public school system improved, the average rose to nineteen by 1988.[104] It is unclear whether the age has risen among other groups. The young woman who ran away from the marriage with her uncle in the Kingston clan in 1998 was sixteen, and in 2000 Thomas Green was charged with rape for allegedly fathering a child with a thirteen-year-old, although he married her, with her parents' consent, when she was fourteen.[105]

This illuminates what is probably the most important difference between nineteenth-century and modern-day polygamy: the social and legal climate in which it is practiced. In the Victorian era, social mores led to legislation to punish adults for behavior that openly flouted those mores. Many polygamists and a few plural wives were imprisoned, and more were fined for persisting in openly living together and calling these relationships marriages. Modern society, however, tolerates, at least legally, a wide variety of sexual practices among consenting adults. But, as a legacy from the Progressive Era, the state is willing to interfere in families to protect what it considers the best interest of the children. After a 1953 government raid on the town now called Colorado City/Hildale, polygamous men were given a year's probation dependent on good behavior. Children, however, were taken away from their families. In 1955, the Utah Supreme Court ruled that the juvenile court had the right to deprive a polygamous couple of its children unless the father stopped living with the mother: "[T]he practice of polygamy and unlawful cohabitation should be weeded out and . . . children should not be subjected to its evil influence and environment."[106] By the 1990s, the legal system generally ignored polygamous marriages unless teenage girls were involved, as in the Kingston and Green cases.[107] Over the twentieth century, the emphasis has changed from punishing adults for living in plural marriage to punishing adults who abuse or marry minors.

Part of the reason some continue to become plural wives at such young ages is the lack of regulation, either by the state, which has difficulty prosecuting such cases, or by the polygamists themselves, especially among secretive groups, independents, and newly formed groups. Independents, those belonging to no specific religious organization, are not regulated by the state or by a social group larger than the family, while the lack of regulation among new groups is perhaps a result of each experiencing its own liminal period.

Such seems to be the case with the True and Living Church (TLC) in Manti. Members talked of the "magnificent and wonderful experiences we had" in the meetings, indicative of the intense comradery of the liminal period. But it was clear new rules for marriage were still developing. One man claimed God had revealed to him that "all marriages were wrong" because in choosing their mates, couples in the church had not been guided by the spirit. The couples should separate, he said, so that God could mate them with more satisfactory companions. When couples split up, however, "it created a lot of bad feelings."[108]

Perhaps to introduce some regulation, Jim Harmston, the church's leader, declared in a May 1994 council meeting that about half the polygamists were sleeping with all their wives at once but that God had revealed to him that the practice was abominable and should cease immediately. Denying that they had engaged in such behavior, the polygamists present told Harmston "to keep his revelations to himself." Some left the church, expressing concern about the group's trying to prescribe behavior for anyone's bedroom. Such resistance to authority makes establishing regulations difficult, if not impossible. The TLC's policy regarding the marital age for young women—if there is one—is not clear, but Harmston has taken a sixteen-year-old bride as a plural wife.[109] Each group creates anew its regulations for polygamous marriages, a process that takes time but leaves a vacuum in which abuses can and often do occur.

These dissenting polygamous groups form as a protest against adaptations to the changing modern world made by the Church of Jesus Christ of Latter-day Saints.[110] Claiming to be the true heirs of the nineteenth-century church, groups such as the TLC reestablish the practice of polygamy. They seek to be—to rework Jan Shipps's phrase—a "latter-day recapitulation" of early Mormonism.[111] But their recapitulation is incomplete: in attempting to recover some practices from the past, they jettison or ignore others. The Fundamentalist Church, for example, does not emphasize temple ordinances for the dead, and most groups recruit new members but do not focus on missionary work. Like others in such groups, members of the TLC see themselves as the elect. By 1999, they no longer sent out missionaries, and they removed everything from their Web site except one official pronouncement. Their mission, they claim, is to gather the elect together; they "feel no obligation to go to 'all the world' since the elect is a remnant and not a majority of the earth's inhabitants."[112]

In contrast, the Church of Jesus Christ of Latter-day Saints has put preaching the gospel and performing temple ordinances for both the living and the dead at the center of its mission. The imminent confiscation of the LDS temples precipitated the announcement of the Woodruff Manifesto. "Which is the wisest course," President Woodruff later asked, "to continue to attempt to practice plural marriage, with the laws of the nation against it . . . at the cost of the confiscation and loss of all the Temples, and the stopping of all the ordinances therein, both for the living and the dead . . . ?"[113] Although missionary work was not mentioned as a reason for discontinuing plural marriage, that effort undoubtedly would have been impeded by persisting in the principle. From 1885 to 1890, when the Manifesto was announced, the church experienced its slowest growth rate of any five-year period from 1860 through 1915.[114]

Moreover, the church had never advocated the practice of plural marriage outside of Mormon strongholds. As the nineteenth century waned, the monogamous family proved more suitable for Utah Saints seeking economic opportunities outside Mormon communities as well as for converts remaining in their homelands. In the Victorian middle-class nuclear family, the church found a family form conducive to social acceptance, increased geographic mobility of its members, and the inculcation of Mormon doctrines and practices. As communities became more diverse and secular, the Mormon home increasingly became a refuge from the outside world, and women were exalted as angel-mothers who taught their children religious precepts and disciplined wayward conduct.[115] The Saints successfully adapted the American nineteenth-century family ideal to their own uses, although the church increasingly faces the challenge of how to incorporate within that ideal growing numbers of single, divorced, and widowed men and women as well as less-than-wealthy women who do not fit the stay-at-home model. In general, however, the ideal of eternal family relationships combined with the adapted Victorian family form has proven remarkably successful in retaining members and making new converts. While consistently emphasizing the eternal nature of marriage sealings since the 1840s, the church has adapted both plural marriage and Victorian middle-class monogamy to changing needs.

APPENDIX:
DESCRIPTION OF DEMOGRAPHIC DATA

No list of those who entered plural marriage is currently available to scholars, and no single source of data exists that can substitute for this deficiency. The Manti data set, which includes all residents of Manti from its settlement in 1849 to 1910, and the subset, which includes all polygamists living in Manti and all their first and plural wives, are based on data gathered from a variety of sources. Individuals were linked across these records to compile as complete a marital history for each as possible.

The following example illustrates how this was done. A family group record from the Patrons Section of the Family History Library in Salt Lake City indicated that Henning Madsen had married Ingalina Johnsen and Katrine Larsen but gave no dates for their marriages. According to the *International Genealogical Index®* (currently the source is Henning Madsen–Ane Catharine Elizabeth Bisheff, 1876, North America, Marriage Search, *Ordinance Index*, CD-ROM, Main File), Madsen married Ingalina on May 2, 1870, and Ane Catharine Elizabeth Bisheff (*sic*) on January 24, 1876. The 1880 Manti manuscript census showed "Engerline Madsen" as head of her household, living with her son from a previous marriage, and listed her as married (1880 U.S. Census, Manti, Sanpete County, Utah, Population Schedule, Enumeration District 65, 25, [stamped 419A], Hemming Madsen household; Niels Pedersen Ipson Family Group Record, Patrons Section, Family History Library, Salt Lake City, Utah). In addition, the Sanpete County Probate Court Record (Book A, 1866–84, 361–62) showed that "Inger Lena" Madsen and Henning Madsen were granted a divorce on September 4, 1883. The 1880 Manti census also listed Henning Madsen as head of household; Christina, age thirty-two, as his wife; and the children, Louisa, thirteen; Maria, ten; Willie, three; and Christian, nineteen (1880 U.S. Census, Manti, Sanpete County, Utah, Population Schedule, 419A). Henning Madsen was clearly a polygamist with two wives from 1876 to 1883.

Using the name Ane Catharine Elizabeth Bisheff from the *International Genealogical Index*, I was able to locate Madsen's plural wife under the name Bischoff in the "Endowment House Record" (vol. H, 306), which listed her as having been born on November 2, 1846, in Viborg, Denmark, to Christian Bischoff and Maria Rasmussen. Although Madsen died in 1890, Ane was in the 1900 census. She was listed as Hannah Marker, born in Denmark in November 1845 and married. In her household were William Madsen, son, born November 1877 (Willie, age three, in 1880 census); Rosetta Madsen, daughter, born May 1883 (*sic*); and Clifford Marker, son, born August 1892 (1900 U.S. Census, Manti, Sanpete County, Utah, Population Schedule, Enumeration District 125, 12 [stamped 140D], Hannah Marker household). Church membership records confirmed that Rosetta Caroline Madsen, born May 11, 1884, was the daughter of Henning Madsen and Ann C. E. Bischoff (Church of Jesus Christ of Latter-day Saints, Manti North Ward, "Record of Members," 9, Family History Library, Salt Lake City, Utah). The cemetery record indicated that Anna C. Marker was born on November 2, 1847, and that she was buried in the same block and lot as Henning Madsen and their daughter (Louisa C. Tatton, "Cemetery Records, Manti, Sanpete County, Utah," 1936, copied from sexton records, typed by the Genealogical Society of Utah, 86, 89, Family History Library, Salt Lake City, Utah).

The Sanpete County Marriage License Records (microfilm reel 1, 1888–94) showed that on August 22, 1889, Peter J. Marker, age fifty-one, married Katrine Madsen, age forty-four (and thus born about 1845). From the information in the "Endowment House Record" that Ane Bischoff's mother was Maria Rasmussen, I was able to link Ane to her mother, Johanna Maria Rasmussen, a resident of Manti, who married Azariah Smith in 1871 (Azariah Smith Family Group Record, Patrons Section, Family History Library, Salt Lake City, Utah). Fortunately, Smith kept a journal in which he noted that Maria's daughter Anne Catherine Elizabeth was married to N. C. Larsen and that in 1874 she immigrated to Utah, expecting her husband to join her the next year. He also recorded that Catherine was sealed to "Maasson" in 1875 and that in 1889 she had left him and married Peter Marker (Azariah Smith, "Journal," January 27, 1872, December 25, 1874, January 6, 1875, and September 1, 1889, Special Collections, Harold B. Lee Library, Brigham Young University).

This journal not only confirmed previous links between records but also provided the name Larsen so that I could find Ane on the Crossing the Ocean Index. She was listed as Ane Larsen, age twenty-nine, immigrating with Louise K., age seven (see Louisa, age thirteen, in the 1880 census), and Johanne M., age four (see Maria, age ten, in the 1880 census), arriving in Utah on September 23, 1874. This corrected the erroneous immigration date, 1873, which was in the 1900 census. Although the birth year varied slightly among the records—1845, 1846, and 1847—other information was sufficient to confirm that records using different names referred to the same woman. This kind of meticulous linking of records provided the data for the Manti data set.

The following are the principal sources used to collect information on individuals in the data set:

1. U.S. Census, Population Schedule, Manti, Utah, 1850, 1860, 1870, 1880, 1900, and 1910, National Archives Microfilm Service. The manuscript censuses provided the core list of those living in Manti. In addition, the censuses yielded other valuable information, including wealth information for 1850, 1860, and 1870, ages of plural wives not found elsewhere, immigration dates, and clues about previous marriages when children in the household had different surnames.

Errors and misspelling of names made linking across these census years difficult at times. The 1860 census was particularly prone to problems.¹ For example, Isaac Herring was listed as Isaac H. Rind, Emeline Cox as Emeline Marble, and Lora Ann Brown as Lorenzo Brown, male. The 1900 census gave the age and birth year of each individual, but for many individuals the birth date was off by one year. Linking by hand, however, overcame these and other problems, so almost all names in the censuses were identified and linked if they remained in Manti.

Because many of the people in the data set did not live their entire lives in Manti and a few never lived there, I also used the census population schedules for Utah (all years) and Iowa (1850). The Utah 1850, 1860, 1870 censuses and the Iowa 1850 census are indexed, and the 1880 census has a Soundex, although it includes only those households with children age ten and under. In addition, a listing of families in the 1880 census, alphabetized by name of the head of household, is available for Utah. The 1856 Utah Territorial Census occasionally provided information about residents in Manti at that time, but it exaggerated the number of people in Utah, is riddled by errors even in recognizable names, and contains no other information besides name and gender.²

2. Church of Jesus Christ of Latter-day Saints, "Record of Members," Manti Ward ([1849]–1877), Manti North Ward (1877–1941), and Manti South Ward (1877–1941), microfilm, 3 reels, Family History Library, Salt Lake City, Utah.³ The records for 1877–1941 listed members in family groups, provided birth dates and birth places, gave parents' names, and occasionally supplied marriage dates and information about excommunications. These records were, however, subject to the efficiency and competency of the clerks keeping them and were initially less complete than they later became. Nevertheless, because most residents were Mormons, these records were a valuable resource.⁴

The record from the early period did not provide lists of members but did give dates of births, marriages, rebaptisms, and occasionally information on divorces.

3. Family Group Records: Patrons Section, Archives Section, and *Ancestral File* (CD-ROM, © data as of January 5, 1998), Family History Library, Salt Lake City, Utah. These family group records contain names, birth dates, birth places, marriage dates, and death dates for the husband, wife, and their children. They also include the parents' names of the husband and wife as well as the names of other spouses each may have had. Each couple has a separate record, so that a man with six wives should have six family group records.⁵

The family group records for each married couple in the core list of Manti residents were photocopied from the Patrons Section, supplemented by records from the Archives Section and the *Ancestral File*, which makes the family group records accessible by computer.

The quality of the data on the family group records is uneven but overall is good. Many records are clearly based on extensive genealogical research, and often those submitting the records had family records inaccessible to scholars. However, dates are sometimes off by one number, indicating typographical errors.

More serious were inaccurate entries and omissions. One family group record erroneously listed the wife's cousin as the wife. In addition, of the 106 family group records in the subset that I was able to check against other records, 10.4 percent (N = 11) listed the wrong number of children.[6] Seven (6.6 percent) were missing one or more children, and four (3.8 percent) attributed children to the couple when either the father or the mother was not the biological parent. One purpose of the family group records is to have children sealed to parents, and children sometimes are sealed to people who are not their biological parents. Nevertheless, such children generally are clearly indicated in these records. Of the four cases in which children were misattributed to a couple, two were children sealed to a man not their biological father, but nothing in the records indicated that. In the other two cases, children of one wife were attributed to another wife of the same man.[7]

Because the listing of other spouses for the husband and wife is not essential to the central purpose of the family group records, these lists were even more prone to error. Thirty (19.3 percent) of the husbands' family group records in the subset gave the wrong number of wives, twenty (12.9 percent) omitting one or more plural wives' names. Such omissions, in combination with missing family groups records, made it difficult to determine if a man was in a plural marriage. Moreover, 5 percent of polygamists had no family group records in the archives. From the family group records alone, it would have been impossible to tell whether 17.9 percent of the data set (N = 28) were in a plural marriage. It was also often difficult to determine whether men whose records listed more than one wife had remarried or entered a plural marriage; their marital histories had to be reconstructed to determine if they belonged in the plural marriage subset.

4. Sexton Records, Manti City Cemetery, early years to 1966, microfilm of the original at the Ogden Pioneer Tabernacle, 2 reels, Family History Library, Salt Lake City, Utah.[8] By using these records, I was able to check the accuracy of other sources and reconstitute some families for whom family groups records were not available.

5. Marriage License Records, Sanpete County, Utah, 1888–1919, microfilm of records at the Sanpete County Courthouse, Manti, Utah, 5 reels, Family History Library, Salt Lake City, Utah. Until 1888, there were no laws requiring records of marriages in Utah; hence, no complete record exists before that date. Some marriage dates, however, may be found in the Justice of the Peace Court Records.[9]

6.Church of Jesus Christ of Latter-day Saints, *International Genealogical Index* (microfiche and without ordinance dates at <www.FamilySearch.org>) and *Ordinance Index*, CD-ROM, FamilySearch®, Family History Library, Salt Lake City, Utah. When this study was begun, the *International Genealogical Index* was a set of microfiche containing the birth, christening, and/or marriage dates of over 118 million deceased persons. These are organized by surname within each country or subdivision of the country. The *International Genealogical Index* is updated and reissued every four years. As of 2001, the *International Genealogical Index* and the *Ordinance Index* can be found at the Family History Library in Salt Lake City and at all family history centers of the Church of Jesus Christ of Latter-day Saints throughout the world. The current *International Genealogical Index*, which lists no temple ordinance dates, can be accessed at <www.FamilySearch.org>. This study relied primarily on the 1984 version, although the 1988 *International Genealogical Index* and the *Ordinance Index* (data to February 1997) were checked for information not found in the earlier version.

The *International Genealogical Index* provided marriage dates of some marriages that took place in Europe, names of spouses and children, and clues about the status of plural wives' fathers. The most important data it provided, however, were sealing dates, which have been extracted from the Endowment House and temple records. At present, the original sealing records for living couples are not available to scholars; thus, family group records and the *International Genealogical Index* (and its successor, the *Ordinance Index*) are the most reliable sources in which sealing dates may readily be found. Because the sealing date was synonymous with the marriage date for many plural marriages, this was an essential source not only for sealing dates but also for names of spouses omitted from family group records. Not all sealings are listed in the *International Genealogical Index*, however; nor is sufficient information about individuals given to distinguish those with the same name from each other. It therefore does not entirely substitute for the lack of the original records.

7. Church of Jesus Christ of Latter-day Saints, "Endowment House Record," microfilm of the original, 7 reels, Family History Library, Salt Lake City, Utah. One rite Mormons consider important is the endowment. With a few exceptions, it can take place only in buildings consecrated for that purpose, usually temples, but in the nineteenth century it also took place in the Endowment House. All individuals receiving the endowment had their names recorded, along with their birth date, place of birth, baptism date, and parents' names. Because all men and most women after 1860 entering plural marriage received their endowments (although not necessarily before entering plural marriage) and because a woman's sealing date was often the same as her endowment date, this record provided a convenient source of information about those who had no family group records.

Unfortunately, volume A, which includes those who received their endowments in Utah before 1855, is currently restricted to Latter-day Saints with temple recommends for genealogical purposes only. All temple records are also restricted, so that no one who received her endowments in the St. George Temple after it was dedicated in 1877, the Logan Temple after 1884, or the Manti Temple after 1888 can be found this way. The exception to this is the Nauvoo Temple Record (FHL), a typescript of which gives the names, birth dates, and birth places of those receiving endowments in Nauvoo from December 1845 through February 1846.

8. Assessment Roll Records, 1873–90, Sanpete County, Utah, microfilm of the original, 3 reels, Family History Library, Salt Lake City, Utah; and Assessment Roll Records, 1900, Basement Archives, Sanpete County Courthouse, Manti, Utah, 2 vols. Wealth information on individuals in Manti was found in the 1850, 1860, and 1870 censuses. For 1880, 1890, and 1900, that

information was gathered from the tax assessment rolls. For 1880 and 1890, those assessed had a single entry giving the total assessment, which was not the case later.

9. Sanpete County, Utah, Probate Court, "Minutes, 1852–1866," Book 1, "Probate Record, including Minutes, 1866–1884," Book A, and "Probate Record, 1884–1890," Book B, microfilm of manuscripts at the Sanpete Country Courthouse, 4 reels; Utah Territory, First District Court Records, "Minutes, 1880–1895," microfilm of manuscripts in Utah County Courthouse, Provo, Utah, 2 reels; and Utah State, Seventh District Court, "Judgment Record, 1896–1910," microfilm of the original at Sanpete County Courthouse, Manti, Utah, 1 reel, all in the Family History Library, Salt Lake City, Utah. Until 1885, civil divorces were usually granted by the county probate courts. From 1885 to 1895, divorces could be granted only by the territorial courts, but after statehood in 1896, divorces were granted in Sanpete County by the district court. The Territorial First District Court Records also include the minutes of prosecutions against polygamists for unlawful cohabitation and adultery.

10. Utah Immigration Card Index [Crossing the Plains Index], 1847–68, microfilm of typed card file, 3 reels; European Emigration Card Index [Crossing the Ocean Index], 1849–1925, microfilm of typed card file, 9 reels; and Scandinavian Emigration Records, 1854–1890, microfilm of the original, 1 reel, all in Family History Library, Salt Lake City, Utah. The alphabetized indexes were convenient for finding the dates of those immigrating to Utah as well as the names of those with whom a person immigrated. They are incomplete, however, especially for the early years and include only those who immigrated in church-sponsored groups. The Scandinavian Emigration Records provide more information, such as age, occupation, and occasionally marital status, but they are not indexed and the Crossing the Ocean Index does not completely make up for this deficiency. Data on emigration from Europe can now be found in the Church of Jesus Christ of Latter-day Saints, *Family History Resource File: Mormon Immigration Index* (N.p.: Intellectual Reserve, 2000), CD-ROM.

11. Early Church Information File, 1830–1920, microfilm of a card file, 74 reels, Family History Library, Salt Lake City, Utah. Although this file does not include all members of the church before 1920 and the amount of information about each person varies, it did provide some information about birth and death dates, names of children, and people's location in Utah.

12. Frank Esshom, *Pioneers and Prominent Men of Utah, Comprising Photographs, Genealogies, Biographies: The Early History of the Church of Jesus Christ of Latter-day Saints* (Salt Lake City: Pioneers Book, 1913). Each entry in the book includes genealogical information and short biographies. It is a convenient place to find data on families in Utah in the nineteenth century, but it is also incomplete—those who have entries paid a fee—and sometimes inaccurate.[10] Of the 155 polygamists in the Manti subset, only 51 (33 percent) had individual entries, and only 49 percent of them had the correct number of wives listed (but not necessarily the correct number of children). Eighteen of those who had entries (35 percent) were listed with one wife

only, even though they were in a plural marriage. In addition to men who had individual entries, six men in the subset were listed in their fathers' entries as children. Five of these six were listed with only one wife, while the sixth was listed with only two of his three wives.

13. W. H. Lever, *History of Sanpete and Emery Counties, Utah: With Sketches of Cities, Towns, and Villages, Chronology of Important Events, Records of Indian Wars, Portraits of Prominent Persons, and Biographies of Representative Citizens* (Ogden, Utah: W. H. Lever, 1898). This source provides biographical information and some genealogical data for those living in Manti in the 1890s. It is less complete and only slightly more accurate than Esshom's work. Only 34 men in the Manti subset had separate listings, and 47 percent of the listings contained errors. Nine percent of the 34 listed no wives when they were in fact polygamists, 3 percent listed too few wives, and 35 percent had only one wife listed or were listed as remarried.[11]

14. Susan Ward Easton Black, comp., *Membership of the Church of Jesus Christ of Latter-day Saints, 1830–1848*, 50 vols. (Provo, Utah: Religious Studies Center, Brigham Young University, 1984–88). Based on numerous published and original sources, this work brings together a great deal of information about individuals who were baptized into the church before 1848. Entries may include not only most of the information in the family group records but also information from censuses, church membership records, biographies, temple records, and the Temple Index Bureau (the last of which is not usually available to scholars). This provided a convenient source of information about the families of those in the data set who resided outside of Manti. This work, however, does not include every person baptized by 1848 and does not provide much genealogical information beyond that included in family group records.

15. M. F. Farnsworth, "History of Manti," 1936, typescript typed by the Genealogical Society of Utah, Family History Library, Salt Lake City, Utah. This history provides not only genealogical information but also lists of those who held important civic and church positions. The historical account of the town supplied additional names of Manti residents.

16. Andrew Jenson, *Latter-day Saint Biographical Encyclopedia*, 4 vols. (Salt Lake City: Andrew Jenson History Company, 1901; reprint, Salt Lake City: Western Epics, 1971). Although this work supplies little genealogical information, it includes biographical sketches of several of those in the Manti data set.

17. Individual journals, autobiographies, and published histories. Several of the people in the data set left some account of their lives. The most important of these, not only for what they told about their own lives but also for what they revealed about other people in Manti, were J. C. A. Weibye, "Diaries," microfilm of the manuscript, LDS Church Archives, Salt Lake City; and Azariah Smith, "Journal," photocopy of the original, Special Collections, Harold B. Lee Library, Brigham Young University, Provo Utah.

NOTES

Abbreviations

AF	Church of Jesus Christ of Latter-day Saints, *Ancestral File*™ (CD-ROM), © data as of January 5, 1998, Family History Library, Salt Lake City, Utah.
BYU	Harold B. Lee Library, Brigham Young University, Provo, Utah.
CHC	B. H. Roberts, *A Comprehensive History of the Church of Jesus Christ of Latter-day Saints,* 6 vols. (Salt Lake City: Church of Jesus Christ of Latter-day Saints, 1930).
COI	European Emigration Card Index [Crossing the Ocean Index], 1849–1925, microfilm of typed card file, 9 reels, Family History Library, Salt Lake City, Utah.
CPI	Utah Immigration Card Index, [Crossing the Plains Index], 1847–68, microfilm of typed card file, 3 reels, Family History Library, Salt Lake City, Utah.
FHL	Family History Library, Salt Lake City, Utah.
History of the Church	Joseph Smith, *History of the Church of Jesus Christ of Latter-day Saints,* 2d ed. rev., ed. B. H. Roberts (Salt Lake City: Deseret Book, 1955).
JD	*Journal of Discourses,* 26 vols. (London: Latter-day Saints' Book Depot, 1854–86).
LDS Church Archives	Historical Department, Church of Jesus Christ of Latter-day Saints, Salt Lake City, Utah.
OI	Church of Jesus Christ of Latter-day Saints, *Ordinance Index*™ (CD-ROM), Main File, © data to March 1993, Addendum, © data to February 1997, FHL.

Introduction

1. Allan Kent Powell, ed., *Utah History Encyclopedia* (Salt Lake City: University of Utah Press, 1994), 436; Gary B. Peterson and Lowell C. Bennion, *Sanpete Scenes: A Guide to Utah's Heart* (Eureka, Utah: Basin Plateau, 1987), 8 (quote);

Albert C. T. Antrei and Allen D. Roberts, *A History of Sanpete County* (Salt Lake City: Utah State Historical Society and Sanpete County Commission, 1999), 280.

2. Antrei and Roberts, *History of Sanpete County*, 285; Chris Jorgensen, "Ex-Mormons Found New Faith, Preach Polygamy and Doom," *Salt Lake Tribune*, August 20, 1994, D1; "Testimony of the Prophet James D. Harmston," [1996], CD-ROM of TLC Web site, in possession of author.

3. John W. Pratt, "Plural Marriage in the True and Living Church of Jesus Christ of Saints of the Last Days (TLC)," March 5, 1999, CD-ROM of TLC Web site.

4. Antrei and Roberts, *History of Sanpete County*, 284; Dan Egan, "Jesus Is a No-Show, So Trio Sues Sect," *Salt Lake Tribune*, April 9, 1998, B2; "3 Sue Church over Lost Possessions," *Deseret News*, April 11, 1998, E2; Dan Egan, "Hex, Wives and Videotape," *Salt Lake Tribune*, April 26, 1998, B1 (quote).

5. Florence Williams, "A House, 10 Wives: Polygamy in Suburbia," *New York Times*, December 11, 1997, B1; "How Can the TLC Believe and Live Plural Marriage When It Is against the Law?" n.d., CD-ROM of TLC Web site (quote).

6. G. Robina Quale, *A History of Marriage Systems* (New York: Greenwood, 1988), 1.

7. Gerald L. Soliday, Tamara K. Hareven, Richard T. Vann, and Robert Wheaton, eds., *History of the Family and Kinship: A Select International Bibliography* (Millwood, N.Y.: Kraus International Publications, 1980); Gail Schlachter, ed., *American Family History: A Historical Bibliography* (Santa Barbara, Calif.: ABC-Clio Information Services, 1984); James Wallace Milden, *The Family in Past Time: A Guide to the Literature* (New York: Garland, 1977).

8. Gerald F. Moran and Maris A. Vinovskis, "The Puritan Family and Religion: A Critical Reappraisal," *William and Mary Quarterly*, 3d ser., 39 (January 1982): 49, 30.

9. Tamara K. Hareven, "Family History at the Crossroads," in *Family History at the Crossroads: A Journal of Family History Reader*, ed. Tamara Hareven and Andrejs Plakans (Princeton, N.J.: Princeton University Press, 1987), xviii.

10. Davis Bitton, *Guide to Mormon Diaries and Autobiographies* (Provo, Utah: Brigham Young University Press, 1977); John F. C. Harrison, "The Popular History of Early Victorian Britain: A Mormon Contribution," *Journal of Mormon History* 14 (1988): 3–15; Lee L. Bean, Geraldine P. Mineau, Katherine A. Lynch, and J. Dennis Willigan, "The Genealogical Society of Utah as a Data Resource for Historical Demography," *Population Index* 46 (1980): 6–19; Patricia Lyn Scott, "Mormon Polygamy: A Bibliography, 1977–91," *Journal of Mormon History* 19 (Spring 1993): 133–55.

11. Robert T. Handy, *A History of the Churches in the United States and Canada* (Oxford: Oxford University Press, 1976), 224; Sydney E. Ahlstrom, *A Religious History of the American People* (New Haven, Conn.: Yale University Press, 1972), 501–2 (quote).

12. Leonard J. Arrington and Davis Bitton, *The Mormon Experience: A History of the Latter-day Saints* (New York: Alfred A. Knopf, 1979), xi, 284–335; Stephan Thernstrom, ed., *Harvard Encyclopedia of American Ethnic Groups* (Cambridge, Mass.: Harvard University Press, 1980), s.v. "Mormons," by Dean L. May; Dean Louder and Lowell Bennion, "Mapping Mormons across the Modern West," in *The Mormon Role in the Settlement of the West*, ed. Richard H. Jackson (Provo, Utah: Brigham Young University Press, 1978), 135–67; James R. Shortridge, "A New Regionalization of American Religion," *Journal for the Scientific Study of Reli-*

gion 16 (June 1977): 143–53; David Brion Davis, "Expanding the Republic, 1820–1860," in *The Great Republic: A History of the American People,* by Bernard Bailyn, Robert Dallek, David Brion Davis, David Herbert Donald, John L. Thomas, and Gordon S. Wood, 3d ed., vol. 1 (Lexington, Mass.: D. C. Heath, 1985), 327.

13. See, for example, Steven E. Ozment, *Flesh and Spirit: A Study of Private Life in Early Modern Germany* (New York: Viking, 1999); Laura McCall and Donald Yacovone, *A Shared Experience: Men, Women, and the History of Gender* (New York: New York University Press, 1998); Linda Kerber, "Separate Spheres, Female Worlds, Woman's Place: The Rhetoric of Women's History," *Journal of American History* 75 (June 1988): 9–39; David Hackett Fischer, *Albion's Seed: Four British Folkways in America* (New York: Oxford University Press, 1989); Margaret Nash, "Rethinking Republican Motherhood: Benjamin Rush and the Young Ladies' Academy of Philadelphia," *Journal of the Early Republic* 17 (Summer 1997): 171–91; and Karen V. Hansen, *A Very Social Time: Crafting Community in Antebellum New England* (Berkeley: University of California Press, 1994).

14. Carle C. Zimmerman, "Family Influence upon Religion," *Journal of Comparative Family Studies* 5 (Autumn 1974): 6.

15. Bruce R. McConkie, *Mormon Doctrine* (Salt Lake City: Bookcraft, 1958), 602, 238.

16. Jan Shipps, *Mormonism: The Story of a New Religious Tradition* (Urbana: University of Illinois Press, 1985), 148–49.

17. Ann Douglas, *The Feminization of American Culture* (New York: Alfred A. Knopf, 1977), 223–26 (quote on 223).

18. *The Doctrine and Covenants of the Church of Jesus Christ of Latter-day Saints* (Salt Lake City: Published by the Church, 1981), 132:6–20 (hereafter cited as Doctrine and Covenants).

19. The contention here is that the term *celestial marriage* meant marriage for eternity, including but not restricted to plural marriages. When the revelation about sealing of marriages and plural marriage was included in the Doctrine and Covenants in 1876, the heading read, "Revelation on the Eternity of the Marriage Covenant, including Plurality of Wives," implying that celestial marriage was a broader term that encompassed plural marriage. *The Doctrine and Covenants of the Church of Jesus Christ of Latter-day Saints, containing the Revelations Given to Joseph Smith, Jun., the Prophet* (Salt Lake City: Published at the Deseret News Office, 1876), section 132, 423. This usage was employed elsewhere in the nineteenth century. In a sermon about celestial marriage on October 7, 1869, Orson Pratt first discussed marriage for eternity, using Adam and Eve (not a polygamous marriage) as his example, and then he dealt with the plurality of wives (*JD* 13:183–96). On August 10, 1873, George Q. Cannon similarly used celestial marriage in its broader sense as the "authority to seal wives to husbands for time and all eternity . . ." (*JD* 16:143). On October 11, 1874, Orson Pratt again used the term to mean eternal marriage: "It will then be known who have been joined together in celestial marriage by divine authority, and who by wicked counsels, and by justices of the peace . . ." (*JD* 17:188). On August 17, 1879, Charles W. Penrose echoed the wording of the heading of Doctrine and Covenants 132: "this doctrine of celestial marriage, or marriage for eternity, including the doctrine of plurality of wives" (*JD* 20:296). A year later, he was more explicit: "our marriage is celestial marriage for time and all eternity—like that with which Adam was

married to Eve in the Garden of Eden . . . when we enter this holy order of marriage, whether it be with one or two, or more wives, we marry in this order . . ."
(*JD* 22:96–97). On February 11, 1883, John Taylor also used the term in the broader
sense: "He has revealed unto us the law of celestial marriage, associated with
which is the principle of plural marriage" (*JD* 24:229). The term, through use of a
synecdoche (a figure of speech by which the whole stands for a part), was also used
to mean only plural marriage, just as government is used to mean federal government, or Celestial Kingdom is used to mean only the highest degree in the Celestial Kingdom. The meaning is determined by the context. This view differs from
that of Carmon Hardy, who argues that beginning in 1882 the meaning of celestial marriage was modified so that it did not mean the same as plural marriage,
while before that it had meant "church-solemnized, polygamous relationships."
He, however, acknowledges that there is "some basis" for questioning the early
use of the term *celestial marriage* solely as plural marriage. B. Carmon Hardy,
Solemn Covenant: The Mormon Polygamous Passage (Urbana: University of Illinois Press, 1992), 52. In my view, the distinction between the whole (marriage
for eternity) and the part (plural marriage) was made clearer in the 1880s, not that
the meaning of the term changed.

20. Doctrine and Covenants 132:1, 29–39.

21. Carl N. Degler, *At Odds: Women and the Family in America from the
Revolution to the Present* (Oxford: Oxford University Press, 1980), 8–51; Robert
L. Griswold, *Family and Divorce in California, 1850–1890: Victorian Illusions
and Everyday Realities* (Albany: State University of New York Press, 1982).

22. Annie Clark Tanner, *A Mormon Mother: An Autobiography by Annie Clark
Tanner* (Salt Lake City: Tanner Trust Fund, University of Utah Library, 1976), 62.

23. This doctrine was fully articulated before the death of Joseph Smith and
stands essentially unchanged in spite of the discontinuation of the practice of
plural marriage.

24. Richard S. Van Wagoner, *Mormon Polygamy: A History*, 2d ed. (Salt Lake
City: Signature Books, 1989); Lawrence Foster, *Religion and Sexuality: Three
American Communal Experiments of the Nineteenth Century* (New York: Ox-
ford University Press, 1981); Todd Compton, *In Sacred Loneliness: The Plural
Wives of Joseph Smith* (Salt Lake City: Signature Books, 1997).

25. Kimball Young, *Isn't One Wife Enough?* (New York: Henry Holt, 1954); Jessie
L. Embry, *Mormon Polygamous Families: Life in the Principle* (Salt Lake City:
University of Utah Press, 1987). Embry acknowledges that her study deals with
the later period, "during the last sanctioned days" of plural marriage (30). For an
assessment of plural marriage based mainly on the writings of polygamous wives
themselves, see Vicky Burgess-Olson, "Family Structure and Dynamics in Early
Utah Mormon Families, 1847–1885" (Ph.D. diss., Northwestern University, 1975);
and Paula Kelly Harline, "Polygamous Yet Monogamous: Cultural Conflict in the
Writings of Mormon Polygamous Wives," in *Old West–New West: Centennial
Essays*, ed. Barbara Howard Meldrum (Moscow: University of Idaho Press, 1993),
115–32.

26. Eugene E. Campbell and Bruce L. Campbell, "Divorce among Mormon Polygamists: Extent and Explanations," *Utah Historical Quarterly* 46 (Winter 1978):
22. Embry has pointed out the erroneous assumptions underlying the Campbells'
estimates of the divorce rate. Embry, *Mormon Polygamous Families*, 176–77.

27. Phillip R. Kunz, "One Wife or Several? A Comparative Study of Late Nine-

teenth-Century Marriage in Utah," in *The Mormon People: Their Character and Traditions,* ed. Thomas G. Alexander (Provo, Utah: Brigham Young University Press, 1980), 53–73; Richard I. Aaron, "Mormon Divorce and the Statute of 1852: Questions for Divorce in the 1980's," *Journal of Contemporary Law* 8 (1982): 5–45. For further information on the family group records, see the appendix.

28. Geraldine P. Mineau, Lee L. Bean, and Douglas L. Anderton, "Migration and Fertility: Behavioral Change on the American Frontier," *Journal of Family History* 14 (January 1989): 43–61; Lee L. Bean and Geraldine P. Mineau, "The Polygyny-Fertility Hypothesis: A Re-Evaluation," *Population Studies* 40 (March 1986): 67–81; Douglas L. Anderton and Rebecca Jean Emigh, "Polygynous Fertility: Sexual Competition versus Progeny," *American Journal of Sociology* 94 (January 1989): 832–55; Lee L. Bean, Geraldine P. Mineau, and Douglas L. Anderton, *Fertility Change on the American Frontier: Adaptation and Innovation* (Berkeley: University of California Press, 1990), 166–79; Douglas L. Anderton, Lee L. Bean, J. Dennis Willigan, and Geraldine P. Mineau, "Adoption of Fertility Limitation in an American Frontier Population: An Analysis and Simulation of Socio-Religious Subgroups," *Social Biology* 31 (Spring–Summer 1984): 140–59; Lee L. Bean, Geraldine Mineau, and Douglas Anderton, "Residence and Religious Effects on Declining Family Size: An Historical Analysis of the Utah Population," *Review of Religious Research* 25 (December 1983): 91–101.

29. D. Michael Quinn, "LDS Church Authority and New Plural Marriages, 1890–1904," *Dialogue: A Journal of Mormon Thought* 18 (Spring 1985): 9–105; Hardy, *Solemn Covenant.*

30. Stanley S. Ivins, "Notes on Mormon Polygamy," *Western Humanities Review* 10 (Summer 1956): 229–39. For an assessment of his sources, see the appendix.

31. James E. Smith and Phillip R. Kunz, "Polygyny and Fertility in Nineteenth-Century America," *Population Studies* 30 (November 1976): 468–71; Lowell "Ben" Bennion, "The Incidence of Mormon Polygamy in 1880: 'Dixie' versus Davis Stake," *Journal of Mormon History* 11 (1984): 27–42; Marie Cornwall, Camela Courtright, and Laga Van Beek, "How Common the Principle? Women as Plural Wives in 1860," *Dialogue: A Journal of Mormon Thought* 26 (Summer 1993): 139–54.

32. Larry M. Logue, *A Sermon in the Desert: Belief and Behavior in Early St. George, Utah* (Urbana: University of Illinois Press, 1988).

33. *Twelfth Census of the United States Taken in the Year 1900,* vol. 1 (Washington, D.C.: United States Census Office, 1901), 392. Alan Macfarlane stated, "The general impression one receives is that the ratio of 1 investigator per 2,000 people or less is essential in order to undertake really intensive 'community studies' by conventional methods." Alan Macfarlane, *Reconstructing Historical Communities* (Cambridge: Cambridge University Press, 1977), 7. Given the necessity of linking multiple records for this project, studying the people in Manti over sixty years was a large undertaking.

34. See chapter 5.

35. This figure was derived by subtracting from the total Utah population Salt Lake City, Ogden, and towns where few Mormons lived (such as Corinne, Park City, Ft. Douglas, and Eureka) and then calculating the percentage of the remainder. *The Seventh Census of the United States, 1850* (Washington, D.C.: Robert Armstrong, 1853), 993; *Population of the United States in 1860: Compiled from*

the Original Returns of the Eighth Census (Washington, D.C.: Government Printing Office, 1864), 576–77; *The Statistics of the Population of the United States* (Washington, D.C.: Government Printing Office, 1872), 275–76; *Statistics of the Population of the United States at the Tenth Census* (Washington, D.C.: Government Printing Office, 1883), 351–53; *Twelfth Census*, 390–93; *Abstract of the Twelfth Census of the United States, 1900*, 3d ed. (Washington, D.C.: Government Printing Office, 1904), 32. On the Mormon village, see Lowry Nelson, *The Mormon Village: A Pattern and Technique of Land Settlement* (Salt Lake City: University of Utah Press, 1952).

36. Ray Rivera and Greg Burton, "Is Time Up for Utah Polygamous Sect?" *Salt Lake Tribune*, December 19, 1999, A1. Three important studies on twentieth-century polygamous groups are Martha Sonntag Bradley, *Kidnapped from That Land: The Government Raids on the Short Creek Polygamists* (Salt Lake City: University of Utah Press, 1993); Irwin Altman and Joseph Ginat, *Polygamous Families in Contemporary Society* (New York: Cambridge University Press, 1996); and Janet Bennion, *Women of Principle: Female Networking in Contemporary Mormon Polygyny* (New York: Oxford University Press, 1998).

37. In 1982, Jerry N. Harrison reconstituted the families of Manti from 1849 to 1948 using only a list of the first settlers, cemetery records, and church membership records. These limited sources led him to conclude erroneously, "The first decade was that in which the pioneers arrived. . . . The next forty years were ones of limited migration of people into Manti." Manti actually experienced considerable in-migration during those years, particularly in the 1880s when the temple was being built. Although Harrison's data were adequate for analyzing mortality, his sources for the period before 1890 were insufficient to provide accurate data on age at marriage or analysis of polygamous marriages. Jerry N. Harrison, *Demographic Transition in a Frontier Town: Manti, Utah, 1849–1948* (New York: Garland, 1989), 181 (quote), 162–69, 147–49.

38. Adelia Cox Sidwell, "Reminiscences of the Early Days of Manti," *Manti Home Sentinel*, August 1, 1889, 1.

39. The appendix contains a list and evaluation of the sources used to construct the Manti data base.

40. See chapter 4 for a full explanation of these marriage types.

41. James B. Allen and Glen M. Leonard, *The Story of the Latter-day Saints*, 2d ed., rev. and enl. (Salt Lake City: Deseret Book, 1992), 160–66, 288–91; Arrington and Bitton, *Mormon Experience*, 127–40; P. A. M. Taylor, *Expectations Westward: The Mormons and the Emigration of Their British Converts in the Nineteenth Century* (Edinburgh: Oliver and Boyd, 1965); William Mulder, *Homeward to Zion: The Mormon Migration from Scandinavia* (Minneapolis: University of Minnesota Press, 1957), 3–185; Gustive O. Larson, "The Mormon Gathering," in *Utah's History*, ed. Richard D. Poll, Thomas G. Alexander, Eugene E. Campbell, and David E. Miller (Logan: Utah State University Press, 1989), 186–87.

42. For evidence that this is the same woman using different names, see the appendix.

43. Bean, Mineau, and Anderton, *Fertility Change on the American Frontier*, 70–90; Logue, *Sermon in the Desert*, 131–39.

44. Wilford Woodruff, Cache Stake Conference, Logan, Utah, November 1, 1891, reported in *Deseret News Weekly*, November 14, 1891, 659; reprinted in Doctrine and Covenants, Official Declaration—1, 292–93.

Chapter 1: Kirtland and Nauvoo

1. Charlotte Brontë, *Jane Eyre,* ed. Richard J. Dunn (New York: W. W. Norton, 1971), 252–83.

2. Obtaining a divorce in England before 1857 involved three court actions after the wife committed adultery. (In addition to adultery, women had to prove their husbands guilty of some misconduct, such as bigamy or incest.) First, the husband had to bring a court action for criminal conversation against the seducer and obtain a damage judgment against him. Second, an action was brought in the ecclesiastical court for divorce *a mensa et thoro.* If the husband succeeded in this second court, he could at last have a parliamentary bill introduced for "Divorcement *a vinculo matrimonii."* The cost for these procedures was sometimes in excess of £1,000. Between 1715 and 1836, only 224 divorces, or fewer than two a year, were granted. Gerhard O. W. Mueller, "Inquiry into the State of a Divorceless Society: Domestic Relations Law and Morals in England from 1660 to 1857," *University of Pittsburgh Law Review* 18 (Spring 1957): 551.

3. Mercy Pitchforth, Early Church Information Card Index, alphabetical listing, microfilm, FHL; Solomon Pitchforth–Ann Hughlings Family Group Record, *AF.*

4. Allen and Leonard, *Story of the Latter-day Saints,* 204–59; Robert Bruce Flanders, *Nauvoo: Kingdom on the Mississippi* (Urbana: University of Illinois Press, 1965), 306–41; *CHC* 2:221–54; B. H. Roberts, ed., *History of the Church of Jesus Christ of Latter-day Saints: Period II, from the Manuscript History of Brigham Young and Other Original Documents* (Salt Lake City: Deseret Book, 1932), 1–243.

5. Solomon Pitchforth–Ann Hughlings Family Group Record, *AF;* 1850 U.S. Census, Salt Lake City, Salt Lake County, Utah, Population Schedule, 54, Samuel Pitchforth household, National Archives Microfilm Publication, M0432.

6. Richard Jenkins–Mercy Pitchforth Family Group Record, *AF;* Samuel Harvey Marble–Celestia Rowley Family Group Record, Patrons Section, FHL; Samuel Harvey Marble and Mercy Pitchforth, 1851, North America, Marriage Search, *OI,* Main File.

7. Richard Jenkins, 1861, North America, Marriage Search, *OI,* Main File; Richard Jenkins–Mercy Ann Pitchforth Family Group Record, *AF;* 1880 U.S. Census, Nephi, Juab County, Utah, Population Schedule, Enumeration District (hereafter E.D.) 24, 400A, Richard Jenkins and Sarah A. Jenkins households, National Archives Microfilm Publication, T0009.

8. The precise definition of *polygamy* is the practice of having more than one wife or husband at a time. *Polygyny* is the correct term to refer to the practice of having more than one wife at a time, while *polyandry* refers to the practice of having more than one husband at a time. The term *polygamy* will be used throughout this study because polyandry, although rare, was allowed in the Mormon marriage system.

9. Doctrine and Covenants 132; Foster, *Religion and Sexuality,* 142–46; Thomas F. O'Dea, *The Mormons* (Chicago: University of Chicago Press, 1957), 138–41.

10. When it was founded, the church was named the Church of Christ. Lyndon W. Cook, *The Revelations of the Prophet Joseph Smith: A Historical and Biographical Commentary of the Doctrine and Covenants* (Salt Lake City: Deseret Book, 1985), 32. For understanding Mormonism and its origins, see Shipps, *Mormon-*

ism; and Arrington and Bitton, *Mormon Experience.* For a history of the earliest years of the church, see Richard L. Bushman, *Joseph Smith and the Beginnings of Mormonism* (Urbana: University of Illinois Press, 1984). For short biographical sketches of the six founders of Mormonism, see Cook, *Revelations,* 4–6, 14, 19–20, 25–27, 34. Biographies of Joseph Smith include Fawn Brodie, *No Man Knows My History: The Life of Joseph Smith, the Mormon Prophet,* 2d ed., rev. (New York: Alfred A. Knopf, 1979); and Donna Hill, *Joseph Smith, the First Mormon* (New York: Doubleday, 1977).

11. *History of the Church* 1:11–18, 39–42. This account was originally printed in the *Times and Seasons,* Nauvoo, Illinois, April 15, 1842, 753–54; May 2, 1842, 771–72; August 1, 1842, 865–66. For the background of Joseph Smith's writing of his history, see Dean C. Jessee, "The Writing of Joseph Smith's History," *Brigham Young University Studies* 11 (Summer 1971): 439–73; and James B. Allen and Leonard J. Arrington, "Mormon Origins in New York: An Introductory Analysis," *Brigham Young University Studies* 9 (Spring 1969): 255.

12. Beginning as Presbyterian ministers, both Alexander Campbell and Barton Stone were influential in the origins of the Christian Church (Disciples of Christ). Stone organized the large revival at Cane Ridge, Kentucky, in 1801, a prototype for subsequent frontier revivals. Stone soon distanced himself from Presbyterian doctrine and polity and took the Bible as his only creed. He and like-minded New Lights took the name "Christian." Alexander Campbell immigrated to the United States in 1809, settling in the Ohio River Valley. He sought to restore primitive Christianity, emphasizing almost exclusively the New Testament at the expense of the Old. The movements led by Campbell and Stone coalesced, as far as their congregational structure would allow, in 1832. Ahlstrom, *Religious History of the American People,* 432–35, 445–52; Handy, *History of the Churches,* 167–69.

13. Milton V. Backman Jr., "Joseph Smith and the Restitution of All Things," in *Joseph Smith: The Prophet, the Man,* ed. Susan Easton Black and Charles D. Tate Jr. (Provo, Utah: Religious Studies Center, Brigham Young University, 1993), 89–91; John Dillenberger, "Restorationism, Protestant," in *Encyclopedia of Mormonism,* 4 vols., ed. Daniel H. Ludlow (New York: Macmillan, 1992), 3:1221. For a comparison of the beliefs of Joseph Smith and Alexander Campbell, see Bushman, *Joseph Smith and the Beginnings of Mormonism,* 180–87.

14. Danel Bachman, "New Light on an Old Hypothesis: The Ohio Origins of the Revelation of Eternal Marriage," *Journal of Mormon History* 5 (1978): 19–32; Danel Bachman, "A Study of the Mormon Practice of Plural Marriage before the Death of Joseph Smith" (Master's thesis, Purdue University, 1975), 54–77; Doctrine and Covenants 132:37, recorded July 12, 1843 (quote).

15. W. W. Phelps to Brigham Young, August 12, 1861, quoted in Foster, *Religion and Sexuality,* 135. For an evaluation of the source, see ibid., 399. See also Bachman, "New Light on an Old Hypothesis," 25; and Van Wagoner, *Mormon Polygamy,* 3–4, 12–13. Van Wagoner finds Phelps's account problematic. In an 1835 letter (by Phelps's time frame about a year after Joseph Smith's comment about marrying plural wives by revelation), Phelps stated that he had "no right to any other woman in this world nor in the world to come." Quoted in Van Wagoner, *Mormon Polygamy,* 12. It is, however, at least as likely that Phelps's memory was faulty about the timing of Smith's comment as about his having said it.

16. *Doctrine and Covenants* (Kirtland, Ohio: F. G. Williams, 1835; reprint, Independence, Mo.: Herald House, 1971), 101:4. See also Van Wagoner, *Mormon Polygamy*, 6, 14.

17. Compton, *In Sacred Loneliness*, 29–36, 25. On the basis of Mosiah Hancock's autobiography, Compton dates the Alger marriage in 1833. The 1835 date fits better with other accounts. See Richard Lloyd Anderson and Scott H. Faulring, "Review of *In Sacred Loneliness: The Plural Wives of Joseph Smith*," *Farms Review of Books* 10, no. 2 (1998): 78–79.

18. Shipps, *Mormonism*, 61.

19. Irene M. Bates and E. Gary Smith, *Lost Legacy: The Mormon Office of Presiding Patriarch* (Urbana: University of Illinois Press, 1996), 5–8, 16–19, 33–44; D. Michael Quinn, *The Mormon Hierarchy: Origins of Power* (Salt Lake City: Signature Books, 1994), 32–34, 46–53.

20. Grant Underwood, *The Millenarian World of Early Mormonism* (Urbana: University of Illinois Press, 1993), 28–33, 46–53; Rex Eugene Cooper, *Promises Made to the Fathers: Mormon Covenant Organization* (Salt Lake City: University of Utah Press, 1990), 69–78.

21. Leviticus 8:6–12.

22. Wandle Mace, "Autobiography," 29, photocopy of MS, Special Collections, BYU.

23. Joseph Smith, *The Words of Joseph Smith: The Contemporary Accounts of the Nauvoo Discourses of the Prophet Joseph*, comp. and ed. Andrew F. Ehat and Lyndon W. Cook (Provo, Utah: Religious Studies Center, Brigham Young University, 1980), 43. See also Underwood, *Millenarian World*, 69–71.

24. Doctrine and Covenants 10:7–9, 38:6.

25. Underwood, *Millenarian World*, 24–57.

26. Milton V. Backman Jr., *The Heavens Resound: A History of the Latter-day Saints in Ohio, 1830–1838* (Salt Lake City: Deseret Book, 1983), 329–41; Stephen C. LeSueur, *The 1838 Mormon War in Missouri* (Columbia: University of Missouri Press, 1987), 1–6, 245–55.

27. Marvin S. Hill, *Quest for Refuge: The Mormon Flight from American Pluralism* (Salt Lake City: Signature Books, 1989), 59; Minutes of High Council and Bishopric Meeting at Far West, Missouri, April 12, 1838, in *Far West Record: Minutes of the Church of Jesus Christ of Latter-day Saints, 1830–1844*, ed. Donald Q. Cannon and Lyndon W. Cook (Salt Lake City: Deseret Book, 1983), 167; *Elders' Journal* (Far West, Mo.) 1 (July 1838): 45.

28. Oliver Cowdery to Warren Cowdery, January 21, 1838, Oliver Cowdery Letterbook, Henry E. Huntington Library and Art Gallery, San Marino, California (see also microfilm in Special Collections, BYU).

29. Ibid.

30. *History of the Church* 3:17 (first quote); Oliver Cowdery to Warren and Lyman Cowdery, February 4, 1838, Oliver Cowdery Letterbook (second quote).

31. Marvin Hill, "Cultural Crisis in the Mormon Kingdom: A Reconsideration of the Causes of Kirtland Dissent," *Church History* 49 (September 1980): 291, 296. Danel W. Bachman designates the apostasies of this period "the first hierarchical split over plural marriage." Bachman, "Study of the Mormon Practice of Plural Marriage," 77–90. In his study of the Mormons in Ohio in the 1830s, Max H. Parkin also argues that plural marriage was a factor in the apostasy. Max H. Par-

kin, "The Nature and Causes of Internal and External Conflict of the Mormons in Ohio between 1830 and 1838" (Master's thesis, Brigham Young University, 1966), 162–74, 348. Lawrence Foster accepts, though tentatively, that plural marriage was a cause of the apostasy. Foster, *Religion and Sexuality*, 138, 302. Although it was a factor, Marvin Hill's argument that it was not the central issue is more cogent.

32. David Whitmer, *Address to All Believers in Christ* (Richmond, Mo.: Privately printed for the author, 1889), 38. Whitmer refers to statements about plural marriage in Nauvoo made by William Marks and Isaac Sheen in *True Latter Day Saints' Herald* 1 (January 1860): 22–24.

33. John Whitmer, *An Early Latter Day Saint History: The Book of John Whitmer Kept by Commandment*, ed. F. Mark McKiernan and Roger Launius (Independence, Mo.: Herald House, 1980), 159–77.

34. *JD*, 5:208 (September 6, 1857) (first and third quotes); Mace, "Autobiography," 178 (second quote).

35. Kathryn M. Daynes, "Mormon Polygamy: Belief and Practice in Nauvoo," in *Kingdom on the Mississippi Revisited: Nauvoo in Mormon History*, ed. Roger D. Launius and John E. Hallwas (Urbana: University of Illinois Press, 1996), 131–32.

36. LeSueur, *1838 Mormon War in Missouri*, 168–79; *CHC* 1:484–87.

37. Flanders, *Nauvoo*, 23–56, 140.

38. *CHC* 1:489–90, 515–17; Roger D. Launius, *Alexander William Doniphan: Portrait of a Missouri Moderate* (Columbia: University of Missouri Press, 1997), 62–66.

39. Joseph Smith, *Words of Joseph Smith*, 8. See also *History of the Church*, 3:385, where the last sentence has been changed to read: "All other sins are not to be compared to sinning against the Holy Ghost, and proving a traitor to the brethren."

40. LeSueur, *1838 Mormon War in Missouri*, 175–77; M. Hill, *Quest for Refuge*, 113, 242n. 121.

41. Robert Wuthnow, "Comparative Ideology," *International Journal of Comparative Sociology* 22 (September–December 1981): 121–40.

42. *JD* 2:31–32 (Brigham Young, April 6, 1853); James E. Talmage, *The House of the Lord*, rev. ed. (Salt Lake City: Deseret Book, 1976), 84.

43. *JD* 4:46 (September 21, 1856). For similar statements by Kimball, see *JD* 3:269 (March 23, 1856), *JD* 4:108 (September 28, 1856), and *JD* 6:126–27 (December 13, 1857).

44. Quoted in Helen Mar Whitney, "Scenes in Nauvoo and Incidents from H. C. Kimball's Journal," *Woman's Exponent* 12 (August 1, 1883): 34.

45. For a historical and doctrinal treatment of this ordinance, see Gordon Irving, "The Law of Adoption: One Phase of the Development of the Mormon Concept of Salvation, 1830–1900," *Brigham Young University Studies* 14 (Spring 1974): 291–314. Whether this sealing ordinance was introduced during Joseph Smith's lifetime is uncertain, although the doctrine supporting it was in place then. Ibid., 293–95.

46. In *Religion and Sexuality*, Lawrence Foster states, "Plural marriage was conceived as a means of strengthening kinship relations and social solidarity" (139–40). Foster, however, puts this into a slightly different context. He indicates that the "sense of increasing tension and imminent crisis" (140) arose from, first,

the Mormons having been driven out of Missouri (whereas I stress the apostasy of the leadership); second, internal social tension created by the high deathrate in the malarial bottoms on which Nauvoo was located and by the extremes of wealth and poverty; and third, the Mormon missionary effort, which took men away from their families. The first two would have affected the entire Mormon community, but plural marriage was practiced by only 30 men and 114 women during Joseph Smith's lifetime. The doctrine having been revealed earlier, the problem is to explain its initial introduction among those select few. (The much larger influx of Mormons into plural marriage in 1845–46 is better explained by the crisis of Joseph Smith's death and especially the opportunity given the Saints by the temple's completion.) Unquestionably, being driven from Missouri created a sense of crisis, as did the internal social tensions, important but not sufficient factors for Mormons' acceptance of plural marriage. Superimposing the apostasy of the leadership helps explain the introduction of plural marriage to a loyal few. The missionary effort undoubtedly worked to make husbands and wives more independent of each other, providing a wedge for plural marriage. At least as important, however, were the converts made by the missionary effort. Female converts separated from husbands and fathers and without means of support would probably have been more accepting of plural marriage in Nauvoo, as they were later in Utah. Nevertheless, Foster's overall exposition of the introduction of plural marriage remains the best from a sociological perspective.

47. Quinn, *Mormon Hierarchy: Origins of Power,* 588; John L. Brooke, *The Refiner's Fire: The Making of Mormon Cosmology, 1644–1844* (Cambridge: Cambridge University Press, 1994), 265–66; Isaac Morley–Lucy Gunn Family Group Record, Patrons Section, FHL; Clare B. Christensen, *Before and after Mt. Pisgah: Cox, Hulet, Morley, Tuttle, Winget, Whiting and Related Families* (Salt Lake City: n.p., 1979), 124.

48. Helen Mar Kimball Whitney, "Autobiography 1881," n.p., LDS Church Archives; Cooper, *Promises Made to the Fathers,* 140–41.

49. Carrie A. Miles, "Polygamy and the Economics of Salvation," *Sunstone* 21 (August 1998): 40.

50. *JD* 3:266 (Brigham Young, July 14, 1855); *JD* 23:64 (John Taylor, April 9, 1882); Helen Mar Whitney, "Scenes in Nauvoo after the Martyrdom of the Prophet and Patriarch," *Woman's Exponent* 11 (March 1, 1883): 148.

51. Mary Elizabeth Rollins Lightner, "Address Delivered at Brigham Young University, April 14, 1905," typescript, Mary Elizabeth Rollins Lightner Papers, Special Collections, BYU (emphasis added); Emily Dow Partridge Young, "Diary," 124, photocopy of typescript, Special Collections, BYU (emphasis added).

52. *History of the Church,* 1:394, footnote; *CHC* 1:337–38; Richard Henrie Morley, "The Life and Contribution of Isaac Morley" (Master's thesis, Brigham Young University, 1965), 29; Isaac Morley–Hannah Blakeslee Finch Family Group Record, Patrons Section, FHL.

53. Quoted in Lyman O. Littlefield, *Reminiscences of Latter-day Saints* (Logan, Utah: Utah Journal, 1888), 46.

54. Ibid., 48. See also Daynes, "Mormon Polygamy," 135–38.

55. Foster, *Religion and Sexuality,* 146–74; M. Hill, *Quest for Refuge,* 115–21; Linda King Newell and Valeen Tippetts Avery, *Mormon Enigma: Emma Hale Smith* (Garden City, N.Y.: Doubleday, 1984), 99–101, 147.

56. "Lectures on Faith," in *Doctrine and Covenants* (1835; reprint, Indepen-

dence, Mo.: Herald House, 1971), 60. The relationship between loyalty and plural marriage in Nauvoo is detailed in Daynes, "Mormon Polygamy," 134–39.

57. Foster, *Religion and Sexuality*, 126.

58. Lawrence Stone, *The Family, Sex, and Marriage in England, 1500–1800* (New York: Harper and Row, 1977), 171–72.

59. Compton, *In Sacred Loneliness*, 12. D. Michael Quinn also uses the term *Mormon dynasticism*, although it includes kinship relations between members of the Mormon hierarchy as well as marriages. D. Michael Quinn, *The Mormon Hierarchy: Extensions of Power* (Salt Lake City: Signature Books in association with Smith Research Associates, 1997), 177.

60. Quoted in Compton, *In Sacred Loneliness*, 465.

61. Helen Mar Whitney, "Scenes and Incidents in Nauvoo," *Woman's Exponent* 10 (October 15, 1881): 74. Laura and Abigail Pitkin, eleven and four years his senior respectively, later became his wives. Heber C. Kimball–Laura Pitkin Family Group Record and Heber C. Kimball–Abigail Pitkin Family Group Record, *AF*.

62. Doctrine and Covenants 132:63.

63. Compton, *In Sacred Loneliness*, 15. Michael Quinn is more temperate in his judgments but nevertheless argues that one cannot assume that marriage with an older wife precluded sexual relations. Quinn, *Mormon Hierarchy: Extensions of Power*, 183–87. While one may appreciate Quinn's disabusing the notion that "widows and middle-aged women lack sexual attractiveness," his argument that plural marriages with lesser-known wives (often assumed to be sealed for eternity only) were sexual ones, though plausible, also rests on assumptions.

64. David Thelen, "Memory and American History," *Journal of American History* 75 (March 1989): 1117–29.

65. Josephine F. Fisher, certificate, February 24, 1915, original in Vault Folder in the LDS Church Archives, quoted in Bachman, "Study of the Mormon Practice of Plural Marriage," 141.

66. See for example, Bachman, "Study of the Mormon Practice of Plural Marriage," 142; Compton, *In Sacred Loneliness*, 183; Richard S. Van Wagoner, "Mormon Polyandry in Nauvoo," *Dialogue: A Journal of Mormon Thought* 18 (Fall 1985): 78; Van Wagoner, *Mormon Polygamy*, 44, 48–49n. 3; and George D. Smith, "Nauvoo Roots of Mormon Polygamy, 1841–46: A Preliminary Demographic Report," *Dialogue: A Journal of Mormon Thought* 27 (Spring 1994): 11.

67. Windsor Palmer Lyon–Sylvia Sessions Family Group Record, *AF*; Compton, *In Sacred Loneliness*, 181, 185.

68. Cooper, *Promises Made to the Fathers*, 143n. 1.

69. Benjamin F. Johnson to George F. Gibbs, [April–October 1903], in Dean R. Zimmerman, *I Knew the Prophets: An Analysis of the Letter of Benjamin F. Johnson to George F. Gibbs, Reporting Doctrinal Views of Joseph Smith and Brigham Young* (Bountiful, Utah: Horizon, 1976), 40.

70. Mary P. Ryan, *Cradle of the Middle Class: The Family in Oneida County, New York, 1790–1865* (Cambridge: Cambridge University Press, 1981), 143–55, 230–41; Paul E. Johnson, *A Shopkeeper's Millennium: Society and Revival in Rochester, New York, 1815–1837* (New York: Hill and Wang, 1978), 43–48, 55.

71. Dallin H. Oaks and Marvin S. Hill, *Carthage Conspiracy: The Trial of the Accused Assassins of Joseph Smith* (Urbana: University of Illinois Press, 1975), 25; P. Taylor, *Expectations Westward*, 18–46; Flanders, *Nauvoo*, 57–91.

72. Caroline Barnes Crosby, "Memoirs," in *Women's Voices: An Untold History of the Latter-day Saints, 1830–1900*, ed. Kenneth W. Godfrey, Audrey M. Godfrey, and Jill Mulvay Derr (Salt Lake City: Deseret Book, 1982), 48–52; Karl Ricks Anderson, *Joseph Smith's Kirtland: Eyewitness Accounts* (Salt Lake City: Deseret Book, 1989), 13–14; William Clayton, *Manchester Mormons: The Journal of William Clayton, 1840 to 1842*, ed. James B. Allen and Thomas G. Alexander (Santa Barbara, Calif.: Peregrine Smith, 1974), 201, 217; Newell and Avery, *Mormon Enigma*, 89, 91, 132; C. Christensen, *Before and after Mt. Pisgah*, 118, 120.

73. Parley P. Pratt, *Autobiography of Parley Parker Pratt* (Salt Lake City: Deseret Book, 1979), 47–50, 67, 72, 127, 292, 310.

74. Steven Mintz and Susan Kellogg, *Domestic Revolutions: A Social History of American Family Life* (New York: Free Press, 1988), 43–64; Stephanie Coontz, *The Social Origins of Private Life: A History of American Families, 1600–1900* (London: Verso, 1988), 169–97.

75. George Smith, "Nauvoo Roots of Mormon Polygamy," 16; Annette P. Hampshire, *Mormonism in Conflict: The Nauvoo Years* (New York: Edwin Mellen, 1985), 135–55; D. Hill, *Joseph Smith*, 297–302, 319–20, 358, 387–416.

76. Brigham Young, Address, October 8, 1866, LDS Church Archives, quoted in Andrew F. Ehat, "Joseph Smith's Introduction of Temple Ordinances and the 1844 Mormon Succession Question" (Master's thesis, Brigham Young University, 1982), 58.

77. William Clayton testimony, February 16, 1874, in Andrew Jenson, "Plural Marriage," *Historical Record* 6 (May 1887): 226.

78. Doctrine and Covenants 132:20, 37, 63.

79. *History of the Church*, 6:432–631; Van Wagoner, *Mormon Polygamy*, 63–71; M. Hill, *Quest for Refuge*, 142–51; Oaks and Hill, *Carthage Conspiracy*, 12–21; Quinn, *Mormon Hierarchy: Origins of Power*, 132–41. Quinn's account stresses that Joseph Smith was more concerned with the *Expositor*'s revealing secret information about political negotiations than about plural marriage.

80. Flanders, *Nauvoo*, 306–41; David E. Miller and Della S. Miller, *Nauvoo: The City of Joseph* (Santa Barbara, Calif.: Peregrine Smith, 1974), 130–208; Hampshire, *Mormonism in Conflict*, 181–214; John E. Hallwas, "Mormon Nauvoo from a Non-Mormon Perspective," *Journal of Mormon History* 16 (1990): 53–65; Kenneth H. Winn, *Exiles in a Land of Liberty: Mormons in America, 1830–1846* (Chapel Hill: University of North Carolina Press, 1989), 176–222; M. Hill, *Quest for Refuge*, 119–21, 142–51, 171. Hill states, "Plural marriage was a factor, but it was not decisive any more than it had been in Kirtland or Missouri. Anti-pluralism was the main cause of persecution" (181).

81. Ehat, "Joseph Smith's Introduction of Temple Ordinances," 194; Quinn, *Mormon Hierarchy: Origins of Power*, 143–243. Quinn argues that Joseph Smith, in the last few days of his life, turned away from plural marriage and the secret temple ordinances. Quinn, *Mormon Hierarchy: Origins of Power*, 145–48.

82. George Smith, "Nauvoo Roots of Mormon Polygamy," 14–15, 29–30; Compton, *In Sacred Loneliness*, 4–8. Smith attributes ten marriages to Joseph Smith during 1843, but Compton's evidence suggests those marriages were performed earlier.

83. Allen and Leonard, *Story of the Latter-day Saints*, 225–27; Flanders, *Nauvoo*, 326–29; *History of the Church*, 7:439–42.

84. Irving, "Law of Adoption," 296–99; C. Christensen, *Before and after Mt. Pisgah*, 122–23; Edwin Parker Merriam Family Group Record and John Buchanan Family Group Record, Patrons Section, FHL; Terry Tuttle Family Group Record, Archives Section, FHL; Susan Ward Easton Black, comp., *Membership of the Church of Jesus Christ of Latter-day Saints, 1830–1848*, 50 vols. (Provo, Utah: Religious Studies Center, Brigham Young University, 1984–88), 9:3–5, 28:152–53; Milton V. Backman Jr., comp., *A Profile of Latter-day Saints of Kirtland, Ohio and Members of Zion's Camp, 1830–1839: Vital Statistics and Sources* (Provo, Utah: Department of Church History and Doctrine, 1982), 15; John Carter Family Group Record, *AF*; Frederick Walter Cox–Calista Cordelia Morley Family Group Record, Patrons Section, FHL; George Smith, "Nauvoo Roots of Mormon Polygamy," 29–30.

85. C. Christensen, *Before and after Mt. Pisgah*, 124; Morley, "Life and Contribution of Isaac Morley," 104–5. Fawn Brodie erroneously assumed that because Cordelia Cox was sealed to Joseph Smith in 1846, she must have been married to him when he was still alive. Brodie, *No Man Knows My History*, 457, 486.

86. Morley, "Life and Contribution of Isaac Morley," 105; Allen and Leonard, *Story of the Latter-day Saints*, 229–34; Richard E. Bennett, *Mormons at the Missouri, 1846–1852: "And Should We Die . . ."* (Norman: University of Oklahoma Press, 1987), 26–67.

Chapter 2: Plural Marriage under Mormon Control

1. Bennett, *Mormons at the Missouri*, 90, 51–63, 257–58 ftn. 45; Flanders, *Nauvoo*, 303–4; Leonard J. Arrington, *Great Basin Kingdom: An Economic History of the Latter-day Saints, 1830–1900* (Lincoln: University of Nebraska Press, 1958), 21, 47–48.

2. W. H. Lever, *History of Sanpete and Emery Counties, Utah: With Sketches of Cities, Towns, and Villages, Chronology of Important Events, Records of Indian Wars, Portraits of Prominent Persons, and Biographies of Representative Citizens* (Ogden, Utah: W. H. Lever, 1898), 184, 194; Bennett, *Mormons at the Missouri*, 122–25.

3. Bennett, *Mormons at the Missouri*, 136–42; Isaac Morley–Lucy Gunn Family Group Record and John Sweat Family Group Record, Patrons Section, FHL; Isaac Morley, CPI.

4. Bennett, *Mormons at the Missouri*, 194–98.

5. E. Young, "Diary," 3–4, 103, 119 (quote).

6. C. Christensen, *Before and after Mt. Pisgah*, 182–86.

7. *JD* 1:53–66 (August 29, 1852) (quotes on 62 and 54).

8. David J. Whittaker, "Early Mormon Polygamy Defenses," *Journal of Mormon History* 11 (1984): 43–63. See also Davis Bitton, *The Ritualization of Mormon History and Other Essays* (Urbana: University of Illinois Press, 1994), 34–53.

9. Unsigned manuscript, LDS Church Archives, quoted in Bitton, *Ritualization of Mormon History*, 35.

10. Belinda Marden Pratt, *Defence of Polygamy, by a Lady of Utah, in a Letter to Her Sister in New Hampshire* (Salt Lake City: n.p., 1854), 4–6.

11. Hardy, *Solemn Covenant*, 87–90, 110n. 43.

12. *JD* 4:278 (January 25, 1857).

13. William Alcott, *The Physiology of Marriage* (Boston: John P. Jewett, 1859), 115–20; Louis J. Kern, *An Ordered Love: Sex Roles and Sexuality in Victorian Utopias — The Shakers, the Mormons, and the Oneida Community* (Chapel Hill: University of North Carolina Press, 1981), 47–48; Charles A. Cannon, "The Awesome Power of Sex: The Polemical Campaign against Mormon Polygamy," *Pacific Historical Review* 43 (February 1974): 67 (quote).

14. Ryan, *Cradle of the Middle Class*, 157 (quote); Paul A. David and Warren C. Sanderson, "Rudimentary Contraceptive Methods and the American Transition to Marital Fertility Control, 1855–1915," in *Long-Term Factors in American Economic Growth*, ed. Stanley L. Engerman and Robert E. Gallman (Chicago: University of Chicago Press, 1986), 307–79; Degler, *At Odds*, 181.

15. Ryan, *Cradle of the Middle Class*, 18–51, 65–75; Mary P. Ryan, *The Empire of the Mother: American Writing about Domesticity, 1830–1860* (New York: Institute for Research in History and the Haworth Press, 1982), 19–70, 97–114; Joan Smyth Iversen, *The Antipolygamy Controversy in U.S. Women's Movements, 1880–1925: A Debate on the American Home* (New York: Garland, 1997), 133–57.

16. An excellent study of this topic is Edwin Brown Firmage and Richard Collin Mangrum, *Zion in the Courts: A Legal History of the Church of Jesus Christ of Latter-day Saints, 1830–1900* (Urbana: University of Illinois Press, 1988). See also Edwin B. Firmage, "Reflections on Mormon History: Zion and the Anti-Legal Tradition," *Dialogue: A Journal of Mormon Thought* 31 (Winter 1998): 53–64; Mark P. Leone, *Roots of Modern Mormonism* (Cambridge, Mass.: Harvard University Press, 1979), 111–47; and Raymond T. Swenson, "Resolution of Civil Disputes by Mormon Ecclesiastical Courts," *Utah Law Review* 1978, no. 3 (1978): 573–95.

17. Elizabeth D. Gee, "Justice for All or for the 'Elect'? The Utah County Probate Court, 1855–72," *Utah Historical Quarterly* 48 (Spring 1980): 129–47; Allen and Leonard, *Story of the Latter-day Saints*, 363–64; James B. Allen, "The Unusual Jurisdiction of the County Probate Courts in the Territory of Utah," *Utah Historical Quarterly* 36 (Spring 1968): 132–42.

18. Poland Act, chap. 469, sec. 3, 18 Stat. 254 (1874); Thomas G. Alexander, *Utah, the Right Place: The Official Centennial History*, rev. ed. (Salt Lake City: Gibbs Smith, 1996), 175–76; Utah Historical Records Survey, Division of Community Service Programs, Works Projects Administration, *Guide to the Public Vital Statistics of Utah* (Salt Lake City: Utah Historical Records Survey, November 1941), 42.

19. Arrington, *Great Basin Kingdom*, 45–50; Eugene E. Campbell, "Governmental Beginnings," in *Utah's History*, ed. Poll et al., 153–64; Bennett, *Mormons at the Missouri*, 227–28.

20. Eugene E. Campbell, "Early Colonization Patterns," in *Utah's History*, ed. Poll et al., 133–52; Arrington, *Great Basin Kingdom*, 84–95.

21. Milton R. Hunter, *Brigham Young, the Colonizer*, 4th ed., rev. (Santa Barbara, Calif.: Peregrine Smith, 1973), 260, 266; C. Christensen, *Before and after Mt. Pisgah*, 106–7, 113, 122–23, 194; Terry Tuttle Family Group Record, Archives Section, FHL; John Buchanan Family Group Record and Edwin Parker Merriam Family Group Record, Patrons Section, FHL; Black, *Membership of the Church*, 28:152–53; Leah B. Lyman, "On to Manti," *Saga of the Sanpitch* 1 (1969): 8–11.

22. Sidwell, "Reminiscences of the Early Days of Manti"; C. Christensen, *Be-*

fore and after Mt. Pisgah, 194; Albert Antrei and Ruth D. Scow, eds., *The Other Forty-Niners: A Topical History of Sanpete County, Utah, 1849–1983* (Salt Lake City: Western Epics, 1982), 490.

23. William L. Knecht and Peter L. Crawley, comps., *History of Brigham Young, 1847–1867* (Berkeley: MassCal Associates, 1964), 57–58; *CHC* 3:460–64, 481; S. Lyman Tyler, "The Indians in Utah Territory," in *Utah's History,* ed. Poll et al., 361.

24. Dean L. May, *Utah: A People's History* (Salt Lake City: University of Utah Press, 1987), 101–10; Eugene E. Campbell, *Establishing Zion: The Mormon Church in the American West, 1847–1869* (Salt Lake City: Signature Books, 1988), 93–111; *CHC* 4:36–40; Tyler, "Indians in Utah Territory," 360.

25. Daniel W. Jones, *Forty Years among the Indians* (Salt Lake City: Juvenile Instructor Office, 1890), 51 (quote); Morley, "Life and Contribution of Isaac Morley," 181–82.

26. *CHC* 4:38–40; Historical Records Survey Project, Utah, *Inventory of the County Archives of Utah,* vol. 20 (Ogden, Utah: n.p., 1940), 12–15.

27. Will of Madison D. Hambleton, Sanpete County, Utah, "Probate Record including Minutes, 1866–1884," Book A, December 13, 1869, 30, microfilm of original, FHL; Last Will and Testament of Christian Nielsen, File of Wills, County Clerk's Office, Sanpete County Courthouse, Manti, Utah; Jane Anderson, "An Indian Who Became as a White," in Centennial Committee, Manti, Utah, *Song of a Century* (Provo, Utah: Community Press, 1978), 38; James Tilman Sanford Allred Family Group Record, Patrons Section, FHL; James Tilman Sanford Allred and Fanny Shantaquint, 1862, North America, Marriage Search, *OI,* Main File; Church of Jesus Christ of Latter-day Saints, Endowment House, "Endowments of the Living, 1851–1884," vol. D, 188, microfilm of MS, FHL (hereafter cited as "Endowment House Record"). For an assessment of taking Indian children into Utah Mormon households, see Brian Q. Cannon, "Adopted or Indentured, 1850–1870: Native Children in Mormon Households," in *Nearly Everything Imaginable: The Everyday Life of Utah's Mormon Pioneers,* ed. Ronald W. Walker and Doris R. Dant (Provo, Utah: Brigham Young University Press, 1999), 341–57.

28. Allen and Leonard, *Story of the Latter-day Saints,* 280; *CHC* 4:40.

29. Albert Antrei, *High, Dry, and Offside* ([Manti, Utah]: Manti City Council, 1995), 149–59; Andrew Jackson Judd and Fannie Kenner Anderson, "A History of Manti's Progress," 1958, 10, typescript, Special Collections, BYU; Centennial Committee, Manti, Utah, *Song of a Century,* 28–29.

30. Ella L. Turner, ed., *The Ancestors and Descendants of Abraham Daniel Washburn and His Wife Flora Clarinda Gleason, Utah Pioneers, 1805–1962* (N.p.: Privately printed by author, 1963), 25; Abraham Daniel Washburn Family Group Record, Patrons Section, FHL. See also Azariah Smith, "Journal," 86, photocopy of original, Special Collections, BYU.

31. C. Christensen, *Before and after Mt. Pisgah,* 281; Frederick W. Cox–Emeline Whiting Family Group Record, Frederick W. Cox–Jemina Losee Family Group Record, and Frederick W. Cox–Calista Cordelia Morley Family Group Record, Patrons Section, FHL; Frederick W. Cox and Lydia Margaret Losee, 1854, North America, Marriage Search, *OI,* Main File.

32. C. Christensen, *Before and after Mt. Pisgah,* 237–38.

33. Ibid.

34. *CHC* 3:464.

35. Adelia B. Sidwell, "Reminiscences of Early Manti," in Centennial Committee, Manti, Utah, *Song of a Century*, 35.

36. Sidwell, "Reminiscences of the Early Days of Manti," *Manti Home Sentinel*, August 22, 1889, 1.

37. Sidwell, "Reminiscences of Early Manti," 34–36; *CHC* 3:464–65; George Peacock–Mary Artemisia Lowry Family Group Record, Patrons Section, FHL. Chief Wahkara also told the parents of Eunice Warner that he wished to marry her. Her husband had recently been found killed by Indians at his mill near Manti. Not surprising, she also refused. Peter Gottfredson, *History of Indian Depredations in Utah* (Salt Lake City: Press of Skelton Publishing, 1919), 78.

38. John Alton Peterson, *Utah's Black Hawk War* (Salt Lake City: University of Utah Press, 1998), 1–41, 119–22, 329–35; *Inventory of the County Archives of Utah*, 18–27; Centennial Committee, Manti, Utah, *Song of a Century*, 32; R. Warren Metcalf, "A Reappraisal of Utah's Black Hawk War" (Master's thesis, Brigham Young University, 1989), 11–29, 33–35; Walker Lowry, *Wallace Lowry* (n.p.: Stinehouse Press for Walker Lowry, 1974), 53–56; Gottfredson, *History of Indian Depredations*, 130; Jens C. A. Weibye, "Diaries," April 18, April 23, April 24, 1867, LDS Church Archives.

39. A. E. M[erriam], "History of Sanpete County," *Manti Home Sentinel*, April 11, 1890, 1.

40. Sidwell, "Reminiscences of the Early Days of Manti," *Manti Home Sentinel*, August 1, 1889, 1; A. E. M[erriam], "History of Sanpete County," *Manti Home Sentinel*, March 28, 1890, 1; George W. Bradley, "Sketch of the Life of Ex-Bishop Bradley, Moroni, Utah," *Manti Home Sentinel*, March 4, 1890, 1; Davis Bitton and Linda P. Wilcox, "Pestiferous Ironclads: The Grasshopper Problem in Pioneer Utah," *Utah Historical Quarterly* 46 (Fall 1976): 345–47; Arrington, *Great Basin Kingdom*, 148–56.

41. Heber C. Kimball to William Kimball, February 29, 1856, *Millennial Star* 18 (July 1856): 395–96.

42. Lever, *History of Sanpete*, 78; Daniel A. Christensen, "Life Story of Andrew Poulsen," 1933, photocopy of typescript, copy in possession of author.

43. Paul H. Peterson, "The Mormon Reformation of 1856–1857: The Rhetoric and the Reality," *Journal of Mormon History* 15 (1989): 59–87; Gustive O. Larson, "The Mormon Reformation," *Utah Historical Quarterly* 26 (January 1958): 45–63; E. Campbell, *Establishing Zion*, 181–200; Thomas G. Alexander, "Wilford Woodruff and the Mormon Reformation of 1855–57," *Dialogue: A Journal of Mormon Thought* 25 (Summer 1992): 25–39; David L. Bigler, *Forgotten Kingdom: The Mormon Theocracy in the American West, 1847–1896* (Spokane, Wash.: Arthur H. Clark, 1998), 121–33. For the relationship between the agricultural disasters and the reformation, see P. Peterson, "Mormon Reformation of 1856–1857," 62–63. See also Arrington, *Great Basin Kingdom*, 152, 459.

44. See chapters 5 and 6 for evidence that new plural marriages considerably increased during the reformation.

45. Peter Madsen, "Journal and Autobiography of Peter Madsen, Ephraim, Utah," 28, microfilm of MS, LDS Church Archives.

46. Church of Jesus Christ of Latter-day Saints, "Manti Ward Record," Book C, March 20, 1861, microfilm of MS, LDS Church Archives.

47. Donald Bruce Johnson and Kirk H. Porter, comps., *National Party Platforms, 1840–1972* (Urbana: University of Illinois Press, 1973), 27.

48. Gustive O. Larson, *The "Americanization" of Utah for Statehood* (San Marino, Calif.: Huntington Library, 1971), 57–58, 65–66, 72–73, 94.

49. Gavin Wright, *Old South, New South: Revolutions in the Southern Economy since the Civil War* (New York: Basic Books, 1986), 29; Arrington, *Great Basin Kingdom*, 201–2; G. Larson, *"Americanization" of Utah*, 32–33.

50. *An Act to Punish and Prevent the Practice of Polygamy in the Territories of the United States and Other Places, and Disapproving and Annulling Certain Acts of the Legislative Assembly of the Territory of Utah*, U.S. Statutes at Large, 12, secs. 1–3, 501 (1862).

51. Arrington, *Great Basin Kingdom*, 257–70; Conway B. Sonne, *Saints on the Seas: A Maritime History of Mormon Migration, 1830–1890* (Salt Lake City: University of Utah Press, 1983), 141; Richard L. Jensen, "Steaming Through: Arrangements for Mormon Emigration from Europe, 1869–1887," *Journal of Mormon History* 9 (1982): 3–23.

52. Laura Christensen McCurdy Clark, *Others* (n.p., n.d.), 8–10; Sonne, *Saints on the Seas*, 150; "Journal History of the Church of Jesus Christ of Latter-day Saints," September 30, 1853, LDS Church Archives; Richard Hayes, COI.

53. Dean L. May, "Towards a Dependent Commonwealth," in *Utah's History*, ed. Poll et al., 219; Emil Hartvigsen, COI.

54. David Herbert Donald, "Uniting the Republic, 1860–1877," in *Great Republic*, by Bailyn et al., 500.

55. Quoted in Richard D. Poll, "The Political Reconstruction of Utah Territory, 1866–1890," *Pacific Historical Review* 27 (May 1958): 118.

56. Orma Linford, "The Mormons and the Law: The Polygamy Cases, Part I," *Utah Law Review* 9 (Winter 1964): 316; Arrington, *Great Basin Kingdom*, 356–57.

57. *Reynolds v. U.S.*, 98 U.S. 145, 166 (1879). For a discussion of the case, see Linford, "Mormons and the Law, Part I," 331–41.

58. *An Act to Amend Section Fifty-three Hundred and Fifty-two of the Revised Statutes of the United States, in Reference to Bigamy, and for Other Purposes*, U.S. Statutes at Large, 12, sec. 1–4, 30–31 (1882).

59. Ibid., sec. 5, 31 (1882).

60. Ibid., secs. 8–9, 31–32 (1882); Linford, "Mormons and the Law, Part I," 317–21.

61. *JD* 25:312 (John Taylor, October 6 and 7, 1884). In 1885, the Supreme Court ruled that those who were no longer polygamists could vote. *Murphy v. Ramsey*, 114 U.S. 15 (1885).

62. Lawrence M. Friedman, *Crime and Punishment in American History* (New York: Basic Books, 1993), 127–32.

63. "An Act to Punish Adultery," California Penal Code, 1872, sec. 266a, 380; *People v. Gates*, 46 Cal. 52 (1873); *Collins v. State*, 14 Ala. 608 (1848). See Friedman, *Crime and Punishment*, 127–32.

64. Allen and Leonard, *Story of the Latter-day Saints*, 413–14, 416–19.

65. Rosa Mae McClellan Evans, "Judicial Prosecution of Prisoners for LDS Plural Marriage: Prison Sentences, 1884–1895" (Master's thesis, Brigham Young University, 1986), 24–39, 73. Evans verified that these men were imprisoned for their involvement in plural marriage by checking the names of the men punished for

these crimes against family group records. Stan Larson gives figures slightly different from Evans's: 766 for unlawful cohabitation, 135 for adultery, 6 for unlawful cohabitation/adultery, 6 for polygamy, 5 for polygamy/unlawful cohabitation, 1 for adultery/polygamy, 1 for bigamy, and 1 for incest. Stan Larson, ed., *Prisoner for Polygamy: The Memoirs and Letters of Rudger Clawson at the Utah Territorial Penitentiary, 1884–87* (Urbana: University of Illinois, 1993), 209–31. The numbers reported by the Utah Commission are 988 convicted for unlawful cohabitation, 149 for adultery, 43 for fornication, and 1 for incest. Linford, "Mormons and the Law, Part I," 366. Stewart L. Grow, in his study of the Utah Commission, however, gives slightly different numbers: 1,004 convictions for unlawful cohabitation and 31 for polygamy. Stewart L. Grow, "A Study of the Utah Commission, 1882–1896" (Ph.D. diss., University of Utah, 1954), 268. Evans's figures include only those who were imprisoned, while the Utah Commission counted all those convicted, regardless of whether they were imprisoned. Moreover, Evans claims that none of the men or women imprisoned for fornication was convicted because of involvement in plural marriage (24).

66. *An Act to Amend an Act Entitled "An Act to Amend Section Fifty-three Hundred and Fifty-two of the Revised Statutes of the United States, in Reference to Bigamy, and for Other Purposes," U.S. Statutes at Large,* 24, secs. 1–6, 635–36 (1887).

67. Ibid., sec. 17, 638. The Morrill Anti-Bigamy Act had annulled the laws that incorporated the church; this section of the Edmunds-Tucker Act dissolved the corporation and provided for the enforcement of that dissolution.

68. Ibid., 12, secs. 15–16, 637–38.

69. Ibid., sec. 20, 639. For a discussion of the act, see Linford, "Mormons and the Law, Part I," 322–27.

70. Arrington, *Great Basin Kingdom,* 360–79; 136 U.S. 1 (1890).

71. *CHC* 6:203–22; Edward Leo Lyman, *Political Deliverance: The Mormon Quest for Utah Statehood* (Urbana: University of Illinois Press, 1986), 124–49.

72. Shipps, *Mormonism,* 115. See also Jan Shipps, "The Principle Revoked: A Closer Look at the Demise of Plural Marriage," *Journal of Mormon History* 11 (1984): 65–77.

73. Some plural marriages were still performed in Mexico and the United States, however. Hardy, *Solemn Covenant,* 389–425; Quinn, "LDS Church Authority and New Plural Marriages," 9–105.

74. Utah Constitution, art. 3, sec. 1; "An Act to Enable the People of Utah to Form a Constitution and State Government, and to Be Admitted into the Union on an Equal Footing with the Original States," *U.S. Statutes at Large,* 28, sec. 3, 107 (1894).

75. May, "Towards a Dependent Commonwealth," 225–41; Thomas G. Alexander, "Integration into the National Economy, 1896–1919," in *Utah's History,* ed. Poll et al., 409–46.

76. Antrei and Scow, *Other Forty-Niners,* 60 (first quote); L. Clark, *Others,* 105 (second quote). "States" carpets were those manufactured and shipped from states further east.

77. Allen and Leonard, *Story of the Latter-day Saints,* 267–72, 303–21, 350–55, 361–65, 402–7; Russell R. Rich, *Ensign to the Nations: A History of the Church from 1846 to 1972* (Provo, Utah: Brigham Young University Publications, 1972), 188–282, 294–97, 303, 371–77, 633–35.

Chapter 3: Nineteenth-Century Marriage Law in Utah

1. Norma S. Wanless, "So Be It," *Saga of the Sanpitch* 8 (1976): 26–31; 1860 U.S. Census, Manti, Sanpete County, Utah, Population Schedule, 12, F[rederic]k Cox household, National Archives Micropublication M653.

2. Mary Ellen Tuttle would have been thirteen at the time she and Fred Cox wanted to marry. Marrying at age thirteen was not common in the 1850s in Utah, but several did so. None of Mary Ellen's siblings entered plural marriage. John Henry Tuttle Family Group Record, Patrons Section, FHL.

3. Wanless, "So Be It," 26–31. Howard Cox, son of Fred Cox, and his plural wife Alvira, were the sources for this story; a niece of Fred Cox verified it (31). Although the story was written down long after the events, it does not conflict with those facts that can be checked. Lucy did not conceive her first child until December 1857, although she was married April 20 of that year. Her four subsequent children were born regularly at two-year intervals, indicating little difficulty in conceiving children. Such data support the assertion that she and Fred Cox did not begin living together as husband and wife until sometime in October. Frederick W. Cox Jr.–Lucy Allen Family Group Record, Patrons Section, FHL.

4. Frederick W. Cox Jr.–Lucy Allen Family Group Record, Patrons Section, FHL; 1900 U.S. Census, Manti, Sanpete County, Utah, Population Schedule, E.D. 125, 10 [stamped 138A], Lucy Cox household, National Archives Micropublication T623; Walter Stringham Family Group Record, Patrons Section, FHL.

5. Wilford Woodruff, *Wilford Woodruff's Journal, 1833–1898*, 9 vols., ed. Scott Kenny (Midvale, Utah: Signature Books, 1983–84), 4:11. See also Thomas G. Alexander, *Things in Heaven and Earth: The Life and Times of Wilford Woodruff, a Mormon Prophet* (Salt Lake City: Signature Books, 1991), 167.

6. *Acts, Resolutions, and Memorials Passed at the Several Annual Sessions of the Legislative Assembly of the Territory of Utah* (Salt Lake City: Joseph Cain, 1855), chap. 17, sec. 3, 104 (emphasis added).

7. Lyman D. Platt, "The History of Marriage in Utah, 1847–1905," *Genealogical Journal* 12 (Spring 1983): 30–31.

8. Hosea Stout, *On the Mormon Frontier: The Diary of Hosea Stout, 1844–1861*, 2 vols., ed. Juanita Brooks (Salt Lake City: University of Utah Press, 1964), 2:428.

9. The act incorporating the church had been reenacted on January 19, 1855, by "An Act in Relation to the Compilation and Revision of the Laws and Resolutions in Force in Utah Territory, Their Publication, and Distribution." See *An Act to Punish and Prevent the Practice of Polygamy*, 12, sec. 2, 501 (1862).

10. James A. Brundage, "Concubinage and Marriage in Medieval Canon Law," *Journal of Medieval History* 1 (April 1975): 1–17 (quote on 7); Michael M. Sheehan, "Christian Marriage: An Historical Perspective," in *Christian Marriage Today: Growth or Breakdown?* ed. Joseph A. Buijs (New York: Edwin Mellen, 1985), 18–23; Michael M. Sheehan, "Choice of Marriage Partner in the Middle Ages: Development and Mode of Application of a Theory of Marriage," in *Marriage, Family, and Law in Medieval Europe: Collected Studies*, ed. James K. Farge (Toronto: University of Toronto Press, 1996), 87–176; Eric Josef Carlson, *Marriage and the English Reformation* (Oxford: Blackwell, 1994), 14–21; Michael M. Sheehan, "Family and Marriage, Western European," in *Dictionary of the Middle Ages* (New York: Charles Scribner's Sons, 1988), 608–12; Kenneth M. Boyd, *Scottish Church*

Attitudes to Sex, Marriage and the Family, 1850–1914 (Edinburgh: John Donald, 1980), 47–48.

11. Carlson, *Marriage and the English Reformation*, 24–33; Sheehan, "Christian Marriage," 22–23.

12. Carlson, *Marriage and the English Reformation*, 3–8; Steven Ozment, *When Fathers Ruled: Family Life in Reformation Europe* (Cambridge, Mass.: Harvard University Press, 1983), 28–44.

13. Sheehan, "Christian Marriage," 24.

14. Carlson, *Marriage and the English Reformation*, 66–180; R. B. Outhwaite, *Clandestine Marriage in England, 1500–1850* (London: Hambledon, 1995), 1–49; Lawrence Stone, *Uncertain Unions: Marriage in England, 1660–1753* (Oxford: Oxford University Press, 1992), 12–32.

15. Edmund S. Morgan, *The Puritan Family: Religion and Domestic Relations in Seventeenth-Century New England*, new ed., rev. and enl. (New York: Harper Torchbooks, 1966), 31–32; John B. Boles, *The South through Time: A History of an American Region*, vol. 1 (Englewood Cliffs, N.J.: Prentice Hall, 1995), 155.

16. Michael Grossberg, *Governing the Hearth: Law and the Family in Nineteenth-Century America* (Chapel Hill: University of North Carolina Press, 1985), 66–75, 88–89. Marriage law replaced the term *irregular marriage* with *common-law marriage*, which had more positive connotations. Ibid., 69. See also George Elliott Howard, *A History of Matrimonial Institutions*, vol. 3 (Chicago: University of Chicago Press, 1904), 170–85.

17. James Kent, *Commentaries on American Law*, 4 vols., 12th ed. (Boston: Little, Brown, 1873), 2:87. For a discussion of the nineteenth-century legal view of consent, see Sarah Bassinger Gordon, "'The Liberty of Self-Degradation': Polygamy, Woman Suffrage, and Consent in Nineteenth-Century America," *Journal of American History* 83 (December 1996): 832–40.

18. *U.S. v. Simpson*, 4 Utah 227, 229 (1885).

19. While the weight of the common law stood behind the validity of common-law marriages, ministers and magistrates who performed the marriages for young couples without parental consent could be taken to court by the unhappy parents. Grossberg, *Governing the Hearth*, 78, 96.

20. *Compiled Laws of Utah, the Declaration of Independence and Constitution of the United States and Statutes of the United States Locally Applicable and Important* (Salt Lake City: Herbert Pembroke, 1888), sec. 2584, sec. 2592.

21. Later law cases supported this decision that the marriage was valid. The U.S. Supreme Court ruled, "The fact of marriage being proved, the presumptions of law are all in favor of good faith." *Gaines v. New Orleans*, 73 U.S. 707 (1867). In *Fisher v. Fisher*, the Court of Appeals of New York decided, "A formal ceremony of marriage, whether in due form or not, must be assumed to be by consent, and, therefore *prima facie* a contact of marriage *per verba de presenti.*" 250 N.Y. 316 (1929).

22. Jerrold S. Jensen, "The Common Law of England in the Territory of Utah," *Utah Historical Quarterly* 60 (Winter 1992): 4–26; Michael W. Homer, "The Judiciary and the Common Law in Utah Territory, 1850–61," *Dialogue: A Journal of Mormon Thought* 21 (Spring 1988): 97–108; Shane Swindle, "The Struggle over the Adoption of Common Law in Utah," *Thetean: A Student Journal of History* 13 (May 1984): 76–97; Orma Linford, "The Mormons, the Law, and the Territory of Utah," *American Journal of Legal History* 23 (April 1979): 224–28; G. W. Bar-

tholomew, "Recognition of Polygamous Marriages in America," *International and Comparative Law Quarterly* 13 (July 1964): 1024–30; Carol Cornwall Madsen, "'At Their Peril': Utah Law and the Case of Plural Wives, 1850–1900," *Western Historical Quarterly* 21 (November 1990): 426.

23. Emmeline B. Wells, Ellen B. Ferguson, Emily S. Richards, and Josephine M. West, letter to the Honorable Committee of the Senate on Education and Labor, May 12, 1886, Hearings, Interior Department, Territorial Papers of Utah, microfilm roll 4, Letters Received relating to Polygamy, January 27, 1879, to December 17, 1897, 540, National Archives and Records Service.

24. Church of Jesus Christ of Latter-day Saints, "Manti Ward Record," Book B, Orson Hyde on February 7, 1857, and A. P. Rockwell on May 15–17, 1857. See also William Chandless, *A Visit to Salt Lake; Being a Journey across the Plains and a Residence in the Mormon Settlements at Utah* (London: Smith, Elder, 1857), 251.

25. Fred C. Collier, ed., *The Teachings of President Brigham Young*, vol. 3, *1852–1854* (Salt Lake City: Collier's, 1987), 292. For a similar comment by Brigham Young, see *JD* 6:307 (April 8, 1853).

26. William Kilshaw Barton, *Copy of Diary and Missionary Journal of William Kilshaw Barton, Pioneer of 1852* (Salt Lake City, n.p., n.d.), 12–13; William Kilshaw Barton–Malinda Jane Hewitt Family Group Record and William Kilshaw Barton–Ann Lane Cook Family Group Record, Patrons Section, FHL.

27. Emmeline B. Whitney to Daniel Wells, March 4, 1852, Emmeline B. Wells Papers, LDS Church Archives, cited in Patricia Rasmussen Eaton-Gadsby and Judith Rasmussen Dushku, "Emmeline B. Wells," in *Sister Saints*, ed. Vicky Burgess-Olson (Provo, Utah: Brigham Young University Press, 1978), 459.

28. John D. Lee, *Journals of John D. Lee, 1846–47 and 1859*, ed. Charles Kelly (Salt Lake City: University of Utah Press, 1984), 12, 99 (quote).

29. Azariah Smith, "Journal," August 2, 1903, Special Collections, BYU. See also K. Young, *Isn't One Wife Enough?* 137.

30. "Celestial Marriage," *Seer* 1 (April 1853): 59.

31. Susa Young Gates, "Biography of Lucy Bigelow Young," 16, typescript, box 14, folder 5, Susa Young Gates Collection, Utah State Historical Society, Salt Lake City, Utah.

32. Personal letter from Sydney C. Mickelsen, Karen Kirstine Poulsen's granddaughter, November 5, 1988, Herman Julius Christensen–Karen Kjerstina Poulsen Family Group Record, Patrons Section, FHL. During the reformation, Emma Lynette Richardson also was pressured by her father to marry an older man in polygamy; it was an unhappy marriage that ended in divorce. Emma Lynette Richardson Conover, "Autobiography, 1841–1903," 5, typescript, Utah State Historical Society.

33. Virginia C. Keeler, *Cheney Garrett Van Buren and His Family: A Presentation of Their Lives and Times* (Provo, Utah: J. Grant Stevenson, 1962), 180.

34. George D. Peacock, "Diary," December 14 and 17, 1865, Special Collections, BYU.

35. Annette W. Farr, *The Story of Edwin Marion Whiting and Anna Maria Isaacson* (Provo, Utah: J. Grant Stevenson, 1969), 124.

36. Ibid., 120, 125–27.

37. "Celestial Marriage," *Seer* 1 (October 1853): 152; *JD* 19:167 (November 11, 1877).

38. Karen Lystra, *Searching the Heart: Women, Men, and Romantic Love in Nineteenth-Century America* (New York: Oxford University Press, 1989), 7–8.

39. *JD* 3:360 (June 15, 1856).

40. "Celestial Marriage," *Seer* 1 (October 1853): 154. In the 1940s, Joseph Fielding Smith echoed this view of marriage in a sermon at a Rigby, Idaho, Stake Conference, when he stated that if a man and woman were both really living the gospel, they could live together as husband and wife. Interview with Sydney C. Mickelsen, June 6, 1998, Idaho Falls, Idaho, copy of audiotape in possession of author.

41. Orson Pratt, "Celestial Marriage," *Seer* 1 (February 1853): 31 (emphasis added). For an earlier version of the ceremony, see Fred C. Collier, ed., *Unpublished Revelations of the Prophets and Presidents of the Church of Jesus Christ of Latter Day Saints*, 2d ed., vol. 1 (Salt Lake City: Collier's, 1981), 96. Consent is also at the heart of the ceremony in its earlier form.

42. *The Book of Common Prayer, and Administration of the Sacraments; and Other Rites and Ceremonies of the Church, according to the Use of the Protestant Episcopal Church in the United States of America: Together with the Psalter, or Psalms of David* (Philadelphia: King and Baird for the Bishop White Prayer Book Society, 1848), 120. Baptists and Methodists also included a similar giving of the bride by her parents as part of their wedding ceremonies. See Perry H. Biddle Jr., *A Marriage Manual*, rev. ed. (Grand Rapids, Mich.: William B. Eerdmans, 1994), 109, 117.

43. O. Pratt, "Celestial Marriage," 31; "Celestial Marriage," *Seer* 1 (March 1853): 41.

44. Grossberg, *Governing the Hearth*, 75–83.

45. *Chambers v. Dickson*, 2 S. & R. 475, 477 (Penn. 1816), quoted in Grossberg, *Governing the Hearth*, 80.

46. Grossberg, *Governing the Hearth*, 92–93.

47. O. Pratt, "Celestial Marriage," 32.

48. Carroll D. Wright, *Marriage and Divorce in the United States, 1867 to 1886* (Washington, D.C.: Government Printing Office, 1897; reprint, New York: Arno, 1976), 73.

49. Church of Jesus Christ of Latter-day Saints, Manti Ward, "Record of Members, [1849]–1877," 38½–45, microfilm of original, FHL.

50. Many justice of the peace records have been destroyed or are difficult to locate, while some justices of the peace kept records in their personal journals. *Research Outline: Utah* (Salt Lake City: Family History Library, 1997), 23–24.

Chapter 4: The Nature of Mormon Marriages

1. Grossberg, *Governing the Hearth*, 79.

2. Quoted in C. Wright, *Marriage and Divorce*, 26 (emphasis added).

3. *Book of Common Prayer*, 119–20 (quote); O. Pratt, "Celestial Marriage," 31–32.

4. *Acts, Resolutions, and Memorials*, chap. 64, sec. 1, 260.

5. Edwin Stacey Oaks and George S. Gulick, eds., *American Jurisprudence: A Compendium Text Statement of American Case Law, as Developed in the Cases*

and Annotations in the Annotated Reports System, Being a Rewriting of Ruling Case Law to Reflect the Modern Developments of the Law, vol. 35 (San Francisco: Bancroft-Whiteney; Rochester, N.Y.: Lawyers Co-operative Publishing, 1942), "Marriage," sec. 103; Lynn D. Wardle, "Rethinking Marital Age Restriction," *Journal of Family Law* 22, no. 1 (1983–84): 5–6.

6. Grossberg, *Governing the Hearth,* 105–8; *Compiled Laws of Utah* (1888), sec. 2584; *Laws of the State of Utah, Passed at the Second Regular Session of the Legislature of the State of Utah Held at Salt Lake City, the State Capital, in January, February, and March* (Salt Lake City: Star, 1897), chap. 23, 40.

7. Collier, *Teachings of President Brigham Young,* 3:292.

8. Jane Brown to Brigham Young, n.d., quoted in Jessie Embry, "Ultimate Taboos: Incest and Mormon Polygamy," *Journal of Mormon History* 18 (Spring 1992): 104. See also Chandless, *Visit to Salt Lake,* 193–94.

9. Embry, "Ultimate Taboos," 104–5; George D. Watt and Jane Brown, CPI; Ronald G. Watt, "Sailing 'The Old Ship Zion': The Life of George D. Watt," *Brigham Young University Studies* 18 (Fall 1977): 48–65; Susan Easton Black, comp., *Early Members of the Reorganized Church of Jesus Christ of Latter Day Saints,* 6 vols. (Provo, Utah: Religious Studies Center, Brigham Young University, 1993), 5:244; George Darling Watt–Molly Gregson Family Group Record, *AF;* 1860 U.S. Census, 14th Ward, Salt Lake City, Salt Lake County, Utah, Population Schedule, 41, George Watt household. Some descendants of Watt believe he married Brown on January 5, 1852. That is the date Jane Brown and her mother, Mary Ann Wood, received their endowments, but the *Ordinance Index* does not show a sealing for Brown and Watt on that date.

10. James Allred Family Group Record, Archives Section, FHL; "Endowment House Record," vol. H, 294; Henry Sudweeks Family Group Record and John Sudweeks Family Group Record, Archives Section, FHL. Sudweeks was the only polygamist to serve in prison for incest. Evans, "Judicial Prosecution," 24.

11. Ebbe Jessen Family Group Record, Archives Section, FHL; Jes Olesen Family Group Record, Archives Section; FHL; Anna Maria Berthelsen, COI.

12. Samuel Smith (1818) Family Group Record, *AF;* George Smith (1816) Family Group Record, *AF;* Frank Esshom, *Pioneers and Prominent Men of Utah, Comprising Photographs, Genealogies, Biographies: The Early History of the Church of Jesus Christ of Latter-day Saints* (Salt Lake City: Pioneers Book, 1913), 1169–70, 967; Aaron Johnson (1806) Family Group Record, *AF;* Lorenzo Johnson (1813) Family Group Record, *AF; History of the Church,* 5:17; Rose W. Malmar, "Springville Is Colonized," in *Heart Throbs of the West,* vol. 11, ed. Kate Carter (Salt Lake City: Daughters of the Utah Pioneers, 1951), 394; Winniefred Spafford Manwaring, "Aaron Johnson," in *An Enduring Legacy,* vol. 3, comp. Lesson Committee, Daughters of Utah Pioneers (Salt Lake City: Daughters of Utah Pioneers, 1980), 320–25.

13. Among the families Jessie Embry surveyed, one-quarter involved sororal plural marriage, while Kimball Young found sororal polygamy among nearly one-fifth of the families he studied. Embry, *Mormon Polygamous Families,* 141; K. Young, *Isn't One Wife Enough?* 126. Both studies are nonrandom and weighted toward the later period during which plural marriage was practiced. On the permission necessary for a mother and her daughters to marry the same man, see Annie Eliza Berry, "Reminiscences, 1899–1907," 4, microfilm of typescript, LDS

Church Archives. Other examples of mothers and daughters sealed to the same man are in Embry, "Ultimate Taboos," 102–3.

14. Grossberg, *Governing the Hearth*, 112.

15. Ibid., 121, 344–45.

16. Hugh B. Brown, "The Latter-day Saint Concept of Marriage," in *Selected Readings in the Latter-day Saint Family*, ed. Blaine R. Porter (Dubuque, Iowa: Wm. C. Brown, 1963), 167.

17. Frederick W. Cox Jr.–Lucy Gunn Allen Family Group Record and Frederick W. Cox–Alvira Coolidge Family Group Record, Patrons Section, FHL.

18. C. Wright, *Marriage and Divorce*, 66. See also Jeffery Ogden Johnson, "Determining and Defining 'Wife': The Brigham Young Households," *Dialogue: A Journal of Mormon Thought* 20 (Fall 1987): 57–70.

19. After the Manifesto, some plural marriages were civil marriages but were without church authorization. Quinn, "LDS Church Authority and New Plural Marriages," 52–55; Hardy, *Solemn Covenant*, 323–24.

20. C. Wright, *Marriage and Divorce*, 71–73; Brown, "Latter-day Saint Concept of Marriage," 169–71; Joseph Fielding Smith, "Celestial Marriage," in *Selected Readings in the Latter-day Saint Family*, ed. Porter, 179–84; James T. Duke, "Eternal Marriage," in *Encyclopedia of Mormonism*, ed. Ludlow, 2:857–59; Thomas B. Holman, "Marriage," in *Encyclopedia of Mormonism*, ed. Ludlow, 2:855–57.

21. Doctrine and Covenants 132:16.

22. C. Wright, *Marriage and Divorce*, 72–73. See also *History of the Church*, 5:391–92; and Doctrine and Covenants 132.

23. Quinn, "LDS Church Authority and New Plural Marriages," 24–32.

24. *JD* 20:29 (July 7, 1878).

25. *JD* 3:265 (July 14, 1855).

26. Woodruff, *Journal*, 8:126–27.

27. Quoted in Charles Lowell Walker, *Diary of Charles Lowell Walker*, 2 vols., ed. A. Karl Larson and Katharine Miles Larson (Logan: Utah State University Press, 1980), 2:629.

28. David John, "Journal," vol. 1, 418, microfilm of original, Special Collections, BYU.

29. Quinn, *Mormon Hierarchy: Extensions of Power*, 180–82.

30. Arrington and Bitton, *Mormon Experience*, 204.

31. *JD* 1:54 (August 29, 1852) (first quote, emphasis added); *JD* 20:29–30 (July 7, 1878) (second quote). See also *JD* 3:266 (Brigham Young, July 14, 1855); *JD* 21:41–42 (Henry W. Naisbitt, November 23, 1879); and *JD* 24:146 (George Q. Cannon, May 6, 1883).

32. *JD* 24:161 (June 24, 1883).

33. *JD* 16:166 (August 31, 1873). The parable is found in Matthew 25:14–30. Erastus Snow said that Joseph Smith had interpreted that parable this way. Woodruff, *Journal*, 8:126–27 (October 14, 1882).

34. *JD* 11:269 (August 19, 1866).

35. *JD* 24:161 (June 24, 1883).

36. *JD* 24:170 (May 19, 1883) (emphasis added). See also *JD* 24:146 (May 6, 1883), where George Q. Cannon refers to "new and everlasting covenant concerning patriarchal marriage," indicating that the new and everlasting covenant encompasses more than plural marriage. An unpublished revelation (whose authentic-

ity has been questioned) given through John Taylor, president of the church, in 1886 about how binding the new and everlasting covenant was on the Saints states, "All commandments that I give must be obeyed by those calling themselves by my name unless they are revoked by me or by my authority and how can I revoke an everlasting covenant." John Taylor, "A Revelation on Celestial Marriage Given through President John Taylor at Centerville, Utah, on September 27, 1886," in *Unpublished Revelations of the Prophets,* ed. Collier, 145. The same ambiguity about the term *new and everlasting covenant* in the Erastus Snow quotation applies to this as well. Quinn, however, argues that John Taylor understood the term in this context as plural marriage. Quinn, "LDS Church Authority and New Plural Marriages," 29–30.

37. *JD* 11:268–69 (August 19, 1866) (emphasis added).

38. Woodruff, *Journal,* 7:31 (October 24, 1871).

39. *JD* 1:64 (August 29, 1852) (first quote, emphasis added); *JD* 17:224 (October 7, 1874) (second quote, emphasis added). See also *JD* 3:266 (Brigham Young, July 14, 1855).

40. *Oxford English Dictionary,* 2d ed., s.v. "reject."

41. *JD* 3:266 (July 14, 1855) (emphasis added).

42. *JD* 17:224–25 (October 7, 1874). This reading differs from that given by B. Carmon Hardy, who interprets this passage to mean "one could not . . . rightfully call himself a Latter-day Saint without accepting and *practicing* polygamy." Hardy, *Solemn Covenant,* 19 (emphasis added).

43. *JD* 20:31 (July 7, 1878) (emphasis added).

44. *JD* 23:278 (October 8, 1882).

45. *JD* 22:124 (October 31, 1880).

46. Genesis 22:1–13. The early Latter-day Saints often used the command given to Abraham to sacrifice his son and his willingness to do so as the type of trials the Saints would have to endure to prove their perfect obedience. See, for example, *JD* 4:120 (Heber C. Kimball, October 5, 1856); *JD* 4:249 (Heber C. Kimball, March 1, 1857); *JD* 4:369 (Brigham Young, June 28, 1857), *JD* 8:164 (Brigham Young, September 2, 1860); *JD* 12:164 (Brigham Young, February 16, 1868); *JD* 12:206 (Brigham Young, May 10, 1868); *JD* 16:245 (George Q. Cannon, October 6, 1873); and *JD* 20:259 (John Taylor, March 2, 1879).

47. *JD* 22:124–25 (October 31, 1880). Lorenzo D. Barnes, born March 22, 1812, in Massachusetts, was baptized into the church on June 16, 1833. He served a mission to Ohio before becoming a member of Zion's Camp. After a mission to Virginia, he became a member of the Adam-ondi-Ahman High Council and then served another mission from 1838 to 1841. Shortly after arriving in Nauvoo, he was called on a mission to England, where he died on December 20, 1842, the first missionary of the church to die on foreign soil. His body was brought to Utah in 1852 to be reinterred. Andrew Jenson, *Latter-day Saint Biographical Encyclopedia: A Compilation of Biographical Sketches of Prominent Men and Women in the Church of Jesus Christ of Latter-day Saints,* 4 vols. (Salt Lake City: Andrew Jenson History Company, 1901; reprint, Salt Lake City: Western Epics, 1971), 3:307–8; Andrew Jenson, *Church Chronology: A Record of Important Events Pertaining to the History of the Church of Jesus Christ of Latter-day Saints,* 2d ed., rev. and enl. (Salt Lake City: Deseret News, 1914), 46.

48. Quoted in Woodruff, *Journal,* 8:235 (March 9, 1884).

49. *JD* 24:46 (June 25, 1882).

50. Tanner, *Mormon Mother*, 62; Brian H. Stuy, ed., *Collected Discourses, Delivered by President Wilford Woodruff, His Two Counselors, the Twelve Apostles, and Others*, 5 vols. (Burbank, Calif.: B.H.S. Publishing, 1987–92), 1:142 (June 2, 1888). See also Charles Smith, "Diary," 259, typescript, Special Collections, BYU.

51. *JD* 20:28 (Joseph F. Smith, July 7, 1878); *JD* 22:124 (George Q. Cannon, October 31, 1880).

52. *JD* 3:264 (Brigham Young, July 14, 1855); *JD* 12:312 (Brigham Young, November 29, 1868); *JD* 13:189 (Orson Pratt, October 7, 1869); *JD* 16:166 (Brigham Young, August 31, 1873); *JD* 16:235 (Orson Hyde, October 5, 1873); *JD* 18:249 (Brigham Young, June 23, 1874); *JD* 24:162 (Erastus Snow, June 24, 1883); *JD* 25:309 (John Taylor, October 6 and 7, 1884).

53. C. C. Harris, *The Family and Industrial Society* (London: George Allen and Unwin, 1983), 16–29. See also George Peter Murdock, *Social Structure* (New York: Free Press, 1949), 4–11.

54. George Edward Grove Taylor Family Group Record, Archives Section, FHL; Ann Taylor, COI.

55. William Black Family Group Record, Patrons Section, FHL. Ann Wickes was again sealed to William Black on March 12, 1857. William Black and Ann Wicks, 1856 and 1857, North America, Marriage Search, *OI*, Main File.

56. 1860 U.S. Census, 13th Ward, Salt Lake City, Salt Lake County, Utah, Population Schedule, 11, John Edward Taylor household; 1870 U.S. Census, Rockville, Kane County, Utah, Population Schedule, 458, William Black household, Micropublication M593; Salt Lake City, Utah, Office of Vital Statistics, "Death Records, 1890–1908," FHL.

57. The historian D. Michael Quinn has stated that, although he has searched thousands of records, he has not seen the expression *eternity only* in original nineteenth-century records of sealings. Quinn, *Mormon Hierarchy: Extensions of Power*, 184. I have found that some eternity-only marriages, while not designated as such, are listed on a different page in the record book than the one containing other marriages performed on the same day, indicating an awareness that these marriages were somehow different from the others. In addition, Melissa Willis testified in 1892 that "sometimes they are married for time and eternity, and some times only for time. Sometimes for time, and some times for eternity," indicating those in the nineteenth century acknowledged that some sealings were for eternity only. Melissa Willis, testimony in United States Circuit Court (8th circuit), Court proceedings, 1892–94, typescript of part of the court proceedings and testimony in the case called the "Temple Lot Case," #575, Special Collections, BYU.

58. James Cook Family Group Record, Patrons Section, FHL; Louisa C. Tatton, "Cemetery Records, Manti, Sanpete County, Utah," 1936, 37, copied from sexton records, typed by the Genealogical Society of Utah, FHL.

59. 1870 U.S. Census, Manti, Sanpete County, Utah, Population Schedule, 44, Maria Davenport household; John Mackey-Maria Davenport Family Group Record, Patrons Section, FHL; Tatton, "Cemetery Records," 32; John Mackey and Maria Davenport, 1862, North America, Marriage Search, *OI*, Main File.

60. 1880 U.S. Census, Manti, Sanpete County, Utah, Population Schedule, E.D.

65, 32 [stamped 422D], Samuel Davenport household, and E.D. 65, 30 [stamped 421B], James Cook household; Lever, *History of Sanpete*, 112 (quote).

61. [Martin] Morten Mortensen and Mary Jorgansen, 1878, North America, Marriage Search, *OI*, Main File; "Endowment House Record," vol. I, 20; Martin Axelsen Family Group Record, Patrons Section, FHL.

62. 1880 U.S. Census, Manti, Sanpete County, Utah, Population Schedule, E.D. 65, 5 [stamped 409A], Maria Axelsen household, and 36 [stamped 424D], Morten Mortenson household; Morten Axelsen, COI; 1900 U.S. Census, Manti, Sanpete County, Utah, Population Schedule, E.D. 125, 9 [stamped 137B], Morten Axelsen household; 1910 U.S. Census, Manti, Sanpete County, Utah, Population Schedule, E.D. 155, 2B, Morten Axelsen household, National Archives Micropublication T624. Maren's and Morten's use of different surnames does not appear to be an attempt to hide their relationship. Despite the Supreme Court's ruling in the *Reynolds* case the year before, seventeen Manti households in the 1880 census contained two or more wives, and their relationship to their husbands (head of household) was stated.

63. Nels Anderson, *Desert Saints: The Mormon Frontier in Utah* (Chicago: University of Chicago Press, 1942), 352–53. Michael Quinn states that because older women are still attractive, one should not assume that sex was not a part of a marriage to "widows and elderly spinsters." Quinn, *Mormon Hierarchy: Extensions of Power*, 185. This issue, however, is not attractiveness but what rights and obligations were involved in the commitments a couple made to each other. Although Quinn is persuasive that too many marriages have been termed eternity only but in fact were conjugal ones, even he acknowledges that "some lesser-known wives may not have been in a sexual relationship with their sealed husband" (185).

64. Mosiah Lyman Hancock, "Autobiography," 31, microfilm of typescript, LDS Church Archives.

65. Ibid., 38.

66. Black, *Membership of the Church*, 14:708–10; "Nauvoo Temple Endowment Record," microfilm of typescript, FHL.

67. C. Wright, *Marriage and Divorce*, 66; Van Wagoner, "Mormon Polyandry in Nauvoo," 67–83.

68. Frederick Walter Cox–Calista Cordelia Morley Family Group Record, Patrons Section, FHL.

69. *Complainant's Abstract of Pleading and Evidence . . . the Reorganized Church of Jesus Christ of Latter Day Saints, Complainant, v. the Church of Christ at Independence, Missouri . . .* (Lamoni, Iowa: Herald Publishing House, 1893), 350 (hereafter cited as *Abstract of Temple Lot Case*). Such marriages were commonly called proxy marriages early in the church's history. See J. Johnson, "Determining and Defining 'Wife,'" 58. See, for example, *JD* 26:15 (George Q. Cannon, November 20, 1884).

70. K. Young, *Isn't One Wife Enough?* 32.

71. George Washington Snow Family Group Record, Patrons Section, FHL; John Ely Warner and Eunice Billings, 1849, North America, Marriage Search, *OI*, Addendum; M. F. Farnsworth, "History of Manti," 1936, 157, typescript typed by the Genealogical Society of Utah; Tatton, "Cemetery Records," 152; George Washington Snow–Eunice Billings Family Group Record, Patrons Section, FHL; 1870

U.S. Census, Provo, Utah County, Utah, Population Schedule, 289, Diantha Billings household; 1880 U.S. Census, Provo, Utah County, Utah, Population Schedule, E.D. 81, 48 [stamped 142B], Eunice Warner household.

72. George Washington Snow–Mary Wells Family Group Record, Patrons Section, FHL; Sanpete County, Utah, "Marriage License Records, 1888–1894," May 10, 1893, 407, microfilm of original, FHL; 1900 U.S. Census, Manti, Sanpete County, Utah, Population Schedule, E.D. 125, 9 [stamped 137A], Alexander Tennant household.

73. Deuteronomy 25:5–10.

74. *JD* 6:358 (July 24, 1859). See also "Celestial Marriage," *Seer* 1 (September 1853): 142.

75. C. Christensen, *Before and after Mt. Pisgah*, 233.

76. Typescript of letters in possession of author. See Foster, *Religion and Sexuality*, 312–13; and Lawrence Foster, "Sex and Prophetic Power: A Comparison of John Humphrey Noyes, Founder of the Oneida Community, with Joseph Smith, Jr., the Mormon Prophet," *Dialogue: A Journal of Mormon Thought* 31 (Winter 1998): 80. In neither work does Foster have the context for this letter, and he erroneously uses the Richardson example as support for the idea that early Mormon leaders were toying with providing proxy husbands for wives whose husbands were temporarily away on missions. Foster acknowledges that there is "no conclusive manuscript evidence explicitly supporting such a practice." Foster, *Religion and Sexuality*, 163. As I have shown, the term *proxy husband* was used in an entirely different context, and in the early church the term *proxy* was used almost exclusively in relation to the temple. (Of the twenty-one times the word *proxy* is used in the *Journal of Discourses*, seventeen are clear references to vicarious ordinances, two are to the Atonement, one is to Boaz as a proxy or levirate husband to Ruth, and one is to proxy voting. See, for example, *JD* 5:90 (Heber C. Kimball, July 26, 1857); *JD* 5:291 (Erastus Snow, October 4, 1857); *JD* 6:242 (Joseph Young, April 18, 1857); *JD* 6:307 (Brigham Young, April 18, 1853); *JD* 12:73 (D. H. Wells, June 30, 1857); *JD* 13:328 (Brigham Young, April 24, 1870); *JD* 16:187 (Brigham Young, September 4, 1873); *JD* 18:92 (Joseph F. Smith, October 6, 1875); *JD* 18:191 (Wilford Woodruff, April 16, 1876); *JD* 21:294 (Orson Pratt, July 18, 1880); *JD* 22:166 (Charles W. Penrose, July 17, 1881); *JD* 24:97 (Charles W. Penrose, March 4, 1883); *JD* 25:235 (F. D. Richards, May 17, 1884); *JD* 26:15 (George Q. Cannon, November 20, 1884); and *JD* 5:183 (John Taylor, August 30, 1857). In addition, the quotations Foster uses as support for his argument come from critics of the church. Although there was more than one "convenience" marriage, the context of the Richardson case, the only one for which we currently have credible documentation, does not support his conjecture that such marriages were to provide sexual partners for wives whose husbands were absent temporarily on missions.

77. Annie Richardson Johnson and Elva Richardson Shumway, *Charles Edmund Richardson: Man of Destiny* (Tempe, Ariz.: Publication Services, 1982), 6–10, 26–29 (quote on 29).

78. Frederick Walter Cox–Mary Ann Darrow Family Group Record, Patrons Section, FHL.

79. C. Christensen, *Before and after Mt. Pisgah*, 234; Johnson and Shumway, *Charles Edmund Richardson*, 29; Edmund Richardson Family Group Record, Patrons Section, FHL; 1860 U.S. Census, Manti, Sanpete County, Utah, Popula-

tion Schedule, 1, Edm[un]d Richardson household, census information taken June 1, 1860.

80. C. Christensen, *Before and after Mt. Pisgah*, 385.

81. Johnson and Shumway, *Charles Edmund Richardson*, 29, 35; Agreement for Settlement of Estate, January 3, 1882, Frederick W. Cox File, File of Estates, Basement Archives, Sanpete County Courthouse, Manti, Utah.

82. Johnson and Shumway, *Charles Edmund Richardson*, 37.

83. Foster, "Sex and Prophetic Power," 77. See also B. Carmon Hardy, "Lords of Creation: Polygamy, the Abrahamic Household, and Mormon Patriarchy," *Journal of Mormon History* 20 (Spring 1994): 119–52.

84. C. Wright, *Marriage and Divorce*, 25–26.

85. 5 Eng. Rul. Cases 833, 839 (1866). See also Kenneth L. Cannon II, "A Strange Encounter: The English Courts and Mormon Polygamy, *Brigham Young University Studies* 22 (Winter 1982): 73–83. For a critique of the case and how American courts have decided similar cases not related to Mormons, see Bartholomew, "Recognition of Polygamous Marriages in America," 1022–75.

86. John Hyde and Lavinia Hawkins, 1853, North America, Marriage Search, *OI*, Main File. For a brief biography, see Lynne Watkins Jorgensen, "John Hyde, Jr., Mormon Renegade," *Journal of Mormon History* 17 (1991): 120–44.

87. John Hyde, *Mormonism* (New York: W. P. Fetridge, 1857); 5 Eng. Rul. Cases 833, 834, citing *Hyde v. Hyde and Woodmansee* (1866).

88. *JD* 4:165 (January 11, 1857).

89. 5 Eng. Rul. Cases 833 (quote), 834, 837; 12 Eng. Rul. Cases, 735. See K. Cannon, "Strange Encounter," 76.

90. 5 Eng. Rul. Cases 838–39.

91. The court specifically declined to rule on the rights of legitimacy and succession in polygamous marriages. Ibid., 841.

92. *Acts, Resolutions, and Memorials*, chap. 12, sec. 24, 153 (emphasis added).

93. Carole Shammas, Marylynn Salmon, and Michel Dahlin, *Inheritance in America from Colonial Times to the Present* (New Brunswick, N.J.: Rutgers University Press, 1987), 86. For general background on dower rights, see John D. Lawson, *Rights, Remedies, and Practice, at Law, in Equity, and under the Codes: A Treatise on American Law in Civil Causes; with a Digest of Illustrative Cases*, vol. 2 (San Francisco: Bancroft-Whitney, 1889), secs. 775–77; and Tapping Reeve, *The Law of Baron and Femme*, 3d ed. (Albany, N.Y.: William Gould, Law Publishers, 1862; reprint, New York: Source Book Press, a Division of Collectors Editions, 1970), 98–108.

94. *Compiled Laws of the Territory of Utah Containing All Statutes Now in Force* (Salt Lake City: Deseret News, 1876), sec. 1022. By a statute approved February 18, 1876, in settling intestate estates the surviving spouse received one-third of the estate for life if there was only one child, but if there was more than one child, the surviving spouse received only one-fourth of the estate for life. The homestead exemption remained in force (Title 14, chap. 2, sec. 19, sec. 703, 275–76), but it was restricted in 1884.

95. *Acts, Resolutions, and Memorials*, chap. 12, sec. 25, 153 (emphasis added).

96. *Compiled Laws of the Territory of Utah* (1876), sec. 714.

97. Grossberg, *Governing the Hearth*, 200–218.

98. George D. Peacock Family Group Record, Patrons Section, FHL; Church

of Jesus Christ of Latter-day Saints, Manti Ward, "Record of Members, [1849]–1877," 2.

99. Sanpete County, Utah, Probate Court, "Probate Record, including Minutes, 1866–1884," Book A, 265–67, microfilm of MS, FHL; Petition for Final Distribution of Estate, June 24, 1882, George Peacock File, File of Estates, Basement Archives, Sanpete County Courthouse, Manti, Utah.

100. Agreement for Settlement of Estate, January 3, 1882, Frederick W. Cox File, File of Estates.

101. Decree of Distribution of Estate, February 19, 1881, Orson Hyde File, File of Estates.

102. K. Young, *Isn't One Wife Enough?* 267–69.

103. Last Will and Testament of Madison D. Hambleton, Sanpete County, "Probate Record, including Minutes, 1866–1884," Book A, 31–32; Last Will and Testament of Christian Nielsen, File of Wills, County Clerk's Office, Sanpete County Courthouse, Manti, Utah.

104. Sanpete County, "Probate Record, including Minutes, 1866–1884," Book A, 412.

105. Firmage and Mangrum, *Zion in the Courts,* 336.

106. C. Madsen, "At Their Peril," 436–37. Both Kimball Young and Jessie Embry discuss inheritance in polygamous families, although their examples, with the exception of John Taylor, are drawn from the late, post-Manifesto period, when Mormons no longer had exclusive control over the laws and courts that controlled inheritance. K. Young, *Isn't One Wife Enough?* 261–76; Embry, *Mormon Polygamous Families,* 182–86.

107. Grossberg, *Governing the Hearth,* 121, 95–102, 141–49 (first quote on 97, second on 121).

Chapter 5: The Marriage Market

1. Although the church officially forsook plural marriage, some new marriages were sanctioned after 1890. Hardy, *Solemn Covenant,* 389–425; Quinn, "LDS Church Authority and New Plural Marriages," 57–103.

2. For the sources used to create the Manti data set, see the appendix.

3. Quinn, "LDS Church Authority and New Plural Marriages," 57–59; Hardy, *Solemn Covenant,* 389–425.

4. The population used to calculate these rates is women in any Manti census who were twenty years or older and never married as well as those women who spent some of their married life in Manti. The latter group of women did not necessarily live in Manti when they married, but their first marriage took place in Utah; thus, although the base of the study is Manti, the women represent the wider social patterns in Utah. In addition, for the last period, the population used for calculation also includes early twentieth-century Manti residents' daughters who were born before 1890 but who married after 1910. This was done so that the marriage rates would reflect the reality of the Manti marriage rates and not be biased downward: excluding some women in the same birth cohorts as those who did marry before 1910 would have misrepresented the experience of women in the last cohort. As with monogamous wives, only plural wives who spent some

of their married life in Manti and whose first marriages were performed in Utah were included in the calculations; not all wives of polygamists in the Manti subset are therefore represented in these rates. Plural wives whose marriage ended before the polygamist moved to Manti or who married after the polygamist moved from Manti are excluded. In addition, some Utah polygamists had wives who lived apart in different towns. This was especially the case when the polygamist carried general church responsibilities that required him to travel throughout the territory. Had a Manti citizen's plural wives who lived elsewhere been included, the number of plural wives in Manti would have been out of proportion to monogamous ones. Of the 1,084 women in the data set, 10 women, or less than 1 percent, were excluded because not enough information could be found to determine their ages at marriage. Seven percent of women included lacked an exact birth date or marriage date, but their marriage ages could be estimated based on census data, birth of first child, or endowment date, which was usually also the marriage date.

5. For example, each woman who was in Utah on her fifteenth birthday and who did not marry that year contributed one person-year to the age fifteen category. A woman who married would contribute only that portion of the year during which she was single, and similarly, an immigrant would count only during the time she resided in Utah. For example, Louisa Griffin arrived in Utah in 1884 at age twenty-three years and six months. Her arrival therefore added only .50 to the person-years at age twenty-three. She married the next year, when she was twenty-four years and nine months old; she thus contributed .75 person-years to the count for twenty-four-year-olds. Anna Maria Myrup married the day she arrived in Utah: this means she contributed one marriage to the twenty-year-old category but nothing to the person-years.

6. The marriage registration states were Alabama, Alaska, California, Connecticut, Delaware, Florida, Georgia, Hawaii, Idaho, Iowa, Kansas, Kentucky, Louisiana, Maine, Maryland, Michigan, Mississippi, Montana, Nebraska, New Hampshire, New Jersey, New York (excluding New York City), Ohio, Oregon, Pennsylvania, Rhode Island, South Dakota, Tennessee, Utah, Vermont, Virginia, and Wisconsin, and Wyoming. U.S. Department of Health, Education and Welfare, *Vital Statistics of the United States, 1960,* vol. 3, *Marriage and Divorce* (Washington, D.C.: U.S. Government Printing Office, 1964), I-3. Marriage registrations states are those whose records fully cover all marriages and include a minimum list of such items as age at marriage. Hugh Carter and Paul C. Glick, *Marriage and Divorce: A Social and Economic Study,* rev. ed. (Cambridge, Mass.: Harvard University Press, 1976), 9–11.

7. Women in 1960 were used because comparable marriage rates for nineteenth-century United States are not available. Adequate and accessible records for migration and marriage in general do not exist for that period. Michael R. Haines, "Long-Term Marriage Patterns in the United States from Colonial Times to the Present," *History of the Family* 1, no. 1 (1996): 22–23; Irene B. Taeuber and Conrad Taeuber, *People of the United States in the 20th Century,* a Census Monograph (Washington, D.C.: U.S. Government Printing Office, 1971), 295; Degler, *At Odds,* 457; Mintz and Kellogg, *Domestic Revolutions,* 178–80.

8. For those immigrants without known dates of immigration, a date was estimated based on the average lapse of time between arrival and marriage for their period.

9. Percentages of American women who never married are from Daniel Scott Smith, "Family Limitation, Sexual Control, and Domestic Feminism in Victorian America," in *Clio's Consciousness Raised: New Perspectives on the History of Women*, ed. Mary S. Hartman and Lois Banner (New York: Octagon Books, 1976), 121.

10. U.S. Bureau of the Census, "Population Characteristics: Marital Status and Family Status: March 1967," *Current Population Reports*, series P-20, no. 170 (February 23, 1968): 4; Haines, "Long-Term Marriage Patterns," 23.

11. This is in accordance with Carlson's findings that women who immigrated before age fifteen had nuptial patterns similar to those of native-born women. Elwood D. Carlson, "The Impact of International Migration upon the Timing of Marriage and Childbearing," *Demography* 22 (February 1985): 61–72. I reduced the age to fourteen because Mormon women married at a very young age in the initial settlement period.

12. G. P. Mineau, L. L. Bean, and M. Skolnick, "Mormon Demographic History II: The Family Life Cycle and Natural Fertility," *Population Studies* 33 (November 1979): 439.

13. Mineau, Bean, and Anderton, "Migration and Fertility," 50.

14. Logue, *Sermon in the Desert*, 56.

15. M. Skolnick, L. Bean, D. May, V. Arbon, K. De Nevers, and P. Cartwright, "Mormon Demographic History I: Nuptiality and Fertility of Once-Married Couples," *Population Studies* 32 (March 1978): 14; Orville Vernon Burton, *In My Father's House Are Many Mansions: Family and Community in Edgefield, South Carolina* (Chapel Hill: University of North Carolina Press, 1985), 118; Logue, *Sermon in the Desert*, 46.

16. U.S. Bureau of the Census, "Population Characteristics," 4.

17. Mineau, Bean, and Anderton, "Migration and Fertility," 47; John Hajnal, "European Marriage Patterns in Perspective," in *Population in History: Essays in Historical Demography*, ed. D. V. Glass and D. E. C. Eversley (Chicago: Aldine, 1965), 108–15; George Alter, *Family and the Female Life Course: The Women of Verviers, Belgium, 1849–1880* (Madison: University of Wisconsin Press, 1988), 40.

18. For evidence that women on the frontier tended to marry earlier than in areas that had been settled longer, see Richard A. Easterlin, George Alter, and Gretchen A. Condran, "Farms and Farm Families in Old and New Areas: The Northern States in 1860," in *Family and Population in Nineteenth-Century America*, ed. Tamara K. Hareven and Maris A. Vinovskis (Princeton, N.J.: Princeton University Press, 1978), 22–84.

19. Lee L. Bean, Geraldine P. Mineau, Yung-chang Hsueh, and Douglas L. Anderton, "The Fertility Effects of Marriage Patterns in a Frontier American Population," *Historical Methods* 20 (Fall 1987): 163–64.

20. Ivins, "Notes on Mormon Polygamy," 239. (For an evaluation of the sources on which his work is based, see the appendix.) Using the 1860 census, Nels Anderson found that 8.5 percent of households (25 of 293 households) in twelve communities in southern Utah were polygamous. N. Anderson, *Desert Saints*, 394–95. Because the 1860 census listed neither family relationships nor marital status, it is impossible to identify all polygamous families from census data alone. An undercount of polygamists is likely even using the 1880 census, which does list family relationships. L. Bennion, "Incidence of Mormon Polygamy in 1880," 32. Smith and Kunz calculate that 8.8 percent of males practiced polygamy in 1885.

This is, as they note, based on a figure given by the historian Hubert Howe Bancroft, although the source of the figure is unknown. Smith and Kunz, "Polygyny and Fertility," 470–71.

21. Cornwall, Courtright, and Van Beek, "How Common the Principle?" 148; Jan Shipps, Cheryll L. May, and Dean L. May, "Sugar House Ward: A Latter-day Saint Congregation," in *American Congregations*, vol. 1, *Portraits of Twelve Religious Communities*, ed. James P. Wind and James W. Lewis (Chicago: University of Chicago Press, 1994), 307. Polygamous households tended to be larger than monogamous ones. This explains the difference between 30.0 percent of households in 1870 that were polygamous but 36.0 percent (shown in table 3) of the population living in polygamous households.

22. L. Bennion, "Incidence of Mormon Polygamy," 31.

23. In the calculations for table 3, wives not enumerated in Manti but not included in the census indexes anywhere else were added, while duplicates in the census were subtracted. The total for each census year may vary slightly from official census reports because families with no ties to the church have also been eliminated.

24. L. Bennion, "Incidence of Mormon Polygamy," 31, 36–37; Dean L. May, "People on the Mormon Frontier: Kanab's Families of 1874," *Journal of Family History* 1 (Winter 1976): 172. On the basis of his St. George data, Larry Logue argues that there was not a dramatic decline in the number of plural marriages because in St. George there were only ten fewer plural marriages in the 1870s than in the 1850s. Logue, *Sermon in the Desert*, 118. His figures, however, are apparently based only on the plural wives who lived in St. George, which was founded in 1861. Those wives who had been divorced or died before the husband moved to St. George were apparently not counted, which would have undercounted the number of marriages in the St. George data set for the 1850s. Also, as Ben Bennion has shown, St. George had a relatively high incidence of polygamous families in 1880.

25. On the Mormon reformation, see chapter 2.

26. Note that the percentage in plural families is slightly smaller than the percentage of women who were in plural marriage. Since many of these plural marriages had occurred not long before the 1860 census was taken, many of these women had few if any children. Thus, monogamous families generally had more children, which accounts for the low proportion of the population in polygamous families compared with the high percentage of women who were polygamous wives.

27. One family whose status is ambiguous has been omitted from the figures for polygamous families. Had the family been included, the figure in table 3 for 1900 would have been 7.3 percent, and those who were still living in polygamous families in 1900 would rise to 6.8 percent. When Andrew Nelson became disenchanted with Mormonism and joined the Presbyterian church, his first wife divorced him. The other two, who were sisters, remained, although he lived with only the younger one, Sophia. Nevertheless, Camilla, the older sister, is listed in the 1900 census as married for forty-one years. In addition, she is included on the Nelson family tombstone, although Sophia is designated as wife, while for Camilla only years of birth and death are given and no relationship is mentioned. Lever, *History of Sanpete*, 163; Sanpete County, Utah, Probate Court, "Probate Records, 1884–1890," Book B, 313, FHL; 1900 U.S. Census, Manti, Sanpete Coun-

ty, Utah, Population Schedule, E.D. 125, 16 [stamped 144A], Camilla Nelson household; Andrew Nelson tombstone, Manti City Cemetery.

28. Ivins, "Notes on Mormon Polygamy," 231–32.

29. For the way the listing was compiled, see Esshom, *Pioneers and Prominent Men of Utah*, 1, 11–12.

30. Jenson, *Church Chronology*, 87; *CHC* 5:442–43.

31. Jenson, *Church Chronology*, 103.

32. Ruth B. Dixon, "Explaining Cross-Cultural Variations in Age at Marriage and Proportions Never Marrying," *Population Studies* 25 (July 1971): 215–33.

33. Tanner, *Mormon Mother*, 62 (quote); Burgess-Olson, "Family Structure and Dynamics in Utah Mormon Families," 69–82.

34. One visitor to Salt Lake City claimed that no man was allowed to marry if he could not support another wife properly, and even in the humblest class the man had to provide a separate bedroom for each wife. Chandless, *Visit to Salt Lake*, 191. In the outlying areas where living in forts was considered necessary, however, separate bedrooms for each wife was not always possible.

35. *JD* 12:144 (October 9, 1867); *JD* 19:166 (November 11, 1877).

36. The line for foreign immigrants in figure 3 is similar to that on a graph prepared by Richard L. Jensen, although he calculated the number of immigrants from different sources. R. Jensen, "Steaming Through," 20.

37. Foreign immigration virtually ceased in 1858 because of the uncertainty about the future of the Utah settlements with the arrival of Johnston's army. The Utah militia was mobilized to resist the army's efforts to enter the Salt Lake Valley before an agreement had been reached, and the Saints abandoned their northern settlements pending a compromise with the army. The best account of the Utah War is Norman F. Furniss, *The Mormon Conflict, 1850–1859* (New Haven, Conn.: Yale University Press, 1960).

38. Bennett, *Mormons at the Missouri*, 228; Wayne L. Wahlquist, "Population Growth in the Mormon Core Area: 1847–1890," in *Mormon Role in the Settlement of the West*, ed. Jackson, 115.

39. Smith and Kunz, "Polygyny and Fertility," 469.

40. Five-year moving averages are calculated by averaging the number for the target year with the numbers for the previous two years and the following two years. This smooths out the line so trends are more discernible.

41. Lee, Mineau, and Anderton, *Fertility Change on the American Frontier*, 136, 243–44, 250.

42. Lever, *History of Sanpete*, 104–5; Thomas Boyington Family Group Record, Patrons Section, FHL; 1860 U.S. Census, Manti, Sanpete County, Utah, Population Schedule, 16, Wm F. Mailet household; 1870 U.S. Census, Manti, Sanpete County, Utah, Population Schedule, 39, Thomas Boynton household.

43. Cornwall, Cartwright, and Van Beek also found that there were few young unmarried women in 1860. Cornwall, Cartwright, and Van Beek, "How Common the Principle?" 148–49. See also Gary Wyatt, "Mormon Polygyny in the Nineteenth Century: A Theoretical Analysis," *Journal of Comparative Family Studies* 20 (Spring 1989): 17.

44. In their articles on the reformation, Paul H. Peterson and Gustive O. Larson never mention Manti. P. Peterson, "Mormon Reformation," 59–87; G. Larson, "Mormon Reformation," 45–63.

45. Charles S. Peterson, "Imprint of Agricultural Systems on the Utah Land-

scape," in *Mormon Role in the Settlement of the West,* ed. Jackson, 98; Lever, *History of Sanpete,* 61.

46. Azariah Smith, "Journal," June 6, 1869, March 6, 1870, April 3, 1870, December 1871.

47. Manti data set; note on Lyness Bemus Family Group Record, Patrons Section, FHL.

48. Logue, *Sermon in the Desert,* 46, 56; Larry M. Logue, "A Time of Marriage: Monogamy and Polygamy in a Utah Town," *Journal of Mormon History* 11 (1984): 16. The figures for Manti are not calculated in the same way Logue calculated his for St. George, but they are similar.

49. Kathryn M. Daynes, "Single Men in a Polygamous Society: Male Marriage Patterns in Manti, Utah," *Journal of Mormon History* 24 (Spring 1998): 106; Taeuber and Taeuber, *People of the United States,* 301; Hajnal, "European Marriage Patterns in Perspective," 101–43.

50. Taeuber and Taeuber *People of the United States,* 305; Logue, *Sermon in the Desert,* 46.

51. Daynes, "Single Men in a Polygamous Society," 106–9; Logue, *Sermon in the Desert,* 63.

52. Leonard J. Arrington, *Brigham Young: American Moses* (New York: Alfred A Knopf, 1985; reprint, Urbana: University of Illinois Press, 1986), 315.

53. Church of Jesus Christ of Latter-day Saints, "Manti Ward Record," Book A, December 12, 1852, and January 2, 1853.

54. Melvin Ember argues that variations in sex ratios are important in explaining polygamy. Melvin Ember, "Warfare, Sex Ratio, and Polygyny," *Ethnology* 13 (April 1974): 197–206. Polygamy, however, overcorrects for a shortage of males and causes a marriage squeeze against males; that is, since there were fewer single women than men, it was difficult for males to find mates. Gary R. Lee, *Family Structure and Interaction: A Comparative Analysis,* 2d ed., rev. (Minneapolis: University of Minnesota Press, 1982), 80; Daynes, "Single Men in a Polygamous Society," 89–111.

55. E. Campbell, "Early Colonization Patterns," 134–35; Hunter, *Brigham Young,* 65–67.

56. It was similar in St. George, where women in their twenties outnumbered men in 1870, although the ratio evened by 1880. Logue, *Sermon in the Desert,* 70.

57. Daynes, "Single Men in a Polygamous Society," 90; 1850 U.S. Census, Manti, Sanpete County, Utah, Population Schedule; 1860 U.S. Census, Manti, Sanpete County, Utah, Population Schedule; 1870 U.S. Census, Manti, Sanpete County, Utah, Population Schedule; 1880 U.S. Census, Manti, Sanpete County, Utah, Population Schedule; *Seventh Census of the United States, 1850,* 988–93; *Population of the United States in 1860,* 574; *Ninth Census,* vol. 2, *The Vital Statistics of the United States* (Washington, D.C.: Government Printing Office, 1872), 608–18; *Compendium of the Tenth Census (June 1, 1880)* (Washington, D.C.: Government Printing Office, 1883), 618, 624, 630, 636, 642, 648; *Compendium of the Eleventh Census: 1890, Part 3* (Washington, D.C.: Government Printing Office, 1897), 244. For population pyramids showing a non-Mormon town with a preponderance of men and a Mormon town with a majority of women, see N. Anderson, *Desert Saints,* 431. See also Dean L. May, "A Demographic Portrait of the Mormons, 1830–1980," in *After 150 Years: The Latter-day Saints in Sesquicentennial Perspective,*

ed. Thomas G. Alexander and Jessie L. Embry (Midvale, Utah: Signature Books for Charles Redd Center for Western Studies, 1983), 62–63.

58. May, "A Demographic Portrait of the Mormons, 1830–1980," 51, 67.

59. Edward L. Kimball, "The History of LDS Temple Admission Standards," *Journal of Mormon History* 24 (Spring 1998): 135–41.

60. The ordinance of the endowment was suspended during the Utah War, from May 18, 1858, to August 20, 1859. "Endowment House Record."

61. This gender difference was not simply the result of women's being endowed so that they could become plural wives. The pattern of gender differences does not coincide with that for plural marriages. For example, the sex ratio for those endowed in 1869–70 is 73 during a year where there was a large number of plural marriages, which would suggest women were being endowed just before sealings into plural marriage. But the sex ratio is also that low in 1875 and 1884, when the number of plural marriages was fairly low.

62. Helena Chojnacka, "Polygyny and the Rate of Population Growth," *Population Studies* 34 (March 1980): 104.

63. Hardy, "Lords of Creation," 119–52; Woodruff, *Journal*, 3:131 (first quote); *JD* 5:291 (October 4, 1857) (second quote).

Chapter 6: Women Who Became Plural Wives

1. Eliza Maria Partridge Lyman, "Journal, February 1846–December 1885," 13–14, microfilm of MS, LDS Church Archives; "Journal of Sarah De Armon Pea Rich," 44, typescript, Special Collections, BYU. See also Arrington and Bitton, *Mormon Experience*, 199.

2. Gordon Shepherd and Gary Shepherd, *A Kingdom Transformed: Themes in the Development of Mormonism* (Salt Lake City: University of Utah Press, 1984), 78.

3. Burgess-Olson, "Family Structure and Dynamics in Utah Mormon Families," 69–82; Davis Bitton, "Mormon Polygamy: A Review Article," *Journal of Mormon History* 4 (1977): 105; Embry, *Mormon Polygamous Families*, 41–52; K. Young, *Isn't One Wife Enough?* 103–19; Foster, *Religion and Sexuality*, 198, 211–12; Marie Cornwall and Laga Van Beek, "The Mormon Practice of Plural Marriage: The Social Construction of Religious Identity and Commitment," *Religion and the Social Order* 5 (1995) 18–23; Logue, *Sermon in the Desert*, 62; Wyatt, "Mormon Polygyny in the Nineteenth Century," 13–20.

4. Lever, *History of Sanpete*, 50–51, 78; Arrington, *Great Basin Kingdom*, 148–56.

5. See figure 4.

6. Larson, "Mormon Gathering," 181–82; Wallace Stegner, *The Gathering of Zion: The Story of the Mormon Trail* (New York: McGraw Hill, 1964; reprint, Salt Lake City: Westwater, 1981), 221–48; LeRoy R. Hafen and Ann W. Hafen, *Handcarts to Zion* (Glendale, Calif.: Arthur H. Clarke, 1976), 53–141; Howard A. Christy, "Weather, Disaster, and Responsibility: An Essay on the Willie and Martin Handcart Story," *Brigham Young University Studies* 37, no. 1 (1997–98): 5–74. Not all who pulled handcarts were poor. Lynne Watkins Jorgensen, "The Martin Handcart Disaster: The London Participants," *Journal of Mormon History* 21 (Fall 1995): 175–76.

7. Alexander, "Wilford Woodruff and the Mormon Reformation of 1855–57," 25–39 (quotes on 28, 31); Lever, *History of Sanpete*, 51, 78; P. Peterson, "Mormon Reformation of 1856–1857," 65–77.

8. Ivins, "Notes on Mormon Polygamy," 239.

9. E. A. Wrigley and R. S. Schofield, *The Population History of England, 1541–1871: A Reconstruction* (London: Edward Arnold, 1981), 158, 349–50, 421–22.

10. Parents probably preferred such men as husbands for their daughters. Embry, *Mormon Polygamous Families*, 49.

11. K. Young, *Isn't One Wife Enough?* 126; Bean, Mineau, and Anderton, *Fertility Change on the American Frontier*, 111.

12. Patty Bartlett Sessions, *Mormon Midwife: The 1846–1888 Diaries of Patty Bartlett Sessions*, ed. Donna Toland Smart (Logan, Utah: Utah State University Press, 1997), 29.

13. Maureen Ursenbach Beecher, "Women's Work on the Mormon Frontier," *Utah Historical Quarterly* 49 (Summer 1981): 276–90.

14. Women in the "unknown, women over 30" category have not been identified on the Crossing the Ocean Index or Crossing the Plains Index using their maiden names. This means that they probably came to Utah using another surname, but former marriages for these women have not been found, often because the name is too common to clearly distinguish the woman searched from others of the same name. Probably most had been previously married and, in any case, had no father living in Utah.

15. Mulder, *Homeward to Zion*, 148.

16. Donald K. Grayson, "Human Mortality in a Natural Disaster: The Willie Handcart Company," *Journal of Anthropological Research* 52 (Summer 1996): 185–205. Women, Grayson explains, are normally better able than men to survive under conditions of little food, because females over five years of age have a lower basal metabolism. They are also generally smaller and have a higher proportion of body fat than men. In addition, women endure cold conditions better than men because their body fat is distributed subcutaneously and thus serves as a good insulator. Men have greater decreases in core temperatures, and their basal metabolism increases more than women's, while they maintain higher skin temperatures. Men thus suffer greater heat loss because of the greater difference between their higher skin temperatures and the temperature of the air. Grayson, "Human Mortality," 189. Various figures have been given for the number of deaths and the number of people in the company. Those given in the text are Grayson's. Howard Christy gives 74 deaths for the Willie Company. Christy, "Weather, Disaster, and Responsibility," 51.

17. Azariah Smith, "Journal," November 30, 1856; Albert Smith Family Group Record, Patrons Section, FHL; Arrington, *Great Basin Kingdom*, 158.

18. Lever, *History of Sanpete*, 151; John Lowry Sr. Family Group Record, Patrons Section, FHL; Elizabeth Haydock, CPI; Christy, "Weather, Disaster, and Responsibility," 51. Josiah Rogerson, who was fifteen when he was a member of the Martin Company, estimated that between 135 to 150 of the company died. Hafen and Hafen, *Handcarts to Zion*, 140.

19. Church of Jesus Christ of Latter-day Saints, Manti South Ward, "Record of Members, 1877–1941," 22, microfilm of MS, FHL; William Bench Jr. Family Group Record, Patrons Section, FHL.

20. Niels Peter Domgaard and Metta Christina Christiansen, 1859, North

America, Marriage Search, *OI*, Main File; "Endowment House Record," vol. C, 90; 1860 U.S. Census, Manti, Sanpete County, Utah, Mortality Schedule, Mette C. Dungar; International Society, Daughters of Utah Pioneers, *Pioneer Women of Faith and Fortitude,* 4 vols. (N.p. [Utah]: Publishers Press, 1998), 1:825.

21. "Family History: Taken from a History Written by Joseph Hansen, Price, Utah," 11, typescript, Manti City Library; Jens Hansen Family Group Record, Patrons Section, FHL.

22. Hans Jensen Hals, "Reminiscences and Diary, 1867–1910," 7, trans. Lauritz G. Peterson, microfilm of typescript, LDS Church Archives; Juanita Brooks, *Emma Lee* (Logan, Utah: Utah State University Press, 1975), 4 (quote).

23. Embry, *Mormon Polygamous Families,* 89–98.

24. Dean L. May, *Three Frontiers: Family, Land, and Society in the American West, 1850–1900* (New York: Cambridge University Press, 1994), 107–41.

25. Quinn, *Mormon Hierarchy: Extensions of Power,* 187–92.

26. Gary S. Becker, *A Treatise on the Family,* enl. ed. (Cambridge, Mass.: Harvard University Press, 1991), 87.

27. Burgess-Olson, "Family Structure and Dynamics in Utah Mormon Families," 71–74, 84.

28. Seven unknown monogamous wives have been eliminated in this figure.

29. Jessie L. Embry and Martha S. Bradley, "Mothers and Daughters in Polygamy," *Dialogue: A Journal of Mormon Thought* 18 (Fall 1985): 99–101.

30. See chapter 4.

31. Farr, *Story of Edwin Marion Whiting and Anna Maria Isaacson,* 120; Logue, *Sermon in the Desert,* 62–63; Embry, *Mormon Polygamous Families,* 54, 66–71.

32. See chapter 9.

33. Of the 19,017 Latter-day Saints emigrating from Britain between 1841 and 1868, 47.0 percent were male and 47.5 were female; the remainder were infants not listed by sex. Before 1855, male immigrants outnumbered female. Of the 12,477 emigrants from Scandinavia, 46.5 percent were male, and 53.5 percent female. Single women over fourteen made up 15 percent of the emigrants, and single men over fourteen accounted for 12 percent. Before 1869, of the immigrant companies studied by William Mulder, 80 to 85 percent of both British and Scandinavian emigrants came in family units. Mulder, *Homeward to Zion,* 108–9.

34. Arrington, *Great Basin Kingdom,* 211–13.

35. K. Young, *Isn't One Wife Enough?* 124–25.

36. *JD* 26:72–73 (November 30, 1884).

Chapter 7: Economics and Plural Marriage

1. D. Michael Quinn, "The Mormon Hierarchy, 1832–1932: An American Elite" (Ph.D. diss., Yale University, 1976), Abstract, n.p., 81–157.

2. Linda Mealey, "The Relationship between Social Status and Biological Success: A Case Study of the Mormon Religious Hierarchy," *Ethology and Sociobiology* 6, no. 4 (1985): 249–52. See also Steven F. Faux and Harold L. Miller Jr., "Evolutionary Speculations on the Oligarchic Development of Mormon Polygyny," *Ethology and Sociobiology* 5, no. 1 (1984): 22–24; and Wallace Gardner Blackhurst, "Wealth, Polygamy, and Fertility in a Polygamous Society: Utah County Mormons, 1851–1870" (Ph.D. diss., University of Chicago, 1990), 49.

3. Arrington and Bitton, *Mormon Experience,* 199–200; Embry, *Mormon Polygamous Families,* 62–65; Quinn, "Mormon Hierarchy," 61–63.

4. Warren Stone Snow was included in this calculation, although he was listed in the Moroni manuscript census. His usual residence was Manti, where he was a church leader.

5. Nathan Lewis–Jemima Sydom Family Group Record, *AF;* Daniel Allen–Mary Ann Morris Family Group Record and Henning Madsen–Karen Tennesen Pedersen Family Group Record, Patrons Section, FHL; Henning Madsen, CPI.

6. Johannes Alder–Anna Barbara Alder Family Group Record, Patrons Section, FHL; Adam Craik Smyth–Emily Brown Family Group Record, *AF.*

7. Soren Christoffersen monument inscription, Manti City Cemetery, Manti, Utah; Soren Christoffersen Hansen–Ane Nielsen Family Group Record, *AF;* Soren Christophersen Hansen and Wilhelmina Stick, and Soren Christopher Hanson and Anna Jenson, 1859, North America, Marriage Search, *OI,* Main File.

8. Sanpete County, Utah, Probate Court, "Minutes, 1852–1866," Book 1, 103, 105 (March 14, 1865, April 4, 1865), microfilm of MS, FHL; Johannes Alder and Matilda Sophia Schramm, 1865, North America, Marriage Search, *OI,* Main File; Johannes Alder–Matilda Sophia Schramm Family Group Record, *AF.*

9. Ivins, "Notes on Mormon Polygamy," 230, 233.

10. Calculated from the real and personal wealth figures in the 1860 Manti manuscript census.

11. May, "People on the Mormon Frontier," 79–180.

12. Of the polygamists listed in the 1860 Manti census, only one, Eric Ludvigsen, had no property listed. That may have been an omission by the census taker, however, because a biography of Ludvigsen indicated that after he arrived in Utah in 1854, "he located in Manti and took up ten acres of land," to which he eventually added an additional one hundred acres. Lever, *History of Sanpete,* 149–50.

13. This is somewhat higher than the Gini coefficient of 0.394 derived from a schedule of assets and income for each household head completed by bishops at the end of 1857. Lee Soltow and Dean L. May, "The Distribution of Mormon Wealth and Income in 1857," *Explorations in Economic History* 16 (April 1979): 155. This coefficient is lower than that for 1860 Manti because income is more evenly distributed than wealth, and the list probably did not include the poorest families. Ibid., 154, 158. Kearl, Pope, and Wimmer calculated that the Gini coefficients for all of Utah for 1850 and 1870 were 0.69 and 0.74, respectively. J. R. Kearl, Clayne L. Pope, and Larry T. Wimmer, "Household Wealth in a Settlement Economy: Utah, 1850–1870," *Journal of Economic History* 40 (September 1980): 484–85. Those single and without wealth were, however, not included in their calculations. Moreover, those living outside Salt Lake County had considerably less wealth, which increased inequality overall for Utah. Kearl, Pope, and Wimmer, "Household Wealth," 490. The Gini coefficient for Kanab, Utah, based on wealth assessed for taxes in 1874–75 was 0.456. May, "People on the Mormon Frontier," 179–80.

14. Lee Soltow, *Men and Wealth in the United States, 1850–1870* (New Haven, Conn.: Yale University Press, 1975), 103.

15. Jeremy Atack and Fred Bateman, *To Their Own Soil: Agriculture in the Antebellum North* (Ames: Iowa State University Press, 1987), 89–91, 282.

16. Both coefficients for Manti are calculated using figures in the 1860 Manti

manuscript census. I assume, however, that the value of real estate given for Daniel Henrie was incorrect. It was listed at $30,000. Because it was listed at $3,000 in 1870 and $1,200 in 1850 and because there is no evidence that he gained and lost so much land over that period of time, I assume that the census taker added one extra zero and that the true amount should be $3,000. Had I not made that change, the Gini coefficient for family wealth would have been 0.627, and the coefficient for wealth per capita within families would have been 0.493.

17. Atack and Bateman, *To Their Own Soil*, 51–52, 67–68.

18. Gordon W. Kirk Jr., *The Promise of American Life: Social Mobility in a Nineteenth-Century Immigrant Community, Holland, Michigan, 1847–1894* (Philadelphia: American Philosophical Society, 1978), 16–20; Howard McKinley Corning, ed., *Dictionary of Oregon History* (Portland, Oreg.: Binford and Mort, 1989), 224; *Historical Atlas Map of Marion and Linn Counties, Oregon* (San Francisco: Edgar Williams, 1878; reprint, Salem, Ore.: Marion County Historical Society, 1976), 24.

19. Atack and Bateman, *To Their Own Soil*, 94. There is no indication that women "brought appreciable amounts of wealth to their marriages." Blackhurst, "Wealth, Polygamy, and Fertility," 23.

20. Moreover, a total of 58 (45.0 percent) of those 129 married men were in plural marriage at some time in their lives. 1860 U.S. Census, Manti, Sanpete County, Utah, Population Schedule; Manti data set. All the calculations for polygamists and their wealth in 1860 Manti have excluded Soren Hansen Christoffersen. He was in Denmark on a proselyting mission, although his two wives lived in Manti and his wealth is listed as his first wife's.

21. Kearl, Pope, and Wimmer, "Household Wealth," 484–85.

22. James R. Clark, ed., *Messages of the First Presidency of the Church of Jesus Christ of Latter-day Saints, 1833–1964*, 6 vols. (Salt Lake City: Bookcraft, 1965), 2:268.

23. *JD* 13:204 (October 9, 1869).

24. Lucy Meserve Smith, excerpt from her "Historical Narrative," in *Women's Voices*, ed. Godfrey, Godfrey, and Derr, 267.

25. Catharine Cottam Romney, *Letters of Catharine Cottam Romney, Plural Wife*, ed. Jennifer Moulton Hansen (Urbana: University of Illinois Press, 1992), 166 (quote), 174.

26. Maureen Ursenbach Beecher, "Under the Sunbonnets: Mormon Women with Faces," *Brigham Young University Studies* 16 (Summer 1976): 479–83.

27. Ellis Shipp, *The Early Autobiography and Diary of Ellis Reynolds Shipp*, comp. and ed. Ellis Shipp Musser (Salt Lake City: Deseret News, 1962), 210–11.

Chapter 8: Civil and Ecclesiastical Divorce

1. Sanpete County, "Probate Record, including Minutes, 1866–1884," Book A, April 19, 1873, 65–66.

2. Ibid.; Cyrenus Henry Taylor Family Group Record, Patrons Section, FHL.

3. Lawson, *Rights, Remedies, and Practice*, secs. 778–93; Kent, *Commentaries*, 2:95–105; Roderick Phillips, *Putting Asunder: A History of Divorce in Western Society* (Cambridge: Cambridge University Press, 1988), 439–70; C. Wright, *Marriage and Divorce*, 73–206; Howard, *History of Matrimonial Institutions*, 3:3–

160. Deeds of separation—contracts between husbands and wives stipulating provisions for their separation from each other—were, however, upheld in the majority of cases if their object was an actual and immediate separation. Lawson, *Rights, Remedies, and Practice,* sec. 778.

4. For another example of a divorce granted when the couple did not appear, although the wife's father did, see Washington County, Utah, "Court Records," Book A, 1854–72, 15–16, microfilm of MS, FHL.

5. George Carlos Johnston Family Group Record, Patrons Section, FHL; Logue, *Sermon in the Desert,* 78–79.

6. Johnston Family Group Record, Patrons Section, FHL; Emily Melissa Taylor and George Carlos Johnston, 1867, North America, Marriage Search, *OI,* Main File.

7. 19 Utah Reports 470 (1899).

8. Lawrence Foster, "A Little-Known Defense of Polygamy from the Mormon Press in 1842," *Dialogue: A Journal of Mormon Thought* 9 (Winter 1974): 23–24.

9. Udney Hay Jacob, *The Peace Maker* (Nauvoo, Ill.: J. Smith, 1842; reprint, Kearns, Utah: Deseret Publishing, 1975), 10.

10. Ibid., 15, 18, 44.

11. Aaron, "Mormon Divorce," 8.

12. Ibid., 11; Jane Turner Censer, "Smiling through Her Tears: Antebellum Southern Women and Divorce," *American Journal of Legal History* 25 (April 1981): 28; Howard, *History of Matrimonial Institutions,* 3:13. North Carolina's supreme court interpreted its omnibus clause so narrowly that the state legislature began granting divorces again. Phillips, *Putting Asunder,* 448.

13. *Compiled Laws of the Territory of Utah* (1876), sec. 1151 (emphasis added).

14. Quoted in Aaron, "Mormon Divorce," 11–12.

15. Sanpete County, Probate Court, "Minutes," Book 1, 59, 68; Sanpete County, "Probate Record, including Minutes, 1866–1884," Book A, 12, 13, 20, 22, 25–26, 36, 39, 42, 43, 45, 47, 53–54, 60–61, 63–64, 70, 71, 81, 95, 121, 123, 128, 129, 136, 142, 143, 144, 148, 149, 152, 153, 154, 159, 160.

16. Sanpete County, "Probate Record, 1884–1890," Book B, 136, 143. See also 123, 148, 152.

17. Ibid., 49, 95, 168.

18. *Compiled Laws of the Territory of Utah* (1876), sec. 1152.

19. Sanpete County, Probate Court, "Minutes," Book 1, and "Probate Record, including Minutes, 1866–1884," Book A. Another eleven of the divorces had too little information recorded to determine whether the husband or the wife filed for divorce.

20. Calculated from table 3 in Martin Schultz, "Divorce Patterns in Nineteenth-Century New England," *Journal of Family History* 15 (January 1990): 107.

21. C. Wright, *Marriage and Divorce,* 170.

22. Sanpete County, "Probate Record, including Minutes, 1866–1884," Book A, 159.

23. Joel Prentiss Bishop, *Commentaries on the Law of Marriage and Divorce, with the Evidence, Practice, Pleading, and Forms; Also of Separation without Divorce, and of the Evidence of Marriage in All Issues,* 6th ed., rev. and enl., vol. 2 (Boston: Little, Brown, 1881), sec. 685.

24. Griswold, *Family and Divorce in California,* 1–23.

25. C. Wright, *Marriage and Divorce,* 164.

26. Glenda Riley, *Divorce* (New York: Oxford University Press, 1991), 143; Lawson, *Rights, Remedies, and Practice,* sec. 790, sec. 792; Bishop, *Commentaries on the Law of Marriage and Divorce,* secs. 28–32. The Civil Code of the First French Empire, however, permitted men and women to divorce by mutual consent or unilaterally. Phillips, *Putting Asunder,* 266–67, 405–6.

27. Phillips, *Putting Asunder,* 90, 440–61; Lawson, *Rights, Remedies, and Practice,* sec. 792.

28. As late as 1958, the New York assembly considered making collusion in matrimonial actions a misdemeanor, though it did reject the bill. Nelson Manfred Blake, *The Road to Reno: A History of Divorce in the United States* (New York: Macmillan, 1962), 224.

29. Sanpete County, "Probate Record, including Minutes, 1866–1884," Book A, 36–37 (first quote), 37 (second quote).

30. C. Wright, *Marriage and Divorce,* 204.

31. Quoted in ibid., 324.

32. Ibid., 124.

33. Ibid., 124–25. For another example, see Weibye, "Diaries," July 30, 1868.

34. *Compiled Laws of the Territory of Utah* (1876), sec. 1151.

35. Quoted in C. Wright, *Marriage and Divorce,* 204.

36. Ibid., 204–5.

37. *Compiled Laws of Utah* (1888), sec. 2602.

38. C. Wright, *Marriage and Divorce,* 414–17.

39. *Compiled Laws of Utah* (1888), sec. 2602.

40. Sanpete County, "Probate Record, including Minutes, 1866–1884," Book A, 163. See also p. 165 and File 23, Divorce Case Files, 1869–87, Basement Archives, Sanpete County Courthouse, Manti, Utah.

41. File 9, File 8, File 20, Sanpete Divorce Case Files.

42. File 24, File 52, File 16, File 62, ibid.

43. See, for example, File 29 and File 35, ibid.

44. U.S. deputy marshals made their first raid on Manti in search of men practicing polygamy on November 29, 1885. Lever, *History of Sanpete,* 66.

45. File 4, Sanpete Divorce Case Files; Herman Julius Christensen–Karen Kjerstina Poulsen Family Group Record, Patrons Section, FHL; personal communication from Sydney C. Mickelsen, November 5, 1988.

46. 3 Utah 431 app., 436 (1861); 1 Utah 112 (1873).

47. *An Act in Relation to Courts and Judicial Officers in the Territory of Utah, U.S. Statutes at Large,* 18, sec. 3, 254 (1874); *Whitemore v. Hardin,* 3 Utah 121 (1881); *Amy v. Amy,* 12 Utah 278 (1895).

48. "In the Matter of the Estate of Herman J. Christensen, Deceased," 4–5, typescript of Hearing, Seventh Judicial District Court, Sanpete County, Utah, File of Estates, Basement Archives, Sanpete County Courthouse, Manti, Utah; L. Clark, *Others,* 25.

49. 17 Utah 412 (1898). Because the family generally used the spelling Christensen, that spelling is used in the text.

50. *In re Herman J. Christiansen,* 17 Utah 412, 422–32 (1898).

51. No divorce files for divorces before 1869 are currently among the nineteenth-century divorce files in the Archives of the Sanpete County Courthouse. Because

the file for this case was not produced for the court in 1898, it would appear that the early divorce case files were no longer in existence by that date.

52. *In re Herman J. Christiansen*, 425.

53. Phillips, *Putting Asunder*, 471–72; Blake, *Road to Reno*, 130–50.

54. Aaron, "Mormon Divorce," 18–19.

55. Firmage and Mangrum, *Zion in the Courts*, 325.

56. Ibid., 329.

57. For a description of the *Ordinance Index*, see the appendix. Of the ninety couples granted a divorce between August 3, 1852, and December 26, 1870, thirteen could not be identified. For twelve of the couples, only a surname was given in the probate court records, and no divorce case files exist. In addition, one Danish couple could not be identified because the names were too common.

58. Church of Jesus Christ of Latter-day Saints, Manti Ward, "Record of Members, [1849]–1877," 36; Sanpete County, Probate Court, "Minutes, 1852–1866," Book 1, 30.

59. Sanpete County, "Probate Record, including Minutes, 1866–1884," Book A, 43; Mads Peter Kjar and Maria Sophia Vose Petersdeck, 1870, North America, Marriage Search, *OI*, Main File; 1870 U.S. Census, Manti, Sanpete County, Utah, Population Schedule, 45, Mads Kjar household.

60. Sanpete County, "Probate Record, including Minutes, 1866–1884," Book A, 55; Jens Frederick Steck Family Group Record, Patrons Section, FHL.

61. Sanpete County, "Probate Record, including Minutes, 1866–1884," Book A, 104; Joseph Smith Wing Family Group Records, *AF*; Joseph Smith Wing and Elizabeth Marshall, 1863, Joseph Smith Wing and Sarah Adelia Wright, 1863, Joseph Smith Wing and Mary Josephine Allen, 1864, Joseph Smith Wing and Sophia Anina Bone, 1866, and Joseph Smith Wing and Sophia Maria Amalie Hendrickson, 1872, North America, Marriage Search, *OI*, Main File; 1880 U.S. Census, Springville, Utah County, Utah, Population Schedule, E.D. 82, 165, 167, 168, 158, 156.

62. Firmage and Mangrum, *Zion in the Courts*, 325, 329–30.

63. See David L. Bigler, ed., *The Gold Discovery Journal of Azariah Smith* (Salt Lake City: University of Utah Press, 1990).

64. Azariah Smith, "Journal," April 12 and 29, 1853.

65. Ibid., October 19, 1854.

66. Firmage and Mangrum, *Zion in the Courts*, 359; Lawson, *Rights, Remedies, and Practice*, sec. 789; Bishop, *Commentaries on the Law of Marriage and Divorce*, sec. 36.

67. Azariah Smith, "Journal," February 10 and 20, 1855.

68. Ibid. This is the same statement used by John R. Park and Annie Armitage in 1873 (*Hilton v. Roylance*, 25 Utah 129, 135 [1902]) and Elbridge Tufts and Eleanor Bringhurst in 1870 (*Tufts v. Tufts*, 8 Utah 142, 144 [1903]). See also C. Wright, *Marriage and Divorce*, 125; and Firmage and Mangrum, *Zion in the Courts*, 327–28.

69. Azariah Smith, "Journal," February 20, 1855; 1860 U.S. Census, Manti, Sanpete County, Utah, Population Schedule, 18, Esariah Smith household.

70. Deuteronomy 24:1.

71. C. Wright, *Marriage and Divorce*, 125; Firmage and Mangrum, *Zion in the Courts*, 323.

72. C. Wright, *Marriage and Divorce*, 124.

73. Jules Remy and Julius Brenchley, *A Journey to Great-Salt-Lake City*, 2 vols. (London: W. Jeffs, 1861; reprint, New York: AMS, 1971), 2:149.

74. C. Wright, *Marriage and Divorce*, 124. See also Firmage and Mangrum, *Zion in the Courts*, 326–27.

75. 1883, Disfellowship Files, Fd. 6, quoted in Firmage and Mangrum, *Zion in the Courts*, 327.

76. Quoted in Embry, *Mormon Polygamous Families*, 178; Arrington, *Brigham Young*, 318; Danel Bachman and Ronald K. Esplin, "Plural Marriage," in *Encyclopedia of Mormonism*, ed. Ludlow, 3:1091–95.

77. JD 4:55–57 (September 21, 1856); Woodruff, *Journal*, 4:451, 464.

78. JD 4:55, 56 (September 21, 1856).

79. "Journal History," December 15, 1858, microfilm, Brigham Young University; Nicholas Groesbeck–Elizabeth McGregor Family Group Record, *AF*.

80. JD 17:119 (June 28, 1874).

81. K. Young, *Isn't One Wife Enough?* 227. See also ibid., 452.

82. *Abstract of Temple Lot Case*, 380.

83. 1 Corinthians 7:14–15. For background on the Pauline Privilege, see Phillips, *Putting Asunder*, 18, 67, 70.

84. Church of Jesus Christ of Latter-day Saints, Manti Ward, "Record of Members, [1849]–1877," 38½.

85. Azariah Smith, "Journal," December 25, 1874, January 6, 1876.

86. *Abstract of Temple Lot Case*, 380.

87. For a similar example, see Steven Pratt, "Eleanor McLean and the Murder of Parley P. Pratt," *Brigham Young University Studies* 15 (Winter 1975): 225–56.

88. C. Christensen, *Before and after Mt. Pisgah*, 118, 135.

89. 1882–83, Disfellowship File, Fd. 1, quoted in Firmage and Mangrum, *Zion in the Courts*, 359.

90. JD 7:317 (October 6, 1859) (emphasis added).

91. James Beck Notebooks, 1859–65, vol. 1, LDS Church Archives, quoted in Foster, *Religion and Sexuality*, 162. An unauthorized version of this is found in Dennis R. Short, *For WoMen Only: The Lord's Law of Obedience* (Salt Lake City: Dennis R. Short, 1977), 85–90. See also JD 17:119 (Brigham Young, June 28, 1874). The idea, however, that one righteous husband was better able than another to save a woman in the next life was soundly condemned by Jedediah M. Grant in 1856. JD 4:128 (October 26, 1856).

92. Brodie, *No Man Knows My History*, 465–66; Compton, *In Sacred Loneliness*, 79–101.

93. JD 4:165 (January 11, 1857).

94. JD 24:171 (May 19, 1883). "Signing the divorce" meant signing the standard divorce agreement, as Azariah and Camilla Augusta Smith did.

95. 19 Utah 470 (1899); 25 Utah 129, 159 (1902).

Chapter 9: Incidence of Divorce and Remarriage

1. Campbell and Campbell, "Divorce among Mormon Polygamists," 5. The records the Campbells examined did not state whether the marriages being dissolved were polygamous or monogamous.

2. C. Wright, *Marriage and Divorce*, 125.

3. Ibid., 125, 416–17. The number of civil divorces has been adjusted downward from the 4,078 Wright lists for the period to eliminate the nonresident divorces.

4. Ibid., 147–48.

5. Ibid., 147.

6. Ibid., 149.

7. Geraldine P. Mineau, "Utah Widowhood: A Demographic Profile," in *On Their Own: Widows and Widowhood in the American Southwest, 1848–1939*, ed. Arlene Scadron (Urbana: University of Illinois Press, 1988), 163n. 27.

8. Kunz, "One Wife or Several?" 68–69.

9. Warren Snow to Sarah Snow, December 3, 1862, and September 24, 1863, Warren S. Snow Papers, Special Collections, BYU.

10. For 10 of the 425 women, I found too little information to know whether they had been divorced. Since they have not been counted in the numerator but have been in the denominator, the percentages may be slightly low.

11. Four polygamists were excluded from this calculation because their second marriages were nominal or eternity only.

12. *Statistical Abstract of the United States, 1998: The National Data Book*, 118 ed. (Washington, D.C.: Government Printing Office, 1998), 111–14.

13. *JD* 6:356 (Orson Pratt, July 24, 1859); *JD* 13:39 (George Albert Smith, October 8, 1869); *JD* 16:231 (Orson Hyde, October 5, 1873).

14. *JD* 24:171 (John Taylor, May 19, 1883); Berry, "Reminiscences," 8.

15. One other wife divorced her polygamous husband for apostasy when he left Utah. She then became the plural wife of the bishop of Manti.

16. File 35, Divorce Case Files; Lever, *History of Sanpete*, 163; 1900 U.S. Census, Manti, Sanpete County, Utah, Population Schedule, E.D. 125, 16A, Camilla Nelson household; Nelson tombstone, Manti Cemetery.

17. Note on Titus Billings Family Group Record, Patrons Section, FHL.

18. Lucinda Lee Dalton to D. H. Cannon, August 24, 1884, John Taylor Correspondence, LDS Church Archives, quoted in Lavina Fielding Anderson, "Lucinda L. Dalton," in *Sister Saints*, ed. Burgess-Olson, 160–61.

19. John Taylor to Lucinda Lee Dalton, March 17, 1887, John Taylor Letterbook, no. 14, 346, LDS Church Archives, quoted in ibid., 162–63.

20. L. Anderson, "Lucinda L. Dalton," 163.

21. Utah Territory, First District Court, "Minutes," Book 4, 6, 48, microfilm of MS, FHL; "Sanpete County Marriage Record," November 26, 1888, microfilm of original, FHL; 1880 U.S. Census, Manti, Sanpete County, Utah, Population Schedule, E.D. 65, 3–4 [stamped 408C–408D], Christian Madsen and Elsina Madsen households.

22. Evans, "Judicial Prosecution," 124; Utah State, Seventh District Court, Sanpete County, "Judgment Record, 1896–1936," Book 1, 48, microfilm of original, FHL; Joseph L. Jolly Family Group Record, Patrons Section, FHL.

23. Jesse Ordean Washburn, *Hyrum Smith Washburn, 1853–1924: Pioneer of Manti and Monroe, Utah, with Near Ancestors and Descendants* (Salt Lake City: Crabtree, 1983), 24–25; Benjamin F. Johnson, *My Life's Review* (Independence, Mo.: Zion's Printing and Publishing, 1947), 106, 113, 121–23.

24. Church of Jesus Christ of Latter-day Saints, Manti Ward, "Records of Members, [1849]–1877," July 5, 1854, 45; Paul Ernest Kofford Family Group Record,

Patrons Section, FHL. The Record of Marriages also contains a copy of the bill of divorce that Levi Hancock wrote for Fanny Myrick.

25. Thomas Woolsey Family Group Record, Patrons Section, FHL; Henry God-futz Rabel Family Group Record, Archives Section, FHL; 1850 U.S. Census, Utah County, Utah, Population Schedule, 134, Henry Rabel household.

26. Dean C. Jessee, "Brigham Young's Family: The Wilderness Years," *Brigham Young University Studies* 19 (Summer 1979): 499.

27. N. Anderson, *Desert Saints*, 408–9.

28. J. R. Kearl and Clayne L. Pope, "Wealth Mobility: The Missing Element," *Journal of Interdisciplinary History* 13 (Winter 1983): 469.

29. "Katherine Hulet Winget Autobiography," in *Our Pioneer Heritage*, vol. 13, comp. Kate B. Carter (Salt Lake City: Daughters of Utah Pioneers, 1970), 492.

30. J. R. Kearl, Clayne L. Pope and Larry T. Wimmer, comps., *Index to the 1850, 1860, and 1870 Censuses of Utah: Heads of Households* (Baltimore: Genealogical Publishing, 1981), 344.

31. Anderton and Emigh, in their article studying Mormon polygamous fertility, wrote, "Families in which a divorce occurred were also excluded, since divorce was relatively rare in these communities and these women were likely to exhibit idiosyncratic behavior." Anderton and Emigh, "Polygynous Fertility," 842n. 8. Neither assertion is supported by this study of divorces.

32. Table 6 includes all remarriages, not just those of divorcées.

33. Cornwall, Courtright, and Van Beek, "How Common the Principle?" 152, found little indication of widows in plural marriage in their 1860 sample. *AF*, the basis of their comments on family relationships, is incomplete. The quinquennia 1855–59, however, did have one of the lowest percentages of divorce or widowed women entering plural marriage in Manti (see figure 7 above), and that probably was also the case in the Salt Lake areas they studied.

34. William Bench Family Group Record, Patrons Section, FHL.

35. "Florence Ellen Fowler Adair," *Our Pioneer Heritage*, vol. 7, comp. Kate B. Carter (Salt Lake City: Daughters of the Utah Pioneers, 1964), 270. This short autobiography does not mention her mother's second marriage.

36. For the experiences of widows in nineteenth-century Utah, see Maureen Ursenbach Beecher, Carol Cornwall Madsen, and Lavina Fielding Anderson, "Widowhood among the Mormons: The Personal Accounts," in *On Their Own*, ed. Scadron, 117–39.

37. Mineau, "Utah Widowhood," 152.

38. Phillips, *Putting Asunder*, 218–19.

Chapter 10: The Decline of Plural Marriage

1. Joan Iversen, "Feminist Implications of Mormon Polygyny," *Feminist Studies* 10 (Fall 1984): 507–19 (quote on 507); Foster, *Religion and Sexuality*, 212–13.

2. M. E. Teasdale, "Correspondence," *Woman's Exponent* 17 (July 1, 1888): 19.

3. See chapter 5.

4. Antrei and Scow, *Other Forty-Niners*, 321–41; Lever, *History of Sanpete*, 63; Bean, Mineau, and Anderton, *Fertility Change on the American Frontier*, 159–80, 244–48.

5. Klaus J. Hansen, *Mormonism and the American Experience* (Chicago: University of Chicago Press, 1981), 176; Ivins, "Notes on Mormon Polygamy," 239.

6. Quinn, "LDS Church Authority and New Plural Marriages," 52–104; Hardy, *Solemn Covenant*, 167–243.

7. Shipps, *Mormonism*, 125.

8. Antrei and Scow, *Other Forty-Niners*, 152.

9. "Francis George Wall—Pioneer of 1863," in *Our Pioneer Heritage*, vol. 7, ed. Carter, 366–67.

10. Utah Territory, First District Court, "Minutes," Book 3, 3; William Braithwaite Family Group Record, Patrons Section, FHL.

11. Weibye, "Diaries," August 19, 1887, November 7, 1889, February 24, 1890; Evans, "Judicial Prosecution," 131.

12. Utah Territory, First District Court, "Minutes," Book 3, 610. See also Linford, "Mormons and the Law, Part I," 364.

13. Grow, "Study of the Utah Commission," 268; Linford, "Mormons and the Law, Part I," 366; Evans, "Judicial Prosecution," 24–39, 73; S. Larson, *Prisoner for Polygamy*, 209–31.

14. Utah Territory, First District Court, "Minutes," Book 3, 267, Book 4, 15.

15. Ibid., Book 4, 299; John D. T. McAllister, "Autobiography and Diary, 1851–1906," vol. 5, 362, typescript, Special Collections, BYU; Federal Writers' Project, "Isaac Jimeson Riddle, Early Son of Pine Valley, Utah," Utah Pioneer Biographies, vol. 24, FHL.

16. Utah Territory, First District Court, "Minutes," Book 4, October 29, 1888, 6; Thomas G. Alexander, "Charles S. Zane: Apostle of the New Era," *Utah Historical Quarterly* 34 (Fall 1966): 307–8; Gustive O. Larson, "The Crusade and the Manifesto," in *Utah's History*, ed. Poll et al., 263.

17. *An Act to Amend*, 22, sec. 7, 31 (1882).

18. *Compiled Laws of Utah* (1888), sec. 2742 (emphasis added).

19. Grossberg, *Governing the Hearth*, 221.

20. *An Act to Amend an Act*, 24, sec. 11, 637 (1887).

21. 7 Utah 49 (1890); *An Act to Punish and Prevent the Practice of Polygamy*, 12, sec. 2, 501 (1862).

22. 7 Utah 63 (1890); 137 U.S. 682 (1891); Orma Linford, "The Mormons and the Law: The Polygamy Cases, Part II, Civil Disabilities," *Utah Law Review* 9 (Summer 1965): 557–59; C. Madsen, "At Their Peril," 437–38.

23. *In re Pratt's Estate*, 7 Utah 278 (1891); Esshom, *Pioneers and Prominent Men of Utah*, 51; Bitton, *Guide to Mormon Diaries*, 280; Jenson, *Church Chronology*, 92, 144, 158, 176; Orson F. Whitney, *History of Utah*, 4 vols. (Salt Lake City: George Q. Cannon and Sons, 1898), 3:602.

24. "An Act to Legitimate the Issue of Bigamous and Polygamous Marriages, Born on or prior to January 4th, 1896, and Declaring Their Heritable and Other Rights," in *Laws of the State of Utah Passed at the Special and First Regular Sessions of the Legislature* (Salt Lake City: Deseret News, 1896), chap. 82, 271–72; "An Act Relative to the Heritable Rights of the Issue of Polygamous Marriages," ibid., chap. 41, secs. 1 and 2, 128–29; *In re Handley's Estate*, 15 Utah 212 (1897).

25. *Rohwer v. District Court*, 41 Utah 279 (1912).

26. Ibid., 292, 287.

27. *The Revised Statutes of the State of Utah in Force Jan. 1, 1898* (Salt Lake

City: State Journal, 1897), sec. 2833; Utah Constitution, art. 3; *Rohwer v. District Court*, 286 (quotes); *Compiled Laws of the State of Utah* (Salt Lake City: Skelton, 1907), sec. 1184.

28. *An Act to Amend an Act*, 24, sec. 18, 638 (1887). If the husband had mortgaged the lands, the widow would only be entitled to dower in such lands after the mortgage was paid, but her right to dower on those lands superseded any other person's right except the mortgagee. Section 18 of the Edmunds-Tucker Act annulled an 1872 Utah statute stating that no right of dower was allowed in the territory. *Compiled Laws of Utah* (1888), sec. 2530.

29. *Compiled Laws of Utah* (1888), secs. 2530–33. For general background on the release of dower, see Joel Prentiss Bishop, *Commentaries on the Law of Married Women under the Statutes of the Several States, and at Common Law and in Equity*, vol. 1 (Boston: Little, Brown, 1873), sec. 451. Under the Edmunds-Tucker Act, dower rights would be in force until the widow "shall have lawfully released her right thereto" or "in case of divorce dissolving the marriage contract for the misconduct of the wife." *An Act to Amend an Act*, 24, sec. 18, 638, 639 (1887).

30. A widow who renounced the will would take her dower right under common law, which was one-third of the realty that her husband possessed at death. Philip Pugsley's first wife, Martha, renounced her testamentary legacy and received one-third of her deceased husband's real estate in 1903. Clarissa Ames, Pugsley's plural wife, objected to the first wife's receiving an allowance during the administration of the estate, but the Utah Supreme Court decided for the first wife's right. *In re Estate of Pugsley*, 27 Utah 489 (1904). See also *Revised Statues of the State of Utah in Force Jan. 1, 1898*, sec. 2897.

31. *An Act to Amend an Act*, 24, sec. 19, 639 (1887).

32. At common law, a deed from a husband directly to his wife was legally void. Lawson, *Rights, Remedies, and Practice*, sec. 716. A Utah law passed in 1872, however, provided that the property owned before marriage or acquired after marriage was the separate property of the spouse who owned or acquired it. In addition, the spouse owning the property could dispose of that property "without any limitation or restriction by reasons of marriage." *Compiled Laws of Utah* (1888), sec. 2528. This statutory law overrode the common law restriction on a deed from a husband to his wife (or wives).

33. The data in this paragraph are based on Sanpete County, Utah, "Assessment Roll Records, 1873–1890," 1886, 1888, and 1890, microfilm of original, 2 reels, FHL. These records are not paginated, but the entries are alphabetized. For additional examples, see K. Young, *Isn't One Wife Enough?* 267–70.

34. *Laws of the State of Utah, Passed at the Special and First Regular Sessions of the Legislature . . . April 1896* (Salt Lake City: Deseret News, 1896), chap. 118, Right of Dower, 356–58; "An Act Relative to the Heritable Rights of the Issue of Polygamous Marriages," chap. 41, secs. 1 and 2, 128–29.

35. *Revised Statutes of the State of Utah in Force Jan. 1, 1898*, sec. 2832, sec. 2826; *Hilton v. Thatcher*, 31 Utah 360 (1906).

36. *Raleigh v. Wells*, 29 Utah 217 (1905).

37. Ibid., 221, 217. The case was decided not only on Emily Raleigh's not being a legal wife but also on the weakness of the evidence about the property being a gift and her title to it by adverse possession.

38. *Riddle v. Riddle*, 26 Utah 268 (1903).

39. Ibid., 282.

40. *Beck v. Utah-Idaho Sugar Co. et al.*, 59 Utah 314 (1921).

41. Kimball Young gives several examples of inheritance by polygamous families, about 50 percent of which he indicates were settled amicably. In his discussion of inheritance, however, all of the estates he examines were settled after the passage of the Edmunds-Tucker Act, and he bases his generalizations about inheritance on the legal situation of those years without qualifications about the period he is discussing. K. Young *Isn't One Wife Enough?* 266–76. See also Embry, *Mormon Polygamous Families*, 182–86.

42. *An Act to Amend an Act*, 24, sec. 9, 636 (1887); C. Wright, *Marriage and Divorce*, 61.

43. Martin Ottenheimer, *Forbidden Relatives: The American Myth of Cousin Marriage* (Urbana: University of Illinois Press, 1996), 31–41.

44. *An Act to Amend an Act*, 24, sec. 4, 636, sec. 17, 638 (1887). Henry Sudweeks was the only polygamist convicted under this provision. Evans, "Judicial Prosecution," 24.

45. *Compiled Laws of Utah* (1888), secs. 2583–84 (quote); Grossberg, *Governing the Hearth*, 103–52; Howard, *History of Matrimonial Institutions*, 2:464–91.

46. *Compiled Laws of Utah* (1888), sec. 2583, sec. 2593, sec. 2594, and sec. 2584.

47. *U.S. v. Simpson*, 4 Utah 227 (1885).

48. *U.S. v. Cannon*, 4 Utah 122 (1885); *Cannon v. U.S.*, 116 U.S. 55 (1885).

49. *U.S. v. Snow*, 4 Utah 280 (1886); *U.S. v. Snow*, 4 Utah 295 (1886); *U.S. v. Snow*, 4 Utah 313 (1886); Linford, "Mormons and the Law, Part I," 359–64; O. Whitney, *History of Utah*, 3:459–75.

50. S. Larson, *Prisoner for Polygamy*, 209–31. The Utah Commission stated that thirty-five men were convicted for polygamy (Linford, "Mormons and the Law, Part I," 347–59, 366–70), but Evans claimed that fourteen of those cases had nothing to do with LDS plural marriage, while the remaining eight, if they were convicted, served no prison sentence. The penalty for polygamy was imprisonment for a term of not more than five years and a fine of not more than $500, while the punishment for unlawful cohabitation was imprisonment for a term of not longer than six months and a fine of not more than $300. *An Act to Amend*, 22, secs. 1 and 3, 30–31 (1882).

51. *An Act to Amend an Act*, 24, sec. 24, sec. 20, 639–40 (1887).

52. Hardy, *Solemn Covenant*, 141–46; Van Wagoner, *Mormon Polygamy*, 123–24, 153.

53. N. Anderson, *Desert Saints*, 415; Quinn, "LDS Church Authority and New Plural Marriages," 50.

54. John D. T. McAllister was cohabiting with and having children by his eighth wife, but his legal wife had died in 1889. His fourth wife, however, was still living. 1900 U.S. Census, Manti, Sanpete County, Utah, Population Schedule, E.D. 125, 2 [stamped 130A], John McAllister household; 1900 U.S. Census, St. George, Washington County, Utah, Population Schedule, E.D. 175, 15 [stamped 207A], Cornelia McAllister household; John D. T. McAllister–Ellen Handley Family Group Record, *AF.*

55. Nelle Spilsbury Hatch and B. Carmon Hardy, eds. and comps., *Stalwarts South of the Border* (n.p., 1985), 67.

56. 1900 U.S. Census, Redmond, Sevier County, Utah, Population Schedule, E.D. 130, 3B [stamped 13B], Johanna Breinholt household; 1910 U.S. Census,

Redmond, Sevier County, Utah, Population Schedule, E.D. 158, 1A, Johanna Breinholt household.

57. Hardy, *Solemn Covenant,* 145.

58. Sanpete County, Utah, "Assessment Roll Records, 1900," Basement Ar-
chive, Sanpete County Courthouse, Manti, Utah. Although the laborer's wife who
rented her house cannot be found in either the 1910 or the 1920 census, she is
listed in the same household as her husband and his wife in the 1914 and 1920
church censuses. Her presence in her husband's household was probably not revealed to the federal census taker to avoid detection of his continuing cohabitation. Church of Jesus Christ of Latter-day Saints, "Church Census Records, 1914–
1935," Schiess–Shipley (alphabetical listings), microfilm, FHL.

59. 1900 U.S. Census, Logan, Cache County, Utah, Population Schedule, E.D.
78, 11 [stamped 253A], Steven Hailstone household.

60. Jessie Embry's study provided similar conclusions. It indicated that only 12
percent of the polygamous wives in her data set received little or no support from
their husbands. Embry, *Mormon Polygamous Families,* 96.

61. Lever, *History of Sanpete,* 179.

62. On September 13, 1890, Inger Marie Schougaard purchased property in
Manti for $488. Probably part, if not all, of that amount was a one-time settle-
ment from her husband. She had married on March 18, 1886, and had two children, sons born May 8, 1887, and September 26, 1888. The younger son had died
on February 11, 1889, about a year and a half before she purchased property at
the height of the campaign against the church. The timing and the amount—
quite large for a woman busy with infants to acquire in a short time—suggest a
settlement from her husband. County Recorder's Office, Deed Book 24, 454,
Sanpete County Courthouse, Manti, Utah; Church of Jesus Christ of Latter-day
Saints, Manti Ward, "Record of Members, [1849]–1877," 78; Tatton, "Cemetery
Records," 128.

63. Embry, *Mormon Polygamous Families,* 190–91.

64. N. Anderson, *Desert Saints,* 416–17; "In re Reed Smoot," Committee on
Privileges and Elections, View of the Minority, Senate, 59th Cong., 1st sess., Report 4253, Part 2, 23.

65. Thomas G. Alexander, "The Manifesto: Mormondom's Watershed," *This
People* 11 (Fall 1990): 21–27.

66. Shipps, *Mormonism,* 116–29; Thomas G. Alexander, *Mormonism in Transition: A History of the Latter-day Saints, 1890–1930* (Urbana: University of Illinois Press, 1986).

67. Whether Mormon belief in plural marriage still persisted by the end of the
twentieth century is ambiguous. In a television interview, Gordon B. Hinckley,
the president of the church, stated, "I condemn it, yes, as a practice, because it is
not doctrinal. It is not legal. And this church takes the position that we will abide
by the law." In that context, whether the pronoun *it* refers to plural marriage itself or to the practice of plural marriage is unclear. That the practice, not the belief,
was condemned seems confirmed in President Hinckley's comments in General
Conference a month later: "More than a century ago God clearly revealed unto
His prophet Wilford Woodruff that the practice of plural marriage should be discontinued, which means that it is now against the law of God." "Gordon Hinckley, Distinguished Religious Leader of the Mormons," *CNN Larry King Live,* Cable

Network News, September 8, 1998, transcript; Gordon B. Hinckley, "What Are People Asking about Us?" *Ensign*, November 1998, 71–72.

Chapter 11: The Nineteenth-Century Mormon Marriage System

1. Evans, "Judicial Prosecution," 31; Arrington, *Great Basin Kingdom*, 371.

2. Burgess-Olson, "Family Structure and Dynamics in Utah Mormon Families," 71–74.

3. Foster, *Religion and Sexuality*, 8, 9.

4. Campbell and Campbell, "Divorce among Mormon Polygamists," 16. See also E. Campbell, *Establishing Zion*, 165–67.

5. Emile Durkheim, *Suicide: A Study in Sociology*, ed. George Simpson, trans. John A. Spaulding and George Simpson (New York: Free Press, 1966), 248.

6. Ibid., 250–56; Peter Atteslander, "Social Change, Development and Anomie," in *Comparative Anomie Research: Hidden Barriers, Hidden Potential for Social Development*, ed. Peter Atteslander, Bettina Gransow, and John Western (Aldershot, England: Ashgate, 1999), 10–14.

7. Robert V. Remini, *The Revolutionary Age of Andrew Jackson* (1976; reprint, New York: Harper Torchbooks, 1987), 4–5.

8. See, for example, Charles Sellers, *The Market Revolution: Jacksonian America, 1815–1846* (New York: Oxford University Press, 1991); Melvin Stokes and Stephen Conway, eds., *The Market Revolution in America: Social, Political and Religious Expressions, 1800–1880* (Charlottesville: University Press of Virginia, 1996); Stuart M. Blumin, *The Emergence of the Middle Class: Social Experience in the American City, 1760–1900* (New York: Cambridge University Press, 1989); Michael Feldberg, *The Turbulent Era: Riot and Disorder in Jacksonian America* (New York: Oxford University Press, 1980); Alice Felt Tyler, *Freedom's Ferment: Phases of American Social History from the Colonial Period to the Outbreak of the Civil War* (Minneapolis: University of Minnesota Press, 1944); P. Johnson, *Shopkeeper's Millennium*; and Ryan, *Cradle of the Middle Class*.

9. Robert K. Merton, "Epilogue: Social Problems and Sociological Theory," in *Contemporary Social Problems*, ed. Robert K. Merton and Robert Nisbet (New York: Harcourt Brace Jovanovich, 1971), 830–31.

10. Foster, *Religion and Sexuality*, 3–18; M. Hill, *Quest for Refuge*; Mario S. DePillis, "The Quest for Religious Authority and the Rise of Mormonism," *Dialogue: A Journal of Mormon Thought* 1 (Spring 1966): 68–88.

11. Foster, *Religion and Sexuality*, 161.

12. Ibid., 159; Van Wagoner, "Mormon Polyandry in Nauvoo," 67–83.

13. Peter Atteslander, Bettina Gransow, and John Western, "Conclusions and Implications for Development," in *Comparative Anomie Research*, ed. Atteslander, Gransow, and Western, 215; R. M. MacIver, *The Ramparts We Guard* (New York: Macmillan, 1950), 84–87; Durkheim, *Suicide*, 254; Foster, *Religion and Sexuality*, 8–9; Emile Durkheim, *The Elementary Forms of Religious Life*, trans. Joseph Ward Swain (Glencoe, Ill.: Free Press, 1954), 10 (quote).

14. Foster, *Religion and Sexuality*, 137, 183, 17; M. R. Werner, *Brigham Young* (New York: Harcourt, Brace, 1925), in which he coined the term *Puritan Polygamy*.

15. Campbell and Campbell, "Divorce among Mormon Polygamists," 21.

16. Jack Goody, *The Development of the Family and Marriage in Europe* (Cambridge: Cambridge University Press, 1983), 48–49.

17. Genesis 29; Doctrine and Covenants 132.

18. Campbell and Campbell, "Divorce among Mormon Polygamists," 21.

19. K. Young, *Isn't One Wife Enough?* 120, 121–22; Embry, *Mormon Polygamous Families,* 53; Burgess-Olson, "Family Structure and Dynamics in Utah Mormon Families," 108.

20. "Celestial Marriage," *Seer* 1 (March 1853): 41.

21. Campbell and Campbell, "Divorce among Mormon Polygamists," 17, 19–20.

22. Ibid., 18.

23. Ibid., 19.

24. Black, *Early Members of the Reorganized Church,* 3:407; George Stringham–Ellen Healey Tofield Family Group Record, *AF;* Campbell and Campbell, "Divorce among Mormon Polygamists," 18 (quotes).

25. Nathaniel George Stringham, ed., *Briant Stringham and His People: Containing Sketches of the Lives of Some Sixty-five People, Mostly Members of the Family of Briant Stringham, Utah Pioneer of July 24, 1847* (Salt Lake City: Stevens and Wallis, 1949), 4. In the 1860 census, George was listed as living with his second wife, Ellen, but that is evidence only that he was residing there on the day the census was taken, not that he resided there from the time he married Ellen in 1857 to the time he was listed with his first wife in the 1870 census—a maximum of thirteen years. It is not clear where Polly, the first wife, was living in 1860 because she is not listed in the index to the 1860 census, nor is she listed in the 13th Ward, where she was living in 1856. Like most Utahns at the time, George was not wealthy; he listed only $150 in real estate and $100 in personal property on the 1860 census, although by 1870 his wealth had increased to $3,500 in real estate and $600 in personal property. 1860 U.S. Census, Salt Lake City, Salt Lake County, Utah, Population Schedule, 221, George Stringham household; 1870 U.S. Census, Salt Lake City, Salt Lake County, Utah, Population Schedule, 632, George Stringham household. The Campbells are mistaken in one other detail. They state that George wed his second wife after all the children of his first wife had married. The two youngest sons were unmarried in 1857, when that plural marriage took place. George Stringham–Polly Hendrickson Family Group Record, *AF.*

26. Embry, *Mormon Polygamous Families,* 73–87, 123–27, 137–49; Burgess-Olson, "Family Structure and Dynamics in Utah Mormon Families," 59–68, 129–31; Foster, *Religion and Sexuality,* 219–20.

27. "Celestial Marriage," *Seer* 1 (March 1853), 41, 1 (October 1853), 153.

28. Campbell and Campbell, "Divorce among Mormon Polygamists," 16.

29. Durkheim, *Suicide,* 259–76 (first quote on 271, second on 272).

30. Doctrine and Covenants 132:7.

31. Kimball, "History of LDS Temple Admission Standards," 141; Arrington, *Brigham Young,* 315; Walker, *Diary,* 1:250. Although Anderson implies that Walker did not receive the necessary permission, he did marry a second wife eleven years later. N. Anderson, *Desert Saints,* 402; Charles Lowell Walker–Sarah Smith Family Group Record, *AF.* The reason for the delay is not clear.

32. *Semi-Annual Conference of the Church of Jesus Christ of Latter-day Saints* ([Salt Lake City]: Deseret News, 1897–1964), April 24, 1930, 185 (hereafter *Conference Reports).*

33. "Journal of Sarah Leavitt," Mormon File, Huntington Library, quoted in Karen Lynn, "Courtship and Romance in Utah Territory: Doing Away with 'The Gentile Custom of Sparkification,'" in *A Sesquicentennial Look at Church History: Sidney B. Sperry Symposium, January 26, 1980, Brigham Young University Campus, Provo, Utah* (Provo, Utah: Brigham Young University Church Educational System, 1980), 219. *Sparkification* is a neologism created from the term *to spark*, meaning to engage in courtship, to neck. *Dictionary of American English on Historical Principles* (Chicago: University of Chicago Press, 1944), s.v. "spark". With the Mormons' emphasis on choosing a spouse for religious reasons, "sparking"—gallant and idle flirting but especially amorously kissing—was obviously discouraged.

34. Chandless, *Visit to Salt Lake*, 259.

35. Embry, *Mormon Polygamous Families*, 67.

36. Tanner, *Mormon Mother*, 50, 63–64 (quote on 64).

37. K. Young, *Isn't One Wife Enough?* 131.

38. Durkheim, *Suicide*, 254.

39. Ibid., 272.

40. JD 24:40 (June 25, 1882).

41. JD 26:217 (May 31, 1885). See also JD 13:185 (Orson Pratt, October 7, 1869).

42. Keith Thomas, "The Double Standard," *Journal of the History of Ideas* 20 (January 1959): 537–47.

43. JD 6:126 (December 13, 1857).

44. JD 13:206–7 (October 9, 1869) (emphasis added). When Cannon said "in consequence of that which has been pronounced upon them," he referred to the scripture from Genesis 3:16: "Thy desire shall be to thy husband, and he shall rule over thee."

45. Heber C. Kimball counseled Mormon men to avoid sexual relations with their pregnant and nursing wives. According to the thought of the day, unborn or breast-fed children were influenced by the thoughts and desires of the mother, and stimulating sexual thoughts in pregnant or lactating women would produce lustful thoughts in their infants. Men also transmitted impressions to the unborn child during coitus. In addition, Kimball also told men to avoid sexual relations with their wives who were not fecund. JD 4:278 (January 25, 1857). See also Hardy, *Solemn Covenant*, 89–94.

46. Nancy F. Cott, "Passionlessness: An Interpretation of Victorian Sexual Ideology, 1790–1850," in *A Heritage of Her Own: Toward a New Social History of American Women*, ed. Nancy F. Cott and Elizabeth H. Peck (New York: Simon and Schuster, 1979), 162–81.

47. Not all Latter-day Saints considered this a curse. See JD 11:268 (Brigham Young, August 19, 1866).

48. N. Anderson, *Desert Saints*, 346–47.

49. JD 11:267–68 (Brigham Young, August 19, 1866).

50. Bertram Wyatt-Brown, *Southern Honor: Ethics and Behavior in the Old South* (New York: Oxford University Press, 1982), 50–55.

51. Richard Burton, *City of the Saints and across the Rocky Mountains to California*, ed. Fawn Brodie (New York: Alfred A. Knopf, 1980), 239–40.

52. Sylvester Mowry to [Edward J.] Bicknall, September 17, 1854 and December 31, 1854, in *Among the Mormons: Historic Accounts by Contemporary Ob-

servers, ed. William Mulder and A. Russell Mortensen (New York: Alfred A. Knopf, 1958), 274–76.

53. Quoted in Woodruff, *Journal*, 4:303 (February 4, 1855). For other warnings to U.S. troops, see *JD* 3:234 (Jedediah M. Grant, March 2, 1856).

54. *CHC* 4:261–62; O. Whitney, *History of Utah*, 1:538; Stout, *On the Mormon Frontier*, 2:554–55.

55. S[ylvester] Mowry to Ned [Edward J. Bicknall], April 27, 1855, in *Among the Mormons*, ed. Mulder and Mortensen, 277–78.

56. Lynn R. Bailey, ed., "Lt. Sylvester Mowry's Report on His March in 1855 from Salt Lake City to Fort Tejon," *Arizona and the West* 7 (Winter 1965): 329–35; *CHC* 4:260–61. Mowry became a mine owner in Arizona and was that area's unofficial delegate to Congress to press for territorial status. A promoter who, in Derrick E. Leasure's words, "mixed financial dishonesty with environmental exaggeration," Mowry was charged with treason in 1862 for associating with Confederate officers and had his mine confiscated. He took his arrest coolly and flouted the seriousness of the charge by bringing along his mistress. Through his political influence, he was able finally to obtain a settlement for the confiscated mine. In the late 1860s, he courted the wealthy Lillian Hitchcock of San Francisco, but her parents spurned the match and said that his engagement to her "was only a joke." He died unmarried at age thirty-nine in 1871. Derrick E. Leasure, "From 'Wasteland' to 'Paradise': Sylvester Mowry and Frontier Development," *Journal of the West* 36 (April 1997): 16–23 (first quote on 18); Benjamin Sacks, "Sylvester Mowry," *American West* 1 (Summer 1964): 14–23, 79; Janet Webb Farnsworth, "Sylvester Mowry: Treason or Treachery?" *Old West* 34 (Fall 1997): 44–47; Frank Love, "The Crime against Sylvester Mowry," *Old West* 10 (Fall 1973): 30–31, 57–58 (second quote on 58). The woman Mowry pursued in Utah was Mary Ann Ayers Young, a twenty-year-old immigrant from England. She was the wife of Joseph Angell Young, Brigham Young's oldest son, who was on a mission to Great Britain from 1854 to 1856. She remained in Salt Lake City and in 1860 is listed in the census as living with her husband in Brigham Young's household. Joseph Angell Young–Mary Ann Ayers Family Group Record, *AF*; Mary Ann Ayrs, 1834, British Isles, Individual Search, *OI*, Main File; 1860 U.S. Census, 18th Ward, Salt Lake City, Salt Lake County, Utah, Population Schedule, 213, Brigham Young household; Jenson, *Latter-day Saint Biographical Encyclopedia*, 1:518.

57. Quoted in N. Anderson, *Desert Saints*, 339–40.

58. There is a positive correlation between prenuptial pregnancy and illegitimate births. Because the level of illegitimacy was low in Manti, the real level of prenuptial pregnancy in Manti was also undoubtedly low. For the correlation between prenuptial pregnancy and illegitimacy in the United States, see Daniel Scott Smith and Michael S. Hindus, "Premarital Pregnancy in America, 1640–1971: An Overview and Interpretation," *Journal of Interdisciplinary History* 4 (Spring 1975): 561; and Daniel Scott Smith, "The Long Cycle in American Illegitimacy and Prenuptial Pregnancy," in *Bastardy and Its Comparative History*, ed. Peter Laslett, Karla Oosterveen, and Richard M. Smith (Cambridge, Mass.: Harvard University Press, 1980), 364.

59. Smith and Hindus, "Premarital Pregnancy," 561; Daniel Smith, "Long Cycle," 370.

60. Harold T. Christensen found in Utah County, a county adjacent to Sanpete,

that 9.0 percent of women had children within six months of marriage for the years 1905–7, 1913–15, 1921–23, and 1929–31. This is not significantly lower than the 9.7 percent of women who did so in Tippecanoe County, Indiana, during the years 1919–21, 1929–31, and 1939–41. Harold T. Christensen, "Cultural Relativism and Premarital Sex Norms," in *Society and Self,* ed. Bartlett H. Stoodley (New York: Free Press of Glencoe, 1962), 188.

61. Sanpete County, Utah, Probate Court, "Criminal Docket," Book 2, 14–18, microfilm of MS, FHL. The crime of seduction involves sexual intercourse as well as assent by the victim. See Oaks and Gulick, *American Jurisprudence,* vol. 47, "Seduction," secs. 6–7. However, seduction generally requires that sexual intercourse was accomplished under a promise of marriage or, at the very least, "by means of temptation, deception, and arts and acts of flattery." Ibid., sec. 9, sec. 11. Nothing in the record indicates that the question of inducement was addressed.

62. Sanpete County, "Criminal Docket," Record Book 2, 17–18. The statute dealing with seduction passed in 1851 prescribed a penalty of not more than twenty years or less than one year imprisonment. If the offender married the woman, it was a bar to further prosecution, but he was liable to be required to give bonds with approved securities for her maintenance. "An Act in Relation to Crimes and Punishments," title 2, sec. 21, in *Acts, Resolutions, and Memorials Passed by the First Annual, and Special Sessions of the Legislative Assembly of the Territory of Utah* (Salt Lake City: Brigham H. Young, 1852), 120.

63. Azariah Smith, "Journal," January 21, 1868; A. W. O. Buchanan–Ane Maria Larsen Family Group Record, Patrons Section, FHL. In the 1870 census, Maria listed $200 in real wealth and $175 in personal wealth. She was the only one of Buchanan's wives to list any wealth that year. 1870 U.S. Census, Manti, Sanpete County, Utah, Population Schedule, 10, Maria Buchanan household.

64. *Revised Statutes of the State of Utah in Force Jan. 1, 1898,* sec. 4221.

65. Hals, "Reminiscences and Diary," 118; Hans Jensen–Secelia Marie Jorgensen, Family Group Record, Patrons Section, FHL; 1910 U.S. Census, Manti, Sanpete County, Utah, Population Schedule, E.D. 155, 22B, Hans Jensen household; Utah State, Seventh District Court, Sanpete County, "Judgment Record, 1896–1936," Book 2, 487, 547–48.

66. M. Farnsworth, "History of Manti," 11; Azariah Smith, "Journal," February 11, 1851; Church of Jesus Christ of Latter-day Saints, "Manti Ward Record," Book A, February 9, 1851.

67. Church of Jesus Christ of Latter-day Saints, "Manti Ward Record," Book A, February 23, 1851; Stout, *On the Mormon Frontier,* 2:381, 393, 396; Brigham D. Madsen, ed., *A Forty-Niner in Utah, with the Stansbury Exploration of Great Salt Lake: Letters and Journal of John Hudson, 1848–1850* (Salt Lake City: Tanner Trust Fund, University of Utah Library, 1981), 107–9; Kenneth L. Cannon II, "'Mountain Common Law': The Extralegal Punishment of Seducers in Early Utah," *Utah Historical Quarterly* 51 (Fall 1983): 310.

68. JD 1:97 ("Plea of George A. Smith, Esq., on the Trial of Howard Egan for the Murder of James Monroe," October Term 1851).

69. Stout, *On the Mormon Frontier,* 2:407–8 (quote on 407); K. Cannon, "'Mountain Common Law,'" 310–14. Although Chelnecha Hambleton and Tamson Egan both remained wives of their respective husbands after these incidents, neither bore another child for ten years, whereas before committing adultery they had

borne children every two or three years. Madison Daniel Hambleton–Chelnecha Smith Family Group Record and Howard Egan–Tamson Parshley Family Group Record, Patrons Section, FHL. The two men's marital histories differed considerably in terms of their other wives. Hambleton married a plural wife a month after he was acquitted of Vaughn's murder, and he took a third wife within two years. Church of Jesus Christ of Latter-day Saints, Manti Ward, "Record of Members, [1849]–1877," 43; 1860 U.S. Census, Nephi, Juab County, Utah, Population Schedule, 193, Madison D. Hamilton household. Church authorities suggested that Egan's plural wife Mary Ann dissolve her marriage to him. Following these events, neither Mary Ann nor his other plural wife bore Egan another child, and within three years both were married as plural wives to other men. Titus Billings–Mary Ann Tuttle Family Group Record, Howard Egan–Tamson Parshley Family Group Record, Howard Egan–Nancy Redding Family Group Record, and Howard Egan–Mary Tuttle Family Group Record, Patrons Section, FHL. Egan's only remaining wife was thus the one who had been unfaithful to him. Since according to Mormon beliefs, children belonged to their mothers and the men to whom their mothers were sealed, the child sired by Monroe listed Howard Egan as his father's name. 1860 U.S. Census, Salt Lake City, Salt Lake County, Utah, Population Schedule, 161, Howard Egan household; "Endowment House Record," vol. G, 210.

70. K. Cannon, "'Mountain Common Law,'" 315–17, 326–27; R. Burton, *City of the Saints*, 476; JD 1:369 (John Taylor, April 19, 1854).

71. *Deseret News Weekly*, November 15, 1851, n.p.

72. Ibid., April 5, 1866, 141, and April 12, 1866, 148; O. Whitney, *History of Utah*, 2:143–47; CHC 5:184–88.

73. *Deseret News Weekly*, April 12, 1866, 149.

74. *Salt Lake Daily Herald*, January 4, 1871, 149.

75. JD 13:206–7 (George Q. Cannon, October 9, 1869). Seduction did not presuppose passionlessness; it assumed only that the chaste woman would be reluctant to submit to sexual relations without some strong and usually deceptive inducement. Oaks and Gulick, *American Jurisprudence*, vol. 47, "Seduction," secs. 5–17, secs. 65–70. Mormon women were not as easily influenced or as helpless as was commonly thought. One dramatic example is the Springville woman who in 1866 was raped at gun point. Awaiting trial, her assailant defended himself by saying she had invited him to her house. Taking her father and her father-in-law to the jail, the victim demanded he retract his accusations, and when he would not, she shot and killed him on the spot. O. Whitney, *History of Utah*, 2:147.

76. JD 24:244 (Wilford Woodruff, July 20, 1883). See also JD 4:175 (Heber C. Kimball, January 11, 1857); JD 16:245 (George Q. Cannon, October 6, 1873); and JD 24:186 (George Q. Cannon, July 15, 1883).

77. JD 24:144 (May 6, 1883).

78. See, for example, Doctrine and Covenants 42:75–83; Woodruff, *Journal*, 2:328 (November 28, 1843); JD 4:143 (Heber C. Kimball, December 21, 1856); JD 24:186 (George Q. Cannon, July 15, 1883); JD 24:270 (John Taylor, June 24, 1883); and JD 25:327–28 (George Q. Cannon, October 5, 1884).

79. Quoted in N. Anderson, *Desert Saints*, 347.

80. JD 7:264 (Orson Pratt, September 11, 1859).

81. Firmage and Mangrum, *Zion in the Courts*, 358; N. Anderson, *Desert Saints*, 347–50.

82. *JD* 11:207 (April 5, 1866).

83. Compton, *In Sacred Loneliness*, 81–92; Woodruff, *Journal*, 3:128 (February 16, 1847).

84. *JD* 1:232 (April 8, 1853); *JD* 6:307 (April 8, 1853) (quote).

85. Woodruff, *Journal*, 3:128–29 (February 16, 1847).

86. C. M. Woolf, F. E. Stephens, D. D. Mulaik, and R. E. Gilbert, "An Investigation of the Frequency of Consanguineous Marriages among the Mormons and Their Relatives in the United States," *American Journal of Human Genetics* 8 (March 1956): 239.

87. Arrington, *Great Basin Kingdom*, 356.

88. O. Whitney, *History of Utah*, 2:70.

89. *Reynolds v. United States*, 98 U.S. 145 (1879); *Conference Reports*, April 5, 1907, 12.

90. *Miles v. United States*, 103 U.S. 304 (1880).

91. *Hilton v. Roylance*, 25 Utah 129, 156 (1902).

92. Ibid., 149.

93. Smith and Hindus, "Premarital Pregnancy," 549.

94. Alexander, *Utah*, 200–201; Doctrine and Covenants Official Declaration 1; Hardy, *Solemn Covenant*, 127–66, 244–309; Van Wagoner, *Mormon Polygamy*, 130–51; E. Leo Lyman, "The Political Background of the Woodruff Manifesto," *Dialogue: A Journal of Mormon Thought* 24 (Fall 1991): 21–39; Alexander, *Mormonism in Transition*, 60–73; J. Clark, *Messages of the First Presidency*, 4:84, 216–17; Martha S. Bradley, "Changed Faces: The Official LDS Position on Polygamy, 1890–1990," *Sunstone* 14 (February 1990): 26–27.

95. Hardy, *Solemn Covenant*, 171 (quote), 207 188; Quinn, "LDS Church Authority and New Plural Marriages," 69–90; M. Bradley, *Kidnapped from That Land*, 23–26.

96. Hardy, *Solemn Covenant*, 188.

97. Stye, *Collected Discourses*, 2:214 (April 6, 1891).

98. Kenneth L. Cannon II, "Beyond the Manifesto: Polygamous Cohabitation among LDS General Authorities after 1890," *Utah Historical Quarterly* 46 (Winter 1978): 30; Stye, *Collected Discourses*, 5:168–69 (Wilford Woodruff, July 26, 1896); *Deseret News*, December 30, 1899, 16; Hardy, *Solemn Covenant*, 143–46.

99. Altman and Ginat, *Polygamous Families in Contemporary Society*, x; "Utah Polygamists Estimated at 25,000," *Deseret News*, April 24, 1999, B5; Williams, "A House, 10 Wives," B11; Ken Driggs, "Twentieth-Century Polygamy and Fundamentalist Mormons in Southern Utah," *Dialogue: A Journal of Mormon Thought* 24 (Winter 1991): 44–58; Tom Zoellner, "Rulon Jeffs: Patriarch, President, Prophet for Polygamy," *Salt Lake Tribune*, June 28, 1998, J8; Ray Rivera, "Family Secrets: When Incest Becomes a Religious Tenet, Inbreeding Key to Doctrine of Keeping Bloodline Pure," *Salt Lake Tribune*, April 25, 1999, A1.

100. Tom Zoellner, "Polygamy on the Dole," *Salt Lake Tribune*, June 28, 1998, A1; Greg Burton, "State Suing Polygamist to Recoup Welfare Aid," *Salt Lake Tribune*, June 18, 1999, C1.

101. M. Bradley, *Kidnapped from That Land*, 98–101, 188; Zoellner, "Polygamy on the Dole," A6; Ray Rivera, "Polygamist Gets Jail Time for Beating His Daughter," *Salt Lake Tribune*, June 20, 1999, A1.

102. J. Bennion, *Women of Principle*, 9.

103. Ibid., 7, 37; Altman and Ginat, *Polygamous Families in Contemporary Society*, 470–71. See also chapter 9.

104. M. Bradley, *Kidnapped from That Land*, 99–100. See also chapter 5.

105. Rivera, "Polygamist Gets Jail Time for Beating His Daughter," A1; Greg Burton, "Law Professor Criticizes Prosecution of Polygamist as 'Unequal Justice,'" *Salt Lake Tribune*, May 2, 2000, B1; Randall Larsen, "Friend Makes a Case for Decriminalizing the Practice of Plural Marriage," *Salt Lake Tribune*, May 14, 2000, A5; Greg Burton, "Family, or Felony?" *Salt Lake Tribune*, June 11, 2000, A22.

106. M. Bradley, *Kidnapped from That Land*, 148–81; *In re State in Interest of Black*, 3 Utah 2d 352 (1955) (quote).

107. An exception to this is the conviction of Mark Easterday, who pleaded no contest to an adultery charge for a polygamous marriage. He was sentenced to six months in jail, with the jail time waived, and a fine of $500. Thomas Burr, "Charged with Bigamy, Father of Nine Instead Pleads No Contest," *Salt Lake Tribune*, June 16, 1999, D2.

108. Chris Jorgensen, "Schism Disrupts the Faithful in Sanpete Valley," *Salt Lake City Tribune*, August 28, 1994, A10.

109. Ibid. (quote); John Halstead, "The Structure of LDS Interpretations of the TLC Apostacy" (Honor's thesis, Brigham Young University, 1999), 68–69; Becky Johns, "The Manti Mormons: The Rise of the Latest Mormon Church," *Sunstone* 19 (June 1996): 32; Egan, "Hex, Wives and Videotape," B1. The TLC claims that in polygamous relationships, "all parties are consenting adults." "How Can the TLC Believe and Live Plural Marriage When It Is against the Law?"

110. John Marshall Day, "A Study of Protest to Adaptation" (Master's thesis, University of Utah, 1963), cited in Driggs, "Twentieth-Century Polygamy and Fundamentalist Mormons in Southern Utah," 52; Armand L. Mauss, "Refuge and Retrenchment: The Mormon Quest for Identity," in *Contemporary Mormonism: Social Science Perspectives*, ed. Marie Cornwall, Tim B. Heaton, and Lawrence A. Young (Urbana: University of Illinois Press, 1994), 36–37.

111. Shipps, *Mormonism*, 61.

112. Antrei and Roberts, *History of Sanpete County*, 284; "How Does the TLC Intend to Fulfill the Charge to Preach the Gospel to All the World?," n.d. [1994–98], CD-ROM of TLC Web site. In May 2000, the TLC Web site contained only one document, an official pronouncement that began: "God has commanded us by revelation to cease our labors of preaching and warning to errant Israel and the nations of the earth."

113. E. Lyman, *Political Deliverance*, 135–36; *Deseret News Weekly*, November 14, 1891, 659 (quote).

114. Rodney Stark, "The Basis of Mormon Success: A Theoretical Application," in *Latter-day Saint Social Life: Social Research on the LDS Church and Its Members*, ed. James T. Duke (Provo, Utah: Religious Studies Center, Brigham Young University, 1998), 32.

115. Hardy, *Solemn Covenant*, 336–62; Kathryn M. Daynes, "Diversity and Adaptation: American Families over Four Centuries," in *Fulfilling the Founding: A Reader for American Heritage*, Fall 1999 ed., ed. Gary Daynes (Needham Heights, Mass.: Pearson Custom Publishing, 1999), 285–92; Dorice Williams Elliott, "Women, the Mormon Family, and Class Mobility: Nineteenth-Century Victorian Ideology in a Twentieth-Century Church," *Sunstone* 15 (December 1991): 22–26.

Appendix

1. Wayne L. Wahlquist, "Population Growth in the Mormon Core Area: 1847–1890," in *Mormon Role in the Settlement of the West,* ed. Jackson, 109–10.

2. Ibid., 109.

3. For a description of the Family History Library's holdings and their usefulness for demographic studies, see Bean et al., "The Genealogical Society of Utah as a Data Resource," 6–19.

4. In 1908, only 21 of the 133 families in the Manti North Ward were not members of the church. Teachers' Meeting Minutes, December 19, 1908, microfilm of original, Manti North Ward Record, LDS Church Archives. Of those 21 families, several had been members of the church or had their children blessed in the church so that their names do appear in the membership records.

5. For information on family group records as sources for demographic research, an evaluation of their representativeness, and the use of these records in the Mormon Historical Demography Project, see Lee L. Bean, Dean L. May, and Mark Skolnick, "The Mormon Historical Demography Project," *Historical Methods* 11 (Winter 1978): 45–53; Skolnick et al., "Mormon Demographic History I," 5–8; and Mineau, Bean, and Skolnick, "Mormon Demographic History II," 431–32.

6. Children in the manuscript censuses but as yet unidentified may be additional omissions from family group records.

7. For an evaluation of the quality of a data set based primarily on family group records, see Logue, *Sermon in the Desert,* 129–49. The statistical tests he used for polygamous families suggested "an omission rate of perhaps 3 percent of all births, but again it cannot be assumed that variations in polygamous intervals are due to missing births." Ibid., 137.

8. For a typed, alphabetized listing of the entries in this record, see Tatton, "Cemetery Records." Several entries on the original are omitted from this typescript.

9. Sanpete County, Utah, Justice of the Peace Court, "Justice Docket for the Manti Precinct, 1866–1891, 1873–1892, 1855–1870," microfilm of original, 1 reel, FHL.

10. Studies that rely wholly or partly on *Pioneers and Prominent Men of Utah* for their data are Ivins, "Notes on Mormon Polygamy"; Smith and Kunz, "Polygyny and Fertility"; Kunz, "One Wife or Several?"; and Faux and Miller, "Evolutionary Speculations."

11. Stanley Ivins's influential article on polygamy is based on the genealogical data in Esshom's and Lever's volumes. Even if he had linked the data from the two sources, Lever would have corrected only one of the entries in Esshom, and Esshom corrected none of the entries in Lever. The influence of Ivins's article is demonstrated by its being selected in a survey of Mormon scholars as one of the two best articles written about Mormon history, as evidenced by "sound scholarship and literary quality." James B. Allen, "Since 1950: Creators and Creations of Mormon History," in *New Views of Mormon History: A Collection of Essays in Honor of Leonard J. Arrington,* ed. Davis Bitton and Maureen Ursenbach Beecher (Salt Lake City: University of Utah Press, 1987), 423–24.

SELECTED BIBLIOGRAPHY

Archival Sources

Berry, Annie Eliza. "Reminiscences, 1899–1907." Microfilm of typescript. LDS Church Archives, Salt Lake City, Utah.

Church of Jesus Christ of Latter-day Saints. "Manti Ward Record." Microfilm of MS. LDS Church Archives, Salt Lake City, Utah.

———, Endowment House. "Endowments of the Living, 1851–1884." Microfilm of MS. Family History Library, Salt Lake City, Utah.

———, Manti South Ward. "Record of Members, 1877–1941." Microfilm of MS. Family History Library, Salt Lake City, Utah.

———, Manti Ward. "Record of Members, [1849]–1877." Microfilm of MS. Family History Library, Salt Lake City, Utah.

Farnsworth, M. F. "History of Manti." Typescript. Family History Library, Salt Lake City, Utah.

Hancock, Mosiah Lyman. "Autobiography." Microfilm of typescript. LDS Church Archives, Salt Lake City, Utah.

Hansen, Joseph. "Family History: Taken from a History Written by Joseph Hansen, Price, Utah." Typescript. Manti City Library, Manti, Utah.

Judd, Andrew Jackson, and Fannie Kenner Anderson. "A History of Manti's Progress," 1958. Typescript. Special Collections, Harold B. Lee Library, Brigham Young University, Provo, Utah.

Lightner, Mary Elizabeth Rollins. "Address Delivered at Brigham Young University." Mary Elizabeth Rollins Lightner Papers. Special Collections, Harold B. Lee Library, Brigham Young University, Provo, Utah.

Mace, Wandle. "Autobiography." Photocopy of MS. Special Collections, Harold B. Lee Library, Brigham Young University, Provo, Utah.

McAllister, John D. T. "Autobiography and Diary, 1851–1906," 7 vols. Typescript. Special Collections, Harold B. Lee Library, Brigham Young University, Provo, Utah.

Peacock, George "Diary, 1862–1875." MS. Special Collections, Harold B. Lee Library, Brigham Young University, Provo, Utah.

Sanpete County, Utah. "Assessment Roll Records, 1873–1890." Microfilm of MS, 2 reels. Family History Library, Salt Lake City, Utah.

———. "Assessment Roll Records, 1900." Basement Archives, Sanpete County Courthouse, Manti, Utah.

———. Divorce Case Files. Basement Archives, Sanpete County Courthouse, Manti, Utah.

———. File of Estates. Basement Archives, Sanpete County Courthouse, Manti, Utah.

Sanpete County, Utah, Probate Court. "Criminal Docket," Book 2. Microfilm of MS. Family History Library, Salt Lake City, Utah.

———. "Minutes, 1852–1866," Book 1. Microfilm of MS. Family History Library, Salt Lake City, Utah.

———. "Probate Record, including Minutes, 1866–1884," Book A. Microfilm of MS. Family History Library, Salt Lake City, Utah.

———. "Probate Record, 1884–1890," Book B. Microfilm of MS. Family History Library, Salt Lake City, Utah.

Smith, Azariah. "Journal." Photocopy of original. Special Collections, Harold B. Lee Library, Brigham Young University, Provo, Utah.

Utah State, Seventh District Court, Sanpete County. "Judgment Record, 1896–1936." Microfilm of MS. Family History Library, Salt Lake City, Utah.

Utah Territory, First District Court. "Minutes." Microfilm of original. Family History Library, Salt Lake City, Utah.

Weibye, Jens C. A. "Diaries," 1861–93. Microfilm of original. LDS Church Archives, Salt Lake City, Utah.

Whitney, Helen Mar Kimball. "Autobiography 1881." MS. LDS Church Archives, Salt Lake City, Utah.

Young, Emily Dow Partridge. "Diary." Photocopy of typescript. Special Collections, Harold B. Lee Library, Brigham Young University, Provo, Utah.

Books, Articles, and Theses

Aaron, Richard I. "Mormon Divorce and the Statute of 1852: Questions for Divorce in the 1980's." *Journal of Contemporary Law* 8 (1982): 5–45.

Adair, Florence Ellen Fowler. "Florence Ellen Fowler Adair." In *Our Pioneer Heritage*, vol. 7, compiled by Kate B. Carter, 269–71. Salt Lake City: Daughters of the Utah Pioneers, 1964.

Ahlstrom, Sydney E. *A Religious History of the American People.* New Haven, Conn.: Yale University Press, 1972.

Alexander, Thomas G. "Charles S. Zane, Apostle of the New Era." *Utah Historical Quarterly* 34 (Fall 1966): 290–314.

———. *Mormonism in Transition: A History of the Latter-day Saints, 1890–1930.* Urbana: University of Illinois Press, 1986.

———. *Things in Heaven and Earth: The Life and Times of Wilford Woodruff, a Mormon Prophet.* Salt Lake City: Signature Books, 1991.

———. *Utah, the Right Place: The Official Centennial History.* Rev. ed. Salt Lake City: Gibbs Smith, 1996.

———. "Wilford Woodruff and the Mormon Reformation of 1855–57." *Dialogue: A Journal of Mormon Thought* 25 (Summer 1992): 25–39.

Allen, James B. "The Unusual Jurisdiction of the County Probate Courts in the Territory of Utah." *Utah Historical Quarterly* 36 (Spring 1968): 132–42.

Allen, James B., and Glen M. Leonard. *The Story of the Latter-day Saints.* 2d ed., rev. and enl. Salt Lake City: Deseret Book, 1992.

Altman, Irwin, and Joseph Ginat. *Polygamous Families in Contemporary Society.* New York: Cambridge University Press, 1996.

Anderson, Lavina Fielding. "Lucinda L. Dalton." In *Sister Saints*, edited by Vicky Burgess-Olson, 141–71. Provo, Utah: Brigham Young University Press, 1978.

Anderson, Nels. *Desert Saints: The Mormon Frontier in Utah.* Chicago: University of Chicago Press, 1942.

Anderton, Douglas L., Lee L. Bean, J. Dennis Willigan, and Geraldine P. Mineau. "Adoption of Fertility Limitation in an American Frontier Population: An Analysis and Simulation of Socio-Religious Subgroups." *Social Biology* 31 (Spring–Summer 1984): 140–59.

Anderton, Douglas L., and Rebecca Jean Emigh. "Polygynous Fertility: Sexual Competition versus Progeny." *American Journal of Sociology* 94 (January 1989): 832–55.

Antrei, Albert. *High, Dry, and Offside.* [Manti, Utah:] Manti City Council, 1995.

Antrei, Albert C. T., and Allen D. Roberts. *A History of Sanpete County.* Salt Lake City: Utah State Historical Society and Sanpete County Commission, 1999.

Antrei, Albert, and Ruth D. Scow, eds. *The Other Forty-Niners: A Topical History of Sanpete County, Utah, 1849–1983.* Salt Lake City: Western Epics, 1982.

Arrington, Leonard J. *Brigham Young: American Moses.* New York: Alfred A. Knopf, 1985. Reprint, Urbana: University of Illinois Press, 1986.

———. *Great Basin Kingdom: An Economic History of the Latter-day Saints, 1830–1900.* Lincoln: University of Nebraska Press, 1958.

Arrington, Leonard J., and Davis Bitton. *The Mormon Experience: A History of the Latter-day Saints.* New York: Alfred A. Knopf, 1979.

Atack, Jeremy, and Fred Bateman. *To Their Own Soil: Agriculture in the Antebellum North.* Ames: Iowa State University Press, 1987.

Bachman, Danel W. "New Light on an Old Hypothesis: The Ohio Origins of the Revelation on Eternal Marriage." *Journal of Mormon History* 5 (1978): 19–32.

———. "A Study of the Mormon Practice of Plural Marriage before the Death of Joseph Smith." Master's thesis, Purdue University, 1975.

Backman, Milton V., Jr. *The Heavens Resound: A History of the Latter-day Saints in Ohio, 1830–1838.* Salt Lake City: Deseret Book, 1983.

Bartholomew, G. W. "Recognition of Polygamous Marriages in America." *International and Comparative Law Quarterly* 13 (July 1964): 1022–75.

Barton, William Kilshaw. *Copy of Diary and Missionary Journal of William Kilshaw Barton, Pioneer of 1852.* Salt Lake City: n.p., n.d.

Bates, Irene M., and E. Gary Smith. *Lost Legacy: The Mormon Office of Presiding Patriarch.* Urbana: University of Illinois Press, 1996.

Bean, Lee L., and G. P. Mineau. "The Polygyny-Fertility Hypothesis: A Re-evaluation." *Population Studies* 40 (March 1986): 67–81.

Bean, Lee L., Geraldine P. Mineau, and Douglas L. Anderton. *Fertility Change on the American Frontier: Adaptation and Innovation.* Berkeley: University of California Press, 1990.

———. "Residence and Religious Effects on Declining Family Size: An Historical Analysis of the Utah Population." *Review of Religious Research* 25 (December 1983): 91–101.

Bean, Lee L., Geraldine P. Mineau, Yung-chang Hsueh, and Douglas L. Anderton. "The Fertility Effects of Marriage Patterns in a Frontier American Population." *Historical Methods* 20 (Fall 1987): 161–71.

Bean, Lee L., G. P. Mineau, Katherine A. Lynch, and J. Dennis Willigan. "The Genealogical Society of Utah as a Data Resource for Historical Demography." *Population Index* 46 (1980): 6–19.

Becker, Gary S. *A Treatise on the Family.* Enl. ed. Cambridge, Mass.: Harvard University Press, 1991.

Beecher, Maureen Ursenbach. "Under the Sunbonnets: Mormon Women with Faces." *Brigham Young University Studies* 16 (Summer 1976): 471–84.

———. "Women's Work on the Mormon Frontier." *Utah Historical Quarterly* 49 (Summer 1981): 276–90.

Beecher, Maureen Ursenbach, Carol Cornwall Madsen, and Lavina Fielding Anderson. "Widowhood among the Mormons: The Personal Accounts." In *On Their Own: Widows and Widowhood in the American Southwest, 1848–1939*, edited by Arlene Scadron, 117–39. Urbana: University of Illinois Press, 1988.

Bennett, Richard E. *Mormons at the Missouri, 1846–1852: "And Should We Die . . ."* Norman: University of Oklahoma Press, 1987.

Bennion, Janet. *Women of Principle: Female Networking in Contemporary Mormon Polygyny.* New York: Oxford University Press, 1998.

Bennion, Lowell "Ben." "The Incidence of Mormon Polygamy in 1880: 'Dixie' versus Davis Stake." *Journal of Mormon History* 11 (1984): 27–42.

Bishop, Joel Prentiss. *Commentaries on the Law of Marriage and Divorce with the Evidence, Practice, Pleading, and Forms; Also of Separation without Divorce, and of the Evidence of Marriage in All Issues.* 2 vols. 6th ed., rev. and enl. Boston: Little, Brown, 1881.

———. *Commentaries on the Law of Married Women under the Statutes of the Several States, and at Common Law and in Equity.* 2 vols. Boston: Little, Brown, 1873.

Bitton, Davis. "Mormon Polygamy: A Review Article." *Journal of Mormon History* 4 (1977): 101–18.

———. *The Ritualization of Mormon History and Other Essays.* Urbana: University of Illinois Press, 1994.

Blackhurst, Wallace Gardner. "Wealth, Polygamy, and Fertility in a Polygamous Society: Utah County Mormons, 1851–1870." Ph.D. diss., University of Chicago, 1990.

Blake, Nelson Manfred. *The Road to Reno: A History of Divorce in the United States.* New York: Macmillan, 1962.

Bradley, George W. "Sketch of the Life of Ex-Bishop Bradley, Moroni, Utah." *Manti Home Sentinel*, March 4, 1890.

Bradley, Martha Sonntag. "Changed Faces: The Official LDS Position on Polygamy, 1890–1990." *Sunstone* 14 (February 1990): 26–33.

———. *Kidnapped from That Land: The Government Raids on the Short Creek Polygamists.* Salt Lake City: University of Utah Press, 1993.

Brodie, Fawn. *No Man Knows My History: The Life of Joseph Smith, the Mormon Prophet.* 2d ed., rev. New York: Alfred A. Knopf, 1979.

Brooks, Juanita. *Emma Lee.* Logan: Utah State University Press, 1975.

Burgess-Olson, Vicky. "Family Structure and Dynamics in Utah Mormon Families: 1847–1885." Ph.D. diss., Northwestern University, 1975.

———, ed. *Sister Saints.* Provo, Utah: Brigham Young University Press, 1978.

Burton, Richard. *City of the Saints and across the Rocky Mountains to California.* Edited by Fawn Brodie. New York: Alfred A. Knopf, 1963.

Bushman, Richard L. *Joseph Smith and the Beginnings of Mormonism.* Urbana: University of Illinois Press, 1984.

Campbell, Eugene E. *Establishing Zion: The Mormon Church in the American West, 1847–1869.* Salt Lake City: Signature Books, 1988.

Campbell, Eugene E., and Bruce L. Campbell. "Divorce among Mormon Polygamists: Extent and Explanations." *Utah Historical Quarterly* 46 (Winter 1978): 4–23.

Cannon, Brian Q. "Adopted or Indentured, 1850–1870: Native Children in Mormon Households." In *Nearly Everything Imaginable: The Everyday Life of*

Utah's Mormon Pioneers, edited by Ronald W. Walker and Doris R. Dant, 341–57. Provo, Utah: Brigham Young University Press, 1999.

Cannon, Charles A. "The Awesome Power of Sex: The Polemical Campaign against Mormon Polygamy." *Pacific Historical Review* 43 (February 1974): 61–82.

Cannon, Donald Q., and Lyndon W. Cook, eds. *Far West Record: Minutes of the Church of Jesus Christ of Latter-day Saints, 1830–1844.* Salt Lake City: Deseret Book, 1983.

Cannon, Kenneth L., II. "Beyond the Manifesto: Polygamous Cohabitation among LDS General Authorities after 1890." *Utah Historical Quarterly* 46 (Winter 1978): 24–36.

———. "'Mountain Common Law': The Extralegal Punishment of Seducers in Early Utah." *Utah Historical Quarterly* 51 (Fall 1983): 308–27.

———. "A Strange Encounter: The English Courts and Mormon Polygamy." *Brigham Young University Studies* 22 (Winter 1982): 73–83.

Carlson, Eric Josef. *Marriage and the English Reformation.* Oxford: Blackwell, 1994.

Censer, Jane Turner. "Smiling through Her Tears: Antebellum Southern Women and Divorce." *American Journal of Legal History* 25 (April 1981): 24–47.

Centennial Committee, Manti, Utah. *Song of a Century, 1849–1949.* Provo, Utah: Community Press, 1978.

Chandless, William. *A Visit to Salt Lake; Being a Journey across the Plains and a Residence in the Mormon Settlements at Utah.* London: Smith, Elder, 1857.

Chojnacka, Helena. "Polygyny and the Rate of Population Growth." *Population Studies* 34 (March 1980): 91–107.

Christensen, Clare B. *Before and after Mt. Pisgah: Cox, Hulet, Morley, Tuttle, Winget, Whiting and Related Families.* Salt Lake City: n.p., 1979.

Christy, Howard A. "Weather, Disaster, and Responsibility: An Essay on the Willie and Martin Handcart Story." *Brigham Young University Studies* 37, no. 1 (1997–98): 6–74.

Clark, James R., ed. *Messages of the First Presidency of the Church of Jesus Christ of Latter-day Saints, 1833–1964.* 6 vols. Salt Lake City: Bookcraft, 1965.

Clark, Laura Christensen McCurdy. *Others.* N.p., n.d.

Clayton, William. *Manchester Mormons: The Journal of William Clayton, 1840 to 1842.* Edited by James B. Allen and Thomas G. Alexander. Santa Barbara, Calif.: Peregrine Smith, 1974.

Collier, Fred C., ed. *The Teachings of President Brigham Young.* Vol. 3, *1852–1854.* Salt Lake City: Collier's, 1987.

———. *Unpublished Revelations of the Prophets and Presidents of the Church of Jesus Christ of Latter Day Saints.* Vol. 1, 2d ed. Salt Lake City: Collier's, 1981.

Complainant's Abstract of Pleading and Evidence . . . the Reorganized Church of Jesus Christ of Latter Day Saints, Complainant, v. the Church of Christ at Independence, Missouri. . . . Lamoni, Iowa: Herald Publishing House, 1893.

Compton, Todd. *In Sacred Loneliness: The Plural Wives of Joseph Smith.* Salt Lake City: Signature Books, 1997.

Cook, Lyndon W. *The Revelations of the Prophet Joseph Smith: A Historical and Biographical Commentary of the Doctrine and Covenants.* Salt Lake City: Deseret Book, 1985.

Coontz, Stephanie. *The Social Origins of Private Life: A History of American Families, 1600–1900.* London: Verso, 1988.

Cooper, Rex. *Promises Made to the Fathers: Mormon Covenant Organization.* Salt Lake City: University of Utah Press, 1990.

Cornwall, Marie, Camela Courtright, and Laga Van Beek. "How Common the Principle? Women as Plural Wives in 1860." *Dialogue: A Journal of Mormon Thought* 26 (Summer 1993): 139–53.

Cornwall, Marie, and Laga Van Beek. "The Mormon Practice of Plural Marriage: The Social Construction of Religious Identity and Commitment." *Religion and the Social Order* 5 (1995): 13–35.

Cott, Nancy F. "Passionlessness: An Interpretation of Victorian Sexual Ideology, 1790–1850." In *A Heritage of Her Own: Toward a New Social History of American Women*, edited by Nancy F. Cott and Elizabeth H. Peck, 162–81. New York: Simon and Schuster, 1979.

Daynes, Kathryn M. "Mormon Polygamy: Belief and Practice in Nauvoo." In *Kingdom on the Mississippi Revisited: Nauvoo in Mormon History*, edited by Roger D. Launius and John E. Hallwas, 130–46. Urbana: University of Illinois Press, 1996.

———. "Single Men in a Polygamous Society: Male Marriage Patterns in Manti, Utah." *Journal of Mormon History* 24 (Spring 1998): 89–111.

Degler, Carl. *At Odds: Women and the Family in America from the Revolution to the Present*. Oxford: Oxford University Press, 1980.

DePillis, Mario S. "The Quest for Religious Authority and the Rise of Mormonism." *Dialogue: A Journal of Mormon Thought* 1 (Spring 1966): 68–88.

Dixon, Ruth B. "Explaining Cross-Cultural Variations in Age at Marriage and Proportions Never Marrying." *Population Studies* 25 (July 1971): 215–33.

Driggs, Ken. "Twentieth-Century Polygamy and Fundamentalist Mormons in Southern Utah." *Dialogue: A Journal of Mormon Thought* 24 (Winter 1991): 44–58.

Eaton-Gadsby, Patricia Rasmussen, and Judith Rasmussen Dushku. "Emmeline B. Wells." In *Sister Saints*, edited by Vicky Burgess-Olson, 456–78. Provo, Utah: Brigham Young University Press, 1978.

Ehat, Andrew F. "Joseph Smith's Introduction of Temple Ordinances and the 1844 Mormon Succession Question." Master's thesis, Brigham Young University, 1982.

Elliott, Dorice Williams. "Women, the Mormon Family, and Class Mobility: Nineteenth-Century Victorian Ideology in a Twentieth-Century Church." *Sunstone* 15 (December 1991): 19–26.

Ember, Melvin. "Warfare, Sex Ratio, and Polygyny." *Ethnology* 13 (April 1974): 197–206.

Embry, Jessie L. *Mormon Polygamous Families: Life in the Principle*. Salt Lake City: University of Utah Press, 1987.

———. "Ultimate Taboos: Incest and Mormon Polygamy." *Journal of Mormon History* 18 (Spring 1992): 93–113.

Embry, Jessie L., and Martha S. Bradley. "Mothers and Daughters in Polygamy." *Dialogue: A Journal of Mormon Thought* 18 (Fall 1985): 99–107.

Evans, Rosa Mae McClellan. "Judicial Prosecution of Prisoners for LDS Plural Marriage: Prison Sentences, 1884–1895." Master's thesis, Brigham Young University, 1986.

Farr, Annette W. *The Story of Edwin Marion Whiting and Anna Maria Isaacson*. Provo, Utah: J. Grant Stevenson, 1969.

Faux, Steven F., and Harold L. Miller Jr. "Evolutionary Speculations on the Oligarchic Development of Mormon Polygyny." *Ethology and Sociobiology* 5, no. 1 (1984): 15–31.

Firmage, Edwin B. "Reflections on Mormon History: Zion and the Anti-Legal Tradition." *Dialogue: A Journal of Mormon Thought* 31 (Winter 1998): 53–64.

Firmage, Edwin Brown, and Richard Collin Mangrum. *Zion in the Courts: A Legal History of the Church of Jesus Christ of Latter-day Saints, 1830–1900.* Urbana: University of Illinois Press, 1988.

Flanders, Robert Bruce. *Nauvoo: Kingdom on the Mississippi.* Urbana: University of Illinois Press, 1965.

Foster, Lawrence. "A Little-known Defense of Polygamy from the Mormon Press in 1842." *Dialogue: A Journal of Mormon Thought* 9 (Winter 1974): 21–34.

———. *Religion and Sexuality: The American Communal Experiments of the Nineteenth Century.* New York: Oxford University Press, 1981.

———. "Sex and Prophetic Power: A Comparison of John Humphrey Noyes, Founder of the Oneida Community, with Joseph Smith, Jr., the Mormon Prophet." *Dialogue: A Journal of Mormon Thought* 31 (Winter 1998): 65–83.

Friedman, Lawrence M. *Crime and Punishment in American History.* New York: Basic Books, 1993.

Furniss, Norman F. *The Mormon Conflict, 1850–1859.* New Haven, Conn.: Yale University Press, 1960.

Gee, Elizabeth D. "Justice for All or for the 'Elect'? The Utah County Probate Court, 1855–72." *Utah Historical Quarterly* 48 (Spring 1980): 129–47.

Gordon, Sarah Barringer. "'The Liberty of Self-Degradation': Polygamy, Woman Suffrage, and Consent in Nineteenth-Century America." *Journal of American History* 83 (December 1996): 815–47.

Grayson, Donald K. "Human Mortality in a Natural Disaster: The Willie Handcart Company." *Journal of Anthropological Research* 52 (Summer 1996): 185–205.

Griswold, Robert L. *Family and Divorce in California, 1850–1890: Victorian Illusions and Everyday Realities.* Albany: State University of New York Press, 1982.

Grossberg, Michael. *Governing the Hearth: Law and the Family in Nineteenth-Century America.* Chapel Hill: University of North Carolina Press, 1985.

Hafen, LeRoy R., and Anne W. Hafen. *Handcarts to Zion.* Glendale, Calif.: Arthur H. Clarke, 1976.

Haines, Michael R. "Long-Term Marriage Patterns in the United States from Colonial Times to the Present." *History of the Family* 1, no. 1 (1996): 15–39.

Hajnal, John. "European Marriage Patterns in Perspective." In *Population in History: Essays in Historical Demography,* edited by D. V. Glass and D. E. C. Eversley, 101–43. Chicago: Aldine, 1965.

Hansen, Klaus J. *Mormonism and the American Experience.* Chicago: University of Chicago Press, 1981.

Hardy, B. Carmon. "Lords of Creation: Polygamy, the Abrahamic Household, and Mormon Patriarchy." *Journal of Mormon History* 20 (Spring 1994): 119–52.

———. *Solemn Covenant: The Mormon Polygamous Passage.* Urbana: University of Illinois Press, 1992.

Hareven, Tamara. "Family History at the Crossroads." In *Family History at the Crossroads: A Journal of Family History Reader,* edited by Tamara Hareven and Andrejs Plakans, viii–xxi. Princeton, N.J.: Princeton University Press, 1987.

Harline, Paula Kelly. "Polygamous Yet Monogamous: Cultural Conflict in the Writings of Mormon Polygamous Wives." In *Old West–New West: Centennial Essays,* edited by Barbara Howard Meldrum, 115–32. Moscow: University of Idaho Press, 1993.

Harrison, Jerry N. *Demographic Transition in a Frontier Town: Manti, Utah, 1849–1948.* New York: Garland, 1989.

Hatch, Nelle Spilsbury, and B. Carmon Hardy, eds. and comps. *Stalwarts South of the Border.* N.p., 1985.

Hill, Marvin. "Cultural Crisis in the Mormon Kingdom: A Reconsideration of the Causes of Kirtland Dissent." *Church History* 49 (September 1980): 286–97.

———. *Quest for Refuge: The Mormon Flight from American Pluralism.* Salt Lake City: Signature Books, 1989.

Homer, Michael W. "The Judiciary and the Common Law in Utah Territory, 1850–61." *Dialogue: A Journal of Mormon Thought* 21 (Spring 1988): 97–108.

Howard, George Elliott. *A History of Matrimonial Institutions.* 3 vols. Chicago: University of Chicago Press, 1904.

Hunter, Milton R. *Brigham Young, the Colonizer.* 4th ed., rev. Santa Barbara, Calif.: Peregrine Smith, 1973.

International Society, Daughters of Utah Pioneers. *Pioneer Women of Faith and Fortitude.* 4 vols. N.p. [Utah]: Publishers Press, 1998.

Inventory of the County Archives of Utah. Vol. 20. Ogden, Utah: n.p., 1940.

Irving, Gordon. "The Law of Adoption: One Phase of the Development of the Mormon Concept of Salvation, 1830–1900." *Brigham Young University Studies* 14 (Spring 1974): 291–314.

Iversen, Joan. *The Antipolygamy Controversy in U.S. Women's Movements, 1880–1925: A Debate on the American Home.* New York: Garland, 1997.

———. "Feminist Implications of Mormon Polygyny." *Feminist Studies* 10 (Fall 1984): 505–22.

Ivins, Stanley S. "Notes on Mormon Polygamy." *Western Humanities Review* 10 (Summer 1956): 229–39.

Jacob, Udney Hay. *The Peace Maker.* Nauvoo, Ill.: J. Smith, 1842. Reprint, Kearns, Utah: Deseret Publishing, 1975.

Jensen, Jerrold S. "The Common Law of England in the Territory of Utah." *Utah Historical Quarterly* 60 (Winter 1992): 4–26.

Jensen, Richard L. "Steaming Through: Arrangements for Mormon Emigration from Europe, 1869–1887." *Journal of Mormon History* 9 (1982): 3–23.

Jenson, Andrew. *Church Chronology: A Record of Important Events Pertaining to the History of the Church of Jesus Christ of Latter-day Saints.* 2d ed., rev. and enl. Salt Lake City, Utah: Deseret News, 1914.

Jessee, Dean C. "Brigham Young's Family: The Wilderness Years." *Brigham Young University Studies* 19 (Summer 1979): 474–500.

Johns, Becky. "The Manti Mormons: The Rise of the Latest Mormon Church." *Sunstone* 19 (June 1996): 30–36.

Johnson, Annie Richardson, and Elva Richardson Shumway. *Charles Edmund Richardson: Man of Destiny.* Tempe, Ariz.: Publication Services, 1982.

Johnson, Benjamin F. *My Life's Review.* Independence, Mo.: Zion's Printing and Publishing, 1947.

Johnson, Jeffery Ogden. "Determining and Defining 'Wife': The Brigham Young Households." *Dialogue: A Journal of Mormon Thought* 20 (Fall 1987): 57–70.

Johnson, Paul E. *A Shopkeeper's Millennium: Society and Revival in Rochester, New York, 1815–1837.* New York: Hill and Wang, 1978.

Jorgensen, Lynne Watkins. "John Hyde, Jr., Mormon Renegade." *Journal of Mormon History* 17 (1991): 120–44.

Kearl, J. R., and Clayne L. Pope. "Wealth Mobility: The Missing Element." *Journal of Interdisciplinary History* 13 (Winter 1983): 461–88.

Kearl, J. R., Clayne L. Pope, and Larry T. Wimmer. "Household Wealth in a Settlement Economy: Utah, 1850–1870." *Journal of Economic History* 40 (September 1980): 477–96.

Keeler, Virginia C. *Cheney Garrett Van Buren and His Family: A Presentation of Their Lives and Times.* Provo, Utah: J. Grant Stevenson, 1962.

Kent, James. *Commentaries on American Law.* 4 vols. 12th ed. Boston: Little, Brown, 1873.

Kern, Louis J. *An Ordered Love: Sex Roles and Sexuality in Victorian Utopias — The Shakers, the Mormons, and the Oneida Community.* Chapel Hill: University of North Carolina Press, 1981

Kimball, Edward L. "The History of LDS Temple Admission Standards." *Journal of Mormon History* 24 (Spring 1998): 135–76.

Kunz, Phillip R. "One Wife or Several? A Comparative Study of Late Nineteenth-Century Marriage in Utah." In *The Mormon People: Their Character and Traditions,* edited by Thomas G. Alexander, 53–73. Provo, Utah: Brigham Young University Press, 1980.

Larson, Gustive O. *The "Americanization" of Utah for Statehood.* San Marino, Calif.: Huntington Library, 1971.

———. "The Mormon Reformation." *Utah Historical Quarterly* 26 (January 1958): 45–63.

Larson, Stan, ed. *Prisoner for Polygamy: The Memoirs and Letters of Rudger Clawson at the Utah Territorial Penitentiary, 1884–87.* Urbana: University of Illinois, 1993.

Lawson, John D. *Rights, Remedies, and Practice, at Law, in Equity, and under the Codes: A Treatise on American Law in Civil Causes; with a Digest of Illustrative Cases.* 7 vols. San Francisco: Bancroft-Whitney, 1889.

Lee, Gary R. *Family Structure and Interaction: A Comparative Analysis.* 2d ed., rev. Minneapolis: University of Minnesota Press, 1982.

Lee, John D. *Journals of John D. Lee, 1846–47 and 1859.* Edited by Charles Kelly. Salt Lake City: University of Utah Press, 1984.

Leone, Mark P. *Roots of Modern Mormonism.* Cambridge, Mass.: Harvard University Press, 1979.

LeSueur, Stephen C. *The 1838 Mormon War in Missouri.* Columbia: University of Missouri Press, 1987.

Lever, W. H. *History of Sanpete and Emery Counties, Utah: With Sketches of Cities, Towns, and Villages, Chronology of Important Events, Records of Indian Wars, Portraits of Prominent Persons, and Biographies of Representative Citizens.* Ogden, Utah: W. H. Lever, 1898.

Linford, Orma. "The Mormons and the Law: The Polygamy Cases, Part I." *Utah Law Review* 9 (Winter 1964): 308–70.

———. "The Mormons and the Law: The Polygamy Cases, Part II." *Utah Law Review* 9 (Summer 1965): 543–91.

———. "The Mormons, the Law, and the Territory of Utah." *American Journal of Legal History* 23 (April 1979): 213–35.

Logue, Larry M. *A Sermon in the Desert: Belief and Behavior in Early St. George, Utah.* Urbana: University of Illinois Press, 1988.

———. "A Time of Marriage: Monogamy and Polygamy in a Utah Town." *Journal of Mormon History* 11 (1984): 3–26.

Ludlow, Daniel H., ed. *Encyclopedia of Mormonism.* 4 vols. New York: Macmillan, 1992.

Lyman, Edward Leo. "The Political Background of the Woodruff Manifesto." *Dialogue: A Journal of Mormon Thought* 24 (Fall 1991): 21–42.

———. *Political Deliverance: The Mormon Quest for Utah Statehood.* Urbana: University of Illinois Press, 1986.

Lynn, Karen. "Courtship and Romance in Utah Territory: Doing Away with 'The Gentile Custom of Sparkification.'" In *A Sesquicentennial Look at Church History: Sidney B. Sperry Symposium, January 26, 1980, Brigham Young University Campus, Provo, Utah.* Provo, Utah: Brigham Young University Church Educational System, 1980.

Lystra, Karen. *Searching the Heart: Women, Men, and Romantic Love in Nineteenth-Century America.* New York: Oxford University Press, 1989.

Madsen, Carol. "'At Their Peril': Utah Law and the Case of Plural Wives, 1850–1900." *Western Historical Quarterly* 21 (November 1990): 425–43.

May, Dean L. "A Demographic Portrait of the Mormons, 1830–1980." In *After 150 Years: The Latter-day Saints in Sesquicentennial Perspective,* edited by Thomas G. Alexander and Jessie L. Embry, 37–69. Midvale, Utah: Signature Books for Charles Redd Center for Western Studies, 1983.

———. "People on the Mormon Frontier: Kanab's Families of 1874." *Journal of Family History* 1 (Winter 1976): 169–92.

———. *Utah: A People's History.* Salt Lake City: University of Utah Press, 1987.

Mealey, Linda. "The Relationship between Social Status and Biological Success: A Case Study of the Mormon Religious Hierarchy." *Ethology and Sociobiology* 6, no. 4 (1985): 249–57.

M[erriam], A. E. "History of Sanpete County." *Manti Home Sentinel,* March 28, 1890, April 11, 1890.

Miles, Carrie A. "Polygamy and the Economics of Salvation." *Sunstone* 21 (August 1998): 34–45.

Mineau, Geraldine P. "Utah Widowhood: A Demographic Profile." In *On Their Own: Widows and Widowhood in the American Southwest, 1848–1939,* edited by Arlene Scadron, 140–65. Urbana: University of Illinois Press, 1988.

Mineau, Geraldine P., Lee L. Bean, and Douglas L. Anderton. "Migration and Fertility: Behavioral Change on the American Frontier." *Journal of Family History* 14 (January 1989): 43–61.

Mineau, Geraldine P., L. L. Bean, and M. Skolnick. "Mormon Demographic History II: The Family Life Cycle and Natural Fertility." *Population Studies* 33 (November 1979): 429–46.

Mintz, Steven, and Susan Kellogg. *Domestic Revolutions: A Social History of American Family Life.* New York: Free Press, 1988.

Morley, Richard Henrie. "The Life and Contribution of Isaac Morley." Master's thesis, Brigham Young University, 1965.

Mulder, William. *Homeward to Zion: The Mormon Migration from Scandinavia.* Minneapolis: University of Minnesota Press, 1957.

Mulder William, and A. Russell Mortensen. *Among the Mormons: Historic Accounts by Contemporary Observers.* New York: Alfred A. Knopf, 1958.

Nelson, Lowry. *The Mormon Village: A Pattern and Technique of Land Settlement.* Salt Lake City: University of Utah Press, 1952.

Newell, Linda King, and Valeen Tippetts Avery. *Mormon Enigma: Emma Hale Smith.* Garden City, N.Y.: Doubleday, 1984.

Oaks, Dallin H., and Marvin S. Hill. *Carthage Conspiracy: The Trial of the Accused Assassins of Joseph Smith*. Urbana: University of Illinois Press, 1975.

O'Dea, Thomas F. *The Mormons*. Chicago: University of Chicago Press, 1957.

Ottenheimer, Martin. *Forbidden Relatives: The American Myth of Cousin Marriage*. Urbana: University of Illinois Press, 1996.

Pace, D. Gene. "Wives of Nineteenth-Century Mormon Bishops: A Quantitative Analysis." *Journal of the West* 21 (April 1982): 49–57.

Parkin, Max H. "The Nature and Causes of Internal and External Conflict of the Mormons in Ohio between 1830 and 1838." Master's thesis, Brigham Young University, 1966.

Peterson, John Alton. *Utah's Black Hawk War*. Salt Lake City: University of Utah Press, 1998.

Peterson, Paul H. "The Mormon Reformation of 1856–1857: The Rhetoric and the Reality." *Journal of Mormon History* 15 (1989): 59–87.

Phillips, Roderick. *Putting Asunder: A History of Divorce in Western Society*. Cambridge: Cambridge University Press, 1988.

Platt, Lyman D. "The History of Marriage in Utah, 1847–1905." *Genealogical Journal* 12 (Spring 1983): 28–41.

Poll, Richard D. "The Political Reconstruction of Utah Territory, 1866–1890." *Pacific Historical Review* 27 (May 1958): 111–26.

Poll, Richard D., Thomas G. Alexander, Eugene E. Campbell, and David E. Miller, eds. *Utah's History*. Logan: Utah State University Press, 1989.

Pratt, Belinda Marden. *Defence of Polygamy, by a Lady of Utah, in a Letter to Her Sister in New Hampshire*. Salt Lake City: n.p., 1854.

Pratt, Orson. "Celestial Marriage." *Seer* 1 (February 1853): 25–32; 1 (March 1853): 41–47; 1 (April 1853): 58–64; 1 (October 1853): 152–60.

Pratt, Parley P. *Autobiography of Parley Parker Pratt*. Salt Lake City: Deseret Book, 1979.

Quinn, D. Michael. "LDS Church Authority and New Plural Marriages, 1890–1904." *Dialogue: A Journal of Mormon Thought* 18 (Spring 1985): 9–105.

———. "The Mormon Hierarchy, 1832–1932: An American Elite." Ph.D. diss., Yale University, 1976.

———. *The Mormon Hierarchy: Extensions of Power*. Salt Lake City: Signature Books in association with Smith Research Associates, 1997.

———. *The Mormon Hierarchy: Origins of Power*. Salt Lake City: Signature Books, 1994.

Reeve, Tapping. *The Law of Baron and Femme*. 3d ed. Albany, N.Y.: William Gould, 1862. Reprint, New York: Source Book Press, a Division of Collectors Editions, 1970.

Remy, Jules, and Julius Brenchley. *A Journey to Great-Salt-Lake City*. 2 vols. London: W. Jeffs, 1861. Reprint, New York: AMS Press, 1971.

Riley, Glenda. *Divorce*. New York: Oxford University Press, 1991.

Roberts, B. H. *A Comprehensive History of the Church of Jesus Christ of Latter-day Saints*. 6 vols. Salt Lake City: Church of Jesus Christ of Latter-day Saints, 1930.

Romney, Catharine Cottam. *Letters of Catharine Cottam Romney, Plural Wife*. Edited by Jennifer Moulton Hansen. Urbana: University of Illinois Press, 1992.

Ryan, Mary P. *Cradle of the Middle Class: The Family in Oneida County, New York, 1790–1865*. Cambridge: Cambridge University Press, 1981.

———. *The Empire of the Mother: American Writing about Domesticity, 1830–1860*. New York: Institute for Research in History and the Haworth Press, 1982.

Schultz, Martin. "Divorce Patterns in Nineteenth-Century New England." *Journal of Family History* 15 (January 1990): 101–15.

Scott, Patricia Lyn. "Mormon Polygamy: A Bibliography, 1977–91." *Journal of Mormon History* 19 (Spring 1993): 133–55.

Semi-Annual Conference of the Church of Jesus Christ of Latter-day Saints. [Salt Lake City]: Deseret News, 1897–1964.

Sessions, Patty Bartlett. *Mormon Midwife: The 1846–1888 Diaries of Patty Bartlett Sessions.* Edited by Donna Toland Smart. Logan: Utah State University Press, 1997.

Shammas, Carole, Marylynn Salmon, and Michel Dahlin. *Inheritance in America from Colonial Times to the Present.* New Brunswick, N.J.: Rutgers University Press, 1987.

Sheehan, Michael M. "Christian Marriage: An Historical Perspective." In *Christian Marriage Today: Growth or Breakdown?* edited by Joseph A. Buijs, 15–32. New York: Edwin Mellen, 1985.

Shipp, Ellis. *The Early Autobiography and Diary of Ellis Reynolds Shipp.* Compiled and edited by Ellis Shipp Musser. Salt Lake City: Deseret News, 1962.

Shipps, Jan. *Mormonism: The Story of a New Religious Tradition.* Urbana: University of Illinois Press, 1985.

———. "The Principle Revoked: A Closer Look at the Demise of Plural Marriage." *Journal of Mormon History* 11 (1984): 65–77.

Shipps, Jan, Cheryll L. May, and Dean L. May. "Sugar House Ward: A Latter-day Saint Congregation." In *American Congregations,* vol. 1, *Portraits of Twelve Religious Communities,* edited by James P. Wind and James W. Lewis, 293–348. Chicago: University of Chicago Press, 1994.

Sidwell, Adelia Cox. "Reminiscences of the Early Days of Manti." *Manti Home Sentinel,* August 1, 1889, August 22, 1889.

Skolnick, M., L. Bean, D. May, V. Arbon, K. De Nevers, and P. Cartwright. "Mormon Demographic History I: Nuptiality and Fertility of Once-Married Couples." *Population Studies* 32 (March 1978): 5–20.

Smith, Daniel Scott. "Family Limitation, Sexual Control, and Domestic Feminism in Victorian America." In *Clio's Consciousness Raised: New Perspectives on the History of Women,* edited by Mary S. Hartman and Lois Banner, 119–36. New York: Octagon Books, 1976.

———. "The Long Cycle in American Illegitimacy and Prenuptial Pregnancy." In *Bastardy and Its Comparative History,* edited by Peter Laslett, Karla Oosterveen, and Richard M. Smith, 362–78. Cambridge, Mass.: Harvard University Press, 1980.

Smith, Daniel Scott, and Michael S. Hindus. "Premarital Pregnancy in America, 1640–1971: An Overview and Interpretation." *Journal of Interdisciplinary History* 4 (Spring 1975): 537–70.

Smith, George D. "Nauvoo Roots of Mormon Polygamy, 1841–46: A Preliminary Demographic Report." *Dialogue: A Journal of Mormon Thought* 27 (Spring 1994): 1–72.

Smith, James E., and Phillip R. Kunz. "Polygyny and Fertility in Nineteenth-Century America. *Population Studies* 30 (November 1976): 465–80.

Smith, Joseph, Jr. *The Words of Joseph Smith: The Contemporary Accounts of the Nauvoo Discourses of the Prophet Joseph.* Edited by Andrew F. Ehat and Lyndon W. Cook. Provo, Utah: Religious Studies Center, Brigham Young University, 1980.

Soltow, Lee. *Men and Wealth in the United States, 1850–1870.* New Haven, Conn.: Yale University Press, 1975.

Soltow, Lee, and Dean L. May. "The Distribution of Mormon Wealth and Income in 1857." *Explorations in Economic History* 16 (April 1979): 151–62.

Sonne, Conway B. *Saints on the Seas: A Maritime History of Mormon Migration, 1830–1890.* Salt Lake City: University of Utah Press, 1983.

Stegner, Wallace. *The Gathering of Zion: The Story of the Mormon Trail.* New York: McGraw Hill, 1964. Reprint, Salt Lake City: Westwater, 1981.

Stout, Hosea. *On the Mormon Frontier: The Diary of Hosea Stout, 1844–1861.* Edited by Juanita Brooks. 2 vols. Salt Lake City: University of Utah Press, 1964.

Stuy, Brian H., ed. *Collected Discourses, Delivered by President Wilford Woodruff, His Two Counselors, the Twelve Apostles, and Others.* 5 vols. Burbank, Calif.: B.H.S. Publishing, 1987–92.

Swenson, Raymond T. "Resolution of Civil Disputes by Mormon Ecclesiastical Courts." *Utah Law Review,* no. 3 (1978): 573–95.

Irene B. Taeuber and Conrad Taeuber. *People of the United States in the 20th Century.* A Census Monograph. Washington, D.C.: U.S. Government Printing Office, 1971.

Tanner, Annie Clark. *A Mormon Mother: An Autobiography by Annie Clark Tanner.* Salt Lake City: Tanner Trust Fund, University of Utah Library, 1976.

Taylor, P. A. M. *Expectations Westward: The Mormons and the Emigration of Their British Converts in the Nineteenth Century.* Edinburgh: Oliver and Boyd, 1965.

Turner, Ella L., ed. *The Ancestors and Descendants of Abraham Daniel Washburn and His Wife Flora Clarinda Gleason, Utah Pioneers, 1805–1962.* N.p.: Privately printed by author, 1963.

Underwood, Grant. *The Millenarian World of Early Mormonism.* Urbana: University of Illinois Press, 1993.

U.S. Bureau of the Census. "Population Characteristics: Marital Status and Family Status: March 1967." *Current Population Reports,* Series P-20, no. 170 (February 23, 1968): 1–16.

Van Wagoner, Richard S. "Mormon Polyandry in Nauvoo." *Dialogue: A Journal of Mormon Thought* 18 (Fall 1985): 67–83.

———. *Mormon Polygamy: A History.* 2d ed. Salt Lake City: Signature Books, 1989.

Wahlquist, Wayne L. "Population Growth in the Mormon Core Area: 1847–1890." In *The Mormon Role in the Settlement of the West,* edited by Richard H. Jackson, 107–33. Provo, Utah: Brigham Young University Press, 1978.

Walker, Charles Lowell. *Diary of Charles Lowell Walker.* Edited by A. Karl Larson and Katharine Miles Larson. 2 vols. Logan: Utah State University Press, 1980.

Wall, Francis George. "Francis George Wall—Pioneer of 1863." In *Our Pioneer Heritage,* vol. 7, compiled by Kate B. Carter, 362–78. Salt Lake City: Daughters of Utah Pioneers, 1964.

Washburn, Jesse Ordean. *Hyrum Smith Washburn, 1853–1924: Pioneer of Manti and Monroe, Utah, with Near Ancestors and Descendants.* Salt Lake City: Crabtree, 1983.

Whitney, Orson F. *History of Utah.* 4 vols. Salt Lake City: George Q. Cannon and Sons, 1898.

Whittaker, David J. "Early Mormon Polygamy Defenses." *Journal of Mormon History* 11 (1984): 43–64.

Winget, Katherine Hulet. "Autobiography." In *Our Pioneer Heritage*, vol. 13, compiled by Kate B. Carter, 489–92. Salt Lake City: Daughters of Utah Pioneers, 1970.

Woodruff, Wilford. *Wilford Woodruff's Journal, 1833–1898*. Edited by Scott Kenny. 9 vols. Midvale, Utah: Signature Books, 1983–84.

Woolf, C. M., F. E. Stephens, D. D. Mulaik, and R. E. Gilbert. "An Investigation of the Frequency of Consanguineous Marriages among the Mormons and Their Relatives in the United States." *American Journal of Human Genetics* 8 (March 1956): 236–58.

Wright, Carroll D. *Marriage and Divorce in the United States, 1867 to 1886*. Washington, D.C.: Government Printing Office, 1897. Reprint, New York: Arno, 1976.

Wrigley, E. A., and R. S. Schofield. *The Population History of England, 1541–1871: A Reconstruction*. London: Edward Arnold, 1981.

Young, Kimball. *Isn't One Wife Enough?* New York: Henry Holt, 1954.

INDEX

Aaron, Richard, 6, 151
Alcott, William, 39
Alder, Anna Barbara, 129, 130
Alder, Johannes, 129, 130
Alexander, Thomas, 117, 187
Allen, Daniel, 129
Allen, Joseph S., 42
Allen, Lucy, 55–56, 60, 62, 70–71
Allred, James T. S., 69
Amy v. Amy, 150
Andersen, Maren, 121
Anderson, Nels, 166
Anderton, Douglas L., 98–99, 108
Apostolic United Brethren Church, 210–11
Arapeen (Chief Wahkara's brother), 42, 45
Attwood divorce case, 146
Axelsen, Maren Jorgensen, 78

Bache, Nancy, 35
Bachman, Danel, 19, 231n.31
Barnes, Lorenzo D., 75
Barton, William Kilshaw, 61
Batchelor, Emma, 122
Bean, Lee L., 96, 98–99, 108
Beck, John, 181
Beck, Matilda, 181
Becker, Gary, 124
Bemus, Ira, 111
Bench, William, 179
Bennett, John C., 28, 32, 33
Bennion, Lowell "Ben," 7; on percentage of Utah in plural marriage, 100
Bertelsen, Anna Maria, 69

Billings, Titus, 112
Black, Susan Ward Easton, 221
Black, William, 77
Book of Mormon, 18–19
Boyington, Thomas, 108
Bradford, Betsey, 35
Braithwaite, William, 175
Brassfield, Newton, 201–2
Breinholt, Johanne, 184–85, 186
Brodie, Fawn, 236n.85
Brown, Emily, 129
Brown, Jane, 68–69
Buchanan, German, 151
Buchanan, John, 175
Burgess-Olson, Vicky, 124, 191
Burton, Richard, 197

Callaway, Levi, 63
Callaway, Mary Frances, 63
Campbell, Alexander, 19
Campbell, Bruce, 6, 160, 189, 275n.25; and normlessness, 191–93
Campbell, Eugene, 6, 160, 189, 275n.25; and normlessness, 191–93
Cannon, George Q., 39, 74–76, 206; on plural marriage, 72, 209; on sexual relations, 196, 202
Carter, John, 37
Carthage, Ill., 34, 79
Cast v. Cast, 149–50
celestial marriage. *See* eternal marriage
Chapman, Welcome, 151–53
Chapman v. Handley, 176

Chase, J. D., 112
Christensen, Hannah, 150
Christensen, Herman Julius, 63, 149–50
Christiansen, Mette Christina, 121
Christoffersen, Ane, 129, 178–79
Christoffersen, Soren C. Hansen, 129, 178–79
Church of Jesus Christ of Latter-day Saints, 186, 213; and economic equality, 133; incorporation of, 57; organization of, 18; and polygamy, 128–29, 183; rank and wealth in, 128
Colorado City/Hildale, 210, 212
Compromise of 1850, 40
Compton, Todd, 6, 231n.17
Cook, Ann, 61–62
Cook, Hannah Massey Davenport, 77
Cook, James, 77
Cook, Marie, 77
Coolidge, Alvira, 71
Coolidge, Elizabeth, 156
Cooper, Rex, 30
Cope v. Cope, 176–77
Cornwall, Marie, 7, 100
Council of Trent (1563), 59
Courtright, Camela, 7, 100
court system: civil, controlled by church, 41; and divorce, 146–47; ecclesiastical, 40, 153; federal control of, 206; and first trial of a polygamist, 38
Cowdery, Oliver, 18, 19, 22
Cowles, Austin A., 33
Cowley, Matthias F., 209
Cox, Cordelia, 35, 43
Cox, Emeline, 43
Cox, Emerette, 43
Cox, Frederick W., Jr., 55–56, 60, 66, 70–71, 178
Cox, Frederick W., Sr., 38, 80–81; estate of, 85; as proxy for Joseph Smith, 35, 79; as settler in Manti, 42, 43
Cox, Harriet, 35

Cox, Jemima, 43
Cox, Lydia, 43
Croshaw, Mary Elizabeth, 195
Cullom-Strubble bill, 50

Dalton, Lucinda, 164
Dana, Richard Henry, 47
deathrate: in Missouri River settlements, 37
divorce, 186, 203–4; and adultery, 157; and age, 166; and apostasy, 156, 158–59, 163–64; and cancellation of sealing, 153; caused by Manifesto, 163–64; church, 142, 151, 153, 160; civil, 142, 151, 160; civil courts and church, 159; de facto, 157–59; desertion as, 156; and economic problems, 166; and exodus from Nauvoo, 165; and government raids, 164; grounds for church, 153–54, 163–67; grounds for civil, 143–44, 148–50; incidence of, 162; lenient laws on, 147–48, 193; and Mormon reformation, 165–66; by mutual petition, 145–46; number of church, 161–62; and plural marriage, 143, 163, 211; rates in Utah, 161–62; and remarriage, 142, 163, 167–69; scriptural justification for, 143, 163; as social regulation, 193–94, 196; state control of, 208; for time, 153; and women, 144–45
Dixon, Ruth B., 103
Doctrine and Covenants, 20, 33, 72
Domgaard, Niels Peter, 121
Dunn, Mary, 78–79
Durkheim, Emile, 193–96; on anomie, 189–90, 208; and religion, 190
dynasticism, 28, 123

Edmunds, George F., 47
Edmunds Act, 150, 206–7; and convictions, 48, 173, 174–76, 183–84
Edmunds-Tucker Act, 14, 49, 58, 173, 208; and inheritance, 175–

76, 177–78; and marriage, 181–82,
183–84, 207
Edwards, Elisha, 129
Edwards, Mariah, 129
Egan, Howard, 201
Egan, Tamson, 201
Embry, Jessie, 6, 191, 246n.13
endowment, 25, 113–14
Endowment House, 5, 56, 81, 113–
14, 142
Ensign, Martin Luther, 79
Esshom, Frank, 220
eternal marriage, 5, 70–71, 225n.19;
purposes of, 71, 76
Evans, Rosa Mae McClellan,
240n.65
exaltation, 169; marriage requisite
for, 4, 71; for monogamists, 72–
75; and polygamy, 73–75; worthy
companion requisite for, 113–14,
163

family models, 3; matriarchal, 40;
patriarchal, 40
Farnsworth, M. F., 221
Farrell, George Lionel, 195
Far West, Mo., 25
Firmage, Edwin, 151, 157
first wife: definition of, 10
Fisher, Josephine F., 29–30
Flint, Kate, 48
Ford, Thomas (governor of Illinois),
34
Foster, Lawrence, 6, 28, 231n.31,
232–33n.46, 251n.76; and the
"liminal period," 188–91, 212; on
polyandry, 81
Fowler, Ellen, 168
Friedman, Lawrence M.: and Victo-
rian compromise, 48–49
Fundamentalist Church of Jesus
Christ of Latter-day Saints, 210–
11, 213

Gentile League of Utah, 103
Gibbons, Nancy, 62
Gleason, Flora, 165

Goss, Bertha, 181
Grant, Heber J., 194
Grant, Jedediah M., 198
Gratian, 58
Green, Thomas, 211–12
Grow, Stewart L., 240n.65

Hals, Hans Jensen, 122, 129
Hambleton, Bergetta, 86
Hambleton, Chelnecha, 86, 200–201
Hambleton, Madison D., 42, 200–
201; will of, 42, 86
Hancock, Levi W., 20, 165
Hancock, Mosiah, 20, 78–79
Hansen, Hans, 200
Hansen, Jens, 121
Hansen, Klaus, 174
Hardwicke Marriage Act, 59
Hardy, B. Carmon, 7, 185, 226n.19,
248n.42
Hareven, Tamara K., 3
Harmston, James, 1, 9, 213
Harris, George W., 22
Harrison, Jerry N., 228n.37
Hawkins, Lavinia, 82
Haydock, Elizabeth, 121
Higgins, Nelson, 42
Hill, Archibald Newell, 201
Hill, Joseph, 200
Hill, Marvin, 231n.31
Hilton v. Roylance, 159
Hinkle, George M., 25
Holdaway, Elizabeth Ann, 165
Hsueh, Yung-chang, 98–99
Huntington, Dimick B., 42
Hyde, John, 82–83, 158
Hyde, Mary Ann P., 85
Hyde, Orson, 157, 192; estate of, 85;
and Mormon reformation, 46, 61
Hyde v. Hyde and Woodmansee,
82, 180

immigrants, 43, 97, 114, 117, 136;
definition of, 95; and mean marriage age, 95–96; and plural marriages, 104–6, 206; proportion of,
in plural marriage, 98

Independence, Mo., 21, 27
Ingalls, Rufus, 198
inheritance laws, 83–87; and children, 84, 175–77; and dower, 178–80, 207; and homestead provision, 84; and plural wives, 177–81, 207
In re Herman J. Christiansen, 150
Isaacson, Anna Maria, 63–64
Iverson, Joan, 173
Ivins, Stanley, 7, 102–3, 118, 130; on demise of polygamy, 174; on incidence of plural marriage, 100; and *Pioneers and Prominent Men of Utah*, 103, 130, 220

Jackson, Charles, 157
Jackson, Harriet, 157
Jacob, Udney Hay, 143
Jacobs, Henry, 158
Jensen, Melinda, 200
Jenson, Andrew, 221
Johnson, Aaron, 69
Johnson, Benjamin F., 165
Johnson, Lorenzo, 69
Johnston, Emily M., 141–42, 147
Johnston, George C., 141–42, 147
Jolly, Joseph, 165
Jolly, Mary, 165
Jorgensen, Cecelia Marie, 122

Kanab, Utah, 100
Kearny, Stephen W., 37
Kent, James, 60
Kenyon v. Kenyon, 149
Kimball, Heber C., 26, 29, 35, 39, 82; on apostasy, 158; on endowment, 25; on sexual relations, 196, 198
Kimball, Helen Mar, 26
King, Austin A., 25
Kingston clan. *See* Latter-day Church of Christ
Kirtland, Ohio, 19, 21, 24
Kofford, Paul, 165
Kolob Guard, 175

Krause, Anna Margaretha Josephine, 130
Kunz, Phillip R., 6, 7, 162

Larsen, Ane, 156, 215
Larsen, Maria, 200
Larson, Stan, 240n.65
The Late Corporation of the Church of Jesus Christ of Latter-day Saints v. United States, 49
Lateran Council: fourth (1215), 58
Latter-day Church of Christ, 210–12
Lauritzen, Cena, 165
Law, William, 33, 34
Lawrence, Maria, 33
Leavitt, Sarah, 195
Lee, Ann, 190
Lee, John D., 62
Lemaster, Emily, 151
Lever, W. H., 221
Lewis, Nathan, 129
Libbey, Hannah, 35
Lightner, Mary Rollins, 26–27
Little, James T., 48
Logue, Larry M., 7, 256n.24; on marriage ages, 96–97
Lowry, John, 45
Lowry, Mary Artemisia, 44
Ludvigsen, Eric, 175
Lund, Anthon H., 72
Lyman, Amasa M., 204
Lyman, Eliza Partridge, 116
Lyon, Windsor, 29–30
Lystra, Karen, 64

Madsen, Christian, 164
Madsen, Henning, 129
Mangrum, Richard, 151, 157
Manifesto of 1890, 13–14, 50, 92, 208–9, 214; and divorce, 163; polygamy after, 101, 174, 184–87, 210; and Second Manifesto of 1904, 209
Manti, 1; and economic development, 98; establishment of, 36,

41; factors of development in, 44–45; fort in, 43; reason chosen for study, 9

Marble, Samuel Harvey, 18

marriage, 122; in America, 59, 67; and availability of mates, 103, 115; and Church of England, 59; civil, 205; and common law, 59–60, 67, 68, 183, 207; desirability of, 103, 115; and economics, 108; encouragement for, 91; feasability of, 103, 115; and free consent, 58–61; history of church and state regarding, 58–60; and parental consent, 58; and the Reformation, 59; and Roman Catholic church, 58–59; and state regulation, 207

marriage age: immigrants and, 95–96; mean, 91, 95, 97, 107, 136, 212; mean, in U.S., 97; median, 95

marriage patterns, 91, 101; comparison of, in England and Utah, 118–19

marriage rates: age-specific, 91, 93–95, 97, 136; age-specific, for monogamous and plural wives, 98–99; by cohort, 93–94

marriage registration: in Utah, 65–66

marriage system: British versus Utahn, 18; definition of, 2. *See also* Mormon marriage system

Marsh, Thomas, 22, 23

Martin Handcart Company, 121

May, Dean, 113; on Kanab, Utah, 100

McAllister, Ann Davis Hailstone, 185

McAllister, John D. T., 175, 185

McArthur, Daniel D., 63

McKean, James B., 206

Merton, Robert: and nonconformers, 190

Mexico, 93, 134, 184, 185, 209

Miles v. United States, 206

Mills, Eleanor, 35

Mineau, Geraldine P., 96, 98–99, 108, 162

Missouri, 24. *See also* Far West; Independence

Mitchell, Sevilla Stoy, 62

monogamy, 18

Monroe, James, 201

Moran, Gerald F., 3

Morley, Cordelia, 35, 79

Morley, Isaac, 79, 175; as founder of Manti, 19, 36, 41–42; in Illinois, 24, 26, 27, 34; sealed to wives, 35, 157

Morley, Lucy, 37

Morley, Theressa, 26

Morley's Settlement, 24, 34, 41

Mormon Battalion, 42, 78; creation of, 37; as source of income, 37

Mormon church. *See* Church of Jesus Christ of Latter-day Saints

Mormon Historical Demography Project, 7, 96, 99

Mormon marriages: and age of discretion, 68; controlled by state, 208; and lack of civil legislation, 57, 193; religious not civil, 56–57 —types of, 10; between affines, 70; civil, 70–71, 82, 205; consanguineous, 68–70, 182, 205, 207; convenience, 77, 80, 82; delayed rights, 78–79, 82; eternal, 70–71; eternity only, 76, 77, 82, 207; levirate, 79–80; nominal plural, 10, 76, 77, 78, 82; polyandrous, 204; proxy, 77, 79, 82; religious, 70–71; time and eternity, 82. *See also* plural marriage

Mormon marriage system, 5, 8, 13, 208; and choice of mates, 68; in nineteenth century, 173; and plural marriage, 92; rules governing, 203; and sources of wives, 112–13

Mormon men: age of, at marriage, 111–12; number of married, 111

Mormon reformation, 107–8, 117–

18; and divorce, 165–66, 205; and
marriage patterns, 101; resulted
in plural marriages, 46, 106; and
scarcity of women, 108–10

Mormon women, 214; and free consent, 64–65; and gender roles,
119, 134; and marital choice, 61;
protection of, 197–99, 200–202;
scarcity of marriageable, 108–10,
114; and sexual relations, 196–97

Morrill Anti-Bigamy Act, 47, 57,
102, 176, 205–6

Mortensen, Morten, 78

Mowry, Sylvester, 197–98, 201

Myrick, Fanny, 165

Native Americans: and children,
42; and settlers, 104

Nauvoo, 17, 24, 27, 79, 165; exodus
from, 34, 106; plural marriage developed in, 36; and protopolygamy, 12, 31; temple in, 34, 78, 102,
106

Nauvoo Expositor, 33

Nauvoo High Council, 32, 33

Nelson, Andrew, 163–64

Nielsen, Christian, 42; will of, 86

Nielsen, Maren, 86

Nielsen, Marie, 86

Norton v. Tufts, 142, 159

Noyes, John Humphrey, 190

Olsen, James, 86

Olsen, Katharine, 86

Oneida Perfectionists, 188, 190–91

Orderville, Utah, 100

Ormsby, O. C., 63

Ottosen, Hans, 111

Panaca, Utah, 100

Parry, John, 119

Partridge, Emily, 27, 38

Patten, David, 22

"Pauline Privilege," 156

The Peace Maker (Jacob), 143–45

Peacock, George, 44, 63, 153; estate
of, 84–85

Peacock, Sarah, 63

Petersen, J., 148

Petersen, Ole, 111

Petersen, Sophia Klauen, 121

Phelps, Elizabeth Stuart, 4

Phelps, W. W., 20

Pinedale, Mont., 211

Pitchforth, Mercy, 17–18, 35

plural marriage, 174, 182; arguments for, 38–39; attitudes in,
173–74; and availability of mates,
103–7; belief of individuals in, 75;
and church leaders, 71–76, 128–
29, 183; and common law, 180;
versus companionate marriage, 5;
and courtship, 195; decline in
number, 102; desirability of, 103–
4; differences between nineteenth-
and twentieth-century, 210–14;
and distribution of wealth, 132–
33; doctrinal foundation for, 71,
116; economic reasons for, 116,
119–23, 124, 211; encouragement
of, 91; equality in, 133–34; and
exaltation, 71, 73–75; feasability
of, 104; as ideal form, 70; and immigration, 104–6; impact on marriage age, 107–8; incidence of
women entering, 99–100, 117;
and living arrangements, 193; and
loyalty, 26; after Manifesto, 92–
93; motivation for, 28–29; nominal, 10, 76, 77, 78, 82; number of
families in, 98–101, 114; in Old
Testament, 20, 38, 191; percentage of families in, 98–101; proportion of, 91; restraints on, 194–96;
sacrificed, 208; second, 167–68,
169; in secret, 209; and shift in resources, 92, 127; status of families in, 186; in twentieth century,
210–13; and welfare, 211. *See also*
polygamy

plural wives, 180; adaptation of,
173–74; attitudes toward, 37–38;
definition of, 10; divorced or widowed, 123, 126–27, 168–69; and

dower rights, 178–80; economically disadvantaged, 91, 119, 123–24, 136, 211; family background of, 123–27; fatherless, 123–24, 126–27; immigrant, 121, 124, 206; marital status of, after Manifesto, 184; and professions, 135
Poland Act, 41, 47, 150, 206
Polk, James K., 37
polygamists, 136, 207; and church rank, 128; and cohabitation, 183–84, 206, 209–10; contemporary, 210, 212; conviction of, 175, 206; disfranchisement of, 206; and divorce, 130; number of wives at a time, 129–30; number of wives during lifetime, 129–30; and wealth, 128, 130–31; and wives after Manifesto, 185–86
polygamous wives. *See* plural wives
polygamy: definition of, 229n.8; sororal, 70, 191. *See also* plural marriage
Poulsen, Karen Kirstine, 63, 149
Powers, Ann Clark, 165
Pratt, Arthur, 176
Pratt, Belinda, 39
Pratt, Milando Merrill, 176
Pratt, Orson, 36, 38, 62, 73; estate of, 176; on love, 64; on polygamy, 74, 191, 193; on proxy marriage, 80
Pratt, Parley P., 32
protopolygamy 12, 31, 204

Quinn, D. Michael, 7, 234n.63, 247–48n.36

"The Raid," 49, 164, 175
railroad, 47, 92, 174
Raleigh, Alonzo H., 179–80
Raleigh, Emily, 179–80
remarriage: of divorcées, 167–69; of widows, 169
Remini, Robert, 189
Reorganized Church of Jesus Christ of Latter Day Saints, 69, 192

research methods, 8–10; and birth cohorts, 92–93; and periodization, 92; and spelling of names, 11
Reynolds, George, 47, 206
Reynolds v. United States, 48, 103, 206
Rich, Charles C., 64, 104
Rich, Sarah D., 116
Richardson, Charles, 81
Richardson, Edmund, 80–81
Richardson, Mary Ann Darrow, 80–82
Richardson, Sullivan, 81
Riddle, Isaac J., 175
Riddle v. Riddle, 180
Rockwood, A. P., 61
Rohwer v. District Court, 177
Romney, Catharine, 134

Salt Lake Valley, 40
Sanpete County Probate Court, 141, 145, 150, 151, 157
Sanpete Valley, 1, 36, 45, 175
Schougaard, Inger Marie, 186
Schramm, Matilda Sophia, 130
sealings, 76, 113–14, 163–64, 204–5, 208; of additional marriages, 205; after civil ceremonies, 71; to create bonds between members, 25–26; defined by court, 207; definition of, 4; eternal nature of, 214
Sessions, Patty, 119
Sessions, Sylvia, 29–30
Sevier Valley, 45
sex ratio, 112–13; men to women, 110; single men to single women, 110
sexual relations: extramarital, 196, 202, 204; and illegitimate children, 199; in Mormon society, 194–97; in nineteenth-century America, 39–40; premarital, 196, 199, 204; and repentance, 202–3; and seduction, 199–202; with underaged, 200
Shakers, 188, 190
Shipp, Ellis, 135

Shipps, Jan, 4, 20, 50, 174, 213
Sidwell, Adelia, 9
Silver Reef, Utah, 198
Silverton, Oreg., 131–32
Skolnick, Mark, 96
Smith, Albert, 37
Smith, Annie D., 145
Smith, Azariah, 37, 62, 221; divorce
    of, 152–53, 157; remarriage of,
    110–11, 113
Smith, Camilla Augusta Taylor,
    152–53, 157
Smith, Emma, 20, 33, 71
Smith, Esther, 37
Smith, George Albert, 104, 155, 201
Smith, Hannah, 134
Smith, Hyrum, 18, 32–33, 34
Smith, James E., 7
Smith, Joseph, 29, 143, 190; alle-
    giance to, 26, 28; death of, 17, 34;
    and Fanny Alger, 20, 22; as head
    of church, 24, 33, 191; and organi-
    zation of church, 18; and polyga-
    my, 20, 32; and restoration of an-
    cient church, 19; and restoration
    of gospel, 73; sealed to wives, 27,
    35, 79, 158
Smith, Joseph A., 145, 200
Smith, Joseph F., 72, 76; on polyga-
    my, 73, 74, 206, 209
Smith, Lucy Meserve, 134
Smith, Samuel, 69
Smith, Samuel H., 18
Smyth, Adam Craik, 129
Snow, Erastus, 73, 115, 196–97
Snow, George W., 79
Snow, Lorenzo, 183, 209
Snow, Minnie, 183
Snow, Sarah, 183
Snow, Warren S., 55–56, 60, 70, 79
spelling of names, 11
St. George, Utah, 96, 112
Staheli, Mary, 130
Steptoe, Edward J., 197–98, 201
Stewart, Nathan, 166
Stone, Barton, 19
Stringham, George, 192–93

Stringham, Polly, 192–93
Stringham, Sabra, 192
Stringham, Walter, 56
Sudweeks, Henry, 69
Sweat, Sophia, 37

Tanner, Annie Clark, 75–76, 195
Taylor, Ann Wickes, 77
Taylor, George, 77
Taylor, John, 26, 35, 48, 195, 204,
    210; and divorce cases, 158, 164;
    estate of, 85–86; on eternal mar-
    riages, 73; on plural marriage, 72;
    on widows, 127
Taylor, Joseph E., 76
Taylor, Joseph H., 141
Taylor, Martha A., 141
temple: in Kirtland, 21; in Nauvoo,
    34, 102, 106; as Old Testament
    practice, 21; ordinances, 213–14.
    See also endowment; sealings
Thompson, Mercy Rachel, 79
TLC. *See* True and Living Church
    of Jesus Christ of Saints of the
    Last Days
Troelsen, Marcus, 111
True and Living Church of Jesus
    Christ of Saints of the Last Days
    (TLC), 1, 2, 187, 210, 213
Tuttle, Luther T., 37
Tuttle, Mary Ellen, 55–56

U.S. Congress, 57–58, 67, 150; and
    antipolygamy acts, 46–48, 49, 86;
    and divorce, 170; and dower
    rights, 14; and marriage, 87, 92,
    174, 181–82; *See also specific acts*
U.S. Constitution, 57; and First
    Amendment rights, 38–39
U.S. government: and antipolygamy
    legislation, 13, 101, 103, 188, 205,
    206, 208; and disfranchisement,
    174; and imprisonment of polyga-
    mists, 36; and Mormon Battalion,
    37; and Utah statehood, 49–51.
    See also U.S. Congress
U.S. Supreme Court, 41, 48, 49,

103; and inheritance laws, 176–
77; and polygamy, 206; and voting
oaths, 50. *See also specific cases*
Utah: economic developments in,
50; non-Mormon men in, 113,
197–99; reconstruction of, 46;
statehood, 50; as territory, 41
Utah Commission, 49, 240n.65
Utah Constitution, 177
Utah legislature, 173; and children,
42, 176; and the courts, 41; and
divorce, 143–44, 148, 159; and
dower, 84, 179; and inheritance,
83–84, 176–77; and marriage, 57,
61, 67, 182–83; and women's voting rights, 47
Utahns: definition of, 95
Utah Supreme Court: on children,
212; on dower, 179, 181; on inheritance, 176–77; on jurisdiction
over divorce, 149–50, 159; on
marriage, 60, 151, 207
Utes: and relations with Mormons,
44; and Sanpete Valley, 45; and
slave trade, 42

Van Beek, Laga, 7, 100
Van Wagoner, Richard, 6, 230n.15
Vaughn, J. M., 200
Vinovskis, Maris A., 3

Wahkara, Chief, 42, 43–45
Waite, Morrison R., 48
Walker, Charles, 194
Walker, Lucy, 26, 27–28
Walker War, 42, 43, 45, 63, 116
Wall, Francis, 175
Ward, Barney, 42
Wareham, James, 153
Warner, Eunice Billings, 79
Warner, John, 79
Washburn, Abraham, 165
Watt, George Darling, 68–69
wealth, 130–33; distribution of,
131–33; Gini coefficients on, 131–

33; median, 130; of monogamists
versus polygamists, 130–31
Webb, Ann Eliza, 103
Weibye, Jens C. A., 175, 221
Wells, Daniel H., 62, 206
Wells, Emmeline Woodward Whit-
ney, 62
Werner, M. R., 190
West, Mary Ann, 157
Whiting, Edwin, 63
Whitmer, David, 18, 23
Whitmer, John, 23
Whitmer, Peter, Jr., 18
Whitney, Newell, 62
Whitney, Sarah Ann, 26
Wilde, James O., 83
Willie Handcart Company, 121
Winget, Katherine, 166, 168
Winter Quarters, 36, 78, 115, 165,
204
Woodmansee, Joseph, 82
Woodruff, Wilford, 72, 74, 117; and
Manifesto, 50, 208, 214
Woolsey, Thomas, 165
Wright, Carroll, 160–62
Wuthnow, Robert, 25

Young, Brigham, 26, 72, 80, 103,
158, 198, 202; and divorce cases,
152, 154–56, 160, 165; on incorporation, 57; as leader of church,
34, 190, 197; on love, 64; on marriage, 56, 66, 69, 112, 192, 194,
204; and polygamy, 73, 74, 206;
on women, 61, 115, 127
Young, Kimball, 6, 191, 195,
246n.13; on divorce, 155–56
Young, Zina Diantha Huntington
Jacobs, 158, 204

Zane, Charles S., 150
Zeeland, Mich., 131–32
Zimmerman, Carle C., 4
Zion's Co-operative Mercantile In-
stitution (ZCMI), 133

KATHRYN M. DAYNES, who received her Ph.D. from
Indiana University, is an associate professor of history
at Brigham Young University. She is also an accredited
genealogist. Focusing on the American family, she
has published essays in *Nauvoo in Mormon History:
Kingdom on the Mississippi*, edited by Roger D.
Launius and John E. Hallwas, and in *Fulfilling the
Founding: A Reader for American Heritage*, edited
by Gary Daynes, as well as articles in the *Journal
of Mormon History* and the *John Whitmer Historical
Association Journal.*

Composed in 9.5/12.5 Trump Medieval
by Barbara Evans
at the University of Illinois Press
Manufactured by Thomson-Shore, Inc.

University of Illinois Press
1325 South Oak Street
Champaign, IL 61820-6903
www.press.uillinois.edu